Bondmen and Rebels

THE JOHNS HOPKINS STUDIES IN
ATLANTIC HISTORY AND CULTURE
Richard Price, General Editor

BONDMEN

A Study of Master-Slave Relations in Antigua

With Implications for Colonial British America

THE JOHNS HOPKINS
UNIVERSITY PRESS

Baltimore and London

DAVID BARRY GASPAR

& REBELS

This book has been brought to publication with the generous assistance
of the Andrew W. Mellon Foundation.

The Johns Hopkins University Press, 701 West 40th Street,
Baltimore, Maryland 21211
The Johns Hopkins Press Ltd, London

The paper in this book is acid-free and meets the guidelines for
permanence and durability of the Committee on Production Guidelines
for Book Longevity of the Council on Library Resources.

LIBRARY OF CONGRESS CATALOGING IN PUBLICATION DATA
Gaspar, David Barry.
    Bondmen and rebels.

    (The Johns Hopkins studies in Atlantic history and culture)
    Revision of thesis (Ph.D.—Johns Hopkins University, 1974), originally
presented under title: Slave resistance and social control in Antigua,
1700–1763.
    Bibliography: p.
    Includes index.
    1. Slavery—Antigua. 2. Slavery—Antigua—Insurrections, etc. 3. Antigua—
History. 4. Slaves—Antigua. 5. Interpersonal relations. I. Title. II. Series.

HT1105.A6G37 1985   306'.362'0972974   85-5222
ISBN 0-8018-2422-2 (alk. paper)

FRONTISPIECE: *Negroes Sunday-Market at Antigua,* by W. E. Beastall
and G. Testolini, 1806.

To My Mother and Father
and the People of the Black Diaspora

Contents

Tables

Preface

In the sugar colony of Antigua, one of the British Leeward Islands in the Caribbean just east of Puerto Rico, two major events that occurred during the first three decades of the eighteenth century drew attention to the tiny island community that had been built up around slavery and shaped by it. In 1710 long-simmering friction between Governor Daniel Parke and the assembly erupted when the assemblymen and their supporters attacked and killed the governor — this was the only such instance in the history of the early modern British Empire. Just how the slave population interpreted, or responded to, such a striking demonstration of open division in the ranks of the ruling class remains an unexplored, and perhaps unexplorable, subject because of the quality of existing sources; we know, however, that three decades later, during a period of severe economic stress, the slaves themselves plotted a spectacular revolt to seize control of the island.

The revolt never materialized. A well-organized, islandwide affair, the slave conspiracy of 1736, had it succeeded, would have catapulted Antigua onto the stage of world history as the first territory in the slave heartland of the Caribbean in which slaves seized full control. And that would have happened a full half-century before the very different (in many respects) upheaval in French St. Domingue, where a combination of powerful forces that emerged both within St. Domingue slave society itself and from the spread of the tremors of the French Revolution into the Caribbean influenced the well-known successful slave revolt that resulted in the establishment of the black Republic of Haiti. The origins of the Antigua conspiracy were, by contrast, overwhelmingly, if not exclusively, internal, and herein lies part of the intrinsic interest of the plot.

Germinated in the fertile soil of the social relations of that slave society, the plot graphically dramatized one possible outcome of the persistent and potentially explosive discordance or competitive struggle between slaveowners' aspirations to control their slaves and the slaves' own conscious efforts to frustrate them in various ways. For the first time in the island's history, after about half a century of development as a slave society, slaveowners faced collective resistance on such an organized and massive scale. Most masters had, of course, long dreaded just such a denouement, the approach of which was, however, difficult to predict, especially as the pattern of general slave resistance was not persistently and openly confrontational, at least from the early 1700s, if not earlier. Still, the expectation of concerted collective violence from the slaves remained. The plot of 1736 forced masters to realize that the elaborate apparatus of control that they had established could not always prevent strongly motivated slaves from openly challenging their power with expectation of success. The plot therefore directs attention to the sets of relations that existed between "two loci of power and two opposing systems of belief," between white dominance and black resistance,[1] between social control and slave resistance, two intertwined dimensions of Antigua slave society that themselves can reveal so much about that society. Just as it is not possible to understand the master class apart from its relations with the slaves, and vice versa, so too are slave resistance and control best studied not separately but together, because of their dynamic interaction. That is the main conceptual thrust of this book in regard to master-slave relations.

As Eric Hobsbawm has pointed out, episodes of social upheaval reveal "important problems [that] cannot be studied at all except in and through such moments of eruption," which expose for examination so much that is normally hidden from view while at the same time dramatizing "aspects of social structure. . . strained to the breaking point."[2] Through the richly documented Antigua slave plot, it is possible to explore the network of interconnections between slave resistance and the hegemonic aspirations of the master class against the background of "crucial aspects" of society, particularly in relation to the slaves' role and status. The plot is used, then, as a window into Antigua slave society to explore questions that are also of relevance to other such New World societies. Departing from many studies that do not preserve the interlocking bonds between resistance and control, and whose penetration is often blunted by a disregard for the unique character of slave societies, the argument of this study is shaped by an appreciation of changes in Antigua slave society with regard especially to relations between masters and slaves, the superstructure of control, the origins and size of the slave population, the expansionary tendencies of slave labor utilization, the development of slave community and culture, and the physical environment itself of the island colony.

Resistance to slavery among the slaves of Antigua began during the early years of the sugar revolution in the second half of the seventeenth century. Later, the slaves made important adjustments in response to a changing physical, economic, and social environment. During the frontier period of the emergent slave society, slave resistance confronted slaveowners with by far their most troublesome internal problem. Along with chronic slave flight to the island's wilds, the activities of organized bands of fugitives who raided plantations, endangered the lives of whites traveling on the highways, and resisted parties sent out after them placed a tremendous strain on the emerging apparatus of control. In the 1680s this maroon type resistance threatened to escalate into full-scale islandwide revolt. But the slaveowners weathered the crisis through search-and-destroy expeditions against the fugitives, exemplary executions of any caught, the enactment of elaborate legislation to stifle resistance, and the expansion of sugar cultivation further and deeper into the wilds. By the late seventeenth century the truly maroon period of resistance had passed, gone along with the forest that had covered hill and valley when the first English settlers arrived in 1632. Henceforth, as the slave system matured and stabilized, slave resistance, while remaining a serious problem, became more accommodative, individual, and less openly confrontational; and within the operating patterns of slave control, consensus gradually emerged to play an important role alongside coercion. Occasionally, however, eruptions of more organized group rebellion warned slaveowners that their power could be more openly challenged. This was the clear message that the 1736 plot carried, projecting in a particularly dramatic way the limitations of slaveowners' so-called control over their slaves. Close analysis of its organization, causes, consequences, objectives, and structure indicate that the plot, deeply rooted in the character of Antigua slave society, was closely related to the tradition of slave resistance, the fragility of the apparatus of control, and the slaves' African culture, particularly among the Akan-speaking slaves from the Gold Coast.

Among the sources from which valuable data have been squeezed and teased in the preparation of this study are plantation inventories and accounts; planters' and merchants' correspondence; censuses; trade accounts; official correspondence between colonial officers and the home government; legislative enactments; minutes of the island legislature; compensation claims; extracts of wills; maps; and travelers' accounts.[3] I was warned when I began this study that I would not find much material. However, as I pushed on and grew more patient with the sources, at the same time reading more widely in the secondary literature on related themes and also discussing my work with encouraging scholars who had interests similar to mine, the sources happily began to yield up their valuable treasures, and the study took some unexpected but fruitful turns. It is somewhat comforting as a result to realize how much we still do not know about the evolution of New World slave societies. While the study covers the period from early settlement to the mid-eighteenth century, its main focus is on the years from the sugar revolution that began in the 1670s up to 1763, when the Seven Years' War ended. In that war between Britain and France, slaves from Antigua and other British sugar islands found themselves in an unaccustomed role: they invaded French territory alongside British troops, though certainly not as fighting men. More importantly, the year of the Treaty of Paris was chosen as a cut-off point also because after about the 1760s, in the West Indies as a whole, internal influences that already shaped the slaves' responses to enslavement were reinforced from outside, as the shock waves of the American and French revolutions and the humanitarian movement for abolition of the slave trade and emancipation spread. These developments belong to a later and certainly more complex phase in the history of Caribbean slave responses to slavery.

This study began as a paper on the causes of the Antigua plot that was presented to the Atlantic History and Culture Seminar at the Johns Hopkins University several years ago — more than I care to remember. The paper, a version of which was later published, expanded almost of its own accord and became my dissertation (1974) at the same university: "Slave Resistance and Social Control in Antigua, 1700–1763." Preliminary versions of parts of this study have also appeared in the *William and Mary Quarterly,* the *Boletin de Estudios Latinamericanos y del Caribe, Caribbean Quarterly,* and *Cimarron.* Further expansion and complete reorganization has resulted in this book, which I am happy to let go of, after many interruptions that greatly slowed down work on it.

Many colleagues and friends, too numerous to mention all by name, have given graciously of their time and knowledge to the metamorphosis of this study, and I am deeply grateful to them all. I am, however, especially indebted to Frederick Cooper, John Cell, Emilia Viotti da Costa, Stanley Engerman, James Epstein, Elizabeth Fox-Genovese, Eugene Genovese, Seymour Mauskopf, Sydney Nathans, and Richard Sheridan for their probing and constructive comments on the final manuscript. Also, Ira Berlin, David Cohen, Michael Craton, Tim Garrard, Franklin Knight, Ray Kea, Michael Louis, Daniel Littlefield, Ann McDougall, Joseph Miller, Michael Mullin, Philip Morgan, Willie Lee Rose, Carl Oblinger, Robert Stewart, Monica Schuler, Peter Wood, Ronald Walters, and Ivor Wilks read and commented on earlier versions, or parts of the study. For bringing certain research materials to my attention I am grateful to Robert Dirks, Richard Dunn, Stanley Engerman, Neville Hall, and especially Richard Sheridan. I would also like to acknowledge the long term support of Bill Abbot, Paul Gaston, Martin Havran, and Anne F. Scott. To teacher and friend Jack P. Greene, under whose direction I worked as a graduate student, and who never let me forget, with criticism and guidance, that I had a book to finish, I owe a special debt. It is easier to acknowledge than to fully measure the contribution he has made to my growth as a historian and to this study, but neither he nor others should be seriously held responsible for what I have written, as I have not always followed their advice. A special thanks also to the students in my seminars and courses at the University of Virginia and Duke University, from whom I have learned so much, perhaps more than they learned from me. Sections of this study were presented to the faculty-student seminars at both places, to the slave society seminar at the National Humanities Center, to the Johns Hopkins seminar in Atlantic history and culture, and at the meetings of several historical associations where careful criticism helped me immensely.

I could not have written this book without access to research facilities, and I am grateful to the staffs of the British Library, London; the Institute of Historical Research, London; the National Register of Archives, London; the Public Record Office, London; the Somerset Record Office, Taunton; Lambeth Palace Library, London; Devon Record Office, Exeter; Gloucestershire Record Office, Gloucester; Essex Record Office, Chelmsford; the Library of Congress, Washington, D.C.; libraries of the University of London, the Johns Hopkins University, the University of Virginia, Duke University, the University of the West Indies, Mona, Jamaica. Research support from the Research Institute for the Study of Man, the University of Virginia, and Duke University is also gratefully acknowledged.

Lottie McCauley, Ella Wood, Elizabeth Stovall, Kathleen Miller, Thelma Kithcart, and Dot Sapp efficiently and patiently typed several drafts of the manuscript, and they must know that my debt to them is great indeed. Henry Tom, my editor at the Johns Hopkins University Press, and Irma Garlick, my copy editor, diligently assisted me in preparing the manuscript for publication. Finally, let me thank Herman and Lorna Boyce, whose generous hospitality helped considerably to ease the pain of research and writing during the longest of my stays in England.

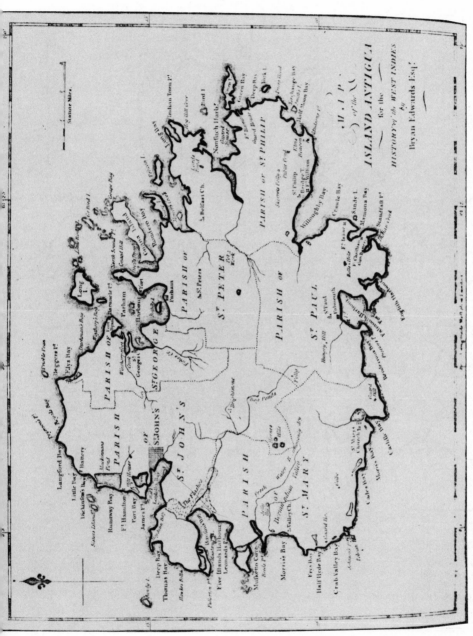

Source: Bryan Edwards, *The History, Civil and Commercial, of the British Colonies in the West Indies,* 3d ed., 3 vols. (London, 1793–1801), 1:facing p. 484.

xix

The Island of ANTEGO

By Herman Moll Geographer.

xx

I

Slave Rebellion, 1736

1

"No People Were Ever Rescued from a Danger More Imminent"

In September 1727, three months after the death of George I, news reached the Leeward Islands that Great Britain had a new king, and their legislatures solemnly proclaimed his accesion. To mark the occasion "an ox was roasted whole" in Antigua "and three hogsheads of beer [were] distributed to the poor inhabitants; while a splendid entertainment was provided for the governor and the gentry. . .at the public expense." William Mathew, lieutenant governor of this group of islands, reported that on September 30 the "Troop of Militia Horse, the Town Militia & five Companys of the Kings Regiment" quartered in Antigua were "all under Arms." The legislature met in special session. "All were Entertained at the Publick Expence," wrote Mathew, "above Two Hundred Pieces of Cannon [were] fir'd among the afternoon rejoicings, [and] a Great Bonfire was Prepar'd in the Markett Place, but the Evening Prov'd Stormy, & 'Twas feard [the fire] might Endanger the Town, being mostly Timber Built. The night concluded the Diversions. The proclamation was Sign'd, And an Address to His Majesty." Similar activities took place in the other three main Leeward Island colonies, St. Christopher, Nevis, and Montserrat.

Later, when George II was crowned, the Leeward Islands gentry celebrated once more, and every October thereafter the Antigua gentry held a ball to commemorate the king's coronation.[1] Preparations for the ball of 1736 were well under way when the authorities unearthed a slave conspiracy "whereby all the White Inhabitants. . .were to be murdered, & a new form of Government. . .Established, by the Slaves, among themselves, and they intirely to possess the Island."[2]

The timely discovery of what turned out to be an elaborate scheme shook the white community. "Here has been a general Stop to all Business occasion'd by the Happy Discovery of an accursed Negro Plot," wrote a distraught resident on October 24. Over several weeks, suspects were arrested, tried, and executed, and many whites, fearing that the slaves would still revolt, remained on their guard and slept uneasily. "You can't expect a long letter from one who hath had but two nights sleep since the 17th instant occasion'd by the providencial Discovery of a Plott among the Negroes here, for a general Massacre," another harrassed resident wrote dramatically seven days later, adding that the plot was "carried on by the very top Negroes of this Island, and such as were indulged in such liberty that

3

they kept one or two Horses a piece and were so entirely trusted by their Masters, that it was with great difficulty, any Crime was believed against them." Most whites would probably have agreed with one observer who confessed, after a number of executions had taken place, that the affair had caught most people by surprise and sown confusion in the tiny colony.[3]

The judges of the first court appointed to try the slaves conceded in their general report that it was difficult to "fix certainly the Person, and precisely the Time, by whom and when, this design was first set on foot . . . it being something, tho not very doubtful, whether Court or Tomboy first moved it; tho generally imputed to the former." They could not be sure when the plans were first laid because it was "most difficult" to determine "from the Evidence given by the Slaves," who, they said, "are not acquainted with our manner, nor indeed Certain manner of Computing it [time]." Although unsure of the slaves' system of time reckoning, the judges nevertheless concluded, after having sifted through slave confessions, testimony, and other information, that the plot was an islandwide affair that had been "undoubtedly in Agitation" since November 1735, if not earlier. The "first Author," or mastermind behind the plot, was the Coromantee slave Court, alias Tackey, aged about forty-five, belonging to Thomas Kerby, justice of the peace and speaker of the assembly. Court's chief accomplice was Tomboy, the Creole (island-born) slave of Thomas Hanson, Antigua merchant and planter.[4]

Court, Tomboy, and the other slave leaders involved in the conspiracy planned an islandwide insurrection to commence on the night of Monday, October 11, when the annual ball commemorating the king's coronation was to have been held in the capital town, St. John's, in a "great house" owned by Christopher Dunbar, probably a prominent island figure.[5] A carpenter by trade, Tomboy was to have secured the job of making the ballroom seats in order to get into the house and plant gunpowder there "to blow up all the Gentry of the Island while they were in the height of their mirth." In their report the judges explained that "when the Company was dancing, fire was to be set to three trains, upon the Notice of firing a Gun and beating a Drum, which were a Notice also to the Negro Musicians and Attendance (who were to be let into the Secret) first to depart." Then, "When the Blast was over, and all in the utmost Confusion, Three at least, if not four Partys, intended to Consist of 3 or 400 men each, were to Enter the Town at Different parts, and to put all the White people there to the Sword." Meanwhile, "Seven Strong Guards [were] to be placed in the out parts of the Town, to prevent Relief" from reaching the beleaguered whites. "St. Johns Fort [was] to be Seized with all the Shipping in the Harbour, and Signals [were] to be given to those in the Countrey, to begin there the same tragical Scene, and proceed onwards to the Town, destroying all in their way." The slaves had also planned to seize Monk's Hill, "our chief Fort and Arsenal" noted the judges, "and the Arms distributed; The Guard there destroy'd, and all the Avenues secured by strong Guards of Slaves."[6]

For months the slave leaders had gone about planning their revolt and recruiting followers. Though they were careful not to arouse the suspicions of whites, their luck ran out when the authorities postponed the ball to October 30, the king's birthday, and forced them to reconsider their plans.[7] A critical dispute arose at this point "whether or not they Should Execute their Plot, by immediately falling on with fire and Sword, or wait for the ball." Tomboy "being young & fiery was for falling on directly, but King Court being of a more phlegmatic temper opposed him, & was willing the business should be done with as little loss of their side as possible." Court obviously preferred not to discard the originally carefully drawn-up plans in favor of a new, hastily devised scheme that might have had to be very differently organized. Had Tomboy had his way, Antigua would probably have been rocked by a full-scale slave revolt at a time when probably no astute observer of Caribbean slave societies would have anticipated such a thing, except perhaps in Jamaica, where the authorities had their hands full trying to pacify the maroons, and even there an islandwide affair was unlikely; but after much deliberation, Court succeeded in persuading the rest to wait for the ball and to proceed with the revolt as originally planned. That decision proved fatal. While the slaves waited, counting the days to October 30 —"the only Preservative to all our Lives," said one Antiguan — the plot was discovered.[8]

As details of the scheme unfolded at the trials, and word about them spread, most whites realized that they had barely escaped the worst consequences of a general slave revolt and must have concluded that, but for the intervention of Providence, they would have been wiped out. As one resident commented, "What Success so well laid a Scheme would have had is plain, had not divine Providence interpos'd." "As no People were ever rescued from a Danger more imminent," reflected the judges soberly, "to whom shall our Deliverance be ascribed but to God, the Father of all Mercies; he cast a Mist before the Eyes of our Enemies, and awakened us from our long and deep Lethargy! He disclosed their most hidden Secrets, and graciously enabled us to take proper Measures for our Safety and the Destruction designed for us, he brought on their own Heads."[9] A large number of slaves were indeed "destroyed" during long weeks of trials and executions.

Was there really a plot? This question should be raised because it is generally much easier to gauge and authenticate a revolt than a conspiracy to revolt. Often carefully planned for some time, but also sometimes spontaneous, a revolt is an identifiable collective outburst of hostility in which lives are frequently lost and property damaged or destroyed; but because there is no comparable outburst in the case of a conspiracy, its existence can sometimes be in doubt. This, for example, has been the fate of Denmark Vesey's conspiracy of 1822 in Charleston, South Carolina, while, for obvious reasons, the same cannot be said about Nat Turner's rebellion in Southampton County, Virginia, nine years later, or the Stono Rebellion in South Carolina in 1739, or the Jamaica rebellion of 1760, or that in the Danish sugar island of St. John in 1733 — all bloody affairs. Referring to some of the problems of interpreting the Vesey affair, Eric Foner has noted that "largely because the plot was betrayed and suppressed, the evidence seems insubstantial. Was Charleston saved at the last minute from a carefully planned insurrection," he asked, "or was all that existed, as the historian Richard Wade has concluded, 'loose talk' among a number of slaves, and hysterical fears among the whites?" Wade, for a number of reasons, came to the conclusion that "no conspiracy in fact existed." But other scholars have taken the opposite view.[10] The obvious difficulties with which scholars must grapple in interpreting the evidence surrounding slave conspiracies also confronted many slaveowners and their contemporaries. It is hardly surprising therefore that whites in the other Leeward Islands doubted that there was a slave plot over in Antigua.[11] But in that island itself, few whites dared do likewise.

Did the Antigua slaves conspire to revolt, overthrow their masters, and take over the island, or was such a confession forced out of them when no such plans had been made? Or if there was a plot, did whites, frightened, perplexed, surprised, eager to see the troublemakers properly punished, exaggerate its scope? One of the disadvantages the student of slave resistance faces, according to Eric Foner, is that whites "frequently succumbed to panic and greatly exaggerated the size and scope of projected uprisings." In many cases too, rumors of intended revolts led to widespread panic and the execution of innocent slaves.[12] Conceivably in Antigua, either through plain fear or overreaction to slave insubordination and suspicious behavior, most whites believed there was a plot when there was none. Or, even if one existed, they may have simply exaggerated it. These issues deserve further exploration.

In constructing a case against the existence of a plot, that it was real only in the minds of whites, attention might be drawn to critical evidence related to frequent slave meetings when conspirators were allegedly recruited and plans laid, the supposed crowning of Court as king during an Akan ceremony, and other developments that convinced the authorities of the rebels' designs. Did such activities, taken together, necessarily indicate that the slaves were plotting a revolt? Could they not have been simply rituals of inversion, intended by slaves as harmless exercises? For their part, whites could have read much more into what was going on and perceived that their security was endangered, because they did not understand the real character of the community based upon African culture that had developed parallel to theirs. The slave community, although shaped by certain limits imposed by slavery and white attempts at hegemony, nonetheless possessed its own peculiar character, which was impenetrable to whites, who were mostly concerned with naked control and exploitation of slaves. What the master class could not understand they ignored, outlawed, or feared. But fear over the significance of slave activities in 1736 flared up, fanned by suspicion of some design afoot, only as bits and pieces of evidence emerged. Several whites had witnessed Court's supposed coronation more than a week before the authorities believed they had enough proof to proceed to arrest and try the rebels; and yet, at that time, no attempt seems to have been made to stop or interfere with the daylight ceremony, nor does there seem to have been any complaint lodged. But very quickly, in an atmosphere of suspicion, slave activities took on a stronger and more specific meaning, and what whites may have earlier dismissed as harmless or construed in symbolic terms they now interpreted literally. When, therefore, Court was believed to have been crowned, it could mean only that he would rule a black Antigua after all whites were slaughtered. And when slaves assumed titles of island gentry, here was more convincing evidence of a planned uprising.

Such developments also helped generate hysteria among whites that may have had political ramifiications; anxiety may have been, therefore, not just simply a disposition shared by all whites. Could some whites, such as justice of the peace Arbuthnot and members of the legislature, who very early believed there was a plot, have had anything to gain from such hysteria? Could they have used fear of revolt for their own purposes? Arbuthnot and other judges of the first court claimed that as a result of interference with proper trial proceedings, slaveowners were barred from attendance at the majority of slave trials; but we must wonder whether there could have been other, unstated motives. Did this also reflect some conflict within the master class? While slaves themselves could have used plot hysteria to settle scores with other slaves, masters could have done the same thing to their slaves who were suspected to be in the plot. Questions related both to the politics of hysteria and to the inability of whites to penetrate the culture of the slaves can be employed, in other words, to suggest that there may have been no slave plot at all. It could have been an invention of some whites who quickly convinced many gullible others.

Even before the trials began, Robert Arbuthnot and his colleagues of the first court believed there was a plot, and as they understood it, their main function was simply to discover the guilty slaves and punish them as they deserved. So far as the council and assembly members themselves were concerned, Arbuthnot's private investigations, carried out even before the bulk of the arrests began, had supplied convincing enough evidence that a plot existed, and most of these owners of slaves and other property, who had a vested interest in the preservation of order, expected to make examples of about 150 of the most involved slaves "both by Death and banishment."[13] There may have been an element of vengeance here. Whatever the case, Arbuthnot and the other judges, with the authority of the legislature, moved quickly to identify and try any slaves under suspicion. If these men were more inclined to revenge than justice, justified doubts must surely arise about the quality of slave witnesses' testimony, especially when it is realized that much of the testimony came from already convicted slaves, and that most of the trials were conducted in closed session. The judges used the evidence obtained to condemn suspected slaves and to prepare their detailed general report on a plot they were convinced existed.

How did these judges justify closed trials? They agreed that the procedure, "not of a Common kind," was only one of the unusual measures adopted. They had barred all whites from the trials, "more particularly the Masters of Slaves, except the Constables guarding the Prisoners and except twice or thrice where some Gentleman of Figure not Master of any Slaves under Tryal, was accidently present" because when they attempted open trials, intending to proceed with "the utmost Dispatch," they found the "Proceedings much retarded by the Spectators asking many Questions of the Prisoners & Witnesses, and some of them not proper." They "soon discovered too, by some Things that happened, how much Masters were prone to countenance & Excuse their Slaves, and that Slaves were imboldened by their Masters presence, and Witnesses intimidated." Arbuthnot and the other judges decided that secrecy was "necessary, which even Oaths of Secrecy might have not effectually procured, considering human frailty and forgetfulness and the common unguardedness of Speech most persons are liable to; For Sometimes a Dangerous Criminal might be mentioned by Witnesses or Party accused in the Course of the Tryal, And this might be talkt of abroad, and occasion Flights, Concealments, and other Inconveniencys not to be foreseen."

The "admitting Slaves to be Witnesses after Conviction of what We termed a Treasonable Conspiracy" was another departure from standard judicial practice. If this exception was considered well, they explained, "there is little or no weight in it For a Slave is not a Person known by the Law of England, and in the Eye of our Laws is the same Person after Conviction as before [,] Slaves being uncapable of giving Evidence, Except against each other (which is always done without Oath) of Sueing or being Sued having no inheritable blood, Masters of no Property, And being the Estate and property of others; So that they can loose no Credit nor have their blood Corrupted, nor forfeit any property, nor suffer any Disability by any Attainder." Moreover, the judges added, "it is expressly left by an Act of Our Island to the Discretion of the Justices to Examine ANY SLAVE as Witness against another Slave, and give what Credit to his Testimony he thinks it in Conscience deserves." Commenting on the use of this discretionary power at the trials, they observed that "we allways made Conscionable Allowances for the hopes & fears of those under Conviction, whom we examined as Witnesses, and for the Ignorance of Prisoners, Acting as their Council as well as Judges, and thro the whole Course of the Inquiry we may venture to Affirm, that we have leaned much more to the Mercifull than Severe."[14]

Did slave witnesses tell the truth in court? Because the vast majority of suspects were tried in closed courts, it should not be surprising that no comment from outside sources has been found to allow critical evaluation of testimony delivered. As there is also nothing on the few open trials, we are left with only the court version, which, needless to say, must be approached with caution.

If some slaves invented stories at their trial or when they gave evidence against others, it is also likely that many others did not do so. Speaking out boldly and describing the complex details of a plot that came close to fruition, when they knew execution was almost certain, may have been a final act of defiance and a declaration of manhood. If, however, many of the slaves' stories and confessions had been supplied by an already prejudiced court, it would help to explain the remarkable consistency of much of the large volume of testimony; but this consistency may also help support the existence of a plot if it can be shown that apprehended suspects awaiting trial, or witnesses, were not in communication with one another in jail or had not conspired to give similar stories if caught. On the second point there is no evidence, but suspects were probably in contact, there being so many held in the jailhouse that on at least two occasions a number were secured on ships in St. John's harbor.[15] But the focus must be on witnesses from whom the bulk of the testimony came, and they appear to have been confined separately and were closely guarded. The judges of the second court believed they could not have entered into "combinations."

In a report to the governor and council on their proceedings against eight slaves whom they condemned to death, these judges felt compelled to refute accusations made by many whites that the slave witnesses, whose testimony had been used to try the eight slaves and others before them, had collaborated in presenting corresponding testimony to incriminate others. These skeptics felt that it was possible that there was no plot at all, or if one existed, that it could not have been as extensive as was imagined. Although "there be not the least Proof of a Generall Combination," the judges complained, "yet the Pretended fears of Some, the Shruggs and Doubtfull words of others, Dropt Purposely in Publick have made men Doubtfull and uneasy." When the "first Whispers of Combination" had reached the governor, they contended, he had sent for the officer of the guard and the twelve constables guarding the witnesses and interviewed them individually before the council. According to the officer of the guard, witnesses were confined in three separate rooms: "they were placed at Such Distance; one from the other, that they Could Not Speak to one another, but that they must be heard, by the Soldiers, and Sentrys, who were night and Day in the Rooms with them, and placed between them." At night also, "besides the Sentrys, Several Soldiers kept between every two Evidences" whose hands and feet were "fast in Irons." The officer of the guard believed it would have been impossible for witnesses to have collaborated, and the constables themselves agreed. Moreover, the judges pointed out, witnesses hardly ever knew what slaves were confined and when they would be tried until they saw them in court, "so that were they Ever so willing it is hardly Possible they could Combine against any Particular Person but from Reasoning."

In the same report, these judges put together an interesting case supporting the existence of a plot. To assert that the "first and most Plausable Probability is that Conspirators will Say, or Swear, any thing of any Body, in Order to Save their Own lives . . . is far from being generally true," they argued. "Wee need not go further than our Own Conspiracy to find above Three Score who Chose the most Cruell Death, rather than Impeach their Fellow Conspirators of what they knew to be true. What reason then have we to Suppose (without some Proof of the Fact) that any one of those who have Confessed to Save their lives, would maliciously give a false Evidence (much less Combine with others who might Detect him) to take away the life of an Innocent Person; but especially when they had it in their Power to Speak the Truth of such Multitudes, the Execution of Every one of whom was Equally Indifferent to the Publick?" Yet even if it were true that conspirators generally tried to save their own skins, continued the judges, "what Temptation can they lye under to Accuse Innocent Persons, after their lives are Secure?"

They explained further that they had adhered to the rule "to Ask Every Prisoner, before he came upon his Tryal, whether he would Confess, and to Promise him his life if he did, without any Stipulation that he should turn Evidence." Furthermore, "all the Old evidences" of the first court "were Secure of their lives before they Came into our hands." These slaves, then, became witnesses after their lives had been spared for admitting to their part in the plot. "What Temptation then would People so Circumstanced lye under to Accuse any one falsely?" the judges asked. Not only was it improbable, they argued, "but almost Impossible for any Men to be Guilty of a great Crime without any Temptation to Serve no End, or Purpose, to gratify no Passion; the most Abandoned Profligates and Villains never did it; but especially in the Present Case where a Detection of such Villany would in all Probability have made them lyable to Forfeit the very lives they were before Secured of." Moreover, "some who gave their Evidence were Actually Acquitted and others sure of being Acquitted." The judges concluded that they could not find a sensible explanation why the slaves would have given false testimony as was alleged, and, if there was one, it "must be a Secret to Every one but those that hatched the Combination."

Aware also that it would be claimed that "some Old Grudge, for an Injury received, might Prompt" witnesses "to take this Opportunity of Satiating their Revenge," the judges had a ready reply. "We answer that it Cannot fairly be Supposed, there Could be such Grudges, against many; or that a Man Secure of his life would run the Risque of losing it, to Gratify a Grudge, much less can it be Supposed that others would Risque their lives that were Secure to them by Combining with them to Gratify their private Malice." They then went on to make some striking observations about slave behavior. "In truth," they reflected, "the Supposition of Old Grudges among Slaves is against fact and Experience." While it was true that slaves sometimes killed one another when they were "Drunk & at a Play. . .yet Considering their Number," this did not happen "so Often as [with] white People." The judges remarked that they had hardly "heard of any Negroes taking any Private Methods to gratifye their Revenge against their own Colour hardly any Such thing as Poisoning, way laying in the Dark or Killing one Another while they Sleep; no, these are Vices of their Betters, and Seldom or never Practiced by them, but upon their Betters." As proof against "a bare Supposition of any Grudges in the Evidence," the judges argued that if it were also taken into account, "how Easily Negroes bear the Highest Injuries, from one another without taking any Notable revenge, such as Thefts, lying with one Anothers Wives; how friendly and Affectionate they are to One Another, to Screen them from Punishment, the affection that naturally arises from a Fellowship in Slavery, the Mutual Tyes that are Contracted in, and Arise from their Joynt Conspiracy, the many friends and Relations they have in it"— these showed that the slaves could "never Voluntarily and Officiously, and to no End or Purpose, take away one anothers lives by giving false Evidence," especially when all the witnesses were "Still in their hearts, well wishers to the Designe that has Miscarried," and "very unwillingly give the Evidence they do, Concealing much more than they Declare." Of all the witnesses used by the two courts, only three, according to the judges of the second court, judging by their "Behaviour and Manner of Giving their Evidence," seemed to give testimony willingly.[16]

These men, then, believed that there was a plot. They were not misled.

Court and Tomboy reportedly confessed their part in the affair, neither of them doing so "till after Condemnation, Court making no Confession, but at the Place of Execution, after having been tied about half an Hour upon the Wheel, and then untied at his own Request, in order to confess," while Tomboy "freely confess'd before he came to the Place of Execution, and without any Pain inflicted."[17] Confronted by the certainty of execution, these two courageous men could have preferred not to misrepresent or lie about the very existence of an affair for which they were responsible, especially if they had no way of knowing whether some of their followers, still at large, planned to stage a revolt anyway. The revolt as planned had not come off, but Court and Tomboy may have decided to accept death with the satisfaction that they could tell their oppressors how close they had come to liquidation. Admitting their role in the affair did not necessarily mean that they felt remorse, as the judges' use of the word *confession* might imply.

The evidence also shows that one courageous slave, Ned, belonging to Jacob Morgan, some time after his trial "Spirited up the other Criminals, who lie in Goal for the Same Crime not to Confess and to keep their minds to themselves and to be true to their Trust," or words to that effect. Two white men, presumably jailers or guards, claimed they overheard these remarks, which they reported to the judges, who earlier had been "inclin'd to have Respited his Execution a little longer," but now quicklly ordered that Ned "be immediately hung up alive in Chains there to Continue till he Dies, then his head to be Cut off and set up in his Masters Plantation upon a Pole, and his [body] to be Burnt, in Otto's Pasture." For what it is worth, the evidence places Ned among the ringleaders, and his behavior in confinement suggests that there may have been a real plot, however much public anxiety may have blown it out of proportion. Another prisoner, Cudjoe, moreover urged "the Parham Plantation Negro's (being four) to Die like Men, and not Confess anything against" two accused free blacks, the brothers Benjamin and Billy Johnson. According to the testimony of the guard and a slave witness, Cudjoe then "Strutted about the Room and Stampd his foot on the Ground" where he was held, exclaiming, "Damn me, I have a heart as Stout as a Lyon. I Dont Care if they come and fetch me now."[18] The rebel slaves also engaged in various well-recorded rituals in preparation for war against the whites (see chap. 11). In the light of such evidence, slave confessions and other testimony should not be dismissed as attempts to escape punishment, or as forced testimony, or even as mere delusions of grandeur, particularly for those who finally forfeited their lives. Nevertheless, they should be used with caution. The plot was not a figment of slaveowners' paranoia. Many of them appeared sane and clear-headed nough at the time of execution to recall how much their slaves were worth.

The idea that they would have accepted massive loss of property, even with compensation, based on the figment of others' imagination seems quite implausible.

Several developments led up to the plot's discovery. According to the general report of the first court, "the suspicions of a Plot were first owing to the uncommon Liberty of behaviour and Speech of some Slaves in and about Town; An unusual Noise of Conckshells Blown in the Dead of Night without any apparent Cause; The assembling of Great Numbers of Slaves, at unreasonable Times; Great Feastings and Caballings, at one of which, Court was then reported to have been crowned and honoured as King; Lists of Officers and Soldiers and Provisions of Ammunitions spoke and inquired after among them." But it was mainly owing to the curiosity and later investigations of Robert Arbuthnot, one of the justices of the peace for St. John's town, that the probable significance of all this was determined early enough for the authorities to take appropriate action. As justice of the peace, Arbuthnot regularly tried slave offenders in his district, so he was in a position to scrutinize their behavior. For months, he said, he had "perceived their Insolence increasing to a very Dangerous Pitch, the many Instances of which had possessed him with a Notion . . . that they were forming a Design of some Attempt or other to throw of their Yoke which appeared to him to be a thing full of Danger Considering their Superiority of Numbers" and the "Over Great Security" of the whites. [19]

On Monday, October 11, Arbuthnot started private inquiries when he and two other justices, Thomas Kerby and Mr. Jennings, met at Kerby's house, where they examined some slaves who had been arrested earlier for gambling. During the proceedings they learned that one of the slaves, Johnny, belonging to Mr. Mercier, had been overheard by Mrs. Browne asking another slave about "a List of officers and Soldiers." Summoned before the justices, Mrs. Browne herself testified "That one Night about three weeks ago she Overheard the said Johnny Speaking to another Slave unknown to her about some Slaves who had Received Public Correction in the Town that Day and saying to him, Hey Day! They have been Punishing Our Officers & Soldiers. To which the other Slave said, I was to have been punished if I had not gone out of the way, and then Asked the said Johnny if the Noise of it was over Johnny made Answer Yes it was, but said he they had whipped One Negro but he was not in Our List." In an attempt to learn more about this list and particularly what names were included, Arbuthnot then took Johnny aside into Kerby's back room, promising to release and reward him if he would give information, but the slave obstinately denied "that he Ever said the words or that he knew or heard of any List or of any Slaves being Officers or Soldiers." Johnny's companions similarly pleaded complete ignorance; but for gambling, they and Johnny "were Ordered Public Correction about the Town."

Arbuthnot, "Being Alarm'd at these expressions and Convinced from all Circumstances that had fallen under his Observation before that Could not be said without a meaning,...could not help Communicating his Sentiments freely and Publickly" to Kerby, Jennings, and other whites present that "the Island appeared to him to be in the Utmost Danger from the slaves." He therefore proposed the immediate preparation of a warrant "to Search all negro Houses not only in the Town but the Plantations Contiguous to it for Gunns Cutlasses Powder, Shott & ca. and Every thing Else of a Suspicious nature and to Apprehend any Slaves on whom any of those things should be found." The warrant was prepared, and the constables assigned to carry out the searches received instructions to move "with the Utmost Dispatch and Secrecy" in order to catch the slaves unawares if possible. At the same time, Arbuthnot promised to recommend compensation for "their Extraordinary trouble" out of public funds. When whites in St. John's town got wind of these developments, several offered information against slaves. News also reached the slaves, one of whom, Jack, belonging to Phillip Darby, became "very Clamorous and impolitick."

Reporting to Arbuthnot the following morning, October 12, Henry James, a white man, said that Jack had made some incriminating remarks in connection with the public punishment of Johnny and others the day before. "What...Do the Baccararas [whites] mean by Punishing the Slaves?" Jack had blazed. "Do they think Negroes Can live upon a Bit and Six herrings a Week?" Jack evidently saw a connection between underfeeding and rebelliousness and resented punishment of hungry and restless slaves. When Mrs. Douglas, Phillip Darby's sister, scolded him "for speaking in this Manner and told him that perhaps he would be taken up by and by," Jack retorted, "what...Can they Do to me, they Can only whip me." But, said Mrs. Douglas, "they can do worse." Defiantly, Jack shot back, "They Can only hang or burn me. What signifies it? I Can but Die." According to Henry James, Jack also admitted to Mrs. Douglas that he was to be one of Court's generals and that the slaves had recently crowned Court king.

Arbuthnot thought Henry James's disclosure "too Material not to be Enquired into" and immediately went over to Thomas Kerby's house to tell him what he had learned about his slave Court. Both Kerby and Arbuthnot then hurried over to Mrs. Douglas's for confirmation of Henry James's story. "Mrs. Douglas Owned Everything Except what Related to Court, in which at that time" Arbuthnot imagined "She had a Reserve And it appeared so, for that same Evening Mr. Darby told the said Arbuthnot the words as Mr. James had related them." When Arbuthnot inquired where the slave Jack might be, Mrs. Douglas said that "he was gone aboard Ship." Anxious to question Jack, Arbuthnot also itched to see, if not yet to question, Court himself, whom he apparently did not know, and Kerby satisfied his curiosity.

According to Kerby, Court, who had been his slave for nearly thirty years, was now head slave "and had always behaved with great Fidelity and honesty." It was unlikely that he could be involved in any "bad Design." Arbuthnot listened, turning this over in his mind. Other persons gave a different picture of Court. The substance of the "very bad Character" they portrayed was that "he was a Dark Designing, Ambitious Insolent Fellow; that upon some Occasions he had threatened Young Mr. Gamble; that if it was not for the Difference of Colour he would tear his Hearts blood Out; That His Master had too good an Opinion of him, [and] was in great Measure blind to his faults; that he allowed him to Carry on trade and many other and greater Indulgencies than ever allowed to any Slave in the island; and that Court had a greater Ascendant and Influence Over the Slaves of this Island than any other Slave whatsoever particularly Over those of his Own Country, the Coromantees who all paid him great Homage and Respect & stood in great awe of him." For the time being, nevertheless, Arbuthnot did nothing about Court. Sometime later that day two constables reported back that they had searched Court's room at Kerby's house, where they only had time to find "a Purse which they thought had more than One hundred Pistoles in it, and an Exceeding fine wrought Drum which they cut to pieces." They had heard Court had a cache of arms, but these were not found because Kerby's clerk, Mr. Milney, and Court prevented them from searching further, claiming that Kerby himself had already gone over Court's room the previous night. Still, Arbuthnot made no move to arrest or question Court.

By afternoon Philip Darby's Jack had been located and Mr. Ambrose Lynch, a merchant in town, brought him before Arbuthnot, who "immediately took the said Slave Aside and Asked him about the Words" alleged against him. At first Jack steadfastly denied everything but admitted "after much sifting" that he was to be one of Court's generals. When Arbuthnot pressed for more details, even offering a reward for "the Whole Truth," Jack "made great Professions of his Innocence and said he only Spoke these words in Jest," meaning no harm. If Jack had hinted at the truth once, would he do so again? Arbuthnot persisted. Jack stuck to his story that he knew nothing about a plot, adding that if he had information "he Certainly would Discover." Unconvinced, Arbuthnot decided to imprison the unyielding slave, whom Mr. Lynch defended, saying he was not a bad fellow, having lived and worked faithfully with him for many years. Arbuthnot would not change his mind. He believed "there was all the Reason in the World to Suspect a Conspiracy of the Slaves" and that Jack was involved.

In regard to the general behavior of the slaves in and about town, Arbuthnot received much information, alarming enough. On either October 11 or 12, James Hanson, a constable, told Arbuthnot that two nights before, when he had lashed a slave with his whip while breaking up "a great Multitude" of them, the slave shouted at him, "God damn your blood! I know you and I will come up with You!" Such threatening language at any other time would probably have meant little, but Arbuthnot believed it ought to be taken into serious account in light of evidence, however circumstantial, that indicated the slaves might be planning something. The justice must have listened intently to Mr. Morgan, another constable, as he made his report "about the Negroes that made a Noise with a Conk Shell and Assembled together, in the Pastures and Out Skirts of the Town," tying the evidence together, searching for some pattern that would confirm what he so far only strongly suspected.

Morgan reported that at about one o'clock on Tuesday morning, October 5, he heard "the blowing of a Conk Shell near his House, which is at the upper End of the Town where there are few Inhabitants." He got out of bed, "Softly Open'd his Window," and in the moonlight "very plainly saw in the Cross Roads by Wavell Smith's House Upwards of One hundred negro Men (so far as he Could Guess)," some armed with cutlasses "brandishing them about and some few with Guns." They fired twice, shattering the stillness of the early morning. Morgan admitted that "he was afraid to Speak to them or Call Out to them to Separate." However, "a Quarter of an Hour after his first Observing them, they all Marched Down towards the Country Pond and Otto's Pasture making hurra's and a great noise as they went along." Morgan was not the only one who had heard the conch shell. Several people living near Otto's pasture, who must also have heard the commotion the slaves made, confirmed the sounding. But unlike Morgan they probably did not stir. Morgan reported further that on Friday night, October 8, at about eight o'clock, while he was chasing several slaves out of town, he "gave one of them a Lick with his Whip, upon which they Separated and made towards Otto's Pasture." One bold fellow from Edward Otto Bayer's plantation stopped, yelling "Damn you boy its your turn now, but it will be mine by and by and soon too!" Arbuthnot took all this as proof of the "Insolence of the Slaves and how much they Despised Common Punishments." One white woman's comment about Mr. Mercier's Johnny, whom Arbuthnot and justices Kerby and Jennings had sentenced to a public whipping of one hundred lashes, only strengthened this belief. Mrs. Murphy said Johnny did not "flinch nor shed a tear at the Whipping," and when it was over he told another slave "it was true it was a Severe Whipping, but he Matter'd it not more than a Musketo Bite."

Arbuthnot, while grateful for whatever information he could find, remained "in great Perplexity of mind to know what to Do or how to proceed to Come to the Bottom of the negros Designs." He finally decided to seek the help of a "faithful Sensible" slave who, he hoped, would know enough about the slaves' secrets. Sometime on October 12, he approached Emanuel, a Portuguese slave belonging to Edward Gregory, a cooper in St. John's. Emanuel "at once Opened such a Scene (without Seeming himself to know the meaning of it) As put it beyond all Doubt that a Conspiracy was formed and near ripe for Execution, and that Court was at the head of it."[20]

Arbuthnot first asked Emanuel "whether he thought the Negroes were not arrived to a much Greater highth of Insolence than he had Ever Observed," to which he replied, "Yes he never had seen Such freedoms as they took, That Droves of them would Often pass by their House in the Night Time, That many of them would Ride a Horse back, That they Often Diced in the Church Pasture and had often heard them Say, I have lost Seven Shillings and Such like Sums at Play." When asked "whether he had not within this Fortnight or three Weeks heard a Conk Shell blow at unseasonable hours of the Night and Seen or heard of Assemblys of Slaves about the town in the Dead of the Night, & what he thought the meaning of all this to be," Emanuel replied in the affirmative, remarking that "he believed the Conck Shells were to Assemble the Negro togather, and that they met & Consulted togather in the Pastures and Places about the Town at and after Midnight." Even so, Emanuel said he could not be sure what specifically the slaves were up to because "he never went Amongst them but kept himself at home and Declined the Company of other Slaves." Perhaps because he thought Emanuel was holding back information, Arbuthnot probed further to know "whether he heard any thing of their Intentions to Rise" and "Whether he Did not Suspect some Such Design within himself." But Emanuel would not be drawn out. He replied only that "he Knew not what to Think, they were grown very Impudent, The White People gave them too much Freedom."

About Court, however, Emanuel had much to say. He remembered that Court "came on Saturday Night Little of this side Last Christmass to their Cooper Shop a Horse Back, and Asked me if I would go to the Widdow Langfords, where he said he was to have a Feast and a Merriment and Attend with his Trumpet there & at the Other Feasts to Sound to their healths." Emanuel claimed he declined the invitation: "I told him my Master was perpetually calling to me in the Night Time being a Sickly Man, & therefore Excused My Self from going to any of their Feasts without my Masters Leave." Throwing his mind back to Court's visit, Emanuel said: "I remember when Court came first that Night. I had my Trumpet in my hand Sounding. I was there Alone; it was a Dark Rainy Night. Court had on a Great Coat but upon his Entering into the Shop he unbuttoned his great Coat and threw it Open & their appeared a fine hanger by his Side with a Red handle. Court Drew it Out and Flourished it, and said Look here you Dog is not this a fine thing. He also had a handsome Green Silk Cap on his head with a Large Bunch of black Feathers Sticking up from it behind." Disappointed at Emanuel's refusal to be his trumpeter, Court next tried to "Speak to my Wife," Emanuel related, "and I Accompanyed him to my Masters Yard where my Wife was." There, Court told her what he wanted Emanuel to do, but she replied that "the Trumpet belongs to the King, and is for the White People, And is not Proper for Negroes." "Well Woman, they say you are not good, and I find you are not good," Court lashed out in disgust. "Take your Husband and Tie him upon your Back." Then Court "in a great passion went to his Mare and Rode to Mrs. Langfords Plantation."

A month or two later, "Of an afternoon," Court returned to ask Emanuel to make him a large umbrella or canopy, explaining, "I want to play my Country Play." He "told me he brought some Sticks to me and wire" to make it, Emanuel recounted. "The Sticks were about Three foot long and an Inch broad and the Wire was to fasten them. He also brought some blew Cloth and White Ozenbrigg to make it of. . .and Pressed me very much to make it, and put it together and stay'd till I Did it, and I made & fasten'd the Frame togather & Cut Out the Cloth, and gave the Cloth to Court to have it Sowed, and then Court went away. So Soon as Court turn'd his Back I took the Frame and threw it behind my house not Caring to be Concerned about making any Such thing." About two days later continued Emanuel, Court brought "the Cloth Sticht togather and Desired me to See it fitted to the Frame, and told me to paint a Pidgeon on Top, and gave me Paint and a Vial of Linseed Oyle to Do it with. I told him I would & he Often Called for it but I put it off, from One time to another, and Never Did it, and was Determined never to Do it, but I Did not tell Court so, I always made Excuses to him of want of time." Finally, "Court fell Out with me upon that Account and for Several Months togather, when-ever I passed by him he Either took no Notice at All of me or Else spoke Abusively to me, As you Damn'd Drunken Son of a Bitch, you Dog, and such Names." But it was obviously important that Court have his canopy, and one day, as Emanuel lay sick in bed, he came to ask for it, deciding, when he discovered it was not finished, to "finish it himself or get some Body Else to do it." Very seriously, he spoke to Emanuel "bending his body to the ground & pointing with his finger to it. WELL EMANUEL if you had taken my Advice and kept Close to me you would be a Better Man than you are Now, if you was to see me do good, you would Do good, If I Do bad You Do Bad." Emanuel replied, "if You go to Hell must I go there to?" Next day Court sent a boy for the canopy materials. The boy took only the frame, leaving the cloth cover behind.

There is a strong suspicion that Emanuel had some idea of Court's intentions but did not wish to give Arbuthnot too much information and implicate himself. When asked why he had not finished the canopy, Emanuel replied quite astutely that "his mind Misgave him that it was for no good Purpose." What did Arbuthnot make of all this? His interpretation was that Court had been "long Since Preparing the badges of Royalty and both by his Habits and his words given Indications of the Success of his Designs and of his future Grandeur and that he wanted Emanuel to partake of his fortune."[21]

Next morning, Wednesday, October 13, Arbuthnot received word that Colonel Samuel Martin's slave Jemmy had asked Mrs. Booth, a white woman in town, to buy him some gunpowder "with promises to pay her for her trouble." The justice immediately sent constables to Martin's plantation to search the slave huts and bring Jemmy to town for questioning. When they found no incriminating evidence, Arbuthnot concluded that Jemmy must have had time to strip his hut and, after questioning him and his brother Tony, imprisoned Jemmy on suspicion of treason. Obviously not inclined to give suspects the benefit of the doubt, Arbuthnot some hours later also had Fortune and Tom Limerick confined "upon his Own private Suspicions Meerly without any Information," reasoning that "if anything Criminal was going forward," these two "bold and Dangerous" slaves were most probably involved.[22]

Later that same day, Arbuthnot also visited Thomas Kerby and met Court, who denied he had a cache of arms or that he kept a large sum of money at his house. But Mr. Robert Delap, another white man who was present, declared that he was "credibly informed that Court had been at Mrs. Parkes' Plantation the Sunday Seven night before and there was Crown'd King of the Coromantees in Presence of the greatest Number of Negroes that were Ever known to be Assembled together, Near Two Thousand." At this gathering Tomboy had held the second place of honor.[23] Kerby could not believe his ears, but he finally offered to hand Court over. Arbuthnot, however, "not knowing what bad Consequences might Attend his Sending the Principal Conspirator (As he looked upon Court to be) to Goal," preferred not to arrest him but let the legislature take all necessary steps against him, and also Tomboy, who had held "a very Sumptuous and Publick feast but the Sunday before [October 10] at his Own Masters House in St. John's to which were invited a great Number of Slaves . . . Several White Persons were spectators to it."[24]

Two days later, Arbuthnot received more information about Court. John Bolan, one of the constables, reported that on the night of October 12, Mr. Farley, the bookkeeper, saw five or six slaves including Court in close consultation near Kerby's house in town. Bolan said that Farley overheard them talking about preparing arms, but they dispersed as he approached. When Farley questioned Court, he firmly denied any conversation about arms, protesting that "he had been a long time in the Island and Could not be supposed to have any bad Design." Farley himself later confirmed Bolan's report. Court's response, calculated to put Farley off the scent, can be compared to a similar remark attributed to Denmark Vesey during his trial, when, addressing the court, "his principal endeavour was to impress them with the idea, that as his situation in life had been such that he could have had no inducement to join such an attempt, the charge against him must be false."[25] Where Vesey stressed socioeconomic status, Court mentioned the many years he had been in Antigua. Vesey, a free Negro and master carpenter, who had been a slave, and Court, a waiting man or personal attendant of his master and living in town, were both privileged blacks whose special status, however, did not prevent them from making common cause with other blacks of lower status to revolt, contrary to what whites may have believed about the behavior of privileged slaves. In Court's ingenious remark itself, we catch a revealing glimpse of the mind of the shrewd and capable leader of the conspiracy. This man had carefully weighed the risks involved and gauged the chances for success. He obviously understood and took into account the psychology of whites, who tended to regard unassimilated slaves as more prone to revolt and open resistance than assimilated ones, African or Creole.

Information about the meeting near Kerby's house reached Arbuthnot on the morning of October 15 just before he reported his findings to the legislature, and he incorporated it into his report. After five days of painstaking inquiry, the justice believed he had uncovered enough to show there was a slave plot now "near ripe for Execution." Acting upon his report, the legislature moved swiftly against slaves and free blacks believed to be involved in the affair.

2

"Our Island Is in Such a Miserable Condition"

When the Antigua legislature met on October 15, few members may have known the full extent of Arbuthnot's discoveries, but before the session ended all had heard enough to be persuaded that a serious crisis loomed. After carefully considering Arbuthnot's report, the most important business on the agenda that day, the legislature turned its attention to how best to proceed. The assembly lost no time in giving a first reading to a bill already prepared by Thomas Stephens "to Restrain and Curb the Insolent behaviour and Tumultuous Meeting of Slaves," which it regarded as "a matter of the utmost Consequence to the publick." It then scheduled a second reading for the next meeting but, before adjourning, supported the governor's order "for the Kings Troops to Patrole thro the streets in Saint John's & places adjoining, and...if they met any Concourse of Negros,...to fire upon them" if they would not disperse. Any slaves killed would be paid for out of public funds.[1]

Four days later, on October 19, the legislature appointed four justices of the peace, Robert Arbuthnot, councillor John Vernon, assemblyman and attorney general Ashton Warner, and assemblyman Nathaniel Gilbert, to conduct full-scale inquiries into the plot within their respective areas of jurisdiction with authority to offer rewards of five pistoles each for any suspects taken up. "Sworn to Act According [to] their knowledge, their Consciences, and the Laws," these four men were to meet again as a court "at such Days and places as they shall agree upon to proceed to Tryal of Such Slaves as they shall think there is Matter Enough against and report their Resolutions from time to time" to the governor. Already, Court, Tomboy, and many other slaves had been detained. The legislature felt that those against whom the evidence was strongest should be tried without delay, while the rest should be kept confined in case more evidence against them should come to light. These, however, the judges could try or release at their discretion.[2]

On October 23 the legislature passed a special act, published in St. John's the same day, that formally authorized Arbuthnot, Vernon, Warner, and Gilbert to investigate the plot and any other disturbances among slaves over the next three months and gave them discretionary power to use slave testimony even if it meant inflicting "pains or tortures not extending to Loss of life or limb" to obtain it.

21

The act justified torture on at least three grounds. First, there was no local law that allowed the justices "to extort or draw Confessions from any Slave charged with the said Conspiracy." Second, there was good reason to believe such a positive law might be useful because "Occasion may soon happen again to make discoverys of Crimes of the like kind, Rebellions and Treasons being of late more frequent among Slaves than heretofore this being the Second plot formed in this Island Within these Seven Years." Third, contended the act, as "no Oaths are found anyway binding upon the said Slaves who are not Christians, nor sensible of the Obligation of oaths," the safety of whites depended "entirely upon the preventing and fully discovering and coming to the bottom and whole truth of the present and other such Conspiracys with the utmost dispatch lest the same may be put in Execution even while" under investigation. Without extensive use of torture, however, (for they later claimed having used it only three times) the judges pushed on with their inquiries, seeking to get to the root of the whole unsettling affair.[3]

While no record of the trials of Court and Tomboy has been found, it is still clear enough that they and ten others executed October 20–27 were convicted largely upon slave testimony, particularly that of Edward Gregory's Emanuel, John Gunthorpe's Coromantee, Robin, and Walter Nugent's Coromantee, Cuffee. It was from Cuffee that the judges first learned about plans to blow up the ballroom on the night of the ball. That part of the planned revolt Court and Tomboy had made known "to few, if any" of the rebels, but Cuffee had overheard the two leaders discussing it, noted the general report, "in a dark Night, at Mr. Kerbys' back door."[4] Satisfied that Court and Tomboy had masterminded the plot, the judges convicted them on October 19 during the night, sentencing them to be broken the following day on the wheel, an instrument of torture similar to the rack, which stretched and dislocated the victim's limbs. Hercules, another ringleader, the slave of John Christophers, received a similar sentence.[5]

On Wednesday morning, October 20, related one observer, "King Court was brought to the Place of Execution, there was laid extended on a wheel, seiz'd by the Wrists and Ancles, and so laid basking in the Sun for the full Space of an Hour and a Quarter, or more, when he begg'd Leave to plead; to which the Justices gave their Assent, and he acknowledged every Thing that was alledged against him, and what his General Tomboy had confess'd in prison the same Morning, when he was assur'd his Time drew near for Execution." At about noon Court was finally executed in the market place evidently before a curious crowd assembled to witness the grim spectacle. His head was severed and stuck up on a pole "of some considerable Height" at the jail door for all to see. The body was burned in Otter's pasture. Whether Court's "Kingly Cap and Canopy" were taken from him just before the execution or earlier is not clear, but somehow, according to one report, a slave had got hold of them. Next day it was Tomboy's turn at the wheel. His head was also cut off and placed beside Court's and the body burned. Before he died, he reportedly "received 35 Strokes with a large Iron Bar as hard as a lusty Negroe Fellow could strike upon the Breast." Hercules was executed the following day. One writer said he lived up to his name, dying "without either remose, or fear. In above four hours torture upon the Rack, not a groan or Sigh came from him, his voice never faltered, and he look'd at the Bar which broke and mangled his Limbs as if he rather enjoyed than feared it. His intrepidity amazed every Body." His head was cut off and displayed, not alongside the other two, but by the customs house, while his body was burned. "He died the bravest of any," said another account, "for he never winched, all the while his Bones were breaking and was more troubled at the Impertinence of a Fly which perched upon his Lip, than all the Torments he endured upon the Rack." One supposed eyewitness, moved by what he saw, was unable to conceal his admiration for the way the three slaves faced their end. They died, he said, "with amazing Obstinacy." Four other slaves deeply implicated in the plot were chained "to Stakes alive and burnt," also on October 22 in Otter's pasture, all of them "valuable Tradesmen and Sensible Fellows." By October 27, five others had also been burned.[6]

After these executions the judges suspended trials while they sought leads on other suspects who might still be at large, not believing, as Court and Tomboy had said in their "imperfect Confessions," that the plot was "stifled in its Birth before the Poyson of it had been far Spread." The breakthrough came when Thomas Hanson's Philida, Tomboy's sister, who had been arrested for making "some virulent Expressions. . .upon her Brother's account," allegedly disclosed voluntarily that several slaves had frequently met on Saturday nights at the house of Treblin, the Creole slave of Samuel Morgan. Philida's brother Jemmy confirmed this after being taken into custody. Treblin, according to the judges, "threw himself into Our hands, without hope of Mercy, making an ample discovery." He admitted when interrogated that many slaves had solemnly sworn to kill the whites, at least fifty binding themselves to do so on October 26, interestingly enough, just three days after the judges had released a number of them for lack of evidence. But now led by the late Thomas Freeman's Coromantee slave, Secundi, "that grand Incendiary," they were still determined to revolt and avenge the deaths of Court and Tomboy. Treblin's information, including details of the slaves' "Oath of Secrecy and Fidelity," which the judges had not known of before, and accounts from Mr. Langford's Billy and others, led them to conclude that "much remain'd to be discovered" of the "most Dangerous Conspiracy cou'd be form'd," and they vigorously pressed on with arrests and prosecutions. Reflecting on all these developments later in their general report, Arbuthnot and the other judges admitted that after the first twelve executions "it might have been reasonably thought, that at least a present Stop might have been put to their prosecuting this bloody Conspiracy, but the Conspirators Spirits seemed rather raised than sunk by it." According to one source, Secundi planned a revolt for the Christmas holidays "when by Law they [the slaves] are to have three Days allowed them."[7] This seems plausible enough, though the judges did not mention it.

When the judges realized that the slaves were determined to revolt even after discovery of the original plot and the execution of some of its leaders, they redoubled efforts to locate and try suspects. Breaking on the wheel and burning, they also concluded, were obviously "too lenative and not Sufficiently Exemplary because the Criminals were not long enough under their Sufferings." Accordingly, they substituted gibbeting alive because it would "lengthen their Pains" and strike "greater Terror into the Slaves that may see their Suffering." The court condemned four slaves "principally and deeply Concern'd" in the plot but who protested innocence "against the fullest evidence" to be "hung up alive with proper Iron Work about their Bodies in the Publick Market Place of St. John's Town upon Jibbets as high as can Conveniently be made and the Execution to be performed as soone as the Gibbets and Irons Can be finished." The condemned were Samuel Martin's Jemmy, James Gamble's Coley, Cuffey of Parham Plantation, one of the biggest in the island, and Quashey, who belonged to Samuel Hoskins.[8] Sentence on Coley, Cuffey, and Quashey was carried out on November 10, and one report says the first two lasted two days and the other three days. Their heads were then cut off and displayed on poles in their master's plantations, while the bodies were burned.[9] Jemmy escaped execution altogether when he became a prime witness. He was later banished.[10] Billy, belonging to widow Langford, had been condemned together with these slaves, but because he "came to a full Confession after Condemnation," the judges stayed his execution "because wee think if he behaves ingenuously to Represent him as fit to be banished, tho, wee have promised nothing to him, but have made use of him already as an Evidence." He was banished in the end. Treblin, whom Philida had implicated, had not yet been tried. But he too, because he made "a very Ample Confession & Discovery," escaped execution and was later banished.[11]

Jemmy, Billy, and Treblin were lucky only because the judges gambled on their usefulness in providing damaging testimony against other rebels. Jacob Morgan's Ned was not as fortunate. On November 11 he was gibbeted as a ringleader. One report noted simply that he died after eight days, while another supplied more vivid detail. According to this account, Ned was gibbeted in the marketplace at about sunset. On November 18 he "got out of his Irons by his Body being wasted and fell down." He was then carried into the prison "and Kept until next Morning by order of the Capt. of the Guard," when the judges paid him a visit. Ned at this point promised them a full confession. They "called some Doctors to him, who gave things proper to raise his Spirits, and ordered him to be put to sleep on a Bed; he was bath'd with warm Water, and had Broths made and given him." On the afternoon of November 19 at about four o'clock, the judges returned to hear what Ned had to say, expecting details about "the Arms and Ammunition" the rebels had secured, but he disappointed them "and continued obstinate, only he acknowledged the Receipt of a half Barrel of Powder (and his Distribution thereof to several Negroes) from Court." Foiled, the judges did not try to stop the hoisting up of Ned at about sunset "into his old Birth," where he died the following day at about two in the afternoon. His body was burned and his head fixed to a pole on his master's plantation. On November 12 the judges also sentenced Jacob Morgan's Jack and Sir William Codrington's Jacko to be "hung in Jibbets in the Market Place there to Remain til they Die of Famine," pointing out that this was "the best sort of Punishment to inflict on the Principal Ringleaders not for Sake of Example only, but in Order to produce Discovery's tending to the Publick Safety." Jack, however, seems to have been burned instead; another ringleader, Thomas Freeman's Secundi, was later gibbeted.[12] In the end six slaves were executed in this manner.

Two other ringleaders, Samuel Martin's Tony, and Colonel Hamilton's Harry, were also broken on the wheel, bringing the number so executed finally to five. In jail after conviction, Harry stabbed himself several times with a knife, hoping to cheat his executioners, but the court quickly ordered his immediate execution before he died of his wounds. All the other slaves finally executed were burned "in Otto's Pasture joyning the Town," at its south end. These, explained the judges, while clearly involved, were not among the main organizers of the plot. The ringleaders had led them astray.[13] The mode of execution therefore reflects the courts' understanding of the rebels' role in the affair, ringleaders either being broken on the wheel or gibbeted, while others were merely burned alive.

No slaves were simply hanged. In the Americas and in Europe of the 1700s, whether for preventive or retributive purposes, authorities preferred execution that caused lingering pain during the enactment of punishment-as-spectacle.[14] After the slave conspiracy in New York City in 1712, for example, several were burned, others hanged, one broken on the wheel, and another sentenced "to be hung in chains alive and so continue from lack of substenance until he is dead." Such executions, said the governor, were "the most exemplary punishments that could be possibly thought of." As a result of another plot in the same city in 1741, thirteen slaves were burned alive and eighteen hanged, two of them in chains. And after South

Carolina's Stono Rebellion two years earlier, some of the rebels had been gibbeted alive.[15] The Antigua pattern was similar. Day after day during the closing months of 1736 and in early 1737, through ritualistic executions that included torture, the authorities were determined to teach the slave population that it was futile to rebel. Many white spectators of such public expression of deliberate cruelty regarded themselves as the real executioners; they indulged a lust for revenge and at the same time found reassurance in the righteous rigor of punishments that vanquished the enemies they feared. Every execution, every head exposed on a pike, reminded or warned whites to be wary of their slaves and at the same time symbolized that, at least for the time being, slaves were reduced to impotence.[16] The slaves themselves may have got a different message.

———————————————

So far as the governor and council were concerned, martial law had automatically taken effect upon discovery of the plot and the mobilization of the militia and other troops "as if a General Alarm had Actually been set about by firing of Cannon," as required by the militia law of 1702, and they believed that it should continue "untill a Law for the Better Government of Slaves should be past."[17] When a number of militiamen, behaving as though there were no martial law, refused to do guard and patrol duty and used up the stores issued to them nevertheless, the council on November 8 brought this to the assembly's attention. The assembly agreed that all militiamen called out to duty since October 22, when that house had consented to the placing of guards, should be subjected to martial law, but that, as many of these men were not aware of the obligations and penalties of martial law, their officers should read them the articles of war. The assembly provided that martial law should continue for only eight more days (November 8–16), with militiamen being notified "by Beat of Drum and Proclamation" in St. John's "and other places where Guards shall be Ordered to be kept and that the same take place against all Persons immediately they are Summoned and to Continue in force against them whilst they are on Duty and no longer." Keen on court-martialing the offending militiamen, however, the council argued that their trials would help confirm the existence of martial law instead of doing so by drumbeat, which "may be attended with many Ill Consequences."[18] What these consequences were they did not say.

At the legislature's meeting on November 15, the council continued to press for the general enforcement of martial law until a new act for the better government of slaves was passed, and not simply to govern the conduct of militiamen, as the assembly all along seemed to prefer. Facing the issue squarely, the assembly now contended that "the putting Martial Law generally in force at this time Will in Our Opinion be of very ill Consequence for it will Destroy the Civil Authority, whilst the other is Existing, and in Consequence the Magistrates Cannot proceed to Tryal of the Slaves now under Confinement. . .or any other that may be taken up." They preferred that martial law apply to "the troop of Carbineers, as well as. . .all others that have been or shall be Summoned by Direction's of His Excellency, to Appear on Duty in any parts of the Island" until the trials ended, "and that it Continues in full force against them whilst on Duty." This arrangement, the assembly believed, would be as effective as general martial law "and at the same time preserve the Civil Order."[19] It seems to have got its way in the end.

Meanwhile, the judges were busy. By mid-November prosecutions had revealed enough about the dangerous extent of the plot that they advised further tightening of security all over the tiny island. In a letter to the assembly, two of them recommended that horse patrols should ride "Every Night Over the whole Island and all Day Sundays" until the trials were over, "and that all Persons in the foot who are not on other Duty do ride the said Patroles in such Numbers, & in such Places in their Several Districts as shall be Order'd by their Proper Officers." Agreeing promptly, the assembly asked the governor to issue the necessary orders, including "that all Masters be Oblidg'd to find Horses for their Servants and Overseers, if they have them not of their Own."[20]

By December 9, by which time thirty-four slaves had been executed, the council asked the presiding judges to submit a report of whatever evidence came before them so they could better assess how dangerous the conspiracy had been and whether it still posed any threat. On December 20, the judges responded that they were preparing a comprehensive report of the affair using the trial record, which was so long that they needed more time to complete it. At the same time, they asked that a new court replace them, "Our private Affairs having greatly Suffer'd by our Continual Attendance for upwards of Nine weeks upon the Enquiry." "These Gentlemen being quite fatigued & Wearyed out by a Long Attendance," wrote Governor Mathew, "I was forced to appoint five others to go on with the Tryalls." These were Vallentine Morris and Josiah Martin of the council, and Benjamin King, Henry Douglas, and Thomas Watkins of the assembly, any three of whom could constitute a court, provided at least one was a council member. By the governor's order, they were to obtain immediately all the evidence in the hands of the first court "that they may Distinguish what Prisoners are already under Condemnation and not Executed, What prisoners are in Custody but not yet tryed, and what Negros they are to Issue their Warrants for." They also had the same authority as the first court and were to report their proceedings periodically.[21]

In five days the slaves' Christmas holidays would begin. The possibility that slave unrest could flare up into open rebellion was always foremost in most slaveowners' minds at this time of festivity, and the legislature usually strengthened security all over the island. They had even more reason to be wary during Christmas 1736, because they believed Antigua was still exposed to the danger of a rebellion originally planned by Court and Tomboy. "Wee are upon Duty every fourth Day" one resident had written on December 13, "that is all white Men, without Distinction above Sixteen; and have about 480 Men on Duty, in the whole Island, per day." Earlier, another had pointed to the "utmost Confusion" into which the plot had thrown the island; "all our People are under Arms, and 'tis believed will continue so til after Christmas." Many slaveowners must have watched the approach of Christmas with increasing apprehension, just as South Carolinians would three years later. Although many of the Stono rebels had been executed after the rebellion that erupted in September, the assembly believed that if others were inclined to revolt "the Christmas Holy Days... being a Time of general Liberty to the Slaves throughout the Province," would be just right, and they asked Lieutenant Governor William Bull for special security precautions during the season.[22]

After more than two months of trials and executions, Arbuthnot and the other judges of the first court submitted to the legislature their comprehensive report (general report), dated December 30, 1736, which, among other things, described the organization and causes of the plot and the steps taken against the rebels. The judges were also careful to point out that the conspiracy had probably not yet been crushed "since undoubtedly there are Hundreds by us undiscovered, who have bound themselves by impious Oaths to destroy us, Man, Woman and Child." The extensive scale of the affair demonstrated, they said, "what must be the Spirit and Inclination of the Slaves, and how weak and vain it would be in us, to say the Country is in Safety," or to advise ending inquiries.[23]

The general report showed that forty-seven slaves were executed by December 15, while fifty more were to be banished, including seven witnesses. Two fugitive suspects, the Coromantee driver, Old Tom, belonging to Edward Byam, and Davy, also a driver, belonging to George Thomas, were still at large, and rewards were offered for taking them dead or alive; four freedmen—John Corteen, Mulatto Tom, Mulatto Jack, and Free Simon—were also confined awaiting trial. By mid-January, the second court had increased the number of slaves tried and executed by twenty-five. Commenting on the frequency of executions up to this time, Governor Mathew observed in a classic piece of understatement, "I hope they will in good time put an end to these Executions, I think they are very numerous." A resident writing about a month earlier had remarked simply, "Such Executions are shocking." But from another, writing just two days before the governor, we catch a much stronger sense of the prevailing atmosphere. "We are in a great deal of Trouble in this Island," this distraught writer lamented. The "Burning of the Negroes, hanging them on Gibbets alive, Racking them upon the wheel, & c. takes up almost all our Time, that from the 20th of October to this Day, there have been destroyed Sixty fine sensible Negroe Men, most of them Tradesmen, as Carpenters, Masons, and Coopers. I am almost dead with watching and warding," he added, "as are many more." Probably the most striking of these remarks is the veiled suggestion that it was senseless to execute so many valuable slaves. That point was also echoed in the *Gentleman's Magazine* of London, which carried an observation in "Fog's Journal" concerning "Whether the selling the prime Conspirators to the Spanish Mines, wou'd not have secur'd the Whites, as well, as to put so many to Death for a Crime, which (if we may guess by what has lately come from the Press) will be deem'd a Pitch of Virtue by not a few in our Mother Nation."[24] Already, it seems, there were people in England who openly sympathized with rebellious slaves in the colonies. Most Antigua slaveowners, however, conscious of the slaves' proneness to resistance and the extent to which they outnumbered whites, obviously dreaded rebellion and supported execution instead of mere transportation for reasons already cited, even if loss of slaves might impose hardship, including finding replacements.

The last executions took place on March 8, 1737, when 11 slaves were burned.[25] The official list of executions (table 2.1) shows that, in all, 5 slaves were broken on the wheel, 6 gibbeted alive, and 77 burned: 88 executions in less than four months. These executed slaves were distributed among 60 owners: 40 lost 1 slave each, 13 lost 2, 6 lost 3, and 1 lost 4. Appended to the execution list were the names of 36 other slaves who were to be banished "so as never to return, or if Possible to be heard of," and 13 witnesses on whom sentence had not yet been passed (table 2.2); 25 of the 43 sentenced to banishment by the first court were still on this final list; of the others, the magistrates of the first court reexamined the cases of 8 on fresh evidence and condemned them to death, while the rest were pardoned or discharged. The second court added 11 more, however, for banishment. It also recommended a pardon for 5 witnesses, but the assembly, believing one of them, Major Martin's Jemmy, to be "a most Dangerous Criminal," voted that he be banished instead along with the rest of the witnesses, all of whom were involved in the plot. Commenting on the favor shown these men, the judges of the first court explained, "because a full Discovery without them could not be made, we have taken the Liberty of preserving some of the Guilty from Death, and assured them of Life upon Terms of Banishment, unless the Legislature, should for any important Reasons dispense with it; not doubting, but the Exigency of Affairs, will excuse and even justify this Conduct, and that it will receive its Confirmation from the Legislature with proper Marks of Favour to such Witnesses, as may distinguish their Case from other Criminals banished."

TABLE 2.1. Slaves Executed, 1736–1737

Master	Slave	Occupation
Thomas Kerby	Court	waiting man
Thomas Hanson	Tomboy	carpenter
John Christophers	Hercules	carpenter
Johana Lodge	Fortune	carpenter & fiddler
Philip Darby	Jack	cooper
Anthony Garrett	Venture	carpenter
Thomas Stephens	Frank	coppersmith
Christopher Hodge	Cudjoe	sugar boiler
Jacob Morgan	Green	waiting man
Edward Gregory	Annimo	cooper
Edward Gregory	Quash	cooper
John Haws	Gift	carpenter
Clement Tudway	Cuffee	mason
Estate of John Gamble	Colley	fiddler & butcher
Mary Hoskins	Quash	carpenter
Jacob Morgan	Ned	mason
Estate of Thomas Freeman	Secundi	driver
Sr. Wm. Codrington	Jacko	driver
Samuel Martin	Tony	—
Josiah Martin	Charles	coachman
Sr. Wm. Codrington	Ghlode	driver
Abraham Redwood	Scipio	driver
Abraham Redwood	Oliver	driver
Lucy Parke	John Guy	"Head field Negro"
Jacob Morgan	Jack	coachman
William Painter	Toney	carpenter
George Thomas	Geoffry	millwright
John Tomlinson	Cuffy	driver
John Tomlinson	Billy	driver
Samuel Martin	Scipio	old driver
Edward Otto Bayer	Jean	driver
Edward Otto Bayer	Collon	driver
Josiah Neufville	Bristol	fisherman
Caesar Rodeney	Kellsey	cooper
Thomas Kerby	Quaco	cooper
Mary Moore	Sampson	cooper
Estate of John Goble	Oliver	driver
Estate of John Goble	Billy	driver
Dr. Sydserf	Saby	driver
Edward Byam	Cudjoe	driver

	Manner of Execution			
Gibbeted	Broken on the Wheel	Burned	Date	Compensation
	x		Oct. 20, 1736	45
	x		Oct. 21	150*
	x		Oct. 22	140
		x	Oct. 22	100
		x	Oct. 22	82*
		x	Oct. 22	120
		x	Oct. 22	50
		x	Oct. 27	70
		x	Oct. 27	96*
		x	Oct. 27	133*
		x	Oct. 27	133*
		x	Oct. 27	90
x			Nov. 2	93*
x			Nov. 2	60
x			Nov. 2	100
x			Nov. 11	96*
x			Nov. 13	82*
x			Nov. 13	76*
	x		Nov. 15	73*
		x	Nov. 15	60
		x	Nov. 15	76*
		x	Nov. 15	72*
		x	Nov. 15	72*
		x	Nov. 15	70
		x	Nov. 15	96*
		x	Nov. 15	
		x	Nov. 27	75*
		x	Nov. 27	110*
		x	Nov. 27	110*
		x	Nov. 27	73*
		x	Nov. 27	135*
		x	Nov. 27	135*
		x	Nov. 27	100
		x	Nov. 27	120*
		x	Dec. 17	70
		x		100
		x	Dec. 17	52*
		x	Dec. 17	52*
		x	Dec. 17	82*
		x	Dec. 17	60

TABLE 2.1. (continued)

Master	Slave	Occupation
Estate of John Kerr	Monday	wheelwright, carpenter, mason, etc.
Thomas Freeman	Natty	coachman
William Yeamans	Quash Cooma	driver
John Wickham	Primus	driver
Philip Darby	Scipio	waiting man
Nicholas Lynch	Only	cooper
Edward Chester	Frank	driver
Estate of Hamilton	Harry	driver
Minnahan	Jack ˙	driver
James Weatherill	Joe	one of
James Weatherill	Pinzance	these a
James Weatherill	Jacob	carpenter
Samuel Harman	Quamina	–
Samuel Harman	Harry	–
William Young	Hanniball	driver
John Fyffe	Richmond	cooper
General Mathew	Caesar	"a sort of an Obia man"
Joseph Lyons	Tim	–
Estate of Parry	Quamino	–
Elizabeth Conner	Richmond	carpenter
Bayer Otto	Quamina	–
Bayer Otto	Malhes	–
Bayer Otto	Robin	"old fellow over ye Rest"
John Green	Saltash	fisherman
John Green	Chelsia	fisherman
Margaret Dayly	Tribling	driver (could write well)
Joshua Archbold	Monday	–
Joshua Archbold	Natty	–
William Young	Quamina	–
George Lucas	Caesar	–
Henry Lyons	Minion	–
John Vernon	Cudjoe	carpenter
Tudway	Watty	old driver
Isaac Royall	Hector	driver
Estate of Warner	Johnno	–
Archbold Cochran	Green	–
Richard Oliver	Quaco	driver
Estate of Goble	English Dick	driver
Benjamin King	Dick	carpenter

Manner of Execution				
Gibbeted	Broken on the Wheel	Burned	Date	Compensation
		x	Dec. 17	200
		x	Dec. 17	82*
		x	Dec. 17	75
		x	Dec. 17	80
		x	Dec. 17	82*
		x	Dec. 17	55*
		x	Dec. 20	150
	x		Jan. 1, 1737	65
		x	Jan. 4	55*
		x	Jan. 4	86*
		x	Jan. 4	86*
		x	Jan. 4	86*
		x	Jan. 4	
		x	Jan. 4	85
		x	Jan. 4	100
		x	Jan. 4	110
		x	Jan. 4	
		x	Jan. 4	85
		x	Jan. 4	55*
		x	Jan. 4	100
		x	Jan. 15	56*
		x	Jan. 15	56*
		x	Jan. 15	56*
		x	Jan. 15	57*
		x	Jan. 15	57*
		x	Jan. 15	60
		x	Jan. 15	60*
		x	Jan. 15	60*
		x	Jan. 15	100
		x	Feb. 18	70
		x	Feb. 18	40
		x	Feb. 18	95
		x	Feb. 18	93*
		x	Feb. 18	70
		x	Feb. 18	100
		x	Feb. 18	70*
		x	Feb. 18	65
		x	Mar. 8	52*
		x	Mar. 8	

TABLE 2.1. (continued)

Master	Slave	Occupation
Archbold Cochran	Jack	—
Archbold Cochran	Prince	carpenter, mason, etc.
John Pare	Vigo	drummer
Caesar Rodeney	Mulatto Ned Chester	carpenter
John Tomlinson, Jr.	Barroman	—
Bayer Otto	Secundi	driver
Estate of Thomas Freeman	Ptolamy	—
William Lavington	Sampson	driver & fiddler
Sr. Wm. Codrington	Sacky	—
Totals		

SOURCE: "A List of the Names of Negros that were Executed for the late Conspiracy, Their Trades, To whom they Belonged, the day and Manner of their Respective Execution," enclosed in Mathew to BT, May 26, 1737, CO 152/23, X7. Some of the execution dates are taken from the legislature's minutes in CO 9/10 and CO 9/11. Compensation payments are taken from minutes in CO 9/12.
*Average amounts where owners received a lump sum for more than one slave executed.

They referred in particular to Samuel Morgan's Treblin, "against whom there was no possitive Proof of Guilt, and whose Confession was free and full, and his manner of giving Evidence appeared steady and honest, and was of great service."[26]

When the official list of executions and banishments was prepared, 3 freedmen were still in custody. Henry Kipp's Parmenio had joined Davy and Tom in flight, bringing the number of fugitives to 3. On April 11, 1737 the legislature passed an act for banishing forty-seven slaves so sentenced and also outlawed the 3 fugitives, who would be executed when caught unless they surrendered within ten days. A reward was offered for taking them dead or alive. Anyone harboring them was guilty of treason and would also be executed. In explaining why it chose to outlaw the fugitives, the legislature noted that if it did not do so, Davy, Tom, and Parmenio might well be caught only after the witnesses against them had been banished or when no witnesses could be found; it would be difficult to try them then. Alternatively, detaining the witnesses until they were brought in, "which may Possibly be many Months, Even Years," would involve much trouble and expense. This statement, incidentally, suggests that it was possible for runaways to remain at large for very long periods even in tiny, compact Antigua, especially if other people (slaves, poor whites, dissident upper-class whites) were willing to help them. Writing in May 1737, Governor

| | Manner of Execution | | | |
Gibbeted	Broken on the Wheel	Burned	Date	Compensation
		x	Mar. 8	70*
		x	Mar. 8	70*
		x	Mar. 8	70*
		x	Mar. 8	120*
		x	Mar. 8	80*
		x		56*
		x		82*
		x		60
		x	Mar. 8	76*
6	5	77		

Mathew reported that one of the fugitives had been caught "and pretended to make some fresh Discoverys of a new Insurrection to Revenge the Deaths of those that were Executed" but that he had not heard anything further. This fugitive may have been Parmenio, who did indeed help with inquiries. He was detained in prison for a long time while the authorities presumably checked on his story about a new plot. Finally, he was banished to North America, preferably Virginia, in 1740.[27]

While the legislature had included the names of slave witnesses in the act that banished forty-seven slaves in 1737, they postponed carrying out sentence on the witnesses while they testified at the trials of a few freedmen accused of being in the plot. By admitting slave evidence against free persons even in an emergency that threatened island security, the legislature had taken a bold and dangerous step, as we shall see. These valuable witnesses were later transported to North America. The other transportees, first intended for Lisbon or "Such other place," were later reported bound for the nearby colony of Hispaniola, the Spanish American mainland or some other territory belonging to Spain.[28] Why the legislature chose these destinations is not clear, but it would be interesting to know how the troublemakers were disposed of. In the act, owners of banished slaves were guaranteed compensation, but the terms of exile were spelled out with care. The conspirators were banished not only from Antigua but

TABLE 2.2. Slaves Banished, Slave Witnesses, and Freedmen in Prison, 1736–1737

Slaves Banished

1	Sydserf's	Robin	19	Osborn's	Cubinna
2	Skerrit's	Billy	20	Delap's	Tom
3	Bondinott's	Dick	21	Delap's	Robin
4	Goble's	London	22	Scandrett's	Baptist
5	Sanderson's	Tony	23	Pare's	John Sabby
6	Pare's	Quaco	24	Pare's	Caesar
7	Freeman's	Troilus	25	Hunt's	Quaco
8	Sutton's	Tom	26	Buckshorn's	Sampson
9	Bawn's	Primus	27	Ditto	Jacob
10	Hunt's	Cuffee	28	Cusack's	Yorke
11	Lynche's	Delmore	29	Parham Driver	Cuffy
12	Lyndsey's	Quash	30	Barton's	Joe
13	Morgan's	Newport	31	Pare's	Billy
14	Monk's	Mingo	32	Pare's	Cudjoe
15	Roache's	Pilgarth Pennezer	33	King's	Kitty
16	Col. Thomas's	Cromwell	34	Weatherill's	Toby
17	Elm's (Senr.)	Jack	35	Sawcolt's	Cudjoe
18	Elm's (Junr.)	Quamina	36	Royal's	Quaco

Slave Witnesses

1 Triblin belonging to
   Mr. Morgan
2 Billy belonging to
   Mr. Langford
3 Jemmy belonging to
   Col. Martin
4 Tom belonging to
   Mr. Lynch
5 Quamina belonging to
   Major Martin
6 Quamina belonging to
   Col. Fry
7 Quaco belonging to
   Capt. Allicock
8 Jemmy belonging to Mr. Elliot
9 Ingham belonging to
   Mr. Godsell
10 Otta belonging to
   Mr. Thomas (Parham
   plantation)
11 Peter belonging to
   Mr. Farlow
12 Cuffee belonging to
   Mr. Langord
13 George belonging to
   Mr. Thomas (Parham
   plantation)

Freedmen in Prison
1 John Corteen
2 Mulatto Tom
3 Simon Nichols

SOURCE: "A List of Negroes to be Banished"; "A List of Negroes that were Evidences"; "A List of Three Free Negroes & their names," in Mathew to BT, May 26, 1737, CO 152/23, X7.

also from the rest of the Leeward Islands. If any were found in these islands after July 1, 1737 and convicted for it, they were to be executed as felons. Any person importing these slaves would forfeit £200 Antigua money a head, a sum "to be recovered with full Costs of Suit of Action of Debt Bill plaint or Information in any of His Majestys Courts of Record in this Island wherein no Essoign or wager of Law shall be allowed." Moreover, the slaves would be seized and used by the government before again being banished. Later, somehow, at least one of the conspirators turned up not far from the Leeward Islands in the Danish island of St. Croix, where, interestingly enough, he was among the leaders of a slave plot in 1759, twelve years after being shipped out of Antigua.[29]

Proceedings against the conspirators had virtually ceased by May 1737. Martial law was still in force, although the slaves were reported to be "pretty quiet." Gradually life returned to normal. Looking back over the dramatic events of the past few months that had so suddenly disrupted their lives, most whites may have quickly agreed that slaves should be more strictly controlled to undermine the potential for revolt. Whether they would have agreed that they, slaveowners or not, had as full a responsibility as the legislature to improve controls is uncertain, but most must have shared the judges' advocacy of stricter enforcement of slave laws. These gentlemen who had sat in judgement over the conspirators also believed encouragement of mutual distrust among slaves could strengthen the overall system of control. "As there must of necessity always be a number of Slaves among us, vastly superior to the Whites, which will be a lasting Temptation to the former to enter into Conspiracies," they contended, "and which cannot better be prevented, than by rendering them distrustful of each other, by generous Rewards and Encouragements given to those who discover their machinations; we submit it to be considered, whether without injuring ourselves, we can neglect duly rewarding those, whom Providence hath made its Instruments in the late Discovery." They recommended rewards for Walter Nugent's Cuffee, John Gunthorpe's Robin, Edward Gregory's Emanuel, Thomas Hanson's Philida, and Samuel Morgan's Treblin, in all of whom, they said "there appeared an honest Zeal for our Preservation, and an Abhorrence of what was intended against us; and to whose free Evidence or Confession, (next to the Goodness of God) our Preservation is owing."[30]

Cuffee and Emanuel had been voluntary witnesses. Cuffee, observed the governor and council, "became an Evidence at the beginning of the Conspiracy," and to him "We Chiefly Owe our Safety." Emanuel also had "made some Discoverys very early, and Refused to make the Conspirators Colours." Treblin, sentenced to be banished, but singled out for a mark of favor, received an award of £14 before leaving. In 1739 a special act emancipated Cuffee and Robin, who were to "enjoy all the Libertys and

Priviledges allowed by the Laws...to free Negroes and no more, and...Subject, as other Free Negroes are to the Same Laws." Along with Emanuel they were also awarded monthly gratuities for as long as they remained in Antigua. The act explained that the legislature, acting in the interest of whites, was bound "not only in Point of Gratitude but in point of Prudence" to recognize the slaves' fidelity, "that other Slaves upon like Occasions, if any Such Should ever happen, which God forbid, may be Encouraged to make timely Discovery's."[31] When it was being drafted, the assembly regarded the act as "Supplementary to the Acts of this Island for the better Government of Slaves."[32] How effective its inherent strategy of divide and rule proved to be is probably not as intriguing as how the slaves may have later treated those who had collaborated with the authorities in any way, particularly Cuffee, Robin, and Emanuel.

Rewarding witnesses was only a fraction of the expense the legislature incurred in connection with the plot. Conscious of mounting expenditure as more and more slaves were hauled up for trial, the assembly, as early as January 8, 1737, after about three months of prosecutions and militia alert, proposed a halt to arrests, except for fugitives from justice, those who were positively implicated in the plot, and others whose arrests had already been ordered. Stopping inquiries, it contended, would "quiet their [the slaves'] minds and...Ease the Publick of the great Expence that now Attends the Same on that Occasion." Also, whites would be spared "the Constant Personal Duty that they are now Oblidg'd to Do." The judges of the second court agreed with this assessment, "not being Inclin'd themselves to make Examples by Execution or Otherwise of more than 150 Exclusive of the Evidences & three or four that have Absconded notwithstanding they can have Information now of half the Negros in one of the Largest Plantations." By this time, too, the assembly suspected collusion among witnesses to implicate slaves perhaps even without foundation. Vallentine Morris succinctly expressed the view of those slaveowners who believed expense should not stand in the way of crushing the existing spirit of rebellion. "It is a maxim in Politicks Drawn from the Experience of all ages," said Morris with telling imagery, "that a Conspiracy deeply laid, & Extended wide, if not Searched to the Bottom, like a Deep wound Skined Over soon Breaks out again with Double Danger." Whether these people were satisfied or not finally with the number of slaves executed and banished, the island was saddled with a burden of expense that compensation claims undoubtedly increased.[33] In 1738 the governor tried to raise £20,000 through taxes, "a vast sum for so small an island, but," he explained, "the great expense the negro plot occasioned and the debts accruing from last year's very small crop made this great tax unavoidable." Twelve years later some of the conspiracy-related debts remained unpaid.[34]

The plot had another important effect. It inspired the legislators to consider seriously the deficiencies of the island's internal security. Their eyes opened, they decided Antigua needed more British troops than the five companies posted there. John Yeamans, agent in London, made the first move when, without authorization, he petitioned for them. Signed by persons in London claiming to be merchants and planters, the petition was turned down, partly because the agent could not show it emanated from the islanders themselves. The real reason, however, was that the Privy Council was not satisfied that the troops would be properly subsisted and quartered.[35] After all, those already in Antigua were poorly taken care of. Only when the Antiguans agreed to increase subsistence, which they had hitherto strongly objected to, and to build barracks for 624 men and officers, and also a hospital, did they get the additional troops. They accepted responsibility for a force of not less than 400 and not more than 624 men. At the same time the legislature voted not to slacken its "Endeavours towards Procuring Such a Number of White Servants as May be thought Proper which together with the Additional Troops will Put us in Such a Situation, as never Again to Apprehend the Danger We have so lately Escap'd and may at all Events Ever Preserve this island to his Majesty."[36]

As for the island militia, in which many able-bodied men were reluctant to serve, the plot revitalized it. "Out of this Evil," wrote Governor Mathew in January 1737, "Antigua has gained an Advantage I long laboured for in vain. The whole Militia now is armed & with bayonets, & have been taught the use of them. God preserve the other islands from such an Attempt. They are hardly Convinced there really was a conspiracy here. Their Militia undisciplined & almost unarmed." Nevertheless, Montserrat, only thirty miles to the southwest, took the precaution of passing a seven-clause act suppressing assemblies of slaves and restricting their economic and commercial activities. According to the preamble, it was apparent "that the Laws now in Force relating to Negroes and Slaves, are not extensive enough to restrain them; and that Lenity and Indulgence, instead of producing the desired Effects, have rather given Encouragement to Robberies and Disorders, by furnishing Pretences, whereby the Offenders often Escape Punishment." Governor Mathew observed that the part of the act "for restraining licentious Negroes has long been wanting." At Nevis, about forty miles to the northwest, the legislature updated the militia regulations with a twenty-six-clause act, the preamble of which referred to the island's exposure "to Invasions of Enemies in Time of War, and Insults of Pirates in Time of Peace, as well as to the Danger of Insurrections of the Slaves." Mathew remarked that the new act was the best the island had passed, "one with Common Sence in it." He "had long litigated this matter with them in vain" he added, "and Still (though I have gaind by this Law allmost Evry point I had proposd, and held fast by, resolving to pass no Law in the old insignificant forms and for but Eight yearly meetings) Yet my Lords The Article of Bayonetts is thrown out, and I was forcd to pass this Law, or have none at all. I hope hereafter they will judge better for their own Preservation." Mathew believed bayonets would be very useful and for years had supported their use in the Leewards militia without success (except in Antigua in 1734) because, as he explained, "in a Negro Warr where You are attackd with Despair & greater Rapidity, can a fire keep of Multitudes from breaking in upon a Few with Bills & Cutlasses, for these are the Negro chief weapons? Is not the Bayonet here the only weapon to Stop Such outsets?" For whatever reason, the Nevis legislature behaved as if it did not think so, but in addition to the militia act it passed another for the better disciplining of slaves. In St. Christopher, just northwest of Nevis and separated from it by a narrow channel, the response to the Antigua affair was not as marked, for here the assembly appointed a committee "to inspect into and Examine the Severall Acts now in being relating to the regulation of Negroes," but no new act seems to have emerged.[37]

In Antigua itself the legislature did not pass any new long-term regulations, although at one point it may have intended to.[38] In most slave societies, at least in British America, harsher laws aimed at tighter control of slaves tended to follow serious plots and revolts.[39] Perhaps the Antigua legislature, rather than pass a new set of Draconian regulations, relied instead upon a stricter enforcement of those in existence, and hoped that the failure of the plot would discourage later collective resistance.

If the wave of anxiety and confusion that swept over whites in Antigua when the plot was discovered did not reach St. Christopher, Nevis, or Montserrat, as Governor Mathew mentioned, that can perhaps be understood. For, after all, nothing of its kind had ever happened in the islands, where the major problem of slave resistance came from sporadic threats by aggressive bands of runaways. In Antigua the unexpected had happened. Fatigued by the long hours of guard and patrol duty he was forced to do and shaken by the immensity of the plot and frequent executions, one Antigua resident confessed that "our island is in a poor miserable condition, and I wish I could get any employment in England to do." He was not alone. Many whites were reportedly quitting the island. "Some of the principal Gentlemen there with their Families," one report stated, "are making Provision to leave the Island, believing the Negroes will accomplish their Designs sooner or later." It should be borne in mind, though, that conditions in Antigua were already unsettling enough because of a recession and a prolonged drought.[40] The conspiracy only worsened the situation.

If some of the escaping whites sought refuge closer to home in the nearby islands of St. Bartholomew, Anguilla, or St. Martin, to the northwest, they would have discovered to their dismay that here too the slaves were exceptionally restive. "The Contagion," reported an alert Governor Mathew, "is spread further among these islands than I apprehend is discovered. By an enclosed affidavit of John Hanson," he told the Board of Trade, "it actually has taken effect in St. Bartholomew, & is discovered in Anguilla & St. Martins." Hanson related that on December 15, 1736, while he was at St. Martin (shared by the French and Dutch), his brother read him a letter from Monsieur Pymon, governor of the French section, in which he said the slaves in the French island of St. Bartholomew "were rose in Rebellion & had killed Eleven men of the white Inhabitants, but that the Remainder. . . kept together being about thirty men not daring to Separate, & waited Succours" from him. But Pymon's hands were tied because a plot had been discovered in his own colony, where eight slaves awaited execution and whites were on the alert. Hanson believed Pymon tried to get help from Martinique, another French island, far to the south. He also said he heard the slaves in Anguilla, one of the smaller Leewards about one hundred miles northwest of Antigua, were "to Join those of St. Martins the 26th" December. Governor Mathew's claim about the spread of a "contagion" of rebellion in the cluster of islands just north of Guadeloupe, where slave disturbances also erupted in late 1736,[41] does not necessarily imply collaboration among the slaves, although that possibility should not be dismissed. Whatever the case, the affair in Antigua was evidently the biggest.

The Antigua plot possesses some of the main characteristics of systematic revolts in the U.S. as they have been analyzed by Marion D. de B. Kilson. According to Kilson these revolts, such as the conspiracies of Gabriel Prosser in Virginia in 1800 and Denmark Vesey in South Carolina in 1822, aimed at "overthrowing the slave system itself and establishing a Negro state." Carefully planned and organized, such revolts ran the risk of discovery the longer the incubation period and the more complicated they were. While the Antigua plot of course had certain unique features, it provoked responses from whites quite similar to the three-step syndrome of systematic revolts that Kilson found common in the United States. In regard to the slavocracy's responses within the area of revolt, Kilson has argued that first came a phase of "much panic and activity" when vengeance was directed at the rebels and often also at innocent blacks; white moderates, as well as outsiders "who were disliked but not directly involved" might also become targets of aggression. In the second identifiable phase, the slavocracy used intensified armed might to preserve stability of the slave system. The third phase brought enactment of harsher preventive legislation.[42] Because they tended to overlap in time, it could be argued that these sequential developments were hardly ever so discrete; at the same time, useful as their isolation may be, they focus primarily on responses of the free population and project a distinctly incomplete picture of the wider society's responses to slave revolt. Antigua's slavocracy responded to the 1736 slave plot roughly according to Kilson's three-step syndrome, but phases one and two were more pronounced than three. The panic phase deserves special attention because it highlights some important dimensions of the plot's impact that were sharply reflected through the Antigua authorities' arrest and unprecedented prosecution of freedmen suspects using slave testimony. Some of the slaves so testifying were even under sentence of death.

3

"Not . . . bound . . . by the Ordinary Rules of Law"

According to the London agent John Yeamans, writing early in 1737, Antiguan whites remained "under the most terrible apprehensions of further attempts" at slave rebellion. A nagging suspicion that the slaves might still revolt kept authorities alert, probing deeper and deeper into the affair, leaving no stone unturned to expose slaves' covert designs. During the hunt for clues and suspects, suspicion fell upon several free nonwhites. Shaken by the plot, councillor Vallentine Morris voiced the fears of many whites who were eager to see the conspirators, slave or free, quickly and deservedly punished. Objecting to a plea to stop the trials because of mounting expenses, he observed, among other things, that by testimony of several slaves later executed, "by the Evidence of 16 Witnesses, by the Examinations taken against above 150 Conspirators. . . there was hardly a Sensible Negro in the Island of either Sex, but was Engaged in it Either as an Actor, Abettor, or Approver; that Most of the free Negros, and free Mullattos were Actually Engaged in it."[1] There must have been only a handful of these free nonwhites or freedmen in the island; however, whatever their politics and sympathies in the ongoing social conflict between slaves and white masters, Morris, who had heard a stream of testimony in his capacity as a judge of the second court, obviously felt that they were in league with the slaves.

By the time the judges of the first court had prepared and submitted their general report at the end of December 1736, freedmen John Corteen, Thomas Winthorp (Mulatto Tom), Mulatto Jack, and Simon Nichols (Free Simon) were in jail awaiting trial for alleged complicity. When Mulatto Jack, who lived with councillor Colonel Nathaniel Crump, appeared before them, the court assumed he was a slave, but Jack pleaded that he had been "free born" in Ireland, where he had been kidnapped fifteen or sixteen years before and sold in Antigua. The court believed his story, but how "far this may be a Mitigation of his Crime, We submit to the Wisdom of the Legislature, his provocation being great." As for Corteen and Winthorp, Robert Arbuthnot and the other judges believed that if the evidence of slaves could be used against them they would undoubtedly be found "as guilty as any Condemned on this Account." Corteen, they said, "appears to have been distinguishably violent for our Extirpation," and, while the evidence against Winthrop was not as strong, it was nevertheless sufficient "to prove him a dangerous person." Not authorized by the terms of their appointment to try free persons connected with the plot, Arbuthnot and his colleagues simply collected evidence that they later put in the hands of the legislature. That evidence came from slaves and was at law not permissible at trials of free persons, black or white. Nevertheless, the judges may have intended to drop a broad hint to the legislature that, because of the extraordinary circumstances, in which no free witnesses were available whose testimony might be used to obtain a conviction "in an Ordinary Course of Justice," it might have to find some way to draw upon slave testimony. To be sure, the situation was tricky; it required a solution that should result in the freedmen's conviction, implied the court, for "the Safety of the Island seems to be inconsistent with their remaining here."[2] Entangled later in the same predicament as Corteen, Winthorp, and others were the free Negro brothers Benjamin and William (Billy) Johnson.

Benjamin and Billy Johnson, natives of Antigua, were born into slavery, the property of a Dutch slaveowner Margaret [Barbara?] Low, who "at her cost and thro' Her care Baptized Principled and instructed" them "sufficiently in the Christian Religion which they professed openly according to the Church of England." She also educated them "in a manner superior to many white People" so that they could not only read and write but knew enough "Arithmetick and Accounts . . . to Qualify them to Trade and keep a shop." In her will Margaret Low had freed Benjamin and Billy and left them everything, "which was so Considerable as to set them up in Shops, and Enable them to Carry on a Trade, wch they had so Considerably improved that Ben Johnson was supposed to be worth fifteen hundred or Two thousand Pounds" in 1736. "Considerable and substantial" traders, the brothers also owned a few slaves and other property. "Easy in their Circumstances" and reportedly sharing in "all the Priviledges that White men Enjoy," they were not suspected of involvement when the plot was first discovered; indeed, for some weeks they did duty guarding apprehended slaves. Later, "by some Words dropping from some of the Evidences" they were "supposed not to be altogether innocent" and were arrested during the early sessions of the second court, probably in December 1736.[3]

On the same day, December 30, 1736, that the legislature received the first court's report, it began deliberating how to proceed against the Johnsons and agreed, on the basis of evidence from the second court, to prepare a bill of attainder to try them for high treason. Following the council's suggestion that the attorney general and a committee of the assembly prepare the bill, the assembly appointed members John Frye and John Murray. They also decided that Corteen, Winthorp, Mulatto Jack, and Simon Nichols should be included in the bill. Completed and presented to the legislature at its next meeting, January 3, 1737, the bill included, however, only the Johnsons. Assemblyman Ashton Warner, who was also attorney general, explained that the committee "did not think proper" to include the rest. Though his reasons must have satisfied the assembly, they were not recorded. The assembly gave the bill a first reading that day and scheduled a second for January 12. At the same time it agreed that the Johnsons should have copies before their arraignment and be issued an order to answer charges pending against them. The house also authorized the speaker to serve summons on anyone willing to give evidence on the Johnsons' behalf. Although the Johnsons were arrested weeks after Corteen and others, the legislature took up their case first.[4]

Arraignment was scheduled for ten in the morning, Wednesday, January 12. It was a most solemn occasion, for the legislature convened as a court. Robert Arbuthnot, who was probably more acquainted than anybody else with the unsettling dimensions of the slave plot, agreed to prosecute for a fee. After the order formally charging the Johnsons with high treason was read, the marshal brought the "Prisoners to the Barr" in chains, which were then taken off. Speaker Thomas Kerby then asked the two men whether they had received the order and copies of the bill against them in good time. They said they had. The bill was next read aloud to them, and the speaker then drew their attention to the seriousness of the charges and assured them a "full and fair Tryal." He "Exhorted them to make a full and free Confession of their Offences if Guilty, and to discover what they knew of the Conspiracy with which they stand, charged, and of the persons concerned therein." Calmly, the Johnsons denied knowledge of the plot or involvement in it and declared themselves ready to stand trial if they would be allowed separate counsel, Frederick Cope for Benjamin, and Harry Webb for Billy. The marshal conducted the prisoners out of the room while the assembly considered their request. Instead of separate counsel, the assembly decided that only one should represent both men and that counsel should confer only once with each prisoner separately. At the same time, the assembly ordered the marshal to hold them in separate rooms so that there would be no communication between them, and to be sure not to permit contact with anyone but counsel. The assembly also agreed that the Johnsons should name their choice of witnesses other than those the speaker had already been authorized to summon but stipulated that no additional witnesses would be permitted thereafter, though the prisoners would be allowed to cross-examine any witnesses against them at the trial set to start at ten in the morning, Monday, January 17. The house next ordered all the defendants' books and papers to be lodged with the speaker for examination by members, the defense, and the prosecuting counsel, and that the clerk of the house supply prosecuting council with a copy of the bill, minutes of the day's proceedings related to the case, and other information already put together against the Johnsons.

The assembly then moved on to the most important part of the preliminaries of the case—justifying the use of slave evidence against free persons—and passed the following resolution:

Resolved by this House that it is the Opinion of this House That Evidence of slaves by the rece'd known usages and practice of this Island cannot be admitted against freed persons in any case Criminal or Civil in the Ordinary Courts of Judicature in this Island, but that this being a Case of the Greatest Moment to the Island, that ever hapned and Concerns the very being of the Government, and the lives and propertys of every white Inhabitant of this Island, and the Proceedings therein against Benjamin Johnson and William alias Billy Johnson two freed Negroes not being in the Ordinary manner but by Bill of Attainder This House will admit Slaves to give Evidence thereupon either for or against the Two Johnsons because this House in its Legislative Capacity doth not Conceive itself bound in this Case by the Ordinary rules of Law, Observed by Inferior Courts, and that this House is at Liberty to give such Credit thereto as they shall think it in their Conscience deserves, because the Treasonable practices charged in the Bill of Attainder were carried on by the Slaves, so that no white persons Evidence in the nature of the thing can be reasonably expected to prove the same.[5]

The last point was the most crucial part of this tortuous justification of a most unusual procedure. If there was little probability of finding white evidence to implicate the Johnsons, then slave evidence would have to do, so long as proper procedures were used. On this basis the assembly acted to prepare an enabling bill to try the freedmen. The prisoners themselves, having gotten a copy of the bill, were already aware of these procedures. Thus, when the marshal brought them back before the house, this part of the proceedings carried no surprises. Nevertheless, they listened intently as the speaker described the assembly's orders and resolutions. They then submitted the names of several witnesses who might be summoned on their behalf. The marshal next took them away, to appear again in court in five days.

Before proceeding with the trial on Monday, January 17, the assembly ruled that neither the Johnsons nor their counsel would be permitted to question its authority to pass bills of attainder and that witnesses for and against the defendants would be examined separately and not within sight or hearing of one another. Frederick Cope, defense counsel, then asked for permission to call as witnesses several white persons then behind bars who could supply material evidence in the Johnsons' favor, but the house ruled to consider the request only after the evidence against them had been heard. Benjamin and Billy Johnson were then brought in. The governor and council were invited to sit in on the proceedings, the governor occupying a seat to the speaker's right. When everybody had taken his place, Robert Arbuthnot rose gravely and opened the case for the prosecution with observations on the substance of the bill and the evidence in his possession.

The first witness to take the stand was Samuel Morgan's slave Treblin, who, we will recall, was implicated in the slave plot and after his arrest made "a very Ample Confession & Discovery"; later the judges used him as a key witness against other slave suspects. Sentenced to be transported out of Antigua, Treblin had, however, been detained pending trial of the freedmen. As Treblin started into his testimony against the Johnsons on January 17, testimony based on information he had picked up from Thomas Freeman's slave Secundi, one of the executed conspirators, an alert assemblyman objected that such evidence was "Improper," being mere hearsay "and not from any of the partys now Accused or from any person who had been Examined as a Witness in any Tryal relating to the same plot, nor from any Witness now produced, nor any posative Evidence yet given as to the point that was offered to be proved by such hearsay Evidence." When another legislator seconded the objection, it seemed contentious enough to be taken into account, and the prisoners were removed and the room cleared temporarily, while members thrashed out the issue of whether all the evidence should be first heard, and then a determination made on what might be material or not. They finally decided to follow that procedure and the trial resumed. Treblin again took the stand and completed his testimony, but neither this testimony nor that of other witnesses was recorded. Several other slave witnesses followed Treblin: John Frye's Quamino, Thomas Stephen's Dick, Atta of Parham Plantation, Jemmy, the property of Colonel John Elliot deceased, the deceased William Paynter's Johnny, Edward Chester's mullato Frank, and Jonas Langford's Cuffey. The defendants cross-examined some of these. The only witness for the Johnsons examined that day was Mary Cummerford, a white woman. The court then adjourned until the following day, January 18.[6]

When the court reassembled, Mary Cummerford again took the stand to complete her testimony. Edward Hatton, a prisoner, next appeared for the defense, followed by several witnesses for the prosecution: Booty, owned by James Weatherill, John Vernon, John Gunthorpe, John Farley's Peter,

Samuel Martin's Jemmy, James Langford's Billy, constables James Hanson and John Boland, Josiah Martin's Quamino, Thomas Hanson's Philida and Quash, John Ayres (planter), Robert Arbuthnot, the slave George of Parham Plantation, Henry Cuyler (merchant), Thomas Hanson's Jemmy, Thomas Hazlewood, Sarah Lenine and her husband, John Lenine. Other witnesses gave evidence against the defendants the following day, January 19: John Fisher (planter), Walter Nugent's Cuffey, John Gunthorpe's Robin. Called back to the stand were Samuel Morgan's Treblin and Samuel Martin's Jemmy; and then followed Robert Stevens, Andrew Lessley, and Ann Ayres (John Ayres's wife). Also appearing a second time were Thomas Hanson's Quash, James Langford's Billy, Thomas Stephen's Dick, who were followed by first-time witnesses Mary Joyce and Elizabeth Thompson. After these two were examined, the confessions of Court and Tomboy were read out as part of the prosecution's case.[7]

When the assembly next convened on Monday, January 24, several white witnesses for the defense delivered testimony. They were Charles Allen (goldsmith), Josiah Neufville (shopkeeper), John Predeux (silversmith), John Thibou (shopkeeper), Edward Hazard (shopkeeper), Charles Gardner (bookkeeper), Anthony Garrett (carpenter), Gustavus Christian (constable), Patrick Wilson (silversmith), John Lambert (mason), Nathaniel Messum (taylor), Henry Spencer (overseer), William Wyne, Esq., Joseph Haws, Duncan Grant (carpenter), John Murphy (indentured servant at Parham Plantation), Henry Blizard (planter), Merrick Turnbull (doctor), and Richard Glover (millwright). After a long day of testimony from these sixteen witnesses, the house resolved to hear the next day as many other witnesses for the defense as time permitted. Any not then examined were to be set aside for the day after, "to the end the prisoners may have the utmost Opportunity of Acquitting themselves if they can, of the Crimes layd to their Charge."[8]

On January 25, before these witnesses appeared, the house heard the evidence of Benjamin King Esq. and James Hanson (constable) against the defendants. Then one after another the witnesses for the defense were called in: the deceased John Goble's English Dick, Herbert Williams (mariner), John Smith (mariner), John Hatton (overseer), Richard Hacker (overseer), Nicholson Darvill (mason), Timothy Clarkly (carpenter), John Legg (overseer), William Chapman (manager at Colonel Samuel Martin's Greencastle Plantation), Nathaniel Gilbert Esq., Peter Monteyro (carpenter), Margaret White (wife of Walter White, mariner), Peter Martino (cooper), Captain David Agnew, Isaac Libert (silversmith), Jacob Morgan's slave women, Penny and Sabra. Following these depositions prosecutor Arbuthnot requested permission to introduce at a later date additional witnesses against the defendants. But the house refused, ruling "that no further Evidence on either Side be Examined as to the Merits of the Bill after this day" except the free mulatto Richard Moore, and Edward Chester's slave woman Sabina, whose testimonies were delivered January 31 at a session of the house devoted largely to other business related to the plot. The following day, February 1, the Johnsons' counsel, Cope, summed up the case for the defense. His opponent, Arbuthnot, deferred a reply until February 5. At that meeting the house resolved to hear more witnesses "for Information of their Consciences in the Matters relating to the Bill against the prisoners."[9]

How many of these witnesses were called remains uncertain, but according to the sketchy assembly minutes, which do not include transcripts of testimony considered during at least eight days over a six-week period, no fewer than 76 witnesses had appeared at the trial: 38 (20 slaves, 17 whites, 1 free mulatto) for the prosecution, and 38 (35 whites, 3 slaves) for the defense. The distribution between free and slave witnesses is immediately striking in that the prosecution relied heavily upon slave testimony, while the defense drew similarly upon that of whites. The pattern is, however, not surprising. Having legislated slave testimony as acceptable, the state made full use of it in order to make the charges against the Johnsons stick. The defense, on the other hand, called mostly whites, many of whom were character witnesses if nothing more, in order to exploit fully the patronage network between influential whites and freedmen and destroy the case against the Johnsons. In chapter 7 we will explore the origins and significance of client-patron relations between freedmen and whites that developed in Antigua partly as a result of legislation that supported such relationships for the social control of freedmen, and partly in response to realities of life in a race- and class-conscious society where freedmen, as descendants of slaves, were seen as inferior to whites. At the Johnsons' trial, the defendants astutely sought to make white-freedmen relations work for them instead of against them, as Antigua legislators had originally intended. The Johnsons' shrewd maneuver reflected in an openly dramatic situation what freedmen must have been practising all along in countless inconspicuous interactions with whites as part of their day-to-day strategy of survival and advancement.[10]

The assembly finally passed the bill of attainder against Benjamin and Billy Johnson on February 28 and sent it up to the council, whose members immediately ordered an inquiry into the legality of the brothers' freedom. While the council considered the bill, John Corteen, Thomas Winthorp, Mulatto Jack, and Simon Nichols still awaited trial, but when, after having tried the Johnsons, the legislature turned to them, Mulatto Jack seems to have been left out of consideration. On March 9 the legislature deliberated whether to proceed against the suspects "by Bill of

Attainder or by Passing a Law to make the Testimony of Slaves Evidence against Free Negroes and Mulattoes in General, or against them in Particular."[11] This was an interesting suggestion. It shows that anxiety following the plot's discovery helped focus attention on freedmen as potential enemies within the state covertly perhaps in league with the open enemy; indeed, some legislators went so far as to consider further limiting their freedom by proposing a general law to admit slave evidence against freedmen. Had such a law been passed, the legal status of freedmen would have been pushed even closer to that of slaves, and the distinction between slavery and freedom would have given way to one even more explicitly based on race and color, thereby increasing the precariousness of their lives as free persons.

For the assembly, a bill authorizing slave evidence against only the four suspects seemed the best solution, but it also wanted an additional clause dealing with the fugitive slave suspects Davy, Tom, and Parmenio, as if the two cases had some close connection. Governor Mathew objected that "it would be very Improper" to add the clause. Because the bill was "of a Most Extraordinary nature" and required the crown's approval before taking effect, Mathew argued, the fugitives would be affected only later, and possibly not at all, if the bill was disallowed. Mathew therefore recommended adding the clause to a new bill for regulating slaves that was under examination, "as was in a former Negro Law." At the same time he did not think it was such a good idea to delay banishing the slave witnesses because of the expense of maintaining them, a burden that would grow heavier until home authorities decided on the bill. One way out of this difficulty was to take the slaves' testimony, "now Pro Memoria," said Mathew, "in a Manner that they may Effectually be made use of when the King Approves of the Bill." Meanwhile, the witnesses could be shipped off. The assembly endorsed this plan as well as the preparation of a bill to try the freedmen "in the Court of the King's Bench, and making the Testimony of Slaves good Evidence against them, and respiting Sentence of Death and awarding Execution against them until His Majesty's Pleasure shall be Signified in the Premisses." To "Prevent further Delays in the matter," the assembly also offered, if the council had not yet started work, to prepare the bill.[12] On March 31 the council ordered the appearance before it on April 7 of all slave witnesses against the Johnsons and on April 9 of all white witnesses for and against them. On April 12 the council passed the bill of attainder against Benjamin and Billy Johnson, and the next day another bill against John Corteen and Thomas Winthorp, the evidence against Simon Nichols presumably being not strong enough to include him. As for Mulatto Jack, the legislature agreed unexpectedly that, because he had already "suffered great hardships" by being kidnapped in Ireland and enslaved, he would not be prosecuted, provided that his owner, Colonel

Crump, would send him back to Ireland; however, Jack was on no account to be discharged from jail until ready to board ship. Altruism may have had little to do with the decision; rather, the legislature may have simply wanted, with as little fuss as possible, to rid the island of a supposed trouble-maker against whom evidence was weak. It went, however, after bigger fish — the Johnsons, Corteen, and Winthorp.[13]

In a report to the Board of Trade of May 1737 in which he promised "a candid, fair sum of the evidence upon which both Houses (but the council especially) were induced to pass" the bill against the Johnsons, Governor Mathew first dealt with the evidence against Benjamin Johnson. In the absence of trial transcripts, we must rely on the governor's observations for the essence of evidence heard. Part of the testimony against Benjamin Johnson given by four slaves "who as they were all very deeply Concerned in the Plot could therefore make the best Discoverys, and whom the Justices all along averrd to have been very Steady in all the Informations they gave," while not stating, said Mathew, any specific time, maintained that "On some Saturday Night or Sunday abot six or seven Months or longer afore," (the witnesses "each of them declared here but to a Seperate Fact at a Seperate time Except That two of them averr That on Such a Saturday night and Sunday"), Benjamin Johnson took the oath twice "to Destroy the Christians." The third witness "only says that Benjamin pledged his Brother Billy without saying anything, when his Brother Bill Drank the health to him, and offering himself to attack the Town Guard, That Benjamin answered Billy that he would be his Friend." A fourth witness testified that Benjamin Johnson remarked about going to England to marry "But now he hoped to Get a White Wife here, That Damn them (meaning the Christians) he did not get his freedom from them, Damn them his Mistress Gave him his Freedom." Yet another slave witness testified that "a Wife of Courts and a Negro Woman went into Benjamin Johnson's with a Kegg and a box." Court's "wife" told Benjamin Johnson that the powder belonged to Court, and she appeared anxious to be rid of it. Johnson replied "no matter for that, I will Say I bought it." The same witness also claimed that Johnson "sent to a Negro Calld Parham Cuffy and told him if he was askd by the Justices he should not own that he had lent his Mare to him. . . . But that it was a long time afore since he lent it to him." Governor Mathew added here that several of the slaves executed for the plot had confessed connections with the Johnsons.[14]

Among whites giving evidence against Benjamin Johnson was merchant Henry Cuyler, who said he sold Johnson eight casks of gunpowder "of about One hundred weight in the whole" at about the time that the plot was believed to have started. Later he tried to sell Johnson more without success. Robert Stevens also claimed that at about the time the first conspirators were arrested, he heard Benjamin Johnson say that "had he known the Plot would have been discovered he would have gone to Barbados and spent thirty or forty Pistoles and would have returned when the plot was Over." At another time, however, said Stevens, he heard Johnson say he was glad not to have gone to Barbados that "he might stand in Defence of the Country." To counter seemingly positive and circumstantial evidence linking him with the plot, especially the charge that he had taken the oath to kill the whites, Mathew noted, Benjamin Johnson faced the difficult task of proving his whereabouts every Sunday over the past year. One white witness testifying on Johnson's behalf declared that for the past eighteen months he had seen him "morning and evening every Sunday to the best of his knowledge going to or returning from Church." Two other white witnesses said they had similarly observed these trips over the past year. From a slave witness who was supported by a respected gentleman in town came one piece of testimony that constable James Hanson, who seemed determined to harm Johnson in some way, had been goading the slave to implicate Johnson in the plot.[15]

The evidence against Billy Johnson, according to Governor Mathew, appeared to be stronger than that against his brother, but because of the "great Intimicies between them, the Guilt provd upon Billy seems to be very Circumstantially against Benjamin." Two slaves stated that Billy drank the "Damnation health" twice at one feast, while two others also swore they witnessed him do so at other times. Several of these slave meetings or feasts at which conspirators took the solemn oath of fidelity to kill the whites were in reality funerals, explained Mathew, and at one of these Billy allegedly told Thomas Freeman's Secundi "It would be better if we had the Country to ourselves." One slave witness claimed that at another funeral meeting Billy "took Court by the hand Declaring aloud to the Negros present That he (Court) was fitt to be King." Another slave placed Billy at a meeting with the conspirator John Obias, where he also took the solemn pledge administered by Secundi, swearing he would "find Powder Ball and flints and would be the first (as he Livd in Town) to attack the Town Guard." According to this witness, Billy Johnson declared at another meeting that "altho he always Livd very well yet he hoped to Live better." Testimony from some white witnesses agreed with that of slave witnesses that Billy attended meetings and solemnly agreed to be part of the plot. Other white witnesses called on his behalf merely affirmed his honesty and reliability at shop-keeping. Such, then, was Governor Mathew's summary of the evidence upon which the Antigua legislature had acted to condemn the Johnsons.

Mathew also supplied useful observations on the bill's passage through the legislature. When the asembly sent it up to the council for considera-tion and it was read a first time, explained Mathew, he informed members that "so Extraordinary a Law" required a suspending clause. "I was pretty much pressd in council by arguings against my objection," stated the governor, "but I have too lately ventured upon such a breach of my instructions to be guilty of it again, and my positively declaring I would not pass the bill without it occasioned its being sent back to the assembly to be amended with such a clause." In the assembly itself the bill had been passed only "very precariously, accidental sickness or other avocations had called away two or three members from attending," explained Mathew. Otherwise, the bill would not have survived to reach the council, "who were almost to unanimity fond of it." It seemed therefore possible that the bill would not come through the assembly a second time. However, continued Mathew, "the same members being absent as before, it escaped to the council again," not with the amendment "but some scrupulous doubt as from people that were ashamed though not a little willing to give a nay to what they afore had given an affirmative to." Mathew told the council that the suspending clause could be left out; however, he would not assent to the bill after it had passed both houses but would send it home, and if it was approved, he would then pass it. "Now," concluded the governor to the Board of Trade, "I submit to you the success of the bill. I have endeavored to inform you the best on it I can, though very little able from being hardly recovered from a most dangerous fit of sickness, much less am I able to present it to you under my own handwriting. Heats and colds during the late troubles that often kept me on horseback many hours at all times of the night," lamented the governor, "have brought this on me with the bad circumstance that my limbs are now affected." Regrettable as the governor's difficulties were, the plight of the Johnsons was more serious. Their lives hung in the balance. What would happen to them depended upon the home government's ruling on the bill of attainder.

Reporting later on the act against Corteen and Winthorp,[16] Mathew said it was of "an extraordinary Nature as the Lives of two Free men are Concerned." As with the bill against the Johnsons, Mathew at first insisted on the insertion of a suspending clause requiring the crown's approval before he would pass it. However, he later changed his mind for two reasons and passed the act, though "still with a Reserve in it, that whatever should be the Sentence of the Court, it should not be pronounced" until the crown's decision was made known. Why did Mathew pass the act? Corteen and Winthorp, he explained, were to be tried largely on evidence from at least ten slave witnesses who, if the act required the crown's approval before trial, would have had to be maintained at the island's expense until such approval arrived. To "an island allready Exhausted by the vast Charges and loss brought on it by the Conspiracy, as well as loosing nine tenths of this years Cropp by Blast and Drowth," the cost of keeping the slave witnesses until the trial, Mathew believed, was burdensome. His second reason for passing the act was because, all the slave witnesses being principal conspirators, " 'twas high time to ridd the Island of such Dangerous Villains by immediate Banishement," they having escaped death only by informing against their comrades.

While no accounts of any sort dealing with the trial of Corteen and Winthorp have been found, it is evident that the legislature was poised to commence proceedings on April 25, when it agreed to retain Robert Arbuthnot as prosecutor if the attorney general could not appear, and to banish the slave witnesses under that sentence as soon as possible "to the North ward, in order to Ease the Publick of the Charge that now attends the keeping of them here. . . and have them sold for the most they will yield, on the Publick Account." Owners, however, could be authorized to transport their own slaves, in which case they would not receive compensation. [17]

The act of attainder against the Johnsons that passed council on April 12, 1737 showed that they had been judged guilty as charged. In clear and forceful language it declared that evidence pointed to their involvement in the "blackest of Treasons" to stage a major slave revolt, a crime "the more monstrous, surprizing and ungrateful" because of the good fortune they had enjoyed as slaves of Margaret Low, and then as free persons who had inherited her wealth and enjoyed "all the Emoluments Privileges and Advantages of. . .white free born Subjects" in Antigua. Yet, "like Apostates [they] have abandoned truth," added the act, invoking an image of barbarism that whites more appropriately associated with African slaves, "and returned to their Original Infidelity and Superstition endeavouring as much as in them lay to erase the very name of Christianity in this Island and in conjunction with other Heathens to Drink the Blood of YOUR MAJESTIES Christian White Subjects." The Johnsons were guilty therefore not simply of the crime of plotting a revolt, but of betraying the trust of whites, a trust implicit in their admission to free status. Stressing the brothers' treachery, the act pointed out how they had conspired to overthrow the lawful government of the island, knowing full well that, because slave evidence could not be admitted against them in the ordinary course of justice, they did not run much risk of being condemned if the revolt failed. However, continued the act, expressing the view of whites who supported the use of slave evidence, "it Appears to us with all Moral certainty imaginable that they are guilty of this Enormous and unpalleled Treasonable Conspiracy So that unless by some extraordinary Method We are relieved against them this Island must see living in it two of the most dangerous Enemies that ingratitude cruelty and Ambition can raise up against it And from the repetition of their Devilish and unheard of Practices may be exposed to the utmost danger of Ruin and destruction and yet not be able to provide According to the first Laws of nature for its own Preservation and safety." But because "by the Policy and practice of all Nations there is in every Government an extraordinary and necessary power some where lodged to guard it against imminent dangers," such as Antigua experienced through the plot, "and to prevent its own destruction and punish out of the common method such daring Criminals as shall by unexampled Treachery and Bloody and intended Paricide endeavour utterly to extirpate whole communitys by an indiscriminate Massacre of Man Woman and Child," the legislature was justified in passing a bill of attainder, however extraordinary the measure, in order "to prevent and deter others from being concerned in" similar crimes "in hopes of being screend from Punishment by the defect of Our Laws" especially in relation to the inadmissibility of slave evidence against free persons.[18]

By repairing what they saw as a deficiency in the law, supporters of the act were setting a precedent for dealing with future attempts to overthrow the government in which free persons and slaves might be involved, or in which it might be necessary to use slave evidence against free rebels. The act obviously recognized the frightening possibility of subversive cooperation between slave and free, a possibility, however, only made more conspicuous by the slave plot, because in the seventeenth century slaves and indentured servants often acted together to undermine servitude, if only on a very limited scale. While the legislature could perhaps see more clearly the potential for slave-freedmen alliances, it did not forget the possibility that whites would not always stand together against slaves. It is not clear, however, whether the island lawmakers fully appreciated how whites, and the distinction between slavery and freedom, might be affected by the new judicial procedures they contemplated. If they were willing to run whatever the risks might be to slave society as presently constituted in Antigua, it was left to the authorities in Britain with jurisdiction over colonial affairs to draw the line. Condemned to "suffer the Pains of Death and incur all forfeitures as Persons attainted of high Treason," Benjamin and Billy Johnson were the first free people in Antigua to be convicted or even tried for involvement in a major effort of slave resistance.

The act against John Corteen and Thomas Winthorp condemned their "unexampled perfidiousness and treachery" which, as with the Johnsons, was "more inexcusable in them than in the very Slaves" because they enjoyed many of the privileges of whites, whose trust they had so abominably abused. Unlike the Johnsons, they were allowed jury trial. According to the act, slave testimony would be accepted viva voce, under oath if witnesses were Christians, without oath if they were not. If Corteen and Winthorp so desired, counsel would be appointed for each. If "convicted upon confession Demurrer or the Evidence of Two Credible Witnesses," they would receive the death penalty for high treason and incur forfeitures if the crown should confirm the act. By a suspending clause, the court's verdict would be recorded, but passing of sentence would depend on the act's confirmation. Corteen and Winthorp would also be remanded in custody until the crown's decision reached Antigua.[19] While that act and that of the Johnsons were en route to England for approval, Corteen and Winthorp were tried.

———————————————•◦•◦•◦—————————————————

In June 1737 the Antigua legislature appointed a five-man committee made up of councillor Vallentine Morris of the second court that tried the slave rebels, councillor John Vernon of the first court, Nathaniel Crump, councillor John Frye, and Samuel Byam. These gentlemen were entrusted to draft a letter to Antigua agent John Yeamans in London urging him to lobby for acceptance of the act against the Johnsons. Sent on its way probably in July, the letter contained much pertinent information, including some of the evidence upon which the Johnsons were condemned. Yeamans learned that a number of prominent citizens of Antigua believed not only that the brothers were innocent but also that there had been no conspiracy at all, "and Consequently," wrote the committee indignantly, "we must have Murder'd near an Hundred Innocent Souls, Banished Fifty, and put Our Selves to above Twenty Thousand Pounds Expence without the least necessity." Moreover, Morris and others warned, they believed some of the Johnsons' sympathizers would try to defend them in Britain and oppose the bill. The committee went on to explain that contrary to what such people believed, the brothers were a dangerous pair "for those Fellows by their Circumstances, are able to Purchase, and by their Trading way of life, can Easily Distribute Such a Quantity of Powder, Bullets, Cutlaces and Arms, Among the Slaves, as may soon be the Means of Destroying the whole Island should they Escape." Furthermore, the committee told Yeamans, who must absorb and act on such information, "we have reason to believe, by a High and Outragious Insolence that has lately hapned, that the thoughts of recommencing their [slaves] Conspiracy is not yet Out of their Heads."[20]

Recognizing the seriousness of the Johnsons' case, the Board of Trade ordered Governor Mathew to submit accounts of all the evidence the legislature had considered. But Mathew was in St. Christopher when he received the order, and he wrote asking the new speaker of the assembly, Stephen Blizard, for the record of testimony taken before the house. The assembly informed Blizard that neither the clerk nor any member had recorded testimony by order of the house. However, noted Blizard replying to Mathew, "there were some few Gentlemen who for their more Serious Consideration took down what was givn in Evidence, but that I believe has not been very carefully preserv'd." Assemblyman Ashton Warner's notes were "more Regular & Correct than most of the Others," but had been handed over to the former speaker, Thomas Kerby, and could not be traced. Blizard promised to comply with the governor's request as soon as he could.

By the time Mathew returned to Antigua, the council itself had done nothing to collect its account of testimony. The clerk had kept no record. Mathew apparently prevailed upon members to appoint a committee "to gather from their memories and from private notes . . . something of a summary of the evidence."[21]

Meanwhile, the Johnsons had forwarded a petition to the king about their predicament.[22] The Johnsons maintained that the bill that condemned them was "unusuall and extraordinary in its Nature as well as in the manner of its passing." They believed it necessary to point out that, during the inquiries of Arbuthnot and others of the first court, they were "almost constantly under arms guarding the prisoners" and were never accused of complicity; such accusations, however, had come later from the second court and had been based upon testimony of slaves already sentenced to die and not pardoned. The Johnsons contended that "the many and manifest Inconveniences that would arise from allowing the Testimony of Heathens and Slaves to be sufficient to convict free men and Christians have occasioned the same to be constantly disallowed in the Ordinary Course of Justice under a full Conviction that the contrary practice might be of the most fatal consequences to the Lives and Fortunes of the best and most innocent of Your Majestys Subjects in the Plantations" because it was "notorious that the Heathen Slaves even to avoid light punishments and much more the Loss of Life will not only contradict themselves but falsely accuse others." They stressed that most of the testimony came not simply from slaves, but worse, from those sentenced to death, "one of whom had been for several hours fastened to a gibbet to starve to death, under which circumstances it may be supposed he would have accused anyone." The bill of attainder itself was passed "by a bare margin of one or two votes," and would not have passed at all if the attorney general and another member had been present. The petitioners pleaded that they were good citizens and stood to lose too much by being in league with the slave rebels: "Your Petitioners have almost constantly resided in the said Island of Antigua and have never by their behaviour shewn any Spirit or Inclination tending to Rebellion but have always as Inhabitants readily and willingly done their Duty in Militia and born their Share of the Publick Levys and Taxes in proportion to their Substance both in Lands and Negroes which they had acquired by their Industry and all which it is scarce credible your Petitioners would sacrifice and become partys to a design which if it had taken effect must have reduced Your Petitioners to a levell with if not to subjection to their own Slaves." Benjamin and Billy Johnson also shrewdly implied that it was unlikely they would be involved in a scheme in which no witness had charged them with having "any place of Command . . . or with being intended to have any place of Command or Profit . . . if their Plot had taken Effect." They asked the king, in conclusion, not to grant his assent to the bill of attainder as "Your Majestys Wisdom and Clemency may seem meet."

The petition, as well as a letter addressed to the Duke of Newcastle on the "Cruell Barbarous and Bloody Conspiracy that was Carryd on Against Two free Black men"[23] were among papers in the Johnson case that came before the Board of Trade. The thrust of the letter, written by John Douncker of Antigua (occupation unknown) and dated March 22, 1738, was that the slave witnesses against Benjamin and Billy were bribed by some persons, including Robert Arbuthnot, to give false testimony that would help condemn them. Douncker believed Arbuthnot and others were part of a conspiracy to destroy the brothers. Drawing attention to the Johnsons as men of "great Quallification, and their Mother is a Christian & Soe that they was born Christians & their Wifes are Christians & their Chilldren are brought up in the Christian Religion, and they Allwayes Behaved Them Selves as Christians, for they are Quallified fitt for Merchants, & are men of great Dealings," Douncker insisted that the entire proceedings against them were outrageous, for "It is Against the Laws of God that a Heathen should be Against a Christian, & Against the Laws of men that A slave should be Against a free Man, Soe that our Island Cryes out." Douncker begged Newcastle to do all in his power to save the Johnsons.

The Board of Trade got down to a thorough examination of all the facts in the case. Appearing before them were the Johnsons' solicitor; agent Yeamans and his solicitor; Thomas Kerby, speaker of the assembly when the bill of attainder was passed; and John Vernon and Robert Arbuthnot, members of the first court that tried the conspirators. From Vernon and Arbuthnot the board learned that the brothers were so far from being suspected during the inquiries of the first court that Arbuthnot employed them "to look out and make further Discoveries"; no mention of their complicity was made during the more than two months the court sat "until within a day or two before the finishing of it, when one of the Blacks under Examination said, that if We should say any thing of the Johnsons? which Expression seem'd then of so little Moment, that no notice was taken of it." Kerby, who had taken notes on the evidence during the Johnsons' trial, told the board that he himself was not satisfied that they were guilty. Kerby also produced a letter from the attorney general and assemblyman, Ashton Warner, who, while not having attended every sitting of the house on account of illness, felt that the evidence in favor of the bill "as far as he went thro' with the remarking of it, was nothing but a heap of Inconsistencys & Incoherencys." One Mr. Lyons, "a Man of Character and Substance" in Antigua, swore before the board that he saw the Johnsons do their duty along with whites during the slave trials even after the accusations against them were made. Arbuthnot and Vernon nevertheless believed the brothers were guilty. To the board, however, reporting to a committee of the Privy

Council on May 11, 1738, there was still some doubt, "the Evidence being almost entirely that of blacks some of whom were under Condemnation and consequently under a double Incapacity both as Slaves and Persons under Sentence of Death." The board therefore advised that the Johnsons should be cleared of the charges and the bill against them disallowed.[24]

Four days later, Francis Fane, legal adviser to the board, gave his report on the Corteen-Winthorp case. Fane prefaced his opinion with the observation that the bill against them was intended "to alter what has always been the unvaried Law of this Country" not to admit slave evidence against free persons. "If the Fact were true upon which this Act is grounded," stated Fane, "I think it might be matter of Doubt, whether it might be expedient or even just to pass this Law which is to Establish an illegal Method in this particular Case of trying and Condemning Persons after the Crime had been long supposed to be committed." Fane contended that the procedure was "highly unjust, unless the Facts recited in the preamble. . .were very fully proved." Whether full proof had surfaced in Antigua he could not tell, but he certainly had not received any; and if the bill was passed because of existence of proof, that evidence should also have been laid before the board. "But as that has not been done," argued Fane, "I must consider it merely as It stands upon the Act itself, and in that light It appears to me to be an Act of a very extraordinary and unprecedented Nature, and highly dangerous to the lives and properties of His Majesty's free Subjects." For, Fane added, "if once the Testimony of Slaves is occasionally to be introduced in criminal Cases against Free Men, It may open a door to the greatest Oppression and Injustice." Fane did not say so, but of course, while that door should be kept firmly shut, the door to injustice against slaves inherent in the acceptance of all manner of white testimony against them was to be kept ajar. In any case, because the slave witnesses had already been convicted, Fane said, they were incompetent witnesses in point of law even if they had been free persons. The board communicated these observations to the king on June 21 and recommended the bill's disallowance, adding that it ought to have carried a clause suspending application until the king approved; instead the suspending clause related only to the actual carrying out of sentence.[25]

Issued July 20, 1738, the order-in-council that disallowed the bill against the Johnsons and restored them "to the same state and condition as they would have been in had the said Bill never been" passed received the Antigua's legislature's approval five months later, November 29. On November 30 another order-in-council repealed the bill against Corteen and Winthorp, stating that if they had been tried and convicted, (for the home authorities had no official information about that), they should be allowed bail pending further orders from the king, to whom all accounts of proceedings against them should be forwarded.[26] While authorities in England did not receive official notice regarding the court's verdict, news from Antigua indicated Winthorp had been acquitted and Corteen convicted.[27] This could have been accurate for, when the legislature considered the order-in-council in April 1739, only Corteen's name came up. The legislature agreed to free Corteen outright, believing that he could not easily "find Securities in which Case he Would be Committed to Goal, and the Publick charged with his Maintenance Perhaps as Long as he Lives, as it has already happn'd in two or three instances of Late." Indeed it appears that even before receiving the order-in-council, the legislature, sensing the trend of things from the outcome of the Johnsons' case, had already agreed to discharge Corteen without bail.[28] The freedmens' long ordeal had come to an end at last. The Antigua authorities had gambled and lost.

The Antigua freedmen could have been involved in the slave plot. Calculating that only slave evidence could convict them because the plot was secretly planned and coordinated by slaves, Benjamin and Billy Johnson, John Corteen, and perhaps Thomas Winthorp as well, even if he was acquitted, associated themselves with the slave rebels knowing that such evidence was not, by law, permitted against free persons, black or white. They apparently did not anticipate that the legislature would make a bold exception in their case if the plot failed. In the end they escaped not because they were not guilty or because the charges against them were not proved, but on a technical point regarding the use of slave evidence, and because of the apprehension of higher authorities in England that to allow such testimony would set a dangerous precedent that would "open a door to the greatest Oppression and Injustice." While the freedmen's plight as described in this chapter throws light on the status of freedmen generally and also illustrates one important dimension of the internal impact of the slave plot's discovery, the orders-in-council that freed the Johnsons and others undeniably invest their cases with added significance.

By defending primarily the rights and status of "His Majesty's free Subjects" in the slave colony, a mere handful of whom were freedmen, the home authorities conveyed a conception of freedom that was based on class and different from that of the island legislature, which was based on race and class. The authorities in Britain supported the position that freedom for whites as well as blacks should not be easily jeopardized, and that a clear distinction should exist between the meaning of free and slave status. They correctly feared that, in cases involving slaves, once lawfully free blacks were subjected to treatment before the law as if they were not, even free whites risked similar hazards in the future. Among whites this could lead to the oppression of the weak by the powerful and influential, men such as those of the legislature, who invoked race to prosecute the Johnson brothers and others. Their actions reflected and reinforced their belief that freedom for freedmen was not the same as that for whites.

In slave societies in the Americas, the worst fears of slaveowners were realized when their restless bondmen rose in revolt or plotted to do so. On such occasions in North America, according to Winthrop Jordan, because "the colonists dreaded slave insurrections they were quick to excoriate persons they conceived to be potential fomenters of revolt." Such *agents provocateurs* might be outsiders, or whites from within the community itself. Retributive action taken against such subversives, particularly the latter, clearly reflected "white anxiety over lack of cohesion" among whites in the community. Ordinarily, however, during slave disturbances, it was easier for whites to be persuaded, if the slightest suspicion existed, that freedmen were involved. Whites generally assumed that in any strife with slaves, freedmen would stand against them in support of "their brethren in color." Most Antigua slaveowners held similar assumptions of freedmen's behavior that could be traced in the various laws that limited relations between freedmen and slaves. Still, the very titles of the pivotal 1697 and 1702 acts for the better government of slaves and freedmen, who were lumped together and marked for subordination, also reflect these assumptions.[29] Whites saw freedmen and slaves as branches of the same troublesome tree, which should be therefore kept apart. The overwhelming tendency was to emphasize the slave origins of freedmen rather than incline toward according them the full free status of whites, to see them not as allies but as potential enemies of a different race and class who must be kept in their separate place. Such assumptions about, and attitudes toward, freedmen help explain why the legislature, after the discovery of the slave plot, did not lose much time debating the propriety of trying the freedmen suspects as if they were slaves.

Acute concern over the slave conspiracy of 1736 forced to the surface with sickening suddenness long-latent anxieties about general slave rebellion and freedmen's probable role. That the Antigua authorities arrested ownerless blacks who, they believed, had dared plot along with slaves to challenge white power, and had tried them using slave testimony, clearly shows how far they were inclined to go to root out the plot and punish in exemplary fashion all those believed to be principally connected. Alarmed at the *bouleversement* the conspiracy had intended, these men were prepared to risk undermining local judicial practice and ultimately to jeopardize the freedom even of whites in order to defend and reinforce their racial conception of freedom. Such reactions expose the island authorities' fearful awareness of the enormous crisis Antigua faced as a result of the plot.

Although the preceding chapters on the Antigua slave plot are largely concerned with describing the event and its consequences, they do open a window onto the slave society that nurtured it, offering glimpses of several features of that society that merit further investigation in order to account not only for the development of the plot but, more importantly, for slave resistance in its widest sense in relation to whites' attempts to establish effective patterns of control. If slave resistance and control dominated master-slave relations, they can best be studied in relation to each other and also to the dynamics of slave society. Accordingly, the following four chapters of part II explore the implications for Antigua of the forced migration of large numbers of Africans as slaves; the diverse roles of slaves in the developing sugar colony; and the emergence of patterns of control of both slaves and freedmen devised by whites in response to slave resistance, but also as a way of organizing race and class relations between blacks and whites.

II

Slaves and Slave Society

4

African Recruitment

Slaves began to arrive in Antigua in growing numbers as labor for the sugar plantations after the sugar revolution took root and expanded rapidly during the later seventeenth century. From small beginnings the trade developed into a vital link with Africa in the following century. Surviving evidence, though not plentiful, makes it possible to evaluate connections between the trade and problems of slave resistance and control through such related themes as origins and nature of the demand for slaves, mechanisms of trade, size and frequency of supply, buyer preferences, composition of cargoes, and slave population growth.

Before sugar and slavery began to exert their powerful influence on the economy and society of the Leeward Islands, settlers in the four main islands cultivated tobacco as the primary cash crop, with St. Christopher, "the mother island," leading the way. Other crops included cotton, indigo, cocoa, ginger, and provisions. When the price of tobacco fell on the European market in the 1630s, the islanders faced disaster. In a vain effort to raise the price, Governor Thomas Warner, who had pioneered settlement in the islands, imposed a ban on tobacco production in May 1639, which succeeded in impoverishing the planters and lasted for only two and a half years. When the ban was finally lifted, the planters returned to tobacco, but on a much reduced scale, later switching to sugar as the main cash crop. In the 1630s Dutchmen brought the sugar cane to Barbados, further south, and from there it spread north to the Leeward Islands, where, as in Barbados, its large-scale production soon initiated a social, economic, and political transformation so sweeping and rapid that historians have appropriately called it the sugar revolution. Basically, the revolution transformed the individualistic, predominantly white settler society of the tobacco period into a racially stratified society of whites and blacks, the entire institutional structure and value complex of which quickly centered on black slavery. To use Elsa V. Goveia's definition, a "slave society" emerged, a "community based on slavery, including masters and freedmen as well as slaves."[1]

Nothing remotely resembling the sugar revolution that Richard Ligon described as starting in Barbados around the 1640s (two decades after the English colonized it) was apparent in any of the Leewards that early. But by the 1650s the switch from tobacco to sugar had begun. Nevis seems to have been first to make a decisive move. In all four Leewards the plantation system began slowly, and one historian has described the rise of the plantocracy as "a slow and turbulent process," reminiscent in some ways of the rise of the Chesapeake tobacco planters on the American mainland. Though they together had more arable land than Barbados, it was difficult to clear and work. The result was that the Leeward Islands shifted slowly and uncertainly to sugar. But internal political factions, attacks by Carib Indians and European enemies, and the scarcity of capital and credit also account for the failure of the colonists to invest more rapidly in sugar and slaves. Thus, traders in African slaves and European supplies bypassed these northern islands in favor of more commercially sound Barbados, which was already beginning to ride high on a sugar bonanza by the 1650s. Barbados continued to attract both immigrants and capital as the economy thrived. In carving out their future, the colonists in the Leewards had "to pull themselves up by their own boot-straps."[2]

Antigua's development was slow, Richard B. Sheridan has noted, "until near the end of the seventeenth century when it moved ahead of the other Leeward Islands and later outstripped Barbados to become Britain's leading sugar island in the Lesser Antilles." Historians believe the sugar industry received a boost after 1674, when Colonel Christopher Codrington, son of Christopher Codrington, who had settled in Barbados in 1649, migrated from that island, taking along a number of slaves. Codrington, who had some experience in sugar cultivation, is said to have established the first real sugar plantation in Antigua, covering 725 acres, at Betty's Hope, near the center of the island and later part of the Parish of St. Peter. According to the Jamaican planter-historian Bryan Edwards, Codrington "applied his knowledge in sugar-planting with such good effect and success, that others, animated by his example, and assisted by his advice and encouragement, adventured in the same line of cultivation."[3]

For more than a century, the Codringtons remained the leading planter family in the island, owning in 1740 at least six sugar plantations: Betty's Hope, the Garden, the Folly, Roomes's, the Cotton, and the Cotton New Work. Credit for getting the sugar industry started, however, should not all go to Codrington. Already in Antigua when he arrived were some Surinam refugees who brought capital, useful connections, and considerable experience with plantation agriculture and were willing to settle down again to planting in their new home. Among them were the Willoughby, Martin, and Byam families, whose descendants became leading figures in the Caribbean islands. Writing to a friend in 1668, William Byam said he had "deserted our unfortunate colony of Surinam, war and pestilence having almost consumed it. As it is to revert to the Dutch, I have with great loss removed to Antigua, where I am hewing a new fortune out of wild woods."[4] His fortune could probably have been more quickly made in Nevis, where prospects were brighter.

Nevis was the most advanced of the Leewards by the 1670s, although still "not half planted for want of negroes." Already it exported "a great deal of sugar and indigo each year, which would all be sold for the growth and manufacture of England," ran a report, "if the English merchants would do their part, but great part is bartered for beef from Ireland and fish from New England." Its performance contrasted with that of Antigua, where, as reported in 1670, "Their present condition is sadly deplorable, all his Majesty's islands supplied with negroes except poor Antigua...they languish and decline for want of hands, and it is his Majesty [who] will feel it in the end; the strength of the planters consists in single men, who have neither servant nor slave."[5] Antigua and Montserrat lagged so far behind Nevis that they "were sending their freight there in shallops." All these would change for Antigua by 1700, but until it showed greater promise, the home authorities would continue to neglect it. The colony still produced tobacco "in great quantity" in 1671. But Governor Charles Wheler recognized its potential to surpass Nevis and asked the king for his favor because it was "as large as Barbados and the best land in the West Indies."[6] In 1672 the island was still not "half populated" and in common with Montserrat and St. Christopher could not adequately staff its legislature; of the 100,000 acres suitable for cultivation, only 70,000 had been patented. But three years later Antigua obviously began to assume stature as a new frontier for the would-be sugar planter, for in that year, out of 593 emigrants quitting Barbados, where all the good land had been absorbed into sugar cultivation, Antigua alone attracted 67 or 43.5 percent of the 154 who went to other Caribbean islands, thus bearing out the truth of Governor Wheler's claim made eight years earlier.[7]

The 1678 census points to some changes that had taken place in population size, ethnic composition, and property distribution. While the plantocracy was evidently developing, it was still small. Only 6 planters had as many as 60 slaves, but 47 percent of householders were slaveowners, indicating that sugar and slavery were gaining ground. Still, the majority of landowners cultivated subsistence crops or were cane growers without mills. But perhaps the most striking changes were in the size of both the white and slave populations. In 1646 there were only 750 people in the island; by 1655 there were 1,200 and by 1676 the number was 3,500. By 1678 it had grown to 4,480, or 2,308 whites and 2,172 blacks. Six years earlier there had been only 570 blacks and 600 or 800 English inhabitants, "very mean" and living "much scattered."[8] The near trebling of the slave population in six years is a sure indication of the spread of sugar culture. As the pace of economic life quickened in the 1680s, there developed a hectic race among planters to acquire land and slaves because sugar was more economically cultivated on a large scale.

Large sums of capital were needed to purchase both. Proprietors with little resources were at a disadvantage; unable to compete with others more able, many sold out, and the consequent aggregation of small farms or plantations into much larger units was characteristic of the early years of the sugar revolution. As the average unit of cultivation grew larger, land values climbed, while land tended to accumulate more and more in the hands of a relatively small elite, who became the backbone of the island plantocracy.

In every parish during the first half of the eighteenth century the plantocracy extended its power and influence over the life of the colony, taking up every available acre for sugar cultivation. By 1724 there was no unpatented land left, although the island was not under full cultivation. As early as 1708, Antigua accounted for more than half of the overall slave population and sugar output in the Leewards. In 1725 it was said to exceed Nevis, Montserrat, and St. Christopher "both in extent and Trade and by Consequence more business is done here." Writing in 1728, Governor William Mathew noted, "But now and for Years Past the chief Trade . . . is at Antego, next and very near to it at St. Christophers, Nevis has quite lost its Trade, & is a desert Island to what it was Thirty Years ago." From an annual average of 64,996 cwt. in 1706–10, English sugar exports from Antigua climbed to 167,760 cwt. in 1756–60. Antigua rose to prominence as a sugar colony on the backs of the slaves.[9]

The formation of the Royal African Company in 1672 with the monopoly to supply the English colonies with slaves did not immediately result in direct shipments to Antigua. More than a decade elapsed before they began to arrive. In the interim, Nevis was the company depot in the Leewards, and there its sole agent was stationed. As a result, in proportion to its 36 square miles, Nevis, the smallest of the four main islands, was for a time far better supplied with company slaves than the rest, whose planters were forced to sail over to buy "refuse Negroes at intolerable and immoderate rates," according to the St. Christopher council, "and even these only when they could not be sold elsewhere." Governor William Stapleton reported in 1676 that the islands were able to purchase 1,000 slaves annually, valued at £20,000 sterling. Slave prices, however, varied "according to their condition," said Stapleton, but he estimated that "from 3,500 to 4,000 lbs of sugar [was] given to the Royal Company's factors, no certain rate but as agreed from 20 L to 22 L sterling." K. G. Davies calculated that the company auctioned off in Nevis more than 6,000 slaves from 1674 to 1688; that island alone received 40 out of 45 company shipments (nearly 8,000 slaves) consigned to the Leewards between 1674 and 1686, with Montserrat and St. Christopher receiving two cargoes each, and Antigua only one. By 1692 no more than 800 had been shipped directly to Antigua.[10]

With most of the company trade at Nevis, it is not surprising that the other islands soon complained of neglect and demanded direct shipments. The St. Christopher council protested in 1680 that the company's monopoly impeded the island's growth. "Since its incorporation," it complained, "the Company has never vouchsafed to supply this island with more than one inconsiderable vessel, but rather has put hardships and difficulties in the way of the planters." Intent on effecting a change in company policy if they could, the councillors asked the Lords of Trade to make the company "shew cause why the people of this Colony, who have always striven to give it good satisfaction and compliance for everything received, should be thus discouraged and oppressed." They hoped to influence the company "to supply us properly in future or permit us to take other measures herein. For," they argued, "it is as great a bondage for us to cultivate our plantations without Negro slaves as for the Egyptians to make bricks without straw." From Montserrat came similar complaints, the council there noting that since the island "was wholly destroyed by the French and Dutch in 1666 . . . but two small ships have been sent by the Royal African Company with little more than three hundred Negroes, half of whom are already dead." While the Antigua legislature joined in the chorus of protest, it also issued an act in 1675 urging the company to appoint a local agent. The act outlined specific measures for safeguarding company interests. In setting forth the planters' grievances, it stated, "in regard this is the Windermost of His Majesty's Islands, so that the Negroes which are brought to Nevis are sold and disposed of, before any notice can be given us; and moreover for the inhabitants here to go down to Nevis to buy Negroes, and to carry afterwards their Goods to make Payment is a matter very disadvantageous to the Inhabitants here, who are altogether disappointed of the Common Advantage and Conveniences of His Majesty's Gracious Intentions towards them in his Royal Charter Grant to the Said Royal Company." Ten years passed before Antigua finally got an agent, albeit one shared with Montserrat. But that made little difference, for, while slave supplies increased, the planters continued to grumble and find fault.[11]

Slaves not obtained from the company at this early date were delivered by interlopers or separate traders or were simply smuggled in from neighboring Dutch island depots, mainly St. Eustatius. Fully aware of the interloping traffic, Governor Nathaniel Johnson wrote from Nevis in 1688: "Another interloper has been here, and had landed some sixty slaves at Montserrat, when the lieutenant Governor rode up to the landing place and she sailed away. All the slaves were seized. She landed some men, if not all, a few days later, and some of them also were seized. I have condemned the first sixty as lawful seizure, and await evidence to condemn the rest." There being no man-of-war to send after the slavers, they escaped. The governor also noted that the company's employees, who must certainly have been unpopular, "were riotously opposed when seizing these Negroes, and I have ordered a prosecution of the offenders, which I hope will have a good effect. These Negroes are the first that were ever condemned here." Such cases had previously been tried at common law "when juries should not be satisfied with any evidence," but now Johnson had begun to use the Admiralty Court.[12] Confiscated slaves, however, were still sold in the islands. With a growing demand for slaves that apparently the company alone could not satisfy, these islands, with the probable exception of Nevis, explored other channels.

After 1689 the Royal African Company could no longer successfully maintain its monopoly, so seriously had separate traders eroded it. From 1698 to 1712 the trade to the English colonies was thrown open to all private traders who paid the company for the upkeep of its African forts a 10 percent ad valorem duty on exports to the coast. The agreement expired, was not renewed, and the trade became open to all. It should be possible therefore to form some picture of the slave trade to Antigua after 1689 using accounts of company and separate traders' shipments. In 1708 Governor Daniel Parke, on orders from the Board of Trade to supply returns for the Leewards since June 1698, prepared the first detailed accounts of slave imports for the eighteenth century. Parke submitted one for the company (table 4.1) and another for "Permition Shipps" or separate traders (table 4.2) covering the period June 24, 1698 to December 25, 1707.

Both lists give importation dates, names of vessels, masters' names, and size of slave cargo. These early estimates show that a total of at least 1,805 company slaves (8 shipments), or about 200 a year, arrived, while the separate traders, more active, did much better at 549 a year, or a total of 4,945 (41 shipments), more than twice the company figure, making a grand total of 6,750 slaves delivered. This figure pales to insignificance alongside the 34,583 slaves Barbados imported over the same period, 9,006 credited to the company and 25,577 to the separate traders. Barbados, however, had already reached its peak of development and had the capacity to absorb more than five times the number of slaves Antigua got.[13]

Parke also sent home in 1708 a detailed account of company imports for Antigua over a shorter period — February 2, 1702–August 26, 1707 — prepared by Edward Chester, the company agent (table 4.3). While the period covered in this list and Parke's overlap, shipment dates and number of slaves delivered do not always agree. Further, Parke omits three shipments that Chester records. In some ways Chester's account is more valuable, containing information on individual sales, showing not only to whom these were made but also how much was spent per group, broken down into men, women, boys, and girls; also listed are the ships' coastal points of departure. Altogether Chester shows that in 10 shipments 2,176 slaves were imported (931 men, 820 women, 297 boys, and 128 girls), and

TABLE 4.1. Slaves Imported by the Royal African Company, June 24, 1698–December 25, 1707

Date	Vessel	Master	Slaves
Jan. 24, 1701	Ship Bridgewater Frigat	John Bridger	221
Dec. 14, 1702	Ship Lucitania	Paul Sorrell	
Nov. 15, 1704	Ship Lucitania	John Hayes	224
Dec. 10, 1705	Ship Royall Africa	Thomas Mackey	538
May 17, 1706	Brig. Constant Rachell	George Lorrinon	176
Oct. 12, 1706	Ship Regard	Richard Abbott	361
Aug. 23, 1707	Sloop Flying Fame	Henry Hooper	114
	Ship Gaulkin Bird	John Luke	171
Total			1,805

SOURCE: "An Account of what Negro Slaves have been Imported into this Island By the Royall African Company of England from Africa & by what Vessells from the 24th. of June 1698 to the 25th. of December 1707," enclosed in Parke to BT, August 23, 1708, CO 152/7, L97.

sold to 524 buyers. Only 18 were cash purchases; the rest presumably were on some kind of credit arrangement. Combining the Chester and Parke accounts for company shipments (1698–1707), it would appear that close to 2,400 slaves were delivered.[14]

Davies has estimated that of the 60,000 slaves the Royal African Company transported to the West Indies between 1673 and 1711 the majority were adults, mostly males. This might be taken to reflect plantation labor

TABLE 4.2. Slaves Imported by the Separate Traders, June 24, 1698–December 25, 1707

Year	Shipments	Slaves
1698 (Oct. 22)	1	18
1699 (June 3)	1	212
1700	7	164[a]
1701	15	1,618[b]
1702	12	1,795
1703	2	319
1704	2	550
1705 (Jan. 20)	1	269
Total	41	4,945

SOURCE: "An Account of what Negro Slaves have been Imported into this Island by Permition Shipps from Africa or by what Vessells from the 24 of June 1698 to ye 25th. of Decemr. 1707," enclosed in Parke to BT, August 23, 1708, CO 152/7, L96.
[a]Only one shipment recorded.
[b]One shipment unaccounted for.

TABLE 4.3. Slaves Sold by the Royal African Company, February 2, 1702–August 26, 1707

Date	Vessel	Point of Departure	Slaves	Men	Women	Boys	Girls
Feb. 2, 1702	Bridgewatter Friggatt	New Callaborr	221	101	38	20	12
July 24, 1702	Ship Will'm and Jane	Wedaugh[a]	155	95	45	14	1
Aug. 17, 1702	Ship Canterbury	Old Callaborr	94	29	37	18	10
Dec. 9, 1702	Lucitania	Angola	92	34	40	12	6
Oct. 27, 1703	Bridgewater	Accra	218	82	89	35	12
Oct. 12, 1704	Lucitania	Cape Coast Castle & Widaugh	224	142	68	11	3
Nov. 20, 1705	Royall Affrica	Cape Coast Castle	528[b]	219	200	80	29
May 20, 1706	Briga. Constant Rachel	Cape Coast Castle	172	51	65	32	24
Oct. 25, 1706	Regard	Gold Coast	358	119	144	66	29
Aug. 26, 1707	Sloop Flying Fame.	Gold Coast	114	59	44	9	2
Total			2,176	931	820	297	128

SOURCE: Parke to BT, Aug. 23, 1708, CO 152/7, L98.
[a]Whydah.
[b]In the original, the number of women, boys, and girls is incorrectly given as 201, 79, and 31 respectively, which makes a total of 530. The grand total of slaves for November 20, 1705 was thus given as 2,178.

requirements, but, as Herbert S. Klein has pointed out, it could more correctly be a reflection of supply conditions on the African side, where, in many societies, there was a "systematic bias against removing women."[15] That Chester's list should show sales of 56.4 percent males (adult and young), or 42.8 percent adult males compared with 37.7 percent adult females hardly implies a stronger demand for women. Neither does the figure of 425 nonadult sales or 19.5 percent of all sales imply a preference for younger slaves. The pattern of sales might be the result of observed high levels of demand for slaves around the turn of the century, which forced a higher proportion of females and younger slaves onto the market.[16] In any case, the planters, who normally seemed to have little or no influence on the quality or regularity of supply, generally bought whatever slaves were delivered regardless of ethnic, sex, and age preferences. Moreover, slave traders on the African coast had to take what was available or else sail away empty-handed. The composition of a slave cargo therefore was more often related less to specific demand preferences of Antiguans and more to supplies on the coast, as the variability in age and sex composition of individual cargoes in table 4.3 seems to show.

As a result of increased demand around 1700, adult slave prices in Africa also rose. Slave prices of the Royal African Company increased sharply during the first decade of the century, from £16 10s. in Barbados in 1698, for example, to £25 15s. in 1710, perhaps chiefly because of high wartime freight and insurance costs. According to Sheridan, slave prices, which tended to rise and fall together with sugar prices except in wartime, "declined after the War of Spanish Succession, rose in the 1720s, and declined again during the depression of the early 1730s." In the late 1730s prices rose again "and levelled off at about £35 sterling per head during the third quarter of the 18th century." Thomas Kerby, the Antigua company agent in 1724, noted that the Royal African Company, while it held the monopoly, sold slaves at from £23 to £25 colonial currency in the Leewards, but largely as a result of the "interferring Interests" of separate traders, slaves were now sold at "very great Rates" of from £40 to £60 a head. Kerby probably exaggerated because his observations were part of an attack on the separate traders and in support of company monopoly. During the period September 29, 1707–September 29, 1710, the company delivered 956 slaves to Antigua, selling them at £30 3s. a head between 1707 and 1708 and £38 1s. between 1708 and 1710. Corresponding prices for 1707 and 1708 were in Jamaica £24 4s., Barbados £25 4s., and Virginia £23 17s.[17] The separate traders brought 970 slaves to Antigua from Michaelmas 1708 to July 1709. In 1709 and 1710 they sold their slaves in the Leewards for between £30 and £35 a head, but the corresponding prices in Jamaica were between £16 and £20.[18] Slave prices in the colonies were influenced by a number of factors, including the value of currency. In

Antigua prices tended to be higher than in Jamaica and Barbados largely because of currency inflation. In 1710 the separate traders claimed Leewards currency was "20 per cent worse than that of Jamaica."[19]

Antigua planters nevertheless continued to stock their plantations with slaves at existing prices. Returns on slaves imported from May 1, 1711 to May 1, 1712 place the number at 1,008.[20] From then up to the 1720s no figures have been found. Arriving in 32 shipments from December 20, 1721 to December 25, 1726 were 4,633 slaves, or an average of 1,148.25 a year. The detailed account (table 4.4) shows the names of vessels, date of entry at Antigua, master's names, vessels' owners, coastal origins of cargoes, number of slaves delivered, and shipment consignees. Table 4.5 summarizes the data on cargo size and distribution. The largest single cargo of 355 arrived in 1725, delivered by the *Sarah Gally* to Messrs. George and William Thomas; this was also the largest cargo of the eleven arriving in 1725, of which six consisted of over 100 slaves. In 1726 nine out of ten were of that size. The original account of imports appears to be a compilation of consignments made through the Royal African Company and separate traders. Among the latter were some Antiguans trading on their own account. The name of the Antigua planter Thomas Kerby, for example, who was also agent for the company, appears thirteen times on the list of consignees, but only four times as the company's agent. The other nine times Kerby was either individually involved in a slaving venture or in partnership with other people. He is even listed as owning the sloop *Great Caesar,* captained by Henry Lavibond, which made a trip apparently for the Royal African Company, delivering 142 slaves to Kerby in his capacity as agent. If the four consignments to Kerby as agent out of a total of thirty-two are a correct indication of the company's share of the 4,633 slaves imported, then it was a mere 13.8 percent, which underlines the relatively small extent of the company's business after the trade was thown open. While most of the slaves came from the African coast, 32 came from Nevis and 1 from Boston, a reminder that in the eighteenth century there was a small intercolonial traffic.

The account also points to some seasonality in cargo arrivals. While traders avoided the coast in the rainy season (June to August) because of the higher incidence of disease among the slaves, the full impact of which appeared in heavy mortality during the Atlantic crossing, they also tended to stay away from the West Indies during the hurricane season (July to September). The two seasons roughly coincided and explain why, during those months generally, comparatively few shipments arrived in the West Indies, although sometimes, because the traders experienced difficulty in timing their operations, they did arrive in the hurricane season.[21] Only six (832 slaves or 18.08 percent) of the thirty African shipments (4,600 slaves) arrived during the hurricane season, five in September, near the end of the season, and one at its height in August. The remainder, spread out from October to June, show a marked concentration of twenty-two (3,457 slaves or 75.15 percent) from January to June. The pattern of seasonality for 1727 (table 4.6) is roughly similar.[22] Of eight African shipments (1,578 slaves) only two (229 slaves or 14.5 percent) arrived in the hurricane season. November was a good month, three ships transporting 789 slaves between them. With the exception of cargoes in July and August, all others were of over 100 slaves, so Antigua was fairly well supplied that year, 1,658 slaves being landed, including 80 from Barbados, and sold at an average of about £20 sterling or £30 Antigua currency a head.[23] A report for the longer period Christmas 1720–Christmas 1729 gives 11,278 slaves imported, or 1,253.11 a year. Totals were given for 1721 (251), 1728 (1,365), 1729 (2,846); the total for 1727, a period longer than that in table 4.6, was larger by 525. Imports reported for 1730 alone were about 2,288. Information for the remaining years to the mid-eighteenth century is extremely scanty and uncertain, but the annual average import was estimated in 1750 at 2,000.[24]

How many slaves had probably been delivered to Antigua by 1763? Using Philip Curtin's estimates of imports to the Leewards for 1671–1807 broken up into four periods (table 4.7), we can estimate Antigua's share for 1671–1763. Antigua probably received 10 percent in the period to 1671 and roughly 30 percent thereafter. Curtin points out that if "the Leewards followed the demographic trend of Barbados, imports should have been climbing during the 1720s to a peak in perhaps the 1760's or 1770's after which they would have dropped gradually." Frank W. Pitman's estimate of 3,750 slaves a year for 1720–55 therefore seems reasonable and is used to calculate Antigua's share for 1734–63.[25] Table 4.7 shows an estimated 60,820 slave imports for 1671–1763, or 29.3 percent of the Leewards total.

Imports did not, however, swell the slave population proportionately. Between 1720 and 1729, while 11,278 slaves were imported, the slave population grew by only 3,425, from 19,186 to 22,611. Scattered evidence indicates a small re-export trade, but the inability of the slave population to show more significant increase in the 1720s may be put down largely to a high mortality rate, not at all surprising during a period of intense sugar cultivation when production climbed from 5,658 tons in 1720 to 10,276 tons in 1729.[26] Slave mortality rate for the period is estimated at 4.13 percent. Richard Sheridan has estimated an annual percentage decline in the Leewards slave population of 4.4 percent for 1701–25 and 4.8 percent for 1716–50, higher than Jamaica for both periods.[27] Low fertility levels and high male-female ratios help explain low or negative rates of natural increase, which also retarded slave population growth. Possible reasons for high mortality include low-protein diet, accidents, disease, poor infant care, overwork, and malnutrition.[28] Precisely where emphasis should be

TABLE 4.4. Slaves Imported, December 20, 1721–December 25, 1726

Date of Entry	Vessel	Owner	Point of Departure	Slaves	Consignee
Mar. 9, 1722	Ship Lady Rachel	Charles Lansdell	Africa	244	Thomas Kerby, Agent to R.A.C.
June 12, 1722	Ship Margaret	Samuel Bonham	Coast of Africa	205	Thomas Kerby, Agent to R.A.C.
Mar. 14, 1723	Sloop Great Caesar	Thomas Kerby	Coast of Africa	143	Thomas Kerby, Agent to R.A.C.
Sept. 7, 1723	Sloop John & Elizabeth	John Green	Coast of Africa	242	John Barbottain & John Green
Sept. 12, 1723	Snow Lady's Adventure	Francis Ploisted	Coast of Africa	97	Baker from Nevis
Sept. 13, 1723	Snow Unity	John Smallwood	Africa	102	Capt. Henry Baker of Bristol
Jan. 28, 1724	Snow Mary	John Smallwood	Coast of Africa	30	Capt. Henry Baker of Bristol
Apr. 7, 1724	Brigantine Ruby	Stephen Godin	Coast of Africa	79	Thomas Kerby
Apr. 21, 1724	Sloop Success	Royal African Company	Coast of Africa	47	Thomas Kerby, Agent to R.A.C.
May 12, 1724	Brigantine Negroes Nest	Gerrish & Chester	Coast of Africa	154	Edward Chester, Jr.
May 27, 1724	Ship Gaboone	William Gerrish et al.	Coast of Africa	120	Thomas Kerby
Jan. 18, 1725	Ship John & Elizabeth	John Green et al.	Coast of Africa	272	John Barbottain & owners of ship
Jan. 28, 1725	Sloop Charles	William Wanton et al.	Nevis	32	Baker from Nevis
Feb. 22, 1725	Sloop Newport	William Griffith	Coast of Africa	78	Capt. William Griffith
Apr. 23, 1725	Ship Sarah Galley	Samuel Bonham et al.	Africa	355	Messrs. George & William Thomas
May 15, 1725	Brigantine Negroes Nest	William Gerrish & Edward Chester	Coast of Africa	167	Edward Chester, Jr.

Date	Vessel	Owner(s)	Destination	No.	Master/Owners
June 11, 1725	Ship Gaboone	William Gerrish et al.	Coast of Africa	192	Thomas Kerby
June 16, 1725	Snow Hester & Jane	William Gerrish et al.	Coast of Africa	147	Thomas Kerby
July 17, 1725	Brigantine Sarah & Rebecca	Samuel Clark et al.	Boston	1	
Aug. 28, 1725	Ship Byam Gally	Edward Byam & others	Coast of Africa	70	Gov. Edward Byam & Owners of the Ship.
Oct. 8, 1725	Brigantine Ruby	Stephen Godin	Coast of Africa	45	Thomas Kerby
Dec. 13, 1725	Ship Sea Nymph	William Gerrish	Africa	166	Thomas Kerby
Jan. 4, 1726	Ship Betty Gally	Humphrey Morice & G. Smith	Coast of Africa	226	George Byam
Feb. 5, 1726	Snow Kingfisher	Richard Harris	Coast of Africa	197	Edward Chester, Jr.
Mar. 30, 1726	Snow Gold Coast Gally	Thomas Kerby & John Burke	Coast of Africa	180	Thomas Kerby, John Burke & the Captain
Apr. 18, 1726	Ship John & Elizabeth	John Green & others	Coast of Africa	150	John Green & Owners of the Ship.
Apr. 18, 1726	Brigantine Negroes Nest	William Gerrish & Edward Chester	Coast of Africa	140	Edward Chester, Jr.
June 2, 1726	Brigantine Catherine & Elizabeth	Humphrey Hill et al.	Coast of Africa	176	John Burke & Ambrose Lynch
June 22, 1726	Sloop Three Friends	John Green et al.	Coast of Africa	155	Capt. John Green & the Owners of the Ship.
Sept. 6, 1726	Ship Stannage	Thomas Tarleton et al.	Coast of Africa	180	Capt. Thomas Tarleton
Sept. 13, 1726	Snow London Spy	William Gerrish	Coast of Africa	141	Thomas Kerby
Nov. 7, 1726	Snow Flying Horse	William Gerrish & Arthur Lowe	Coast of Africa	200	Thomas Kerby

SOURCE: Enclosure in Hart to BT, Feb. 15, 1727, CO 152/15, R190.

TABLE 4.5. Annual Importation of Slaves to Antigua, 1722–1726

Year	Slaves	Shipments	Mean Cargo Size
1722	449	2	225
1723	584	4	145
1724	430	5	85
1725	1,525	11	140
1726	1,645	10	165

SOURCE: Enclosure in Hart to BT, Feb. 15, 1727, CO 152/15, R190.

placed for the Leewards is not yet clear, but it might be pointed out that compared with Jamaican slaves, who produced much of their own food, those in the Leewards were fed on imported supplies that were often deficient in both quantity and nutritive value. Malnutrition therefore could have played a very important role in poor demographic performance especially during periodic subsistence crises brought on by drought and interruption of supplies. A large number of new Africans, or salt-water slaves, as they were called, also died during the seasoning period in the colonies as psychological and physical troubles caused by the adjustment process took their toll among slaves already weakened and demoralized by the trip from Africa.[29] The Reverend Robert Robertson, clergyman and plantation proprietor in Nevis, stated in 1731 that the "loss of Slaves (not including those immediately from Guinea, of which about two Fifths die in the Seasoning) may well, one year with another, be reckoned at One in Fifteen." Increase by births was "not great, or nothing near so great as Strangers to the Colonies are apt to think" he added, while not many new Africans survived even though owners took "all imaginable Care." Robertson agreed that high rates of mortality made "the Continuance of fresh Supplies absolutely necessary."[30]

Mortality also slowed down the growth rate of the slave population in the sugar colonies, but it was nevertheless clear that, as the sugar revolution progressed, the number of blacks increased rapidly until blacks outnumbered whites by significantly wide margins. Such black majorities would have important consequences for the island societies. In Antigua by 1720, nearly one out of every five whites (19.1 percent) was an indentured servant, and white bondage was more common there than in Nevis, Montserrat, or St. Christopher; but already Antigua had long begun to rely heavily on slave labor, which would ultimately make indentured labor marginally significant. At 84.0 percent of overall population in 1720, slaves outnumbered all whites including indentured servants.[31] The supply of servants, never encouraging even before the sugar revolution, moved into high gear early in the eighteenth century, and virtually dried up in later years. With the expansion of sugar cultivation, land engrossment left little

TABLE 4.6. Slaves Imported, March 25–November 20, 1727

Date of Entry	Vessel	Registration	Owner	Point of Departure	Slaves
Apr. 8, 1727	Snow Judith	London	Humphrey Morice	Africa	220
Apr. 11, 1727	Snow Gold Coast Gally	Antigua	Thomas Kerby et al.	Africa	160
May 1, 1727	Ship Byam Gally	Antigua	Gov. Byam et al.	Africa	180
July 31, 1727	Ship Stannage	Liverpool	Thomas Tarleton et al.	Africa	152
Aug. 21, 1727	Sloop Catherine	Boston	Peter Papillon	Africa	77
Oct. 14, 1727	Sloop George	Barbados	William Read et al.	Barbados	80
Nov. 4, 1727	Ship Catherine Gally	London	Humphrey Morrice	Africa	550
Nov. 20, 1727	Snow Codrington	Bristol	Sir William Codrington	Africa	139
Nov. 20, 1727	Snow Tryall	London	William Gerrish	Africa	100
Total					1,658

SOURCE: Mathew to BT, Dec. 1, 1727, CO 152/16, S65.

TABLE 4.7. Estimate of Antigua Slave Imports, 1671-1763

Period	Leeward Islands	Antigua	Percentage
1671	7,000	700	10
1672-1706	44,800	13,440	30
1707-1733	43,100	12,930	30
1734-1763	112,500	33,750	30
Total	207,400	60,820	29.3

SOURCES: Philip D. Curtin, *The Atlantic Slave Trade: A Census* (Madison: University of Wisconsin Press, 1969), p. 62; Frank Wesley Pitman, *The Development of the British West Indies 1700-1763* (1917; reprint, New York: Archon, 1967), pp. 76-77.

opportunity for servants who had served out their time to become freeholders. Antigua therefore could not attract servants; and even among those who had completed service, many quit the island, took to the sea, or drifted into idleness in the towns. Others became artisans and plied their trade to stay afloat, but in time even these hopeful tradesmen found themselves in open competition with slave craftsmen, some of whom led a fairly independent existence. Still others who had somehow acquired small lots of land found they could not compete with the sugar planters and sold out. Life for a former indentured servant was hazardous, and unless things improved servants could not be expected to help increase the white population by coming to Antigua or staying to settle there.

In 1734 agent John Yeamans put his finger on some reasons behind the decline of the white population, which had reached a peak of 5,200 in 1724 and thereafter slid steadily downward. "The Decrease of White Men," he told the Board of Trade, "I apprehend to be Owing to Several Causes. Epidemical Distempers have destroyed Numbers, Dry Weather, Want of Provisions, And inability to pay their Taxes have obliged Others to go off." Moreover, "Land has been at So high a price from the Smallness of the Quantity...that the Settlers of Ten or Twenty Acres who formerly rais'd Only Provisions have been tempted to Sell their Possessions to the Sugar Planters & have thereupon quitted the Island." Yeamans believed that another "and a very great cause" was "the Employing Negro tradesmen, Such as Carpenters, Coopers, Millwrights, Masons etc.," and if slaves were prevented from entering these trades whites might be attracted to the island. The way to bring all this about, however, as he quickly pointed out, was not by an "immediate Act against employing Such Negro Tradesmen, (which would be too great inconveniencys that would arise from Obliging the Inhabitants all at once to provide themselves with White workmen, a thing almost Inpracticable)," but rather to discontinue training slave artisans and gradually replace them with white workmen. On paper this idea made some sense, but it would be difficult to win cooperation from slaveowners, some of whom made a living off the earnings of their skilled property. In regard to struggling marginal planters who might be tempted to abandon the island altogether, Yeamans suggested that they might change their minds if the home government reduced duties on island exports "which the Trade is not able to bear" and placed the islands "upon the Same footing with the French as to all those advantages they derive from the favour & Indulgence of their Mother Country."

War and rumors of war also drove whites away from, or deterred their migration to Antigua. "Upon the Whole," Yeamans contended, "While a french War threatens his Majesty's Sugar Colonies in General and While Antigua in Particular lies Extremely Exposed to the Invasions of an Enemy," it would not be easy to attract settlers. Even "numbers of the old Settlers from a despair of being able to Maintain their Ground May retire with their most Valuable Effects" to the greater safety of North America unless a naval squadron stood ready to protect the islands, which badly needed military supplies. Without these, argued Yeamans, "No Encouragements great Enough can be propos'd Either to bring on new, or to induce the Old Settlers to Continue." Many years earlier, in the heat of the Anglo-French war of 1702–13, Governor Nathaniel Johnson had commented that "The common people and Artificers" of the Leewards "whose Fortunes are easily remov'd with them, will for the most part goe to Coracoa, and Saint Thomas's; that is, will turn Privateers during the wars, and Pyrates forever after."[32] Resident sugar planters stayed, only to feel the full effect of a French invasion in 1712.

Governor Parke, who very soon after his arrival in the island fell afoul of the plantocracy, had his own explanation of why new settlers could not be enticed to immigrate. The law, he claimed, was hardly enforced against residents. "As to Criminall matters one Would think ye inhabitants . . . Could be guilty of No Crime, for Except Soldiers, sailors or Strangers No inhabitants has ever been punish'd Since I Came, And yett this town of St. Johns is ye most wicked town I ever was in, No justice of peace ever punishes anybody or binds them over to ye Sessions." The governor himself had "bound Some Over, t'is true, butt all were brought in not Guilty." These, he said, "are ye Reasons no Strangers will Settle among them Except he Can att once buy an Estate." Antigua, in other words, was no place for a new settler without means; entry into white society was possible but only at the top. The money and property interest dominated. "Ye rich oppress ye poor to yt. degree, that should there come a peace for Seven Years, noby would be here butt Negroes and their Masters or Overseers." The governor said that Barbados had a law by which planters were to keep one white person for every ten slaves or acres, and "I have often desir'd ye same here, butt to no purpose." The note of despair in Parke's comments grew stronger. "I now desire yr Lordps.' directions how to remedy all these disorders," he wrote. "I have indeavour'd it, so did Sir Wm. Mathews" before him, "butt in vain." Parke lamented that all he had succeeded in doing was stirring up "a wasps' nest about my ears. . . If I would yett take no notice of all these abuses," he concluded, "in a little time I should have Addresses of thanks from them." An industrious if also officious administrator, Parke under-stood that the socioeconomic character of Antigua slave society militated against white population growth through migration or the development of a sizable class of whites not tied directly to sugar and slaves. Complaint brought little help from the Board of Trade, who simply told Parke to do his best to prevent white depopulation especially by discouraging "the breeding up of Slaves to handicraft Trades."[33]

Far less accusatory in tone than Parke's, Yeamans's observations of 1734 were incorporated in a Board of Trade report to the committee of the Privy Council. The Board, however, went further to mention "the non-observance of the laws which oblige the owners of land to keep certain num-bers of white servants in proportion to the numbers of their Negroes." One possible way therefore to increase the number of whites seemed to be to enforce white servant acts. In 1724 Governor Hart had recommended en-forcing the 1716 act, which contained elaborate provisions governing ser-vant recruitment.[34] But neither this act nor others before or after it through the eighteenth century, were successfully enforced. From time to time, however, legislators showed a revived interest in the "better strength-ening and settling" of the island with more whites, but that was usually when the slaves seemed particularly restless or war was expected. When the danger subsided so too did the interest in recruitment schemes. All attempts to keep up the white population did not, in the long run, change the trend toward increase in the ratio of blacks to whites. Scattered census returns, for what they are worth, show that while white population reached a peak in 1724 and then declined, black population increased steadily, if unevenly (table 4.8). Even taking heavy mortality into account, black popu-lation almost tripled in the period 1703–56. From 1:3.80 in 1724 the ratio of whites to blacks declined to 1:9.21 in 1756. Blacks represented 79.2 per-cent of the total population in 1724; by 1756 that proportion became 90.2 percent. Accounts of parish registers confirm that burials normally far ex-ceeded births among whites; a high mortality rate contributed not only to the slow growth of the white population in the first quarter of the eighteenth century but also to its absolute decline thereafter.[35]

Antiguan slaveowners were aware of the potential dangers of a growing black majority but resigned themselves to facing them rather than aban-don lucrative sugar cultivation with slave labor. In pursuit of profit they invited such consequences as their own brutalization through management of slaves, degradation of white labor, and slave rebellion. Writing in 1736 to the Earl of Egmont, trustee of the Georgia colony, the Virginian planter

TABLE 4.8.   Population of Antigua, 1672–1774

Year	Whites	Blacks/Slaves	Total Population	Percentage Black
1672[a]	800	570	1,370	41.6
1678[b]	2,308	2,172	4,480	48.5
1703[c]	—	11,000	—	—
1705[d]	—	12,187	—	—
1708[e]	2,892	12,943	15,835	81.7
1711[f]	2,854	11,838	14,692	80.5
1720[g]	3,652	19,186	22,838	84.0
1724[h]	5,200	19,800	25,000	79.2
1729[i]	4,088	22,611	26,699	84.6
1734[j]	3,772	24,408	28,180	86.6
1741[k]	—	27,418	—	—
1744[l]	—	27,892	—	—
1753[m]	3,461	—	—	—
1756[n]	3,435	31,428	34,863	90.2
1774[o]	2,590	37,808	40,398	93.5

SOURCES: [a]CSP 1669-74, no. 896, p. 977; [b]Richard S. Dunn, *Sugar and Slaves: The Rise of the Planter Class in the English West Indies* (Chapel Hill: University of North Carolina Press, 1972), p. 127; [c]Thomas to BT (before Nov. 16, 1703), CO 152/5, H2; [d]Johnson to BT, Sept. 17, 1705, CO 152/6, K8; [e]Parke to BT, Mar. 8, 1708, CO 152/7, L53; [f]St. Leger to BT, Aug. 23, 1712, CO 152/10, O14; [g]Hamilton to BT, Aug. 22, 1720, CO 152/12, O46; [h]Hart to BT, July 12, 1724, CO 152/14, R101; [i]Mathew to BT, Aug. 31, 1734, CO 152/20, V46; [j]ibid.; [k]Mathew to BT, Apr. 15, 1746, CO 152/25, Y154; [l]ibid.; [m]Thomas to BT, Oct. 8, 1753, CO 152/57, Aa86; [n]Thomas to BT, Feb. 20, 1756, CO 152/28, Bb75; [o]Gov. Ralph Payne's account.
NOTE: When the term *blacks* is used in census returns in place of *slaves*, it does not appear that freedmen were included.

William Byrd approved of that colony's exclusion of slaves for those reasons, objections to slavery that were common in the early eighteenth century. Slaveowners in Antigua would have agreed with Byrd that the "private mischiefs" to planters' behavior and white labor were "nothing if compared to the publick danger" of slave revolt. For, Byrd contended, reflecting on slavery and slave population growth in Virginia, "in case there should arise a Man of desperate courage amongst us, exasperated by a desperate fortune, he might be dreadfully mischeivous before any opposition could be formed against him, and tinge our Rivers as wide as they are with blood."[36] However, the real basis for concern was not the existence of a black majority but rather its uncooperative and subversive behavior, which was a threat to the slave system. Just as the emergence of a significant black majority that was difficult to control in South Carolina soon after 1700 made slaveowners regard slaves as the enemy within, so too in Antigua; however, slaveowners in the sugar island seem not to have been as anxious about major slave offensives against them as their counterparts in Jamaica, where the topography aided runaways and maroons. The style of slave resistance in Antigua by the eighteenth century, more covert, individual, and unsystematic, contributed to a less explosive atmosphere and a generally less apprehensive slaveowning class. The plot of 1736 came like a sudden thunderclap, shattering their complacency.

To judge by their frequent complaints, Antigua and other Leeward Islands planters seemed to have been generally in need of more slaves than they received even after the trade was no longer a Royal African Company monopoly. Governor Parke informed the company in 1707 that there was "great Want of Slaves in all ye Islands." War could have interrupted supplies at the time. In 1719 the company reported that the Leewards were not so well supplied as before, while Governor Hamilton elaborated that "the Numbers that are now imported are not near what they were formerly which not only obliges planters to give greater Prices for them. . . but is a great Hindrance to the Improvement of the Sugar Plantations." By 1724 Antigua was still understocked; while no unpatented land remained, some was uncultivated because of too few slaves, a situation brought about, said company agent Thomas Kerby, by "the great discouragements that the Company have met with" since the trade was thrown open to all traders.[37] For the rest of the 1720s, however, the trade revived, only to peter out again. A report of 1734 stated that supplies had declined to "almost nothing"; while the island had about 40,000 acres suitable for sugar cultivation, "want of Negroes occasion'd these acres to be not wholly improved." Two years before, the Reverend Robertson had estimated Antigua needed about 20,000 more slaves, to work especially at manuring land of declining fertility.[38] If these claims for the first four decades of the century are correct, Antigua needed more slaves both to extend the areas of cultivation and to work lands losing their fertility. Complaints about scarcity of supplies continued into the 1740s and 1750s. When Governor George Thomas reported in 1756 on the state of the island, by then fully cultivated, he observed that 1755 had been an unusually good year, and planters were thankful for additional labor "to manure their lands, which are greatly improverished by long Culture."[39]

If slave prices in the Leewards tended to be higher than in Barbados and Jamaica, why were these islands not better supplied? Disruptions of war aside, one reason could be that Barbados, better capitalized, and Jamaica certainly faster growing, were traders' preferred markets. In a memorial to the Board of Trade in 1750, Antiguans supplied their own explanation, which related not so much to numbers as to preferred ethnic groups. Preferring slaves from Whydah (Dahomey) and the Gold Coast, they complained that few had arrived in recent years. "The loss of this most valuable Trade," they explained, "is owing partly to the rivalship of foreign Nation's, but principally to the discretion of Bristol and Liverpool Merchants who chuse rather to trade to Calabar, Angola and the Bite" because slaves from these places, "being much less valuable, are purchased at a cheaper rate." Yet, added the memorialists, such slaves "are imposed upon us for want of better, at the price of the best sort, to the great injury of the Planters, who are deeply involved in debt by the mortality and failure of that kind of Negroes." Plantations "must inevitably be ruined," they contended, "for want of Caramantee, Fantee, and Poppa Negroes" unless Britain regained supremacy in the trade. Samuel Martin, a leading planter, reflected while struggling to restore his plantation, wrecked by bad management while he was away in England, that "for want of Gold Coast Negroes here, I must take measures of supplying my great want of them by being concerned in a Ship for that purpose tho' perhaps it may be a dear, since it is ye only method."[40]

As supplies continued short in the 1750s, Walter Tullideph, attorney for George Thomas's plantations, wrote the absentee in March 1752 that there had "not been a Guinea Cargoe Sold here these Six Months, orders being lodged here for their proceeding to Jamaica," where he believed prices were better, "and I doubt we shall have very few to Stay this year." So few cargoes had been arriving in Antigua that, when "the Salusbury of Liverpool, Capt. Keys, with 100 & odd Slaves" docked in 1757, one resident referred to "a great Market." Two years earlier, although Antiguan planters preferred not to buy Angola slaves, when a French vessel arrived with 500, they quickly bought them up, along with another 300 from another French vessel from Pawpaw, even though smallpox had broken out aboard.[41]

Unable to obtain regular supplies of suitable slaves from the coast, planters tried at least two alternatives: the more enterprising and able sent their own vessels to Africa; an illegal traffic was also carried on with the Dutch at nearby St. Eustatius. Evidence on the direct island slave trade is scattered through such sources as official correspondence from the colony, observations from the Royal African company's agents, planters' private papers, and shipping returns.[42] In 1708 the separate traders claimed that among several plantation vessels trading on the coast were two Antiguan sloops that had transported 260 slaves to the Leewards between Michaelmas 1707 and July 1708. In 1716 Thomas Kerby, on behalf of himself and other owners of the sloop *Frances,* petitioned the governor for a loan of twelve or fifteen barrels of gunpowder to enable them to send the vessel to the Gold Coast for slaves.[43] Table 4.4 shows that planter-merchant Kerby was involved in a number of such ventures in the 1720s. In the minutes of the Antigua legislature evidence can be found that in 1720 George Crump and Samuel Redhead were making preparations to send their "large Commodious Sloop of Ten guns" to the coast. The Codringtons were also involved in the trade. Sir William Codrington in 1720 hoped his sloop would return with more than 150 slaves purchased mainly with rum. All the Leewards traded directly to Africa taking for exchange "small Cargoes from Great Britain" and rum, which in 1724 was cited as the most profitable exchange commodity, selling on the coast "for Five Shillings Sterling per Gallon tho the first Cost is not One Shilling."[44]

The alternative to this trade was an illegal traffic with St. Eustatius, the Dutch emporium. It can be traced back to the late seventeenth century. In 1688 Governor Johnson referred to Mr. Crispe of St. Christopher, whom customs officers and agents of the Royal African Company reported "as a persistent smuggler of Negroes and sugar to and from the Dutch islands." Noting that smuggling adversely affected company trade and the crown's interests because sugar was exchanged for slaves, Johnson suggested that the only way "to check this countraband trade is to authorise the arrest and examination on oath of suspected persons, who, on refusing to answer the accusations, should be esteemed guilty." Indeed, he added, a royal proclamation should impose the measures and would do much "to destroy this trade, but it cannot be utterly put down except by destruction of the Dutch and Danish settlements."[45] Whatever steps may have been taken to destroy smuggling did not prevent its continuation into the eighteenth century. A memorial to the Board of Trade in 1709 placed some of the blame on customs officers who were accused of part ownership of smuggled cargoes. Collector of customs John Helden of St. Christopher reported in 1719 that over the four preceding years the Dutch at St. Eustatius had imported several thousand slaves whom they sold to English and French buyers for sugar and ready money. Similar reports came from the Leewards governors in 1718 and 1724. St. Christopher, closest to St. Eustatius, appears to have been the most deeply involved of the islands, importing, according to Governor John Hart, probably 1,000 slaves from 1721 to 1723, but, as no customs duties were paid and buyers brought them in "at their pleasure," he could not be certain about numbers. Hart, writing in 1727, claimed that the trade had come to a "full Stop" largely because 5,600 slaves had arrived in St. Christopher in five years, "a prodigious number to be Imported into so small an island," and sold below Dutch prices.[46] If this was true, the same thing probably held for Antigua, to which large cargoes were also delivered over the period. It is more likely, however, that the trade was temporarily reduced to a trickle, to be revived later on as times of scarcity again replaced those of plenty. That no reports on the trade for later years have been found does not imply that it had dried up, especially when one source has suggested intensification of the St. Eustatius trade in 1730–40.[47] In any case, when Antiguan and other Leewards planters wanted slaves, they purchased from the Royal African Company until the last days of its active life, from separate traders, and from the Dutch at St. Eustatius, while some also invested in direct ventures to the African coast.

Walter Tullideph's correspondence with George Thomas from 1739 to 1758 offers some insight into the problems confronting an attorney in managing the affairs of an absentee planter, not least among which are those related to the slave force itself, especially keeping up numbers. The letters indicate that new Africans were usually hard to obtain in those years, and that Tullideph seemed determined to purchase young slaves for the plantations in his charge.[48] In 1748 he wrote Thomas that he hoped "Negroes will now be imported here in greater plenty, that there may be an addition of 10 or 20 Young ladds made to N. Sd [North Sound]." In April of the following year he bought six young slaves from the Windward Coast for the same plantation "most of them about 18 years old, one or two perhaps 22 or 23 at most." In June he thought of buying five or six young slaves for Winthorpes, another plantation. "You really want them," he told Thomas, "indeed the Negroe Men are craving for wifes and therefore would advise Girls to be bought for that Estate and boys for No. Sd." Winthorpes still needed ten or fifteen young slaves in 1752, and Tullideph recommended purchasing "Ten Young Girls and Five Young Men."[49] If Tullideph's purchasing strategy was in response to general scarcity of slave cargoes, it could mean that, with long-run consequences of scarcity in mind, he believed it was reasonable to expect longer service from slaves purchased young. Furthermore, buying females could also mean he considered possibilities of natural increase. Writing from Dundee, Scotland when he was an absentee himself in 1759, Tullideph, anticipating confiscation of slaves after the British invaded Guadeloupe, told his attorney, Dr. James Russell, "if any number of French slaves are brot. over, & sold reasonable, buy 10 men boys & 10 Women Girls, creole's & divide them between the two Estates." Attorney Rowland Oliver urged the owner of the Swete plantation in 1745 to authorize purchase of six young slaves every year in order to bring the plantation up to strength. And in the 1740s Benjamin King, attorney for the Codrington plantations, advised the owner that Betty's Hope Plantation badly needed fifty more slaves, but he would not recommend purchasing them "full grown" because "such Slaves are allways Obstinate, and Stubborn, & Seldom comes on kindly to Labour." Slaves from "12 to 15 Years of Age will prove best," he said, "and are most Reasonable," commonly costing £25–£28 a head, while grown slaves cost £30–£42. King added that the plantation was "so weak in Negroes that the Women are obligd to do the Labour of men, such as making fire, Carring Potts of Sugar of 100 Weight wch often Occasions Violent Disorders & Miscarriages, and tends greatly to the Detriment of the General Interest, so yt. some Negroe men of ye best Country (about 15) must be purchas'd, ye Rest may be of ye age as above." Writing from Antigua in 1753, attorney William Mackinen urged absentee proprietor Abraham Redwood of Rhode Island, to buy "some [women] or girls with your men and boys, by which means you [ha]ve your estate stock't with creoles for your children, the [advant]age of which my friend Jonas Langford now reaps the [benefit]."[50]

If these cases are representative, then in the 1740s and 1750s planters facing the prospect of short supply and its consequences shifted from male adult purchases to younger slaves, with a significant addition of females. To what extent changes in cargo composition in relation to the sex and age of slaves on the African market influenced the shift is not clear. Yet, obviously connected with the difficult business of plantation management, the shift had probably started much earlier in the eighteenth century as planters, probably understanding much better the nature of their enterprises, realized it was in their best interest in the long run to invest in younger slaves. David Stalker, an employee on the Stapleton plantations in Nevis, warned in 1730 that when purchased, slaves should not be more than fifteen years old. Buy them, he said, preferably "between 12 and 15. They are fully seasoned by 18 and in full as handy as them that is born in the country [Creoles] but them full grown fellers think it hard to work never being brought up to it they take it to heart and dye or is never good for any things." Further research is needed to determine whether such priorities persisted through the eighteenth and early nineteenth centuries, and what might be the demographic and socioeconomic consequences, as well as what role supply conditions played. But if we concentrate on the period of about 1734–56, it will be seen that for the 23-year period 1711–34, which spanned the good years for slave imports of the 1720s, the slave population increased by 12,570, from 11,838 to 24,408, more than doubling (106.18 percent), while for the 22-year period 1734–56, including many lean years, growth was only 7,020, or from 24,408 to 31,428 (28.76 percent) (see table 4.8). It can be concluded that the slave population was growing more slowly, at least because of effects of irregular trade and continued high mortality as slaves were worked harder. But conceivably many slaveowners had begun taking better care of their workers if earnings on the sugar market permitted. During this period the proportion of Creoles may have also increased significantly. In their general report of 1736 on the slave plot, the judges claimed Creoles were "the most numerous...of our Slaves."[51] If this is correct, growth of the Creole population had started much earlier. In addition to changes in the size of the Creole population in 1734–56, there may also have been changes in the sex and age composition among Africans.

David Stalker's comment points to a preference for Creole slaves because, although generally they cost more, especially if skilled, since they had been born and socialized within the slave system unlike new Africans,

they did not have to be seasoned or broken in before fitting into plantation routine. In 1755 Tullideph wrote the absentee proprietor George
Leonard in Tortola, Virgin Islands that while he had purchased that year
thirteen new Africans for his Antigua plantation, fifteen slaves had died,
reducing the work capability of the labor force as "these new negroes can't
be work't so hard as seasoned ones." Tullideph sent Leonard six slaves in
1756, including two new Africans "that are very low and don't agree with
a Sugar Estate, but may upon a Cotton one." Writing from Dundee in 1760,
Tullideph was delighted "our negroes are healthy and that the New ones
thrive and take kindly to their worke, & that you had so good a provision
of Potatoes for them."[52] Obviously many planters must have been judi-
cious in purchasing new Africans, buying singly or in small batches if
possible. When attorney Samuel Redhead advised the absentee proprietor Sir William Codrington that his plantations needed 120 slaves between
them, Codrington, considering the expense involved, asked Redhead "to
use ye utmost discretion therein" and to buy the slaves in batches, "30 or
40 I shou'd think full enough for a first purchase, & when you See how
they stand to pick a few more as opportunity offers, of a fine Cargo; till
a Sufficient number are got; for you think it worse economy to buy too
many at once than too few." Codrington hoped the "small Gangs will grow
up to ease part of this expence."[53] Cautious as they might have been in
purchasing new Africans, when their need was great, planters took the
risk fully aware of the consequences of harsh treatment or premature
exposure to the full rigor of plantation labor. However, rather than rely
on the slave trade to maintain numbers, planters could hire slaves for specific jobs, buy seasoned slaves, adjust production goals, encourage breeding, and shift slaves from one occupation to another when necessary.[54]

   An assessment of the suitability of certain African groups based to a
large extent upon ethnic origins, supposed capacity for hard work under
direction, and tractability also formed one of the central features of
Antiguan demand. Here, as elsewhere in the Americas, preferences were
largely ethnic stereotypes. "Pray let me take upon [myself] to advise you
about buying negroes" wrote Mackinen to Redwood in 1753, "which is
to buy negro[es] at least of the best countrys. There are some other countrys
[from whi]ch young women and girls do well enough, but it is not the [case
wi]th the men; of some countrys they are not worth the [expe]nce." As in
other parts of plantation America, Antiguan slaveowners showed a definite
preference for certain ethnic groups and an aversion to others. Their first
choices were blacks from the Gold Coast generally, whom they called
Coromantees (Koromantyns, Callamantees), and those imported from
Whydah in Dahomey. Coromantee was not the name of any particular
Gold Coast group but a generic term adopted after the Dutch fort at
Kormantin. The largest ethnic groups in the Gold Coast belonged to the

Akan language group (Fanti, Asante), and here too were to be found the Guang and Ga-Andangme peoples and numerous others of the hinter-land.[55] Of the Coromantees Bryan Edwards wrote: "The circumstances which distinguish the Koromantyn, or Gold Coast, Negroes, from all others, are firmness both of body and mind; a ferociousness of disposi-tion; but withal, activity, courage and a stubborness, or what an ancient Roman would have deemed an elevation, of soul, which prompts them to enterprizes of difficulty and danger; and enables them to meet death, in its most horrible shape, with fortitude or indifference. They sometimes take to labour with great promptitude and alacrity, and have constitutions well adapted for it."[56] Nevis planters' first choice, said the Reverend William Smith, writing early in the eighteenth century, were Coromantees; they were "the most valuable and hardy, on account of the vast Heats, and of course, scarcity of Provisions there." All the Leewards placed Coroman-tees at the top of their scale of preferences, but if Bryan Edwards is cor-rect they were also populating the islands with rebellious Africans. Edwards wrote after a number of Coromantee-led and inspired rebellions had broken out in Jamaica and would have us believe, on the basis largely of the Jamaica experience, that Coromantees were natural rebels. Following Edwards, a modern scholar has also observed how "remarkable" it is that "almost every one of the serious rebellions during the seventeenth and eighteenth centuries was instigated and carried out mainly by Akan slaves who came from a highly developed militaristic regime, skilled in jungle warfare."[57] Many Coromantees also came to Antigua and the other Leewards where, however, their record of revolt is not outstanding. We must therefore look elsewhere than in a supposed ferocious disposition or experience in war-fare for an explanation of Coromantee rebellion. The Leewards contrast suggests we should at least take into account the size and rate of growth of the Coromantee slave population in relation to the sociology of slav-ery, and the probable role the very topography of the territory played.

Africans loaded as Whydah, a port in Dahomey, on the Slave Coast, were Antiguans' choice after Coromantees. These slaves were called Pawpaws or Poppas, a term that referred to the Fon, Gun, and other related groups of that region.[58] Writing to Redwood in 1755, Mackinen and Stephen Blizard noted that Gold Coast slaves "always answer better than any Slaves from Africa except Papaws." Edwards said they took to field labor readily, "unquestionably the most docile and best-disposed Slaves that are imported from any part of Africa."[59] These Antigua preferences for Coromantees and Pawpaws corresponded to the make-up of the British slave trade during the first three decades of the eighteenth century, when most British exports came from the Gold and Slave coasts. Although slaves continued to be shipped from these regions, their share in the overall British trade declined after 1730 in favor of the Bight of Biafra, further down the coast. Curtin's calculations indicate that the Gold Coast, which had contributed 38.3 percent of the export trade during the decade 1721-30, held only 15.8 percent between 1751 and 1760. For the same periods the shares of the Bight of Biafra—where the main groups were the Ibos, Ibibios, Edos, and Ijaws—were 3.2 percent and 40.4 percent respectively. From the Antiguans' memorial to the Board of Trade in 1750 it is quite clear they accepted slaves from the Bight but regarded them as obviously "less valuable" than Coromantees or Pawpaws. "In complexion," Edwards wrote, Ibos "are much yellower than the Gold Coast and Whidah Negroes; but it is a sickly hue, and their eyes appear as if suffused with bile, even when they are in perfect health"; moreover, they were a despondent people and did not make good slaves. When Antiguans bought Ibos, or slaves from Calabar or Angola, they risked "mortality and failure of that kind of Negroes." The Reverend William Smith, who had linked the Coromantees' physical durability to native climate and diet, believed Congo and Angola slaves were less valued in the Leewards because "the Plenty of Provision in their own, more temperate, and cool Countries, renders them lazy, and consequently, not so able to endure Work and Fatigue." In the eighteenth century British traders held such views on the relevance of environment and diet, which suggests that British ethnic characterizations were not wholly whimsical.[60]

The Royal African Company and the separate traders must have brought to Antigua slaves from many areas of the African coast other than those already mentioned, but without accurate records it is not possible to say where and what groups were involved. Because Coromantees and Pawpaws were so highly prized, they receive prominent mention in the records, but little or nothing is said about others. In tables 4.4 and 4.6 there is no way of identifying ethnic composition of cargoes simply because "Africa" or "Coast of Africa" are the vague entries for places of origin. In contrast, table 4.3, which deals specifically with company shipments during the first decade of the eighteenth century, at least shows from what African ports vessels arrived, and in two cases from what general coastal region. According to these entries, of ten shipments, six came from the Gold Coast; the *Lucitania,* which arrived in 1704, loaded at both Cape Coast Castle on the Gold Coast, and Whydah (Widaugh) on the Slave Coast. From Angola came one shipment, while yet another came from Whydah. New Calabar and Old Calabar, both along the Bight of Biafra, furnished one cargo each. Reporting on the Calabar slave trade at the beginning of the century, James Barbot, Jr. described New Calabar slaves as "a strange sort of brutish creatures, very weak and slothful." They were, he said, "cruel and bloody in their temper, always quarreling, biting and fighting, and sometimes choaking and murdering one another without mercy, as happened to several aboard our ship." Barbot warned that "whoever carries slaves from New

Calabar river to the West Indies, had need pray for a quick passage, that they may arrive there alive and in health."[61] Thousands of slaves arrived alive from different parts of the coast and lived long enough to have been part of the machinery of plantation production, however uncommitted they may have been to their occupations.

The character of the slave trade influenced ways in which slave society and economy developed in plantation America. The greater the dependence on slave labor, the greater the impact and role of slavery and the slave trade. In Antigua dependence on slave labor led to an influx of Africans, although irregular, and a black population majority in the eighteenth century, while increasing the potential for social conflict; but that potential and the shape conflict took were primarily determined not so much by growth of the slave population as by the role of slavery as an exploitive labor system based on extra-economic compulsion, and its consequences for slaves and slaveowners ideologically, socially, economically, politically, institutionally, and culturally. Together these consequences, on one level, helped shape the dynamics of master-slave relationships, which centered on an interplay of conflicting interests.[62] In examining, therefore, the Antigua slave system in order to disentangle intertwined patterns of slave resistance and control, we must venture beyond the role of the slave trade to look also at the function of slaves in the economy, wherein resided their fundamental value from the slaveowners' point of view.

5

From the Negroes' Labor

While most Antigua slaves were attached to sugar plantations of varying size in the rural districts, large numbers also held a multiplicity of occupations elsewhere and had no direct contact with plantations. As slavery evolved from a mere labor system, embedding itself into the life of the colony, an increasing number of slaves who were often owned by masters without land worked in the towns and even on vessels trading between the islands and beyond to North America, Africa, and Europe. By the middle of the eighteenth century, during the Seven Years' War, slaves were also part of British forces that invaded French West Indian territory. An appreciation of the broad spectrum of slave employment leads to the realization that slave occupations naturally bred and shaped a complexity of roles and a wider range of relationships with masters and whites generally that must have strongly influenced individual and collective responses to enslavement.

Although generally apprehensive of slave rebellion, slaveowners, once they began to profit from the sugar market, relied heavily on slave labor and skills. They calculated the attendant risks and decided they were worth taking if they could control the potential for slave rebellion. Slavery was so pervasive, however, in Antigua and elsewhere in the Americas, that large-scale revolts or conspiracies predictably sent waves of anxiety surging through the master class, in some cases resulting in hysterical acts of retribution. At such times individual slaveowners worried about whether any of their own slaves could be involved. If the answer was yes, they often could not say why, but it was obvious that they had failed to establish effective control. Where had they fallen short? What must be done? Innumerable questions battered and drastically shook their self-confidence in this moment of crisis. To better understand Antiguan slaveowners' responses to the 1736 plot and the threat it posed, to get some insight into the complexity of slave roles and how they may have shaped slave consciousness and their response to slavery and attempts to discipline them, it is useful to explore the extensive utilization of slave labor. Slaves' lives were conditioned not only by their physical, social, and cultural uprooting but also, especially in terms of their adjustment to slavery, by the work they were made to do, which implied exposure to diverse patterns of subordination. A key element, therefore, in existing master-slave relationships relates to slave treatment, in this case with reference to day-to-day living conditions including "such essentially measurable items as quantity and quality of food, clothing, housing, length of the working day, and the general conditions of labor."[1]

Peter H. Wood has shown how occupations and status of slaves changed as the South Carolina economy became more intimately engaged with the rice staple. In the early frontier days slaves worked at a variety of occupations and were largely unsupervised, but after the successful introduction of rice in the 1690s "pioneering life" gave way to "plantation life as the dominant mode of existence," characterized by rapid increase in the African population and allocation of slaves to plantation labor, particularly as field workers. At the same time the system of slave control grew more repressive, a sure indication that whites considered slaves "less as useful and loyal servants in a rough environment than as degraded and resentful labourers." A similar transition, more abrupt and striking, took place in Antigua as sugar and slavery leaped into prominence. In the frontier days before the sugar revolution, slaves were in demand, according to a report of 1671, "for by negroes only can that island be planted till it be cleared of wood for more health for the English."[2] In the following decades, however, the sugar plantation became the dominant unit of economic and social organization, transforming life and labor.

The tiny island in which this process first gathered momentum during the last two decades of the seventeenth century has a very irregular coastline and is relatively flat, except in parts of the northeast and the hilly southwest corner, where the highest peak, Boggy Peak, rises to about 1,319 feet. The southwest Shekerly Hills, eroded remnants of old volcanic mountains, and the territory extending eastward to Falmouth and English Harbour, comprise the island's volcanic region. There are two other structural regions: a broad, gently undulating central plain of clayey soil bordered on the leeward side by the volcanic hills; and on its windward side, limestone uplands. English colonists, who first settled near sheltered bays in the south at Old Road and Falmouth, and later at St. John's in the west, began clearing and cultivating forested land around the volcanic and central plain districts. In this vicinity the first tobacco farms were probably located, but, as settlement became dispersed and planters later considered ideal sites for sugar plantations, cultivation spread and centered on the less rugged central plain and limestone uplands. Betty's Hope, Christopher Codrington's pioneer plantation, was located in the latter area, "near the western end of the Willikies peninsula." Two other large and well-known plantations were also established in the limestone district, Parham Plantation belonging to the Tudways and situated to the north of Betty's Hope near the town of Parham on Parham Harbour, and Cassada Garden, further west, belonging to the Redwoods. Forest rapidly gave way to plantations, and by the early eighteenth century the volcanic region was the only area of extensive forest and woodland left.

Well over half the island was under cane cultivation by 1700, and by 1734 about 50,000 of its estimated 72,000 acres, "but want of negroes occasion'd these acres to be not wholly improv'd, for by the last return," ran a report, "there were upon it but twenty four thousand four hundred and eight." The number of acres "return'd upon oath to pay the land tax" was 58,342, so 8,342 acres were allocated not to cane but to "pasture, provisions or cotton." Barren areas and the southern hills made up the remaining acreage. By 1751, however, the island was reported to be "improved to the utmost, there being hardly one Acre of Ground, even to the Tops of Mountains, fit for Sugar Canes and other necessary Produce, but what is taken in and cultivated." Sugar output increased from an annual average of 4,835 tons in the decade 1711–20 to 8,067 tons in 1751–60. John Luffman, reporting in 1786, said that from his house in St. John's he could see the Shekerly Hills four miles in the distance to the south, some of them "clothed with the luxuriant verdure of the sugar cane to their very summits. This pleasing assemblage of hills," he added, "ranging as far as the eye can reach, affords a view most charmingly picturesque, and which cannot be seen without rapture and delight." Those covered with canes must have been the least steep, for transportation of the crop from field to factory does place a limit on the steepness of slopes that can be cultivated. Planters evidently put as many cultivable acres as possible under sugar cane, which can tolerate a variety of soils.

Climate does not vary appreciably within Antigua and does not affect soil type, but rainfall increases westward and tends to be heaviest in the southwestern district. Droughts, however, occur often. In regard to seasonal rainfall distribution, David Harris has noted that normally "the 'dry' season lasts from January to April and the 'wet' season from August to November, with May, June, July, and December as transitional months." That sequence, he adds, however, can vary widely from year to year. The dry season tends not to be of uniform length across the island, varying from "9 months on the dry east coast to 5 months in the wetter southwestern district,"[3] a factor that was of major importance in the performance of sugar plantations both in and out of drought.

During the early period of the sugar revolution, to capitalize on economic opportunities that sugar cultivation offered, most planters tried to increase their land holdings and slaves. This development can be traced, for example, among proprietors of the Parish of St. Mary, in the volcanic district, who must have first made maximum use of alluvial valleys between the hills before pushing up the less steep slopes on their land. Recorded tax lists for 1688, 1693, 1696, and 1706 reveal notable alterations not only in population size and composition but in property distribution as well.

Dunn, summarizing the data for 1688, 1706, and 1767 emphasizes that "the chief point to emerge. . . is that the largest planters in the parish dramatically enlarged their holdings during the French wars."[4] Slaveholders increased from 16 in 1688 to 30 in 1706, nearly doubling, taxables fell from 53 to 36 over the same period as property accumulated in the hands of fewer persons, the slave population swelled from a mere 332 to 1,150 (346 percent growth). In 1688 only 6 planters owned 20 or more slaves, the biggest having 73; by 1706, that number was 16, and 4 of these planters owned 100 slaves or more. The proportion of slaveholders among taxpayers increased in 1706 to 84 percent. The number of acres per slave decreased from 17.5 in 1688 to 4.9 in 1706. By 1767 every taxpayer was a slaveowner.

The tax lists show that most taxpayers were on the move, especially the larger planters, who, it seems, maneuvered for an economic balance between acreage and slave force. Estimates of a proper ratio of slaves to acres have been placed at 1:1 or 2:1.[5] John Frye, who had 26 slaves in 1678, increased the number to 70 in 1688, to 72 in 1696, and to 103 in 1706. Meanwhile his plantation, which had been 1,000 acres in 1696, shrank to 560 acres in 1706, bringing slaves and acreage into closer balance. William Dunning, who owned 243 acres and 16 slaves in 1693, was also somewhat better off in 1706, with 288 acres and 66 slaves. Many names recur in the tax lists, but new ones also appear. Three names that do not appear, for example, in 1693 show up in 1696, and, according to their assessment for land and slaves, they were bidding for a place among the parish gentry. Henry Winthorpe, who in 1696 owned 250 acres and 32 slaves, was assessed for 190 acres and 38 slaves in 1706. Both Captain Henry Pearne and Major Samuel Martin owned sizable estates in 1696; Pearne had 750 acres and 74 slaves, while Martin had 550 acres, but no slaves were recorded for him. By 1706 Pearne owned 665 acres and 150 slaves. Martin was assessed for 531 acres and 114 slaves. While the plantation system had not yet fully evolved in St. Mary's Parish by 1706, significant trends were evident.

In every parish during the first half of the eighteenth century, the Antigua plantocracy was taking shape and consolidating its hold on social, economic, and political power. A large portion of a planter's wealth was sunk in slaves, and, because of the monocultural nature of the island economy, plantation workers formed the bulk of the slave population, though there were other categories of slaves as well. But how was wealth in plantations and slaves distributed? Any discussion of the slaves' larger experience, or rebellion, for example, must take into account the objective conditions of their lives, which were shaped by such forces as the size of plantation units on which they lived and worked, patterns of actual ownership, and the extraplantation employment of slave labor. If, for example, the plantation unit was small enough for the resident planter "to know his bondsmen well enough to intervene in their daily existence in a direct and personal way," Stuart B. Schwartz has argued, slaves' lives could be affected in important ways very different from impersonal relationships between masters, or their representatives, and slaves, nurtured by high levels of slave-holding concentration.[6]

No studies exist on patterns of slaveholding in Antigua for any period, and they may be difficult to do for the eighteenth century given the scanti-ness of surviving data, but an observation of agent John Yeamans in 1734 can help throw some light on the case for ownership of plantation slaves. Together, the severely limited amount of cultivable land in Antigua, plan-tation milling capacity, land transportation, and economies of scale, helped determine a plantation's optimum size. Yeamans estimated that "there are very few persons. . . at present of above, or even so much as 300 acres of land fit for sugar; and without Such a quantity or something near it, No Planter can be enabled to bear the great Expence of the Buildings & Uten-sils Necessary for making Sugar." A few large and many middling and small planters cultivated all the "improveable land." If it is true that in the mid 1730s there were more than 150 plantations utilizing about 50,000 acres suitable for sugar cultivation, the average size of a plantation would be less than 333.33 acres. However, the impression is that a small number of big planters cultivated much more, so that Yeamans's estimate rings true. Antigua, according to one source, had more than 300 sugar plantations in 1764, and of about 37,000 slaves in the island at least 25,000 were at-tached to them. Sheridan has concluded that if all of the 60,000 acres of taxable land by that time had been absorbed by these plantations, the aver-age plantation would contain 200 acres and 100 slaves. Few plantations in 1768 were as large as Samuel Martin's Greencastle of 605 acres and 304 slaves. "The greater number," says Sheridan, "were considerably smaller."[7]

Such a pattern of plantation and slave ownership had become the norm probably even before the 1730s. Indeed, a 1720 parish list from St. Philip's Parish, in the eastern limestone district, points in that direction.[8] Drawn up as a result of a controversy over construction of a new, centrally located parish church, the list identifies parishioners in favor of the proj-ect and those against, with land and slaves each owned (table 5.1). Of 71 persons listed, 67 owned land ranging from 10 to 480 acres; 4 persons had no land but between them 7 slaves. The slave population of the parish, 1,329, was nearly 7 percent of the island total of 19,186. The vast majority of plantations, 51 out of 67, were less than 101 acres, with nearly 60 per-cent of them less than 50 acres. Among 40 proprietors with less than 50 acres were 12 with ten acres each (ten acre men), while holdings of the 28 others ranged from 13 to 43.5 acres. It is not clear whether all these people cultivated sugar cane, but if they did they would be marginal producers. Of the total number of names listed, 33, or 46.47 percent of those with land owned less than 11 slaves. The bulk of sugar output must

TABLE 5.1. Distribution of Land and Slaves in St. Philip Parish, Antigua, 1720

Owners	Acreage	Total Acreage	Total Slaves
8 having	200 to 480	2,460½	635
8 having	100 to 200	1,051	287
11 having	50 to 100	803	192
12 having	25 to 50	390	97
14 having	15 to 25	269	89
14 having	1 to 15	146	22
67		5,119½	1,322

SOURCE: Vere Langford Oliver, *The History of the Island of Antigua*, 3 vols. (London: Mitchell & Hughes, 1894–99), 1, pp. 92–93.

have come from the 16 plantations with 101 acres or more, which could afford large enough gangs of slaves. Between them these big proprietors held 3,511.5 acres (219.43 average) and 922 slaves (57.63 average), while the 51 middling and small proprietors owned 1,608 acres (31.52 average) and 400 slaves (7.85 average). Seven of the eight largest proprietors with 200 or more slaves who favored building the church owned about 40 percent of the slaves in the parish and 39 percent of the land. By Yeamans's standards there were therefore few genuinely well-established sugar planters, and if the parish list is fairly representative of patterns in other parishes before the 1730s, his claims would stand.

Maps of early Antigua would also seem to corroborate Yeamans's observations. Probably in 1729, the geographer Herman Moll completed a detailed map showing the principal towns, churches, forts, and, most important of all, sugar plantations with wind and cattle mills.[9] Moll used proprietors' names to identify their holdings; in reality larger properties could contain more than one plantation unit. Three holdings were large enough to have three windmills each, and two others operated two windmills each. Moll assigned six windmills to Christopher Codrington's extensive holdings of "great note" in the limestone district. A network of roads radiated near here to various parts of the island. In the neck of land on the south coast of the volcanic district, between Indian Creek and English Harbour in St. Paul's Parish, was an apparent concentration of small farmers, the area being labeled simply "Ten Acre Men." Scattered all over the island, however, were perhaps 162 plantations with one windmill. Because milling capacity helped determine plantation size, these one-windmill plantations would have been smaller than others with more windmills. There may, of course, have been large plantations with a single windmill, understocked with slaves, and operating at less than full capacity. In all there may have been 178 windmills in use, compared with about 33 cattle mills on an equal number of plantations. Other maps for the first half of the eighteenth century make no obvious improvements on Moll's map.[10] The data presented above suggests that the level of concentration of plantation slaveholding was not high and that most proprietors were probably resident and knew their slaves personally.

Concentrated in rural areas, plantation slaves can be classified according to occupation into three broad categories: field workers, skilled workers, and domestics. Field slaves were the very backbone of the plantation labor force; in many respects they bore the full brunt of the harshness of slavery, and certainly the severities of labor in the field. By the later eighteenth century throughout the West Indies, they were organized according to a gang system and assigned special tasks in relation to physical capability, including planting, cultivating, and harvesting the cane, and a number of other related chores, but for many years after the appearance of sugar plantations, organization of field labor was less standardized, especially on smaller plantations. Craton notes that the "quest for efficiency coupled with a lower expectation of the work force may explain why the gang system became more rigorously standardized in nearly all plantation colonies after 1750." The absentee Barbados planter Henry Drax, writing to his manager in 1755, gave some indication of the form the system might take. "The best way I know of to prevent idleness, and to make the Negroes do their work properly will be upon the change of Work, constantly to Gang all the Negroes in the Plantations in the Time of Planting. All the Men Negroes into two Gangs, the ablest and best by themselves for holeing and the stronger Work, and the more ordinary Negroes in a Gang for Dunging, & c. The Women Negroes also in two Gangs as before, and the lesser Negroes into two Gangs, the least to be followed by some careful old Women, who must use them with Gentleness. Out of these six Gangs of Negroes must the Carters, Stillers, Curing house Negroes, Cooks, Lookers after Stock, Watchers of Provisions, & c be drawn." Drax instructed his manager to be sure the underoverseer had lists of the gangs "under his particular Care, that he may be able to give a particular Account of every one, whether Sick or how employed." At crop time, he added, "after your Watches for your Mills, Boiling-House, and Canecutting Gangs are taken out, all the rest of the Negroes, except the smallest Gangs, must be listed into a running Gang for getting Home and Houseing all sorts of fuel."[11]

While organization of the gang system was flexible, it was based upon how best to get heavy and lighter work performed by all the slaves capable of work, so that there would certainly be one group of the most capable performing such heavy work as planting, cutting, delivering canes to the mills, and holing the ground in preparation for planting, and another for lighter tasks such as weeding, supplying the boiling house with cane trash used for fuel, planting corn or provisions, and preparing manure. Adolescents and weak adults were in this group. Other youths who could work comprised another group, and they helped manure fields at planting time, weed them as the young plants grew, and collect fodder for livestock. By the later eighteenth century, when the gang system crystallized into a more standardized structure, these groups were known as the first or great gang, the second gang, and the third gang.[12]

Antigua's cane fields were not ploughed, but instead holed by slaves using a simple hoe — hoe ploughing. Whatever the real reasons for general neglect of the plough in the West Indies, throughout the colonies it was believed holing cane fields was among the most laborious of plantation work. "In stiff lands like those of Antigua," Goveia has observed, "the work imposed a heavy physical strain on the slaves, and it had the additional disadvantage that it prejudiced the planters against the use of cattle in manuring the field which was to be planted." A number of planters, however, manured or dunged their fields in preparation for planting. Slaves wielding hoes in the open field under a mercilessly hot sun dug cane holes about five or six inches deep and about five feet square into which they placed cane cuttings and covered them with a layer of mold about two inches deep; as the plants began to grow, the slaves filled the holes with mold and compost.[13] Overseers frequently hired out field slaves when they could be spared for work on other plantations where additional labor was needed, especially for holing operations. According to Sheridan, the "labor was so exhausting that planters sometimes saved their own Negroes by hiring others for this work at a rate of £8 or £10 per acre" by mid-century. Accounts of the Swete Plantation for 1739 show that the plantation paid Colonel Burton £43 17s. 6d. for holing done by his slaves on just over 10 acres at £4 per acre. Walter Tullideph recorded hiring several slaves in 1742 to hole 14 acres on George Thomas's Winthorpes Plantation. "The Negroes for Winthorpes are going to hole at N. Sd," another of Thomas's plantations, "for abot. 3 weeks," he wrote in 1745, "& we can spare them that much yearly & work that Estate sufficiently alsoe."[14] A gang of 40 to 60 slaves could often hole an acre a day, each slave completing 60 to 100 holes.[15]

In the British sugar islands rainfall played a major role in regulating plantation operations. Holing and planting took place in the wet season.[16] In his tract on sugar cultivation and plantation management, first published in 1754 and designed not "as a complete system of plantership, but only an essay to farther improvements, and to reform the gross and common errors now in practice," Samuel Martin advised that in stiff, solid soils, where plants took longer to mature, "half the quantity of land intended for the crop should be planted in September; but in hot loose soils in October and November." The planting season should then end in January or February, "when the tops of the first canes cut may furnish the last pieces planted. By strict observance of this method the canes will be at full maturity in the proper season for yielding most sugar, which is from the 1st of January (if the weather permits) to the 29th of July." People who for one reason or another scheduled crop time later not only risked the wrath of hurricanes on mills and fields "but make bad sugar, at infinite expence of time and labour, both of negroes and cattle, when the juice of canes becomes weak and waterish." Canes therefore had to be planted, and reaped, even if ratoons, at the right time to avoid jeopardizing crop after crop. During the dry season, Ward Barret has noted, "sugar content of the canes increases to a maximum, then decreases, a change requiring adjustment of planting schedules to mill capacity for optimum results." Sucrose reduction was even more marked if plant growth in response to rainfall occurred after maximum sucrose storage.[17]

There were factors over which planters, as slaveowners, achieved limited or no control, such as slave behavior and weather patterns, but Martin believed proper plantation management could go a long way to lessen the blow of misfortune. For him, the plantation ought to be considered "a well-constructed machine, compounded of various wheels, turning different ways, and yet all contributing to the great end proposed." If any part of that machine did not keep correct pace with the rest, he wrote, "the main purpose is defeated." Martin believed slaves should be properly fed, clothed, and housed, and not overworked, as essential steps in the fine tuning of a plantation. A planter who excused his own incompetence by pleading "want of hands or cattle" had no real excuse in Martin's view, "because these wants must either be supplied, or the planter must contract his views, and proportion them to his abilities." To attempt to overreach himself would only "lead into perpetual disorder, and conclude in poverty. Indeed when severe droughts or unseasonable rains happen, contrary to the general course of nature, the wise planter must do the best he can, chasing always the least of two evils." When things went wrong, of course, slaves' living conditions deteriorated. Martin wrote of an ideal in plantation harmony that few if any planters realized during the first half of the eighteenth century.

Crop time came with the dry season. Martin recommeded January 1 as ideal for starting operations. The real character of sugar production as agro-industrial enterprise appeared starkest during this interval when the canes were harvested and sugar was made. Plantations hummed with intense activity in field and factory. Under a baking sun, while some field slaves, male and female, sweated to chop down the tall canes with bills or cutlasses, others were equally busy tying them into bundles, loading them on animal-drawn carts bound for the mill. On the many Antigua plantations with few or no draught animals, slaves transported canes to the mills on their heads, a practice Martin condemned as degrading "human nature to the toil of brutes." The schedule of harvesting and grinding for two of the Codrington plantations, Betty's Hope and Cotton, agreed with Martin's prescription in the early eighteenth century. Absentee proprietor Sir William Codrington advised his managers in 1715 "To begin with all the three Mills New years day without fail except it falls on a Sunday." This was good advice probably not for religious reasons but because Codrington did not want the start of hectic harvest to clash with the slaves' market and recreation day.[18] Yet one wonders in what mood slaves recovering or still reeling from Christmas excesses faced the prospect of harvest labor. Unexpected rains in the dry season sometimes interfered with the start of the crop, as happened on Abraham Redwood's plantation in 1733. "Your Mill has binn going night and day this five weeks and has made a great Deel of Sugar," Jacob Long wrote Redwood on March 14, forgetting to add that heavy rain after Christmas, which lasted until mid February, had delayed commencement of harvesting.[19] Heavy rain could also prematurely terminate crop because of decreases in sucrose content and difficulties of harvesting. Grinding operations had been under way for some time in Antigua in 1748 when the rains came and spoiled everything. "We have had a good deal of Rainy weather which hath putt such a Spring in the Canes," reported William Dunbar, attorney to Walter Tullideph, "that it hath putt an end to the Crop sooner than many could have wish't." Abrupt alternations of wet and dry spells were even worse. Tullideph's attorney in 1757, Walter Sydserfe, wrote despairingly that at one point it was "so wett that we could not grind, & it is now so drie that our Canes begin to burn." Whatever the schedule, crop time made especially heavy demands on field slaves, and it was not unusual for regular craftsmen, domestics, and other slaves to be assigned to the field to strengthen the ranks.[20] Such seasonal redistribution of slaves was probably more typical of undermanned plantations, for which additional labor might also have to be hired.

The pace of labor slackened notably at the end of crop season, but the slaves were not encouraged to idle but were assigned various odd jobs around the plantation such as cleaning drains and doing other maintenance work, weeding, trashing, and cutting wood, before the strenuous routine of preparing fields for another crop began again. Slaves also planted provisions around this time.

Proprietors imposed an occupational hierarchy among field slaves that may not have accurately reflected the slaves' own perceptions of status. At the very top were drivers, males, chosen, as with rice drivers in South Carolina, on account of maturity, physical strength and size, intelligence, and knowledge of staple culture. Above all they, through some combination of qualities, were believed to be able to command the slaves' respect and cooperation, and they were likely to be acculturated Africans or Creoles. Selected drivers were probably of the same age range, from the twenties to mid-thirties, as those in South Carolina, and similarly elevated from the ranks of the field gang. In 1737 Parham Plantation had three drivers: old Tony aged 72, Cuffi aged 32, and Attaw aged 33. In 1750 Attaw, now 46, was still a driver and listed first on the plantation inventory; old Tony, if he was still alive, had long since ceased to be a driver, while Cuffi had been banished for his role in the 1736 plot. Two new drivers, however, had been pushed forward: Baby's Cudjo, aged 34, and Kate's Quamina, aged 31, both of whom had been field slaves in 1737. Drivers were valuable slaves: Attaw and Cudjo, each appraised at £110, were exceeded in value only by 4 tradesmen among 69 adult males listed.[21] Every field gang had a driver responsible for directing operations, who carried a whip as a symbol of authority and used it when necessary. Large plantations could have a head driver above others.

There were other field slaves with specialized functions, such as the head cattle and mule man, who was not only generally responsible for the livestock but also in charge of transporting canes to the mills and sugar to the warehouses or wharf. Among skilled slaves on plantations must be included boilermen (or boilers or coppers), coopers, carpenters, smiths, masons, millwrights, doctors, and nurses. Slaves infiltrated these occupations, and their success was proof abundant of abilities other than as beasts of burden and raw muscle. The judges who tried the plotters of 1736 pointed out that training large numbers of tradesmen contributed significantly to the scheme's organization.

Boilermen were among the most valued slaves on a plantation, and Pitman has remarked that the position of head boiler was "of equal importance to that of any other slave official."[22] On one plantation in 1708, a slave doubled as driver and boiler.[23] A competent head boiler was supposed to know "how the cane had been raised and treated, the kind of soil in which it grew, whether that soil had been richly or slightly manured, the age of the cane, its species, whether it had been topped short or long in the cutting, and whether it had been arrowed, bored or rat-eaten." All these things he had to know so as to determine "how much lime temper the cane juice needed and the period of boiling." A boiler's responsibility was obviously enormous, and inexpert execution could ruin a crop. Tullideph, aware of the boiler's critical role, instructed his manager, Ephraim Jordan, in clear language to "choose ye most Sensible of my people to be boylers and firemen, with proper encouragements as feed and their ground of a spare day or ye like and punish when they deserve it."[24] Boilermen must have enjoyed considerable independence, but Tullideph for one did not lose sight of the need to discipline them like other ordinary workers if need be, a tricky exercise, one would imagine, if boilermen were not to turn saboteurs.

Slave boilers' skills helped transform raw cane juice into sugar for shipment. Juice from crushed canes flowed from the mill in conduits into a large receptacle, the receiver, and slaves siphoned or ladled it into the great copper for boiling. Lime was mixed in to prevent souring and promote granulation. After a sufficient period of boiling and skimming, the liquid was ladled again into a number of successively smaller coppers and boiled until it became sufficiently thick for ladling into the "tache," or smallest copper with the hottest fire. Here it was boiled again until ready to crystallize, or "strike." There were various ways to determine this crucial stage. Richard Pares said that in Nevis the plantation owner John Pinney believed "the best way was to dip the forefinger and thumb into the boiling liquor and see whether it would make a thread between them." This was a painful procedure, and Samuel Martin recommended "eye art," at which he said slave boilers had become very skilled from long experience; they, indeed, monopolized sugar boiling. "To that eye art," wrote Martin, "I have attended with all diligence, but could never acquire a critical Exactness; for the sight of all other senses, is most fallible, and subject to deception: a little more or less butter thrown into the tach will alter the whole appearance and often deceive the most attentive and experienced eye; and no doubt there are other causes, less observable which produce the like effect." When the sugar was ready to crystallize, workers reduced the heat under the tache, and its boiled-down contents were cooled in a separate receptacle and then placed in hogsheads or barrels, which were stored in the curing-house to allow molasses to drain out of them into other containers. Slaves working in the still-house used this molasses and skimmings from the boiling-house to manufacture rum.[25]

Accidents on the job were common in the still-houses (distilleries), mills, and boiling-houses, and plantations with large-scale operations lost many slaves. Those engaged in such work, laborious and dangerous as it was important, endured extremely hot and unhealthy conditions especially in the steamy boiling-house and distillery. Attorney Benjamin King, writing of Betty's Hope Plantation probably in the 1740s, noted that the boiling-house needed extending by twenty-five feet and five coppers or boiling pots added "as it would greatly quicken our work, and our crops would be sooner taken off every year, as well as preserve ye Slaves from Night Work wch is very injurious, it being at present common to boil all night, notwithstanding the mills are burn'd out of the wind by seven a Clock every Evening, and Besides the Distruction of Negroes." King added that sugar made at night was of poorer quality than if made in daytime "from ye Impossibility of Skimming the liquor so clean, and ye Sleeping of ye Negroes."[26]

Slave housecleaners, cooks, butlers, washerwomen, waiting men or footmen, coachmen, waiting maids, seamstresses, and nurses were attached to the planter's household and classified as domestics, but many urban slaveowners also owned domestic slaves. It may be true that in general domestics were especially favored slaves who saw themselves as a group apart because of greater intimacy with masters, but as some scholars have noted, there was a negative side to this because domestics were almost constantly under orders and within sight of those in authority in the household and exposed to their whims. Psychologically therefore they were, unlike field slaves, under sustained pressure to behave correctly and in this sense endured great strain, which ultimately they could learn to cope with when they understood the perils of domestic work. Greater intimacy with masters probably made domestics more prone than other slaves perhaps to betray plans of slave resistance, but it should also be borne in mind that we will never know how many times they kept their mouths shut, or, indeed, relayed information about "massa" to the field hands. Quite commonly, female domestics shared sexual intimacy with masters, and the proof lies in the colored offspring some of them bore. Goveia found that by the late eighteenth century most domestics in the Leeward Islands were colored or of mixed blood. At this time, few field slaves and many more plantation tradesmen were colored, indicating that less laborious and more prestigious jobs were saved for colored slaves. Menial tasks on plantations became the undisputed domain of slaves of unmixed African ancestry.[27]

Plantation inventories often disclose the distribution of the work force according to several criteria. Slaves were categorized basically according to sex, age, and occupation, but more detailed inventories included other information on each slave such as value, physical condition, whether of mixed blood or not, and sometimes, in the case of children, who their mothers were. On larger plantations most slaves would be assigned to field work, while on smaller plantations slaves tended to be jacks-of-all-trades, and their occupations were not specified in inventories.[28] On the large Parham Plantation, according to a 1737 inventory, there were 202 slaves: 76 men, 70 women, 7 "great boys," 17 little boys, 7 "great girls," and 25 little girls. Among the men were 3 drivers, 1 doctor, 4 coopers, 5 carpenters, and 3 masons. This elite group constituted 21.05 percent of the adult male work force, while most of the remaining 78.95 percent were field slaves. Among adult females were 3 cooks, 1 nurse, 1 "sempthris [seamstress] for the white servants," 2 domestics — a mere 10 percent of adult females. The majority of others were also in the field. Among the "great boys" aged from 14 to 17 years were two, both aged 14, who were apprenticed to tradesmen, one to a carpenter and the other to a mason. By 1772 the plantation had a total of 348 slaves: 147 males, 183 females, and 18 children whose sex was not specified. Occupations were listed for only some nonfield males, including 4 drivers, 2 doctors, 4 carpenters, 5 masons, 8 coopers, 2 blacksmiths, and 5 boatmen. Table 5.2 is a 1751 inventory for Betty's Hope showing a total of 277 slaves. It is very detailed and thus gives a good picture of the range of slave occupations on a large plantation. As expected, slave

TABLE 5.2. Inventory of Slaves on Betty's Hope Plantation, July 26, 1751

Number	Description
5	Both Sugar & Rum hhd Coopers
4	Sugar hhd Coopers
5	Carpenters and Wheelwrights
10	Carpenters for Windmill and Houses
6	Masons
3	Smiths
1	Doctors Man
2	Nurses of the sick
1	Still house tender etc.
1	Stable groom
4	House maids and employed making clothes for white servants
3	Washer women for the household & servants
1	Cook
1	Scullion
39	Field Gang (men) including 2 drivers: (able, working men)
3	Ordinary workers in the field: (1) elderly & lame. (2) elderly & with bad feet. (3) elderly & weakly.
	Men & boys unfit for the field through Age or Distempers:
6	Employed occasionally on services they are fit for
8	Past labor or fit for no work
1	Able but outlawed for murder
2	Boys, Brothers, but born blind
1	Boy but crippled
59	Field gang (Women); (able, working women)
13	Women belonging to the Field Gang but either elderly or weakly & fit only for light, easy work
13	Women past labor or unfit for work
13	Boys that work in the Small Gang with hoes, Weeding & planting
1	Driver of ditto (able man Driver)
7	Small Boys too small for the hoe, kept to picking Grass
1	Driver of ditto
15	Infant boys
18	Girls who work with Small Gang with hoe, weeding & planting
8	Small Girls too small for the hoe, kept to picking grass
13	Infant Girls
6	Cattle & other stock keepers
3	Children with Mrs. Wills

SOURCE: Betty's Hope inventory, July 26, 1751, Codrington Papers, D1610/E5, Gloucestershire County Record Office, Gloucester, England.
NOTE: hhd = hogshead.

workers at Betty's Hope were concentrated in the field gangs, the core of which consisted of 98 slaves, 39 men and 59 women, or 35.37 percent of the total number of slaves. These slaves, listed as able workers, would comprise the first gang for the plantation's heaviest work. The driver, the 13 boys and 18 girls who worked with the hoe weeding and planting, along with the 13 women and 3 men fit for lighter field work, made up additional gangs. Altogether the plantation could claim 146 field slaves, or 52.7 percent of its work force. But these figures conceal the true picture that Codrington's representative supplied in observations at the end of the inventory. "By the list of Negroes on Betty's Hope," he wrote, "there appears to be forty-two that are called able men for the field and 59 women out of which there are several runaways so that including the number of sick that happens we seldom exceed 60 Negroes able to make cane holes unless it is at particular times when the Tradesmen have been taken in the field to assist." He added that, as the plantation's land was generally poor and had never been manured, the field gangs needed to be reinforced with 60 to 70 more able slaves to work the plantation properly. Had it not been "for the little Negroes that are called the Small gang, consisting of about 30 who do much more work in proportion than the Great gang," he concluded, "the Estate would be greatly distressed." On large, undermanned sugar plantations, therefore, we would expect field gangs to be driven harder if not relieved by allocation of other slaves to field duties, a move, however, that could conceivably leave such slaves very resentful and uncooperative.[29]

Scholars who have studied slavery in urban settings have demonstrated the institution's capacity to adapt to a different labor market. In towns and cities of the Americas trends were broadly similar; within the urban perimeter slaves faced conditions of life different from those on rural plantations.[30] In the six towns of varying size and population density established as places of trade since the late seventeenth century in Antigua, a number of slaves were employed in various skilled and semiskilled occupations. Most commentators on the decrease in the white population mentioned, as did Governor Parke in 1707, that an important reason was that Antiguans "breed up their slaves to all manner of Trades." This of course drastically narrowed opportunities for white employment, so that, as Parke further observed, "no servants now come over."[31] As early as 1700 an act stated that "Taverns, victualling-houses, Punch-houses, Sloops, Shallops, and Boats [which] belong to this Island, are for the most part managed by Negro Slaves, to the great Discouragement of White Men who want Employment."[32] The ensuing years brought no lasting changes, although attempts were often made to bar blacks from certain specified occupations. In 1725, for example, during preparation of an act to attract white settlers, the assembly recommended addition of the following clause: "that all Mulattos or Negroes free upon the date hereof shall not after the expiration of three Kallendar months next ensuing the date hereof work at any of the trades hereby prohibited to slaves or as Saylors, unless their names are first given into the Register with their trades or occupations upon pain of receiving sixty lashes by order of a Justice of Peace."[33] Slave domestics and tradesmen probably made up a larger percentage of the urban slave population than those in all other occupations combined. Unlike their plantation counterparts, large numbers of urban tradesmen and domestics, as well as other jobbing slaves, had been purchased and trained ostensibly for hiring out by their owners, many of whom did not possess land.[34] These slaveowners, like others in towns and cities of other slave territories, helped expand slavery's grip on the economy by investing in such slaves from whose labor they derived an income. Some may also have acquired such property for speculation, hoping to sell later as slave values increased.[35] Some tradesmen worked along with their masters; others lived virtually independent lives while they worked at their trades, sometimes with slave apprentices, and paid their owners a weekly or monthly sum. Such arrangements reflected slaveowner's willingness to count on their slaves' loyalty, but at the same time they nurtured a weakening of bonds of dependence of slaves upon masters, thereby undermining an important element in the social control of slaves.[36]

By the 1740s and 1750s slaveholding outside plantations had developed into a prominent feature of Antigua slave society. Its extent can perhaps be appreciated from the tone and content of certain modified tax acts that included special provisions directed specifically at the large body of landless slaveowners. Enacted yearly from 1755 into the 1760s,[37] all of these acts declared, in the wording of the first, that there were many persons who "are not possessors of plantations . . . producing sugar, Rum, Molasses, Cotton or Ginger but have considerable property in Negroes and other Slaves which are variously employed for the benefit of the proprietors." The act charged these slaveowners with not paying their fair share of taxes and imposed a levy of 13s. 6d. per slave. Raising money for war preparations may have had some bearing on the new taxation, but in explaining their decision the legislature simply indicated that the general poll tax on slaves had become "unequal" because there were many planters with worn-out lands who required more labor per acre than others with more fertile land and hence carried a heavier tax burden. In this and future tax acts the legislature proposed to consider the "Real Abilities" of slaveowners by taxing plantation produce, and slaves of those "not possessor of any sugar, cotton and ginger plantations that shall be cultivated and carried on as such."[38] Dr. Walter Tullideph wrote Dr. Walter Sydserfe in December 1755 that the "new method of Taxation will be continued, I think, in bad as well as good years, although the Black Mould Gentry to windward are greatly against it, Collo. Martin was the Great Advocate for it, which induced them to talk of a dissolution in order to seclude him, but that is now blown over."[39] Whatever the level of the new taxes from year to year, the acts that supported them underscored the widespread utilization of slave labor in other than plantation work.

Many slaveowners in both town and country employed their slaves in hawking and peddling various goods, but numerous slaves apparently also traded on their own account. This independent traffic already existed by 1694, when the Leeward Islands legislature passed a law to prevent Jewish traders from dealing with slave peddlers, whom they were accused of driving to theft, especially in the island of Nevis. The legislature believed that slaves stole "even the coppers (for boyling of sugar) out of the walls where they were affixed." The act stated bluntly that the traders, in order "for them to avoid, and evade all manner against their fraudulent dealings keep several well instructed slaves to that purpose, to buy, barter, and receive all such goods as they can persuade the inhabitants slaves to steale from their masters."[40] It was repealed seven years later after the traders complained about its "pernicious consequence" and promised to avoid such practices in the future.[41]

By 1742 slave hawking and peddling were as widespread as ever. In a petition to the assembly, seventy-seven merchants and traders of the town of St. John's condemned the slaves' activities as a "general grievance" damaging to their own trade. The governor may have viewed their petition sympathetically, for in 1734 he had remarked with concern that slave peddlers and other hucksters who dealt with them "raise and fall the value of our money just as they please. . . I own I speak with resentment to find our slaves and the vile extortioning wretches they deal with have us so much at their disposal." To deal with the "Impertinent Impositions of the meanest Hucksters. . . and their unjust hardships and cheats put on our Negroes" through currency manipulation, the governor asked the assembly for suitable legislation "to keep these folks honest and let a shilling in our pockets be as much a shilling as in theirs."[42]

Much of the concern over independent activities of slaves centered on opportunities for crime they were believed to inspire, and certain clauses in the slave codes dealt with this police problem; but everyone recognized that slaveowners had a right to benefit from legitimate employment of their slaves in the towns and elsewhere. Many urban blacks were fiddlers for gain,[43] and many others were also barbers and peruke makers, to judge from a petition of 1764 by which some whites sought to bar them from these trades.[44]

Slavery in the Americas, though predominantly land-based, also sailed the open sea, and the activities and lives of slave seamen form one of the most intriguingly suggestive dimensions of the institution. Antiguans employed slave seamen on their vessels. In 1700 the legislature tried to prevent or at least to limit employment of black seamen because they deprived white men of work.[45] Table 5.3, a list of all ships belonging to Antigua compiled in 1720, yields valuable information about such atypical slaves and free blacks.[46] Among the 58 vessels recorded were 3 ships, 2 brigantines, 1 snow, 30 sloops, and 22 boats; on these worked 235 whites and 98 blacks, 59 of the blacks on boats compared with only 18 whites, a ratio of more than 3:1. No blacks worked on ships, brigantines, or snows, but 41 were on sloops compared with 135 whites. The median numbers of crewmen were 6 whites and 3 blacks. On 16 sloops there were only whites. In one solitary case, however, the *Plunkett*, of 15 tons, there were 4 blacks and no whites. The crew of 1 sloop was unaccounted for, but 37 blacks and 26 whites manned the remaining 12. Of the boats listed, 17 carried a single white and from 2 to 3 blacks each. Significantly, the remaining 5 boats were manned by from 2 to 3 blacks each, with no whites aboard. The median numbers of whites and blacks on boats were 1 and 2 respectively.

Clearly blacks were concentrated on small, open craft with an average carrying capacity of 2.14 tons, powered largely by oars and used mainly for coastal traffic and trips to nearby islands. Fifty percent of these were built in Antigua although local timber was not plentiful.[47] Most boats would have been "droggers," which merchants and planters used to transport plantation produce from wharves along the coast to waiting ocean-going vessels. Parham Plantation had five boatmen in 1771, and every large plantation with frontage on the sea had its loading wharf and boatmen specialists and others who occasionally worked as such especially in crop time. The Ibo Olaudah Equiano was a boatman while at Montserrat during the early 1760s. He had been sold to a Philadelphia merchant living in Antigua, Mr. King, who had "many vessels and droggers, of different sizes, which used to go about the island; and others, to collect rum, sugar, and other goods. I understood pulling and managing those boats very well," wrote Equiano, for he had already had much experience as a seaman, "And this hard work, which was the first that he set me to, in the sugar seasons used to be my constant employment. I have rowed the boat, and slaved at the oars, from one hour to sixteen in the twenty-four; during which I had fifteen pence sterling per day to live on, though sometimes only ten pence." In this respect, said Equiano, he was much better off than other boatmen who belonged to masters less humane than King, many of whom had purchased slaves to hire out for such work and appropriated most of their slaves' earnings, leaving them little for themselves. It is possible that some slaves or free blacks owned their own boats. Equiano refers to an enterprising slave in Montserrat who had saved part of his earnings as a seaman to have a white man secretly buy him a boat.[48]

As the slave of a big merchant, Equiano worked not only as a boatman but as personal attendant, caretaker of horses, crewman on King's vessels, and clerk "receiving and delivering cargoes to the ships...tending stores, and delivering goods."[49] His experiences afford only a brief glimpse at yet another dimension of urban slavery and its relationship to plantations, part of which was the employment of slaves on ocean-going vessels.

The preferred vessel in Antigua, larger than a boat and capable of long-distance ocean traffic, was the sloop, according to the 1720 list, which showed that these one-mast craft ranged from 2 to 40 tons. Actually, only one sloop was of 2 tons' burden or carrying capacity. The next larger sloop was 6 tons, bigger than all boats. Jay Coughtry has found that Rhode Island slave traders to the African coast preferred sloops during the colonial period,[50] and this might also be true of Antiguan entrepreneurs engaged in the direct trade to Africa or trade with other Caribbean islands, North and South America, and Europe. Just over one quarter of the Antigua sloops, 8, or 26.66 percent, were built in Newport, Rhode Island, while 5 were built in timber-scarce Antigua. Wherever they were built, however, these vessels carried slaves far away, to places where they had opportunity to see and hear much that they later brought back to Antigua and transmitted to other slaves. This clearly was one of the ways in which information of interest to slaves was disseminated.[51] Like Equiano, many slave sailors probably also engaged in petty trading from place to place, developing contacts useful both for regular trade and for collecting information.[52] Slave seamen moved in a different world, less narrowly circumscribed than that of typical plantation slaves and even urban slaves generally, and were exposed to a wider range of influences and experiences that helped shape their lives. However, we need more precise information about these people and their role in the slave community to fill in the details of slavery at sea. Equiano's autobiography is useful in this regard.

As with other occupations already noted in which blacks competed with whites, who progressively lost ground, black seamen aroused the disapproval of their competitors. In 1722 several white seamen petitioned the legislature to put a stop to blacks working on all vessels, including boats.[53] In the long run little came of this, for, reporting on Antigua shipping in 1746, Governor Mathew noted: "The number of shipping that belongs wholly to the Inhabitants (including Coasting Vessels) 47. Their Burthen 1000 Tons & the number of Men Including Slaves employed in navigating them is 230;"[54] an overall decline from 1720.

TABLE 5.3. Vessels Belonging to Antigua, August 8, 1718–May 8, 1720

Vessel	Kind	Burden	Whites	Blacks	Place of Construction
Portsmouth	Sloop	40 tons	8		Newport, R.I.
Two Brothers	Sloop	10	2	4	Antigua
Pidgeon	Sloop	20	7		Bermuda
Success	Boat	3	1	2	Tortola
Edward & Joseph	Boat	2	1	3	Antigua
Princess Anne & Emilia	Boat	4	1	2	Antigua
Friendship	Sloop	40	8		Norwich, New England
Charming Nelly	Ship	70	12		Charles Town
Defiance	Boat	2		3	Beef Island
William & George	Sloop	18	2	5	Newport
Catharine	Sloop	6	2	3	Antigua
Mary	Sloop	30	6		Newberry
Plunkett	Sloop	15		4	New York
Betty & Lydia	Brig	50	7		Boston
Eagle	Sloop	8	2	2	Swansey
Post Boy	Sloop	40	6		Bermuda
Neptune	Sloop	5	1	3	Antigua
Dolphin	Sloop	15	6		Boston
Mayflower	Sloop	25	7		Newport
Providence	Boat (?)	3	1	2	Antigua
Newcastle	Sloop	2	1	2	Antigua
Wheel of Fortune	Sloop	20	6	1	Weatherfield
Stapleton	Sloop	(document torn)			New England
American Wonder	Boat	4	1	3	Antigua
Little John	Snow	40	8		Millford
Phillip & Mary	Sloop	15	2	3	Antigua
Postillion	Sloop	25	7		Maryland

Vessel	Type	Tons			Destination
Jenny	Sloop	30	7		Newport
Anne	Sloop	25	8		New England
Delight	Sloop	10	3	1	Rhode Island
Charles	Boat	3	1	3	Bermuda
Greyhound	Sloop	20	6		New England
Elizabeth	Sloop	25	2	4	Boston
Parham	Sloop	15	2	5	Newport
Friendship	Boat	3		3	Antigua
Benjamin	Boat	2	1	2	Bermuda
Squirrill	Sloop	10	1	4	Newport
Speedwell	Boat	2	1	2	Bermuda
Elizabeth & Mary	Boat	2	1	2	Antigua
Bonadventure	Boat	3	1	3	Bermuda
Doddington	Sloop	30	7		Boston
Traviller	Sloop	35	7		Boston
Hill Galley	Ship	70	12		Boston
Richard & Elizabeth	Sloop	20	6		Virginia
Greyhound	Sloop	30	7		Newport
Anne	Boat	3	2	3	Antigua
William	Boat	2		3	Bermuda
Sarah	Boat	2	1	2	Bermuda
Little Robin	Boat	1	1	2	Bermuda
Sea Flower	Boat	2	1	3	Antigua
Mary	Boat	1	1	2	Antigua
Kings Fisher	Boat	1		2	Antigua
Resolution	Boat	2	1	2	Bermuda
John	Boat	2	1	2	Bermuda
Betty	Boat	1		2	Antigua

SOURCE: Hamilton to BT, Aug. 22, 1720, CO 152/13, Q51, enclosure, no. 62.

Plantation and urban slaves were first and foremost property of private individuals and as such served their particular interests, but under certain conditions such private property could be and was called upon to serve the public interest through attachment to island militia units and employment on public works. As a defense force the Antigua militia was small and inefficient. Naval protection, always sought after, could not always be depended upon; neither could slaveowners commit themselves wholeheartedly to arming their slaves. A few companies of regular troops were customarily stationed in the island, but sickness frequently played havoc in the ranks. In 1749 Lieutenant Colonel Talbot could do nothing but plead in frustration for new troops: "For God's Sake Sr., send Us over 40 or 50 Recruits that we may compleat, and discharge some real Invalides."[55] Antiguan authorities frequently debated ways and means of strengthening defenses; in peacetime they dragged their feet and squabbled over projects, but when war threatened or broke out they managed to pull together to deal with the impending emergency. West Indian strategy in wartime, Richard Pares observed, was necessarily mostly defensive,[56] and the real foundation of Antigua defenses consisted of numerous fortified points, built with slave labor, that dotted the much indented coastline. To construct these defenses the legislature passed numerous acts recruiting slave labor, and these were enforceable for varying periods.[57] A survey of 1746 listed 19 different fortifications.[58]

Before work commenced on the naval dockyard at English Harbour in 1725, most labor requisition acts related to Monk's Hill Fort, the "chief arsenal" of the island by 1734. Begun in 1689, the fort was located in Falmouth Division of St. Paul's Parish on a high hill overlooking Falmouth Harbour on the south coast. During his governorship (1705–10), Daniel Parke, a man of some military experience and evidently obsessed with whipping Antigua's defenses into shape, spent much of his time and energy trying to improve the works. Governor William Mathew after him was also keenly interested. Monk's Hill, he reported in 1734, was "a retreat for women and children, and for ourselves when we can keep the field no longer, a cover for our best effects, a disappointment to the enemy that come for plunder chiefly, and where H.M. sovereignty of this Island must be preserved to the last extremity." He described the fort as having been constructed "on a most ill shaped piece of ground, the summit of a hill, not quite out of command of two others, that lie easterly, and west southerly from it, and the Antigua engineer has so well followed the irregular shape of the hill, that the fort is as ill shaped, and has as little artificial means for defence, as ever was contrived." But it was "so much the darling of the Island that no summes have been spair'd to make it what it is." There were "very high walls, very well built, quite round it," and "in money and Negro labour," Mathew believed it "to have cost, at times, not less than fifty thousand pounds sterling." Mathew admitted, however, that the islanders had begun to "grow cooler now in their opinions of it and are very backward in adding a little to the expense, to justify the rest they have been at." Undaunted, the governor continued "pressing them constantly (but in vain) to provide it with covering for a garrison, as barracks etc."[59]

An act of 1702 required slaveowners to supply one able slave out of every hundred in their possession in order "to Finish and perfect ye Fortifications on Monks hill, a work indispensably necessary for ye retreat and Securitie of our old men, women, and children, in case of an Invasion." Specially appointed commissioners were authorized to impress under warrant blacksmiths, carpenters, and masons, presumably slave as well as free. All slaves employed on the works earned a shilling a day. Masters of slaves killed or maimed were entitled to compensation; two neighboring freeholders appraised the value of such slaves. Masters not supplying their correct quota of slaves were fined five shillings per day for each deficiency. The act was to be in force for only six months. A similar act passed two years later requisitioned two male adult slaves out of every hundred, but as the act itself implied, it was difficult to force compliance to such regulations. It pointed out that for most of the time the laws were in force, many slaveowners did not supply their quota of workers as required but delayed until the laws almost expired and then sent large numbers.[60] This was one way of getting around the law, and slaveowners used it.

Generally, although slaveowners recognized the importance of adequate defenses, they tended, like the assembly itself, to burst into frenzied action in the face of a military threat to the island. All good intentions frequently evaporated when the crisis passed. Governor Parke observed in 1707 that while the threat of a French attack hung over the island, "the People Sent me Negroes to fortyfie Monks Hill, but being Over I can't gett a Negroe to finish what I had begun, but they promise to doe it when the Crop is over."[61] The observation is revealing. If out-of-crop proprietors found it difficult to comply with requisitions for slaves, how much more so must it have been during the hustle and bustle of crop time, when every available hand was needed. Attorney Rowland Oliver wrote the absentee owner of the Swete Plantation in July 1745 that the crop was not yet finished because "the Negroes being so frequently ordered upon Publick work for the Defence of Our Island has prevented the Crop being Taken of Sooner." In May of the same year, Tullideph similarly noted in a letter to Sir George Thomas that he had anticipated making sixty hogsheads of sugar at Winthorpes Plantation "and could have finished the Crop by the 30 June had not the public Workes required so much Negroe Labour, but I fear it may be the middle of July now."[62] Frequently, when it was time to cut and grind canes, private profit took easy precedence over public welfare unless the danger was pressing enough to warrant sudden labor mobilization.

It was certainly not for lack of compensation that slaveowners were reluctant to supply slaves or were negligent in doing so, because in most cases they were paid at a rate stipulated in the enforcing act, which also covered injury or death of workers. If compensation was perhaps not sufficiently encouraging, it was relatively rare for an act to carry no compensation clause at all.[63] Sometimes public expenditure on slave labor was quite considerable, as must have been the case in 1731, when the assembly declared firmly that it would be both easier and cheaper to assign the work to a contractor rather than employ large numbers of slaves at public expense. Slaves did mostly manual work, supplying the brute strength for digging trenches, clearing away bush, and landing, removing, and mounting guns. Carpenters, masons, and blacksmiths were also employed. George Page, a white blacksmith, was paid £11 18s. 6d. in 1707 at the rate of 4s. 6d. a day for 53 days' work his slave blacksmith performed at Monk's Hill.[64]

The naval dockyard at English Harbour, today a tourist attraction called Nelson's Dockyard, was built with the help of slave labor. In 1725 the Antigua legislature, to provide a base where British ships of war might refit and more easily be on hand for defense of trade against French raids in the Lesser Antilles, appropriated land and funds to begin the project. Antiguan self-interest played a key role in this decision because proximity to the French sugar island of Guadeloupe made the inhabitants nervous. By 1729 the legislature had spent £1,250 sterling on the works, including £600 on a fort almost finished; £200 on a completed pond to provide ships with water; £200 on a strong magazine, uncompleted, and capable of holding three or four hundred barrels of powder; and £250 for twenty-five acres of land.[65]

During the 1740s, in preparation for war with France, and even before that, the legislature passed act after act requisitioning slaves for work at the dockyard. "The French are now so superior to us by sea," Tullideph observed in 1745, "that our men of warr have ever since been laid up in English Harbor. We have been working...[there] ½ per cent of our Negroes these 12 months past." At English Harbour, Governor Mathew had written earlier in 1734, "H.M. Ships of warr careen, and [it] is an excellent safe one in the most violent stormes. Here is full room for ten or twelve men of warr or more of any rate, store-houses too are provided... and here the sea stores are laid up, and careening places close to the shore as to a wharf, and many more such careening places may be made in this harbour." The dockyard seems to have superseded Monk's Hill as a major public work by this time. From an act of 1744 and later acts we learn that adult male and female slaves were to work there "from Sun Rise to Noon, Except half an hour between Nine and Ten a Clock in the Morning for Breakfast, and from Two in the afternoon until Sunset." These long hours of toil were no improvement on plantation field labor, and conditions of work, especially among common laborers assigned to menial tasks, could be as brutal on the naval works and fortifications as on some of the worst plantations. In 1707, to take one example, Garret Garret, a white carpenter, petitioned the assembly for compensation for his slave, who, while at Monk's Hill, was "most unmercifully used, by carrying of burthens from the Waterside up the Hill; and that by Kicking, beating, and hard usage from the Overseer. . .languished for about seven days, and afterwards dyed."[66]

Most slaves at English Harbour during its early days of construction and later, an occasion arose, did heavy manual work that was supervised and vaguely resembled field labor organization on large plantations, while slave tradesmen's work was either not supervised or not as closely. In general, labor here was similar to labor on fortifications and as dangerous, especially for slaves handling gunpowder, some of whom died in explosions. Again, as on fortifications, labor at English Harbour was usually but not always paid for at fixed rates, and masters were compensated for loss or injury. In 1757 the Codrington Plantation accounts recorded £53 8s. earned "for 712 days Negro Labour at English Harbour."[67] Whatever the number of slaves attached to the station on a regular basis, Commodore Thomas Frankland, commander in chief of the Leeward Islands Station in the 1750s, complained that the common mechanics there were incompetent blacks.[68]

An important part of the public works consisted of digging and clearing water-ponds, on which residents without other means of storing water for themselves, slaves, and cattle depended. An act of 1702, which superseded another of 1680 intended to be perpetual, authorized the annual appointment of five "knowing men as Commissioners of the publick ponds or watering places" in the political divisions of St. John's and Falmouth. They were empowered to requisition from freeholders one-third of their ablest slaves furnished with "basketts hoes and other proper tooles. . .to Digg and work on the public ponds from time to time." Where old ponds required cleaning, the act obliged freeholders to supply one-sixth of their ablest slaves. Payment for all labor on ponds was fixed at twelve pence a day. "And to the end the Said Negroes. . .may be well followed, and lookt after," the act prescribed that "all masters of Families by themselves or white overseers or for want of Such their Negro overseers are oblidged to attend Said worke constantly where their Slaves shall be ordered to worke on penaltie of being presented att Sessions and being fined Forty Shillings for such default" of civic responsibility.[69]

Here again it is evident the treasury could not always meet overall expenses of slave labor. In 1715, for example, the assembly expressed concern over the cost of slave labor for digging ponds and preferred, at least for a while, to employ free laborers. But the lieutenant governor and council, while agreeing, pointed out that one distinct disadvantage was that free laborers would expect payment in ready cash.[70] Part of the attraction of slave labor was apparently, therefore, greater flexibility in payment. In any case, slave labor was used more often than not. It should surprise no one that slaves built and maintained the island's roads, such as they were, and that provisions similar to those relating to work on fortifications and public ponds governed such employment.[71]

To what extent were slaves used in the defense of Antigua? Here as elsewhere in the Americas, defense was organized under centralized colonial governments, who balked at arming slaves except in serious emergencies and on strictly controlled conditions. The temptation to do so was strongest in colonies with large slave majorities, but arming slaves was never as dominant a feature of colonial security as in East Africa, where weak central authority and the strong bonds of reciprocal obligations between master and slave in Islamic slavery made the political and military importance of slaves possible. Although in both slave systems masters showed confidence in their slaves' loyalty when they allowed them freedom of action and independent employment, slaveowners in the Americas were unwilling, unlike East African slaveowners, to extend such confidence to standardized arming of slaves.[72]

If frontier warfare allowed blacks to play "a full if rather unheralded role" in the early history of South Carolina, the wars of the eighteenth century pushed Antiguan authorities in a similar direction. In discussing the sugar colonies in the eighteenth century, it is virtually impossible not to mention the effects of war, for there were three major conflicts between 1700 and 1763 when England and France, owners of rival sugar colonies, battled each other. This conflict of rival mercantilisms, to borrow Eric Williams's phrase, opened their respective colonies to attack and invasion. When hostilities actually broke out or when rumors of impending attack were in the air, Antiguans understandably shook off their customary indifference and busily prepared to preserve their island; but even in peacetime, as in the early 1730s, they were alarmed by what they described as the increasing strength of their French neighbors at Guadeloupe and especially Martinique, fearing that at some opportune moment they might swoop down upon them.[73]

Governor Mathew responded in 1734 with the suggestion that slaves could be armed for defense and so strengthen the ranks of the small white militia drawn from among adult white males. Page after page in his lengthy report of that year to the Board of Trade revealed a keen appreciation of the need for a properly organized system of defense. "The shipping in our harbours," he explained at one point, "cannot be defended by the ten or twelve men on board each, but must wait their safety from the shore, from these I shall hope to form a battalion of about four hundred men and from among our Negroes, we certainly may arm a thousand sturdy faithful fellows, that with a little encouragement, will I know do eminent service. But," he added significantly, "this is a dangerous experiment for thereafter, however it must be done."[74]

Mathew did not have to explain what he meant to other Antiguan slaveowners, who were all too aware of dangers inherent in his proposal. To put arms in the hands of slaves invited their possible use against masters themselves. Yet for years slaves had done limited militia service alongside and in attendance on whites. When Mathew suggested arming a thousand trustworthy blacks, making practical use of the island's human resources, he probably meant to establish a black contingent separate from black militia recruits. And he was willing to do so for the very good reason that the militia contained only 1,223 men; moreover, he believed there was a real possibility of a French attack. Regular troops consisted of 150 men, while in the whole island there were 24,408 blacks. To Mathew it seemed only common sense, under the circumstances, to gamble on arming some portion of this vast number of slaves, among whom adult males were far more numerous than the white militia. If defense finally devolved almost entirely upon the militia, it hardly constituted an adequate force. Whites may not have responded eagerly to the governor's plans, but they had no real choice. Mathew (1732–53) and Sir George Thomas (1753–66) were two governors of the Leewards who believed the risk of arming slaves for local defense was well worth taking, and to that end they regularly exhorted the legislature to pass the necessary laws.[75]

Social and economic consequences of the sugar revolution, disease, and other factors had all so decreased the white population over the years that there was bound to be a critical decline also in the size and quality of the militia. Already compressed by shortage of whites, the militia was further plagued by the demoralizing tendency for many persons of means to neglect their duty. The militia act of 1702 denounced this behavior as "contrary to the Principles of natural Equity." It was "as unreasonable to exact, as absurd to hope," it declared, "that Men of low Fortune shall cheerfully submit to Fatigues and Hazards, while those who are more deeply interested in the Public, refuse to undergo the same."[76] Accordingly, the act did not allow any exemptions from militia duty, but in 1704, by government order, the marshal, secretary, and customs officers were exempted except in emergencies.[77] The burden of militia duty evidently fell on poorer folk, who did not enjoy it. Mathew took up the case with a stern comment in his speech to the council and assembly in 1739, when war loomed between Britain and Spain. "I am told it has strangely prevailed among the poorer sort, that if in this Cause or any of Warr they are Called upon, tis to defend the Rich and wealthy only, and this at the Expence of their Lives, therefore that such a duty does not belong to them. But we ought all of us to Cure them of this Refractory Error by letting them know that the articles of Warr Established by Law will Certainly bring them to an Ignominous punishment or Death for their avoiding an uncertain Honourable One in the Service of their Country."[78]

To stimulate among them a sense of civic responsibility, the governor proposed to establish a fund out of which to support families of men killed defending the island.[79] Meanwhile islanders of means who shirked their duty had to be motivated also, but no incentives seemed effective enough to curb their customary indifference, which was at its peak in peacetime. Once again, military threats elicited an improved response in that more men showed up for duty, but this did not necessarily improve the quality of the corps. "When we were like to be attacked by A very Powerful Enemy," observed Governor Parke in 1710, "I found my Selfe at the head of A handful of Such Raw Undisciplined men, who as themselves Express it, knew not the Exercise or use of their Arms." Reluctance to perform militia duty is certainly strong evidence of Antiguan whites' lack of public spirit. When militia muster and crop time coincided, the first suffered. The Swete Plantation accounts record a payment of fourteen shillings, "To Cash paid William Sawcolt Adjutant to the Regimt. for the Overseers fines when he could not be spared from the Estate in Croptime."[80]

Ultimately, property was called upon to protect property. Clear evidence that Governor Codrington the elder recognized slaves' military potential in the 1680s comes from an act of February 1689, which stated that slaveowners would be paid five thousand pounds of sugar for each of their slaves "that shall happen to be slain, or mortally wounded, and disabled in Defence of this Island against any of their Majesties Enemies,"[81] during King William's War, which broke out that year. The militia act of 1702, upon which all such subsequent acts were modeled until about 1745, divided the corps into infantry and carbineers serving on foot and horseback, and assigned every officer of the carbineers "two able and trusty Negro Men armed with good Firelocks and a good sharp Bill" to attend them, and "every private gentleman of the same Body, one Negro Man, with red Coats, black Leather Caps, and equally armed."[82] We do not know how many blacks were finally assigned, but the act made it clear that their trustworthiness should be beyond question: "none may serve in the Carbineers, but such as are entirely to be depended upon."[83]

In all slave societies, confidence in certain slaves was a prerequisite to arming them. During the Anglo-French war of 1702–13, a special Antigua act of 1705 required each militia captain of foot to prepare a list of all trusty blacks in his area, free and slave, in order to draft a number for service with the militia. If masters did not cooperate, captains were authorized to choose 6 percent of their most able slaves nonetheless "over whom the said Captain shall appoint Negro leaders, and Cause them to meet within Thirty Dayes. . . and at no other Time but upon Day Allarmes and then that their appearance to be at ye place of Parade with the Capt. of the Severall verges respectively."[84] In the event of attack, these slaves were placed under command of militia captains or superior officers, but masters were responsible for arming them, failure to do which incurred a fine. If masters themselves were to provide arms, they would hardly place these in the hands of slaves whose trustworthiness was doubtful, so this was a good way to get them to cooperate in providing slaves for military service. Masters were also responsible for furnishing each slave recruit with a hat and coat and received twenty shillings for each so equipped: "The coats of the slaves belonging to the verge of the eldest Regiment shall be red, the second Blue, and the youngest green." Attached to the militia of every quarter were to be at least thirty-two slaves, of whom significantly, no more than four should be French. All slaves wounded or maimed in service were eligible for medical attention at public expense and ten pieces of eight compensation, while those serving with distinction, provided it was confirmed either by their militia captains or two reliable witnesses, were to have their freedom. Owners of slaves killed or freed were guaranteed compensation at appraised valued.[85]

In 1711, while the threat of invasion still hung over the island, the legislature felt confident that "As soon as the Allarm is made our poor men will be in armes as our Negroes." The lieutenant governor and council recommended that subsistence be provided for these men "so that they may be ready for service when there is occasion." The behavior of slaves over in Nevis in 1706 probably strengthened expectations of cooperation from slaves. When the French invaded Nevis, writes Richard Dunn, "the commanding officers had hastily surrendered unconditionally, handing over two strong forts without a battle, while their Negroes showed far more courage, keeping up a guerrilla war against the enemy."[86] The lessons of the entire episode were not lost on Antiguans, who, forty miles away, could plainly see terrible signs in the sky that parts of Nevis had been put to the torch.

For the duration of the war of 1739–48, the Leewards were on the alert. France did not enter the war until 1744, but in 1740, anticipating French hostilities, the Antigua assembly once again discussed arming slaves, and two years later the governor reported the existence of 1,018 "Armd. Negroes by Law." White militiamen, regular soldiers from a regiment of seven companies, seamen, and armed slaves made up a total of 2,939 men. Serving this force were 407 carts with slave drivers and 1,662 mules or horses. The legislature took further steps in 1743 with an act aimed specifically at encouraging poorer whites and slaves to behave courageously in defending the island. The act awarded a maximum of £5 12s. Antigua currency to any slave who "shall prove himself faithful and Trusty and shall do or attempt any remarkable Service. . . and if it shall be proved that such slave hath killed or taken prisoner an Enemy invading." Loyal slaves, in other words, were being asked to channel their belligerence, usually concealed, against a foreign common enemy. In 1744 the legislature called upon blacks to assist in patrol duty and the following year discussed proposals to arm and train not less than a thousand men.[87]

The militia act of 1702 had become so thoroughly defective a model by this time that a supplementary act was necessary.[88] The new act reflected strong awareness of the small number of whites living in the island, which contrasted with French increases on other islands. This concern was not new, having been aired at meetings of the legislature in the early 1730s, but it intensified in 1756, leading to a militia act that was plainly meant to prepare inhabitants to repel any attacks launched from French islands. The act ordered all slaveowners to submit to the militia officer in their quarter, once a year, a list of all persons living with the family, slave and free; above all, these registers were to specify all slaves between the ages of eighteen and forty years, as well as a select group of one-twentieth the number of ablest field slaves excluding drivers. In the event of alarms these slaves would be assigned to militia service in their particular districts. The legislature also debated whether to arm slaves with cutlasses or bills upon staves.[89]

Available evidence strongly suggests then, that when the danger was great, slaveowners faced the stark realities of the island's military weakness and gambled on arming some slaves. It was a necessary evil to which they knowingly submitted.

During the Seven Years' War blacks were not only armed to defend Antigua but were also recruited for invasion of both Guadeloupe and Martinique. When news arrived in 1757 that a French fleet had reached Martinique, making the possibility of a French offensive very real, the assembly hastened to order arms from England.[90] In February 1759 Governor George Thomas received a joint letter from Major General Peregrine Thomas Hopson and Commodore John Moore, both in command of British forces, requesting that Antigua raise a number of men, white and black, to assist in the reduction of Guadeloupe, where British troops had occupied the island's western half (Basseterre) since January 24.[91] Aware of the extraordinary nature of the request, and realizing too that slaveowners might well refuse to cooperate, Thomas immediately proposed an act to raise a number of slaves with specific provisions included to allay the fears of owners. "You will observe," he tactfully told the assembly, "that they are to be transported, victualled and armed at the King's Expense, and to be paid for, in case they shall be killed or disabled." "The complete conquest of Guadeloupe," replied the assembly, anxious to see a rival sugar territory of the enemy a few hours' sail away brought low, "is of so great importance to the Navigation, Commerce and Revenue of Great Britain, and the Possession of it by British Subjects, of such security to the Leeward Islands, that we are prompted . . . to Promote every measure that may be conducive to these great ends." Still, they proceeded cautiously enough, passing a resolution to raise no more than three hundred able blacks, on the understanding that slaveowners would receive "payment for such of our Negroes as may die or by any other Means not returned to their proper Owners." They knew slaves could desert once in Guadeloupe, which in terms of property loss was equivalent to their deaths, and therefore compensation was justified. Major General Barrington believed slave reinforcement from the Leewards would be "of the greatest Service to us in carrying on the Attack on the other Side of the Island, [Grande Terre, the eastern half] by going into the Woods and Mountains, where the King's Troops cannot act."[92]

In mid-March Governor Thomas reported making preparations to send Barrington 200 able blacks "as Rangers, to supply the camp with Cattle" of which there were large numbers in Guadeloupe.[93] In addition to such black reinforcements, a number of white volunteers also came forward, but of the 610 men finally sent over from Antigua and St. Christopher only about 150 were white,[94] most of them poorer folk who had done some service on privateers.[95] On the effectiveness of the black contingent, Thomas observed, agreeing with Barrington, that "a number of active able Negroes will be of equal or of more service in a Country so strong by Nature from its almost inaccessible Mountains, violent Torrents and deep Gulleys." There was perhaps something of a boast in his later admission, as if he had achieved the near impossible, that he had raised 800 men, white and black, in the four main islands of his jurisdiction, 200 more than Hopson and Moore had originally asked for. There is no evidence that blacks did any fighting in Guadeloupe, and it is probable that they did not but were used instead as pioneers and general drudges.[96]

Before the war was over Thomas again succeeded in raising slaves for an expedition, against Martinique, further south. Recruiting plans of 1761 intended blacks to serve as "Pioneers, drawers of Cannon, or such other services, as from their accustom'd Labour and exposure to the Sun, they shall be judged better able to undergo, than the natives of other Climates." The legislature subsequently passed two acts in 1761 and 1762 respectively to raise three hundred blacks.[97] According to the 1761 act, slaveowners of fifty or more slaves were required to supply one able, full-grown male for the first fifty, and another for every additional hundred possessed, within ten days after summons from the constable of each of the island's divisions. From these, commissioners would pick three hundred and appraise them prior to embarkation. By stating that no house slaves, tradesmen, drivers, carters, "boatswains of mills," boatmen, boilermen, or distillers would be recruited even though willing, unless owners themselves also consented, the act made an interesting concession to slaveowners in excluding these valuable slaves. A subsequent proclamation encouraged owners to volunteer slaves for recruitment. The act of 1762 made similar concessions with respect to skilled and other privileged slaves and authorized recruiting officers to accept volunteered slaves even though they raised the number of recruits over the three hundred required. The act also authorized the treasurer, at the king's expense, to furnish each slave with the following: a canteen, a new bill, a haversack, a new hoe, and a new basket; and for every five slaves he also had to supply one camp kettle or iron pot for cooking.[98] With such equipment slaves were obviously not meant to fight, yet they played a useful role in the conquest of Martinique in 1762, just as they had before at Guadeloupe. In the end the Antigua legislature warmly congratulated the king for seizing both French islands, from which, they said, the British island colonies had received "more injury and interruption...than from any other of the French dominions."[99]

Imported mainly for hard physical labor on sugar plantations during the first flush of the sugar revolution, blacks before long were also employed in increasing numbers outside plantations as slavery became firmly institutionalized and infiltrated other areas of the economy. This had important social consequences. Blacks were employed as domestics, hired and independent tradesmen, and seamen in the towns; and whenever labor was needed for public projects, or the island was in danger from an external enemy, they were also called upon to play an important role. There were few occupations, it seems, in which slave labor did not compete with free in Antigua, and consequently blacks contributed greatly to the development of the sugar colony. While plantation slaves made the greatest contribution, both because of the nature of their work at the very foundation of the island's sugar economy and because they constituted the largest proportion of the slave population, the wide diversity and value of slave employment generally in the service of masters and the state makes it clear that the role of slavery in Antigua, as in other slave societies, cannot be adequately appreciated or understood with reference only to the lives of plantation-based slaves. Because slavery was far more pervasive, and because blacks did not uncomplainingly submit but constantly, though with varying intensity, displayed their discontent and resentment, sometimes amounting to open defiance, it is no wonder whites frequently expressed grave misgivings about the behavior of those they shrewdly described as the enemy within. For this reason, and also because slave society depended so heavily on the cooperation of slaves in so many spheres of island life, public hysteria, however shortlived, was the predictable response to any discovery of a widespread and well-coordinated slave plot. This is perhaps one of the most obvious conclusions that can be drawn from a close study of extensive slave utilization.

Two related features of slave employment, however, occupations and patterns of slave ownership, draw attention to the slaves' treatment in terms of day-to-day living conditions, and its connections with the development of slave consciousness and how that evolving perception of reality conditioned both the form and the scope of slaves' responses to oppression under slavery.

In regard to plantation slaves, absentee proprietors, whether motivated by economic self-interest, humanity, or both, generally wrote their representatives in the colonies instructing how their slaves should be treated or managed, and this information reflects upon ideals at least, if not realities. "I recommend your prudent Manidgement of my Negrs. & Cattle," Sir William Codrington wrote in his instructions to John Griffith, manager of Betty's Hope in 1715, "and to see ym well fed and kept dry." Codrington also wanted slaves recently arrived from Africa especially well cared for, well fed, and their feet free of chegoes,[100] or small insects. To John Jeffers, manager of his Cotton Plantation, he wrote the same thing that year, instructing him also "To give the Negrs. every Friday afternoon and see that they goe in there ground especially the New Negrs. and let them have ground by ymselves and not with the old Negrs." One of Jeffers's instructions was "not to suffer. . .the wenches to be ill used by any body," and to make his point clearer Codrington added, "you have nothing to do with the house Negrs." Planters generally favored white managers or overseers who could get work out of the slaves without brutal treatment. "As you are pleased to leave it to my discretion to gratifie Mr. Martin for his care and kind usage of your negroes," attorney Tullideph wrote absentee George Thomas in 1749, he gave Martin a cash award for having done "more with the present gang than ever was done before and that without Severity, but by his Own Constant attendance and good Oconomy in the Estate." As an absentee himself in 1758, Tullideph was glad to hear that his slaves were in good health; "tell them," he wrote his attorney, "we all think of them, pray cloth and feed them well and worke them moderately."[101]

When absentees leased or rented their plantations to others, they ran the risk that their slaves would be badly treated. Thomas Farley, one of absentee Charles Tudway's attorneys, had this in mind when he advised against leasing in 1758 unless great care was exercised "to get a Humane

kind master that will feed and cloath your Negroes well, take good care
of them when sick, work them moderately when wll and use them kindely
always; God only knows whether it is right for us to keep these poore
wretches in Slavery all their lives, but as this is permitted, I think it is
Indispensably our duty that have them to make their Slavery as Comfortable to them as the Nature of things will admit of."[102] Many years earlier,
in 1716, when Thomas Fenton left England for Antigua as "Agent and Overseer" of the Tudway family plantation, he was specifically instructed to
inform the absentee of

> "all losses & Crosses of ye Deth of any Negroes and what are
> borne; to Loose Negroes Especially workers are Very great
> Losses therefore I must Recommend them to you. Especiall
> Care and well looking after them that they may be used as
> befitts them and not want what they ought to have, their
> bellys full and planting Enough for them, as it is not Good to
> be Cruell or too severe to them so it is not fitt that they
> should be Leasy & suffered to Neglect there worke, but yt
> they be kept to doe there Duty & Labour as they Ought to
> doe, and will doe if they be well Lookt after at there work &
> have a Deligent Driver yt mindes it."

The absentee owner relied upon Fenton to accomplish all this, "for from
the Negroes Labor all produce must Come."[103]

Every planter, large, middling, or small, realized that success depended
upon, among other things, proper treatment of slaves, the sinews of the
plantations; but the "nature of things" did not always facilitate this especially on large plantations of absentees, who, it is obvious, knew it only
too well. Concern with this aspect of plantation affairs is convincing enough
evidence. If unfettered by specific instructions, managers and overseers,
many of whom were paid a percentage of output, could strive for large
crops at the slaves' expense, promoting their own interests rather than those
of the plantation. On the relatively small number of large plantations in
Antigua that could afford absentee ownership, relations between slaves and
absentees' representatives were more impersonal than on the greater
number of small to middling plantations, on which slaves lived in closer
relationship with resident owners, some of whom worked alongside their
slaves raising provisions or cultivating cane. So far as we can tell, this was
the dominant pattern of slaveholding of land-based slaves during the first
half of the eighteenth century. In general, standards of day-to-day living
conditions measured in terms of living space, food, working conditions,
incidence of punishment, and leisure time tended to be harsher on the large,
impersonally organized plantations, but whatever the particular set of

conditions, they cumulatively helped shape slaves' political outlook or awareness of their situation and the way they would decide to cope with it.[104] The connections between occupations, living conditions, slave consciousness, and resistance can be better appreciated by looking at the slaves who were executed for the 1736 plot, which was not a spontaneous outburst of hostility but a carefully developed scheme knit together by slaves conscious of their individual and collective plight. We will elaborate on this subject in a later chapter, but it is important before doing so to identify the supportive base that made such an undertaking possible, and the extensive utilization of slaves is only one part of it. Persistent slave resistance is another.

Nonplantation slaves, whose lives were generally less circumscribed than those of plantation slaves, nevertheless also developed an awareness of themselves in relation to slavery that was strongly influenced by weakened bonds of dependence on masters, and, as our analysis of the organization of the slave plot will show, such slaves, many of them masterless in the sense that they were independently employed and unsupervised, could be prime recruits for collective resistance.

In classic plantation colonies in which slaves were extensively employed in plantation and nonplantation occupations, as Sidney W. Mintz and Richard Price have observed, (and Antigua can here be mentioned in the same breath as Jamaica and St. Domingue), "the slaves must have known a good deal more about the intimate daily affairs of the masters than the masters could have known about those of the slaves." Mintz and Price contend further that "the institutions created by the slaves to deal with what are at once the most ordinary and the most important aspects of life took on their characteristic shape *within* the parameters of the master's monopoly of power, but *separate from* the master's institutions."[105] Such creative responses from slaves and the evolution of slave consciousness were mutually reinforcing, and it should not be difficult to see the connection between slave consciousness and the scope and form of resistance. Consciousness emerged over time primarily out of the character of slave life as slaves adapted to it. Adaptation itself was heavily dependent upon several factors, including slave culture, occupations, day-to-day living conditions, the presence of unassimilable slaves in the slave population, the general character of slavery, the myriad points of contact between slave and free sectors of society, and all those other features of the total environment of slave society that helped educate slaves about reality, part of which was that slaveowners were dependent on their productive power and that slaves were not completely powerless within the "moral economy" of slave society.[106] At certain critical moments, that situation of reciprocal obligations and shared moral assumptions about what was acceptable and what was not within the master-slave relationship could come under severe strain and precipate open rebellion, the most dramatic form of slave resistance. Slaveowners sought to avert that outcome largely through various techniques of social control, for outright brutality itself was self-defeating.

6

For the Better Government of Slaves

Slaveowners in Antigua confronted the critical problem of slave control early, when the first cargoes of Africans arrived in the seventeenth century. Expansion of the slave system, which brought about large increases in the size of the restless and generally uncooperative slave population, also intensified the need for slave control. To maintain effective authority over these potential rebels and to safeguard the smooth working of island society slaveowners established a system of social control that imposed restraints on slave behavior and at the same time assigned all whites, especially slaveowners, responsibility for ensuring proper slave conduct.

Imposed by the master class, the positive and negative threads of the web of control that gradually emerged were formal and informal. Positive control stressed positive sanctions for conformity such as rewards that were specified by law (formal), or were part of custom, belief, and folkways (informal). Formal and informal as with positive controls, negative controls emphasized negative sanctions such as punishment or the fear of punishment for deviance.[1] Largely through astute manipulation of the authority system they had established to keep the slaves in proper submission, slaveowners hoped to socialize their bondmen into prescribed patterns of behavior through internalization of acceptable norms and values. However, because of countervailing tendencies that included slaveowners' own abuse of authority, the desire of many slaves to gain freedom or to hamper the operation of the slave system if they could, and the addition to the slave population through the slave trade of new, unacculturated Africans who had difficulty adjusting to the new environment — in short, largely because of the psychic warfare waged between master and slave that originated from a fundamental divergence of objectives in regard to slavery as each struggled for mastery over the other — slaves, following their own independent values, remained generally restless, and masters could not achieve the thorough socialization and control they desired. Had they been able to achieve this they would have avoided many headaches regarding the best way to manage slaves.

Slave resistance itself, of course, clearly advertised the failure of whites to knit together fully effective networks of subordination. The slaves were obviously not merely some easily malleable material in slaveowners' hands, to be shaped as they wished. Yet social control as an imposed system of interclass relations was partly successful because the slaves' value system emphasized survival while balancing resistance and accommodation, because the slaves bent themselves to the masters' will up to a point to serve their own interests, forcing elements of their condition to work in their favor while deflecting the most abrasive effects of slavery. Ultimately the obvious flaws of socialization as a basic form of social conditioning drove masters to rely heavily, almost exclusively, upon legally sanctioned forms of intimidation and oppression. These were the more formal aspects of negative social control, and they were enshrined in the slave codes.[2]

But slaveowners also manipulated more subtle and largely informal forms of control in their relations with slaves. In the complex web of master-slave relations, where both master and slave sought to achieve control over the other, but in which, however, slaveowners recognized and asserted their right to such control, that elusive but perhaps universal phenomenon of paternalism helped mold desirable slave behavior. Paternalistic slaveowners endeavored to convince their slaves that, in return for humane treatment, they owed gratitude, which was most suitably expressed in loyalty and submission. Master and slave therefore confronted the other with demands and expectations that in the case of the master were aimed at control of the slaves, but that the slaves themselves could also use for protection from abuse, thus influencing the master's behavior toward them. For both masters and slaves, standing on either side of the fence of slavery, pater-nalism, which could be fostered or contradicted by wider patterns of economic and social life, served as a "fragile bridge across the intolerable contradictions inherent in a society based on racism, slavery, and class exploitation." It helped to tone down what might have been a more flagrant case of constant undeclared war between the two groups.

Paternalism, according to Eugene Genovese, writing about the U.S. antebellum South, "grew out of a necessity to discipline and morally justify a system of exploitation." It was meant to generate in U.S. slave societies and in Antigua tendencies for slaves to cooperate in preserving the sta-bility of society through identification with their owners. Like the nineteenth-century slaveowner James Henry Hammond of South Carolina, about whom Drew Gilpin Faust has written so searchingly, the Antigua slaveowner Samuel Martin understood this well. In his essay on island plantership, he drew attention to "the duties of a planter to his negroes." Martin elaborated on the reciprocal obligations that should ideally exist between masters and slaves by pointing out that a master should treat his slaves with "tenderness and generosity," so that "they may be induced to love and obey him, out of mere gratitude; and become real good beings by the imitation of his benevolence, justice, temperance, and chastity. Nothing influences the conduct of mankind so much as the example of superiors who are always in view, and, therefore a good planter, for his own ease and happiness, will be careful of setting a good example, as the best means of propagating the gospel morality." For Martin and Hammond and many other owners of large numbers of slaves who concerned themselves with working out a cooperative alliance with their bondmen without undue and unproductive reliance on force, it was obviously necessary simultaneously to establish dominance over them and to secure their love and loyalty.[3]

Ultimately, paternalism helped absorb some of the intensity of slave rebelliousness, deflecting its destructive thrust; but that intimacy between master and slave, as Genovese has observed, also turned "every act of impudence and insubordination — every act of unsanctioned self-assertion" by the slaves, many of whom could not or would not adjust their behavior sufficiently, into an act of treason, disloyalty, or ingratitude, "for by repudiating the principle of submission it struck at the heart of the master's moral self-justification and therefore at his self-esteem." This helps explain the benevolent master's lapses into cruelty to his slaves and the predictable rebellious responses of slaves to treatment they saw as unjust. Paternalism itself could feed slaves' rebelliousness.[4]

Within the informal sphere of control, slaveowners used some interesting strategies. On workdays, they kept the slaves working long hours year-round to reduce opportunities for getting into mischief; they granted them customary holidays and also rewards not specified by law for meritorious service to the state or for work well done; they changed the slaves' names either to completely new English substitutes or by anglicizing African names; and they allowed, or sometimes even actively promoted, development of a certain level of discord among the slaves to inhibit growth of solidarity that might lead to collective resistance. Combinations of informal methods of control varied considerably among New World slave societies, but there were also certain similarities. Existing patterns depended upon what seemed to work as a result of a delicate interplay between masters' and slaves' perceptions of realizable objectives in relation to one another.

The naming of slaves deserves special attention here because, while it is a little-studied subject, it allowed masters to define and fully claim slaves as their property while attempting to strip them of an identity associated with their original names. Henceforth, the renamed slaves were extensions of their masters, supposedly also at the mercy of their will. Some insight into this intriguing dimension of the slaves' entry into slave society and community can be derived from the Ibo Olaudah Equiano's experience. Transported first from the Benin province of present-day Nigeria in West Africa to Barbados in the West Indies, Equiano was soon shipped again to Virginia, where his master renamed him Jacob. Even before this his captors had called him Michael. From Virginia Equiano was moved again to England. "While I was on board this ship," he recounted, "my captain and master named me Gustavus Vassa. I at that time began to understand him a little, and refused to be called so, and told him as well as I could that I would be called Jacob; but he said I should not, and still called me Gustavus: and when I refused to answer to my new name, which I at first did, it gained me many a cuff; so at length I submitted, and by which I have been known ever since." By the time his name was changed a third time, Equiano obviously resisted this last attempt to bestow upon him once again a new identity, as if what he had been before, what he had been as an African, did not matter. In the end, he says, he was forced to keep the name Gustavus Vassa, but many Caribbean slaves seemed to have had several names and may never have abandoned their African names, which bound them close to the ancestral culture and homeland. Refusal to relinquish African names was an act of resistance against total domination by slaveowners and their alien culture.[5]

Capitalizing on discord among the slaves as a way to better control the disunited also deserves some elaboration, because it seems to have been one of the more acceptable approaches based on slaveowners' understanding that the slaves represented a potential enemy. We will recall that the Antigua legislature agreed to reward slaves whose testimony helped discover and punish rebels in the 1736 slave plot partly in order to make the slaves "distrustful of each other" and to encourage future "timely Discovery's." Thinking over the potential dangers that whites were exposed to while living among slaves, who greatly outnumbered them, the Reverend Robert Robertson observed in 1729 (extending similar remarks made by Richard Ligon about Barbados in the middle of the previous century) that "Our Safety, as I take it" in the Leeward Islands "lies not a little in this, that as our Slaves are brought from different Countries, so they perfectly hate one another, and are ever clashing and jarring; and tho' for good Reasons we do not encourage or foment their Dissensions, yet it would be ridiculous, as the Case is, to pretend to put a Force on their Temper, and to make them love one another whether we can or no."[6] While ethnic tension was possible among the slaves, Robertson and other like-minded whites probably exaggerated its extent as a kind of psychological reassurance. It was, in any case, with such informal controls, which played an indirect but important role in restraining slaves' negative responses to slavery, that rebel leaders like Court and Tomboy had to contend when they set about organizing collective slave resistance.

The Antigua slave population, compared to that of whites, swelled in the eighteenth century. As a result the dwindling slaveowning class could not expect to acculturate or assimilate the slaves for purposes of better control. Neither did the established church play an active role as an agency of control through christianization of the black majority. In 1723, at the beginning of his episcopate, Edmund Gibson, bishop of London, sent out a questionnaire to the colonial clergy, the replies to which supply interesting information on colonial church life and the attitudes of parishioners to religion. Question 7 dealt with the slaves: "Are there any Infidels bond or free in your Parish; and what means are us'd for their Conversion?" The Reverend Simon Smith, in charge of Falmouth Parish in Antigua, replied succinctly, "There are in the Parish of Falmouth 2,000 or more infidels Negros Slaves Men, Women and children and no care taken for their conversion." From the Parish of St. George in Nevis, the Reverend Henry Pope replied that "We have a great Number of Slaves, but most of them uncapable of the means of Conversion, being natives of Guinea." Neither did he bother to elaborate. Reporting later in 1732, the Reverend James Knox of St. John's Parish in Antigua told the bishop that "There are about twenty five Thousand of them [slaves] in Antigua, and in the other 3 Islands together, there must be that or probably a greater number" who "are all heathens and like to continue so; there are no means used for their Conversion, nor I believe ever will: that," lamented Knox, "is a thing rather to be wished for than hoped or Expected." Knox, on the verge of explaining this last remark, changed his mind, leaving us with the frustrating comment: "I should be too tedious should I enter into detail of the reasons that convince me of this."[7]

Fortunately, Governor Codrington and the missionary Francis Le Jau of the Society for the Propagation of the Gospel in Foreign Parts did not have Knox's reservations when they commented on religious life in the Leewards about thirty years earlier. In 1699, instructed from home to promote "the conversion of negroes," Codrington replied that slaveowners would oppose instruction and baptism of their slaves. Furthermore, he noted, " 'tis evident the few and the very ill-qualified clergymen who go to the islands are not only insufficinet for such a work, but can do no service to the white heathens they find there by their teaching or example." The governor suggested that for "a work of this nature. . . regular clergy who are under vows of poverty and obedience" should be recruited, because the "secular clergy who will be sure of their hire before they set about their task do not think the hope of a reward in another world sufficient encouragement to turn missionaries."[8] Commenting on the attitude of his parishioners in St. Christopher to conversion of slaves during the first decade of the eighteenth century, Francis Le Jau, who later served for many years in South Carolina, noted that they felt "baptism would make negroes free, but I know they don't believe it because of the negroes now in their possession which came from the French or Spaniards & consequently are baptised yet they don't look upon them as free." Le Jau believed that "the true Reason is that if they were baptised by us they would think themselves oblidged to look upon them as brothers in Christ and use them with humanity, whereas as they are they think them to be no men & to take away their life with cruel beating is no murther, in short they use them worse than their Beasts." Generally, slaveowners felt that conversion would interfere with their authority over the slave population. Writing from Antigua in 1744, commissary Francis Byam told Bishop Gibson that he had done "what lies in my power but find it not bless'd with any great success excepting in a few instances of Negroes who have had their freedoms for their faithfull services."[9]

Against this background of church apathy or impotence and slaveowner indifference and, in some cases, hostility to conversion and acculturation, importation of new Africans only reinforced the African-based cultural environment of the slaves, encouraged whites to segregate themselves culturally and socially from them, and reduced some of the force of attempts at domination, especially through legal controls that reflected the immediate political necessities of the master class. It is striking that only a few of the more obvious African elements of slave culture were proscribed where they seemed to pose a possible threat to white security. Otherwise, it seems that by and large Antigua slaves enjoyed much liberty to develop their community life, some elements of which continued to exist in opposition to the world of the slaveowners.

———————————————

The slave laws were aimed largely at more open and obvious opposition to slaveowners' hegemony, and in coercing slaves they expressed various facets of the slave-related ideology of the ruling class. These laws were the backbone of the system of social control; as in other New World slave societies, they "mirror the society that created them," reflecting both "the political traditions of the European colonizers and the political necessities of a way of life based upon plantation slavery." Antiguan slave laws regulated slaves as private property and persons or, more correctly, because of the heavy emphasis on property, which was held sacred also in the law of England, as a "special kind of property." It was obvious that slaves were unlike other property in that they possessed a will of their own and were capable of independent thought and action. When therefore the slave laws dealt with them as rebels and runaways, they were recognized as persons who posed a problem to public order. "The law," according to Elsa Goveia, "was forced to allow the slave some kind of 'persona' for the purpose of dealing with him under this aspect of his activity as a special kind of property," and in the process unmistakably emphasized the potential criminality of the slave. Even so, slave laws were commonly not stringently enforced; but they were on the books, and occasionally, as when there were signs of serious slave unrest, they were activated with some vigor, or new and more severe regulations were enacted. Directly or indirectly, the main function of the slave laws, like the private punishments slaveowners inflicted on their slaves, was repressive—"to make them stand in fear." Many slaveowners throughout British America who bothered to write about the disciplining of slaves stressed the use of fear in breaking their spirits. "A slave being a dependent agent," wrote one Jamaican planter, "must necessarily move by the will of another, which is incessantly exerted to control his own: hence the necessity of terror to coerce his obedience. It is, therefore, by the gross operation of fear, or the dread of punishment, that negroes are wrought upon to action." The Jamaican planter Bryan Edwards had this to say: "In countries where slavery is established, the leading principle on which the government is supported, is fear; or a sense of that absolute coercive necessity, which, leaving no choice of action, supersedes all questions of right. It is vain to deny that such actually is, and necessarily must be, the case in all countries where slavery is allowed."[10] It certainly was the case in Antigua from the inception of slavery.

Slave laws are a useful yet admittedly inadequate source for analyzing social conditions and the character of slavery in Antigua that generated slave resistance because they say little or nothing about objective conditions of slavery on plantations or elsewhere. "Statutes provide a picture of race relations and slave control," writes Winthrop Jordan, "which is too clear cut, too highly rationalized, too formalized, and far too uniform." However, if statutory law is "a distillation of some of the society's most cherished values, or at least of the values of the class that wields the hegemonic power that produces laws," then the Antiguan slave laws clearly reflected in most cases the explicit anxieties and preoccupations of slaveowners, and more particularly those of the wealthy gentry, who, as legislators, enacted the law, perceiving themselves to act in the interest of all whites, and, they would have argued, even in the interest of blacks themselves. Laws disciplining slaves were based on the fundamental principles that the person of all whites was inviolable, that police regulations were necessary to prevent slaves from undermining public order, and that owners' property rights in slaves were to be upheld at all times. Upon this foundation legislators erected a superstructure of slave law that embodied a criminal law of slavery, specifying categories of slave crime and appropriate trial and punishment.[11] While crime and punishment in colonial British America and West Africa were in many cases similar, slaves found that their native conception of justice could vary from their masters', and they experienced some difficulty adjusting to colonial society and its legal system.[12]

Before the enactment of the first comprehensive slave act or code in 1697, the Antigua legislature had passed a number of short acts or policing measures to deal with specific incidents of slave rebelliousness, but the spirit of these acts, if not the actual regulations, was later incorporated into the comprehensive act. The act did not carry a preamble explaining its rationale; but it was modeled on Barbados and Jamaica codes, and Antiguan legislators may have shared the view of their counterparts in Barbados who framed the 1688 code that the large slave labor force required for sugar plantations must be governed by special laws because "the said Negroes and other slaves brought unto the People of this Island for that purpose, are of Barbarous, Wild, and Savage Natures, and such as renders them wholly unqualified to be governed by the Laws, Customs, and Practices of our Nations." Influenced by the strong sense of power over the destinies of others that came with expansion of the slave population, but realizing at the same time the need for their systematic control, Barbados legislators justified subordination in language of debasement, referring to the slaves' barbarism. Special "Constitutions, Laws and Orders," the act's preamble declared, were "absolutely necessary. . . framed and enacted for the good Regulating and Ordering" of slaves "as may both restrain the Disorders, Rapines, and Inhumanities to which they are naturally prone and inclined." The act also stated that regulations governing slaves should include "such Encouragements and Allowances as are fit and needful to" their support;[13] but neither the Antigua code of 1697 nor others of later date took much notice of proper support or protection of slaves.[14] Enacted initially to be in force for only two years, the 1697 code was extended in 1700 for another seven years, but in 1702 another act, in reality the old act with a few changes, superseded it. A third comprehensive act was passed in 1723.[15] These acts, occasionally amended, were at the center of the formal apparatus for slave control, and an analysis of them will show how far they were related to slave resistance, or slave crime, as slaveowners defined it.

The law made it clear that nonwhites, slave or free, were to show full deference to all whites. The act of 1702 laid down that a slave striking a white person of whatever station in society was to be publicly whipped, and "if such White Person be any Way hurt, wounded, or disfigured by any Slave's Resistance, such offending Slave or Slaves shall have their Nose slit, or any Member cut off or be punished with Death" at the discretion of justices, except the slave had acted "by his or her Owner's or Master's Order, or in Defence of his or her Person or Goods." That law was meant to teach blacks that whites, whoever they might be, were their superiors. By 1723 the slave act of that year imposed the death penalty for threatening the lives of whites, or burning or attempting to burn their houses. Slaves knowing of such incidents were encouraged to report them to any justice, who was responsible for apprehending the offenders, and if the offenders were found guilty, informers were entitled to a reward of £3 if they could also produce a "Certificate of the Accusation and Condemnation" from any one of the justices trying the case; if the reports proved frivolous or groundless, however, informers were to receive a whipping of not more than 150 lashes on the bare back. These regulations, aimed at preserving the social order, remained in force throughout our period. That there were no specific laws against slave disrespect through insulting words or menacing gestures, or laws that required slaves to step aside when they met whites on horseback or foot, as the slave act of 1733 had laid down in the Danish Virgin Islands, does not mean that Antiguan slaves were less restricted in their conduct. The clauses just cited from the acts of 1702 and 1723 focused only on physical assault on whites or attempts to destroy their property in order to stress the seriousness of these offences, while custom probably covered a whole range of proper conduct toward whites. [16]

The vast majority of slave laws in Antigua as elsewhere in British America, the core of the codes, were police regulations intended to cover threats to public security. By the act of 1702 slaveowners could not allow their slaves off the plantations on Sundays without a ticket "or White Servant with them, in which Ticket is to be Expressed the Names and Numbers, and also to and from what Place, on Penalty of paying, for taking up such Slave or Slaves as Runaways, three Shillings." Slave coachmen and personal attendants alone were exempted. The law also prohibited the sale of rum "or any Sort of dry Goods, by Barter or otherwise" to slaves on Sundays, the penalty for violation being a fine of £3. But neither these regulations nor indeed the entire act of 1702 were adequately enforced, for in 1715 the assembly remarked that "It is with very great concern, we observe the Act for better Government of Slaves is now entirely neglected, whereby the many mischiefs we apprehended was occasioned for want of such a Law is like to fall on the Island in as great a degree as if the same was not in force." The assembly asked the lieutenant governor to issue immediately "strict orders to the severall Officers concerned, That they may duely execute what is required of them in their respective offices, and more particularly to Constables; That they cause all Negroes taken up by Vertue of that Act, to be whipt agreeable to the Intent thereof." The lieutenant governor and council replied that because of an existing debate concerning the act's validity, "and there being severall Fines and Imprisonments imposed by the said Act, To remove all difficulties" they thought it best that "the same be new drawn in His Majesty's Name and sent to the Lt. General in order to be transmitted to England." The assembly then recommended thirteen amendments to the old act, but no new act seems to have been passed until 1723. The legislature had already taken steps to enforce slave laws before they considered enacting a new code, for in 1714, clearly because slaves had persisted in prohibited pursuits on Sundays unchecked by whites, they passed a special act "for the better regulating Negroes and the suppressing their Conspiracies and Profanation of the Lord's Day." [17] Only the title of the act appears in surviving records, so it is not possible to cite its provisions; still, by itself, the title suggests Antigua authorities faced a very troublesome problem of maintaining public order on Sundays, the slaves' full day off from work on the plantations.

The 1714 act evidently caused more problems than it solved, for it was repealed in 1722, having proved "highly inconvenient and, instead of answering the good Ends proposed by it . . . [had] put the Public . . .to great and unnecessary Charges, begot Riots and Disorders between White Men and Negro slaves, and in a great Measure rendered. . .Slaves a prey to idle and ill disposed persons." The consequences of enforcing the act are stated here quite clearly, and if they are considered along with its title, we can guess at some of its provisions or main intent. Just how far public order on weekends, especially in St. John's, had deteriorated by 1723 is revealed in the act of that year, which declared that "Slaves do frequently on Saturdays in the afternoon, and Sundays, gather and assemble in great Numbers in and about the Town of St. John's, and commit Riots, and sometimes kill one another, to the great Terror and actual endangering of the Inhabitants." On Sundays slaves held their market, and while it was in progress constables and the militia of the town were on duty to maintain order. Fights frequently broke out, and the act ruled that any slaves caught fighting were to be publicly whipped by the order of and at the discretion of a justice; the same applied if "any Slave draw a Knife, either in assaulting another, or in his own Defence."[18] But the authorities were also — indeed, more — concerned about the slaves' activities after the market had broken up.

Instead of returning directly to their quarters as the slave laws had intended them to, many slaves dallied about town to amuse themselves at grogshops. A report of 1740 said that there were ten dramshops for every punch house adjacent to "Ottos Pasture and the Negro Market." It is likely that several of these "Disorderly houses" were already in existence in 1723. While numbers of slaves succumbed to the lure of these places on Sundays, others wandered through the town's unpaved streets in groups, stopping here and there to exchange greetings and converse, prolonging the short hours allowed them on market day for such intercourse. Still others meandered towards "Otto's Pasture, and Long's, or Morgan's Pasture," close to town to engage in other diversions. The act of 1723 required that any gathering of more than ten slaves should be dispersed by two companies of men made up of one constable and six militiamen chosen by the town's justices or such officials of the neighborhood acting under orders from the governor or his designated representative. It also required each householder in St. John's to assist when summoned to disperse such assemblies, or to send a white man "armed with a Gun, Powder, and Ball, upon pain of forfeiting twenty Shillings." Constables and others of the riot squad were further authorized "upon seeing any Number of Negroes assembled in a tumultuous Manner, or playing at Dice, or any Game, Play, or Diversion, to make three Proclamations, requiring such Negroes to separate, and disperse, and to retire to their Homes"; and if they refused it was lawful to seize a few to be dealt with by a justice, who would order the offenders imprisoned and later publicly whipped, the number of lashes to be left to the justice's discretion. However, "if the Constable or any in his Assistance shall apprehend it necessary, in Contempt and Disobedience of the Proclamation," they could lawfully fire upon and kill some of the slaves. Owners of slaves killed would be compensated out of public funds in accordance with regulations governing compensation for slave fugitives killed on the run.[19]

While it was not unusual for a select number of slaves to be armed for militia service alongside their masters, every effort was made to deny slaves general access to and use of arms. By the slave act of 1702 it was lawful for a person to relieve slaves of "any hurtful Clubs or other mischievous weapons whatsoever," unless they were guarding their masters' goods. It would have been very difficult to enforce this regulation if Antiguan slaves, like those in the Virgin Islands, enjoyed the sport of stick fighting so entertaining to white spectators. More detailed regulations governing "mischievous weapons" came into effect in 1723. Now, if slaves were found outside the plantation in possession of firearms, cutlasses, swords, pikes, or lances "or other hurtful Arms," they were to be relieved of them unless they were carrying a ticket from their owner authorizing possession or were accompanied by a white person. Whites were permitted to seize either the arms or the slaves carrying them or both, and present them before a justice, who would award the arms to the person seizing them or making the arrest. If, however, the slave's owner could show that the ticket for carrying arms had been lost or had been taken away from the slave, "or the Slave being attendant that Day on his Master to exercise," then the impounded items were to be restored. The fine for selling, bartering, or giving firearms, cutlasses "or offensive Weapons" to slaves, "except those given for Watching" was £10.[20]

Because slaves could use drums to communicate with one another over distances, and because drums were often used at slave gatherings or festivities where whites feared plots could be hatched, the legislature outlawed drumming in the act of 1723; but as early as the 1680s, during maroon disturbances, anxious authorities had ordered slaveowners not to permit slaves to beat drums or make "such like Noyse." The acts of 1697 and 1702 did not reflect concern with this activity, but the 1723 act, much of which was aimed at runaways, directed all owners of plantations or other persons in charge to prevent slaves beating "any Drum or Drums, or empty Casks, or great Goards" or blowing "Horns, Shells, or loud Instruments." Every violation carried a fine of £10 unless the slaves' activities were suppressed within an hour.[21]

At Christmastime slaves were customarily granted three days' holiday, "Play-Days for their Recreation," extending over Christmas Day and the two following days, when they enjoyed some respite from many of the rigors of slavery. "At this Season," wrote Janet Schaw in 1774, "the crack of the inhuman whip must not be heard, and for some days it is an universal Jubilee; nothing but joy and pleasantry to be seen or heard."[22] The excitement of preparing for the few days of bacchanal reached fever pitch by Christmas Eve, when the strict discipline and routine of plantation life was suspended and the slaves began to enjoy a latitude of behavior so opposite to ordinary life as to constitute what anthropologists call a rite of reversal — "a ritual event in which everyday patterns are turned topsy-turvy."[23] Abandoning themselves to eating, drinking, dancing, and merrymaking, slaves consumed large quantities of supplies, some of which they had obtained themselves and some donated by their owners. On the plantation belonging to the deceased Main Swete, slaves were given in 1741 two barrels of beef costing £3 10s. and twenty-five pounds of biscuits. An entry in the plantation's accounts for December 8, 1738 reads, "To 2 barrells of Beef for the Negroes at Christmas . . . £4." In an analysis of the papers of an Antiguan plantation (1769–1818) Ulrich B. Phillips noted that each December "several, usually four, barrels of salt pork or beef and a similar quantity of flour 'for the negroes' Xmas' " were purchased. The slaves expected their treat at least in beef or pork. "Negroes never have aney beefe but at Christmas," David Stalker wrote absentee Sir William Stapleton from Nevis in 1732, expressing concern that it had been "two years in fine that your negroes had herring for the Christmas Beef."[24]

Commenting on Antigua slaves' Christmas activities in 1787, John Luffman noted that he had been "entertained very much during the last week [of December] by the Negroes paying their highly absurd compliments of the season to every person from whom they think a trifle can be drawn, and their common wish upon these occasions, is — 'Long Life and crosperity' — not prosperity (observe, I mention this, lest you should suppose it to be an error of my pen). [S]o careful are they to prevent any encroachment on" their claim to the holidays "that were their owners to give them double the time in lieu thereof, at any other season of the year, they would not accept it." Luffman cited the example of a slaveowner whose slaves had killed him "purely because he obliged them to work on the days appointed for holidays." This man was Major Samuel Martin, of whom we shall have more to say later. Martin's sudden end may have served as a lesson to slaveowners insensitive to the slaves' experience of Christmas as catharsis, an outlet for aggression that, if not released harmlessly through the ritual of Christmas festivity, could result in revolt. But it should be noted that, even when slaves were certain of their holidays, hostile outbursts still occurred. Anthropologist Robert Dirks has shown, through an examination of revolts and conspiracies real or imagined in the British Caribbean between 1649 and 1833, that of the 70 documented cases, 32 of which were conspiracies, 35 percent took place or were scheduled to take place in December. Dirks explains that the December "rioters and insurgents responded to conditions they themselves did not entirely appreciate." Basically, these conditions were related to the "pronounced seasonality in the slaves' regimen."[25]

The annual cycle of sugar plantations centered on crop time and planting time. During the dry months of crop time, roughly December–June, yields of locally grown provisions were low, and by the time the July–November wet season came along food scarcity grew more severe as shipping avoided the Caribbean and its hurricanes. As a result, writes Dirks, during planting time field slaves "endured a prolonged period of backbreaking labor while subsisting on stingy rations, storable grains and starchy tubers." Life was particularly hard for slave gangs in the Leeward Islands and Barbados, who were fed largely upon imported plantation rations. This was the "hard-time" or "hungry-time" described in Barbados. Drought often worsened their predicament.[26] Writing from Antigua on April 10, 1742 during a spell of drought, Walter Tullideph described the plight of Winthorpes Plantation. "Abot. drie weather, what we planted at Winthorpes dead, we can make no Sugar there next year but what we plant now to use as a nursery, to send flower bread & corn as we expect hard times." Provisions of yams, potatoes, and guinea corn were commonly planted at Winthorpes, but during the severe drought of early 1752, which threw "a damp on People's Minds, especially as there is very little Expectations for a Crop next year," Tullideph complained that the charges "of feeding [the slaves] will run higher than usual . . . by which neither potatoes or great Corn could be raised." And over in Nevis in October 1725, Joseph Herbert, manager of the Stapleton plantation drew attention to a "bad crop of provisions by dry weather and a prospect of a bad crop. No provision from abroad from whence the negroes are likely to suffer." That drought lasted into 1726 and contributed to the deaths of some slaves, who, the manager said, "killed themselves by running away in the hard times." The best description of this period of severe privation came from Governor John Hart. Writing to the Board of Trade on May 20, 1726 he said that Antigua "is in a most deplorable Condition from the Dry weather which has continued for Eight months past; there having been no Rain fallen there, till within this three Days. So that they have not only lost there Crop for this Year and the next, But have been oblig'd to bring all their Water, from Guardeloupe and Mountserrat; Which was sold at fifteen Shillings a Hogshead, which has occasion'd the loss of many of the Cattle and Negroes." Nevis, he continued, "is in the same Condition as to their Crops," but, St. Christopher and Montserrat were more fortunate. "Yet upon the best

Computation that I can make," Hart said, "I do not find there will be more than one third part of the sugar made this Year, in proportion to the last: Which will be a very great loss to the Revenue; And many of the midling and poorer Planters will be utterly undone. For they are not only disappointed of their Crops for Two Years But are oblig'd to buy Provisions for themselves and Negroes, upon Credit, from the Merchants." In August of the same year Hart reported that some rain had recently fallen but had made little difference, for "had not these Islands been well Supply'd with Provisions from the Colonys in North America, it must have produced a Famine." The drought hung on into 1727.[27]

Inadequate nutrition through caloric deprivation and protein deficiency during the annual wet season, and such as field slaves in Antigua and Nevis must have suffered through the prolonged drought just described, affected the slaves' physical health and behavior. Morbidity increased as they became susceptible to such nutrition-related disorders as diarrhea (fluxes), edema, beriberi, ancylostomiasis, and maladies associated with infestation by parasitic worms. These were of course added to other causes of slave mortality including suicides, accidents, and infectious diseases such as yellow fever, influenza, smallpox, yaws, and others. Too much rainfall in the wet season could also add to the ill effects of recurrent hunger, destroying provisions and causing sickness among slaves without adequate clothing. "The Negroes are bare of cloaths and pinch'd in their belly," wrote Herbert from Nevis in December 1728, "having lost abundance of potatoes by the great rains in August and Sept." David Stalker, writing in 1732, asked Stapleton to send out some clothes "that the Negroes may have them before the could weather come in. I assure you sir," he explained, "that they suffered very much without them and the work that they loose by sickness oscasioned from severe colds for want of cloaths amounts to a greater loss than the price of cloaths. In short they may be as well without their victuals but at the same time its easier to be purchased in England than here. In the hurricane time the wind and rain blows so very hard that I myself often wish for a great coat to guard me against the weather." The very wet autumn of 1776 brought an epidemic of fever and dysentery to the Stapleton Plantation in St. Christopher, where one-third of the slaves were affected. To fill the breach in manpower, the remaining slaves were driven harder than usual during the late planting season and crop time, and, not surprisingly, in April 1777 they were reported to be "sullen and rebellious."[28] As a result therefore of inadequate nutrition during the planting season and the strenuous work that field slaves were still required to do, and sometimes also because of illness brought on by exposure to cold and damp during a season of heavy rainfall, the health of the field gangs reached bottom generally in November; but by mid December recovery was under way.

The wasted appearance some masters observed in their slaves began to change at this time. Food supply increased dramatically as crops were ready for harvesting and as ships laden with supplies from Britain and North America began to arrive, the hurricane season being over. In the fields the canes were also nearly ripened, and until crop time the pace of plantation activity slowed down as slaves worked at the less demanding tasks of repairing buildings and equipment, and cultivating provisions. Drawing on the work of other scholars who have studied relationships between hunger and behavior, on observations of plantation owners and others connected with sugar cultivation in the islands, and also on his sample of revolts and conspiracies occurring in December, Dirks argues that "among human populations, the effect of sudden increases on the heels of sustained want can be explosive," and that the "tremendous nutritional increment just before the holidays" contributed to a potentially explosive situation among the slaves which the Christmas celebrations helped to defuse, although in many cases aggression was vented. Sometimes therefore relief from hunger, instead of relieving tensions, intensified them. This phenomenon of what Dirks calls "relief-induced agonism" has been documented by scholars studying behavioral responses to relief in several societies where the typical response to "the early refeeding of famished groups is the sudden appearance of symptoms of irritability, the aggressive voicing of complaints, and the other general, often intense, displays of hostility."[29] Whatever the mechanisms that were responsible for such responses and, in the case of the slave societies, that determined whether aggression would be expressed symbolically in the rituals of Christmas or in open hostility, it is nonetheless clear that slaveowners, conscious of the necessity to control their slaves, had stumbled on a safety valve to relieve social tension.

From the foregoing discussion it can be concluded that Antigua, a heavy importer of slave rations and prone to long bouts of drought, would have faced a potential crisis every Christmas. One report on the Leewards in 1732 painted a stark picture of the hardships drought brought: "the Drought is generally followed by an Army of Worms, flies, and other Insects which eat up what little green things are left on Earth; then comes a scarcity of Indian provisions, and a proportionable Dearth of those from England, Ireland, and the North Continent; then a most dreadful Mortality among the Negroes and the Live-Stock." At such times, in an island where the mean annual rainfall for the 87-year period 1874–1960 was only 43.37 inches,[30] it was customary for the governor to appoint a day for solemn fast and humiliation asking God for rain; and when the rains came "making ev'ry valley sing for joy," to quote from John Singleton's description of the island in blank verse, the islanders gave heartfelt thanks.[31] Every Christmas, however, drought or no drought, it was necessary "to keep a look out during this season of unbounded freedom," observed Janet Schaw, "and every man on the Island is in arms and patrols go all around the different plantations as well as keep guard in the town."[32] Only in war-time, perhaps, did Antigua so nearly resemble an armed camp. Martial law was customarily in effect, not that all concerned took their responsibilities seriously. The governor always ordered out the militia companies, which, by the 1723 slave act passed on December 9, were "to ride the Rounds on every Christmas-day, and the two Days next following, from eight of the Clock every Morning, until ten of the Clock every Evening." A typical order, issued by the governor in 1712, required the militia "to disperse all Negroes that Shall Assemble themselves togeather to Suffer no drum to be beat by them and if they Should happen to come up with any Slave who have not a ticket from his Master or Mistress or other person who hath the Chief Command of any plantation to take him up and Secure him or if Such Slave or Slaves Should make any resistance to shoot them and this you are to See performed with diligence and Exactness, in Order to prevent any Commotions or Insurrections from the Negroes."[33]

Special guards were also posted in certain areas. In 1740 the legislature ordered that, in addition to the regular militia patrols, guards were to be posted in the towns of St. John's and Parham in the north, at Monk's Hill, and at James Fort, overlooking St. John's harbor, "these Guards to be placed on Christmas Eve to be relieved every Twenty Four hours." In 1744, when Britain and France were at war, the legislature also passed a special act governing nighttime and Christmas patrols for the duration of the conflict.[34] These men would not have gone through all the trouble of major police alerts at Christmas if they did not dread the possibility of disruptive slave behavior. Merriment and the possibility of revolt went hand in hand. To keep things under control the legislature prepared for the latter, and in the act of 1723 ruled on the former, that "whereas great Disorders have happened, and Murders have been committed by Slaves, because their Masters have not allowed them the same Number of Days for their Recreation at Christmas, as several of their Neighbors have done," all slaveowners were obliged to allow their slaves (except domestics) the full holidays "and no more, or other Days," or be fined £20.[35] The intention here was not so much to protect slaves' rights to holidays as to regularize them and remove a potential threat to public order. Every "Negro infant can tell you," was Janet Schaw's comment on the slaves' attachment to Christmas, ". . .that Master will die bad death, if he hurt poor Negro in his good day."[36]

So comprehensive was the system of police control meant to be in subordinating slaves to whites that even slave funerals were regulated. For slaves burial of their dead was an important rite. "Negroe funerals," reported Luffman in 1787, "particularly such as are of old Creole families, or in esteem among their fellows, are numerously attended. . .The body is mostly inclosed in a wooden shell or coffin, which during the procession to the grave, is covered with a sheet, by way of pall, and such as have it in their power, bring liquor, fruit, etc, to the house of their deceased uncle or aunt, brother or sister (the common appellations, whether related in consanguinity or not), which are consumed by the company while things are getting into readiness."[37] The slave cemetery in St. John's, according to a report of 1719, was located outside the town to the north, opposite Rat Island, with the cemetery for whites just south of it.[38] Here or wherever else slaves may have been interred, mourners performed their burial ceremonies. The Reverend William Smith reported that at Nevis slaves sang at burials, got drunk and had "no sign of Devotion, calling out to the Dead Person, and asking him, Why he died, when he wanted nothing the World could afford, to support Nature?" No Antigua act regulated that part of slave funerals. Instead, thirty years before Luffman wrote, an act stated that because either "through too great Indulgence of Masters, Mistresses, Owners, Renters, and Overseers . . . or the Ambition of the Slaves themselves," slaves often held "pompous and expensive" funerals in imitation of whites, henceforth, "No Slave or Slaves, in any of the Towns . . . shall be buried after Sun-set . . . or in any other than a plain Deal-board Coffin, without any Covering or Ornament, neither shall there be worn any Scarfs or Favours at any of their Funerals." Citizens were authorized to seize slaves wearing prohibited items and deliver them to a justice, who could order a flogging not to exceed fifty lashes. Persons making arrests were to keep whatever was confiscated. In 1780 the legislature found it necessary to revive these regulations.[39] This, and Luffman's observation seven years later that slave coffins were covered with sheets, suggests that it may not have been easy to enforce these laws that were meant to maintain a social distinctiveness even in death between whites and blacks.

There were also on the statute books regulations restricting slaves' economic activities. At first they were open police laws to prevent theft. The Slave act of 1697, for example, prohibited free persons from trading with slaves "for any Sugar Cotton or Tobacco, or Any other goods whatever (except ground provisions or fruit) without leave given from the Owner . . . by himself or his note, or Some white person, which note, or white person Shall Specify what goods provisions or fruit he Shall so Sell and the quantitie." While the 1702 act kept this clause, it did not make specific exception of ground provisions or fruit.[40]

Slaves, who produced various items for sale or exchange at home in kitchen gardens attached to their quarters or in small plots of marginal plantation land, did most of their trading at the slave Sunday market near Otto's Pasture at the southern end of St. John's on land belonging to John Otto Bayer, according to Luffman, "between three roads, leading to Five Islands, Bermudian Valley, and English Harbour." Writing in 1788,

Luffman said the market was "about as large again as the Royal Exchange." Some slaves also peddled wares from place to place, while others may have also participated in the daily market situated in the middle of town, according to a report of 1740.[41] "The Negroes are the only market people," wrote Janet Schaw nearly forty years later. "No body else dreams of selling provisions. Thursday is a market day, but Sunday is the grand day, as then they are all at liberty to work for themselves, and people hire workmen at a much easier rate, than on weekdays from their Masters. The Negroes also keep poultry, and it is them that raise the fruits and vegetables."[42] Luffman observed that the fruits of Antigua "are highly delicious, and surpass, in richness of flavor, those of the neighbouring islands, of which the pine apple, the orange, and the avocado pear, are allowed to be the principals." Other fruits included cashew nuts and apples ("which are as one fruit, when on the tree, the first being perfixed to the eye of the latter"), sapodilla, granadilla, watermelon, pomegranate, melon, citron, lime, lemon, guava, soursop, mango, tamarind, coconut, shaddock, and star-apple. Slaves also sold yams, edda, Indian corn, poultry, and pigs.[43] Contemporaries often claimed that the slave market encouraged slaves to steal what they could not cultivate themselves for sale, and there was some truth in this, for not all plantations could afford to devote surplus land to cultivation by slaves on their own account.

In Antigua, as elsewhere in the sugar islands, the slaves' critical role in the island's internal economy through attachment to plots of land on which they produced commodities, or their deep involvement in the Sunday market, was both accommodation to the slave system and resistance to it, serving both masters and slaves in obvious and not so obvious ways. Sidney Mintz, who has studied Caribbean internal marketing systems in great depth, has argued that slave subsistence cultivation and marketing were creative adaptations or accommodation to the way in which the slave system worked, and that from one point of view these adaptations "contributed to a more harmonious relationship between slaves and free men, and thus may have served at times to reduce slave resistance to the regimen of slavery itself." Resistance, that is, largely of a kind not directly tied to slaves' involvement in the internal economy; for that involvement itself was, according to Mintz, "no innate predisposition to the capitalist spirit so much as oppressed poor persons, struggling for survival and dignity in the face of very burdensome constraints." Resistance and accommodation in this sense were interwoven intricately. As Mintz has concluded, "in slave societies, the ability to accumulate, like the ability to bequeath, becomes a symbol of freedom; where patrimony can lend dignity to genealogy, individual accumulation can mean individual identity. Because the internal market system, like the subsistence cultivation that underlay it, made such accumulation possible, its growth attests to no instinctive desire for barter or for gain, but to the unquenchable human spirit of the slaves who nourished it."[44]

An early nineteenth-century print, *Negroes Sunday-Market at Antigua*[45] (see frontispiece), captured in one way what John Luffman vividly described in another in the late eighteenth century. According to this observant visitor, "the assemblage of many hundred negroes and mulattoes" would begin to form "by daybreak and the market is generally crouded by ten o'clock," the best time to buy the week's supply of nonperishable items. "The noise occasioned by the jabber of the negroes, and the squalling and cries of the children basking in the sun," Luffman added, "exceeds any thing I ever heard in a London market." The stench was "intolerable, proceeding from the strong effluvia, naturally arising from the bodys of these people, and from the stinking salt-fish and other offencibles sent for sale by hucksters, which the negroes will buy, even when in the last stage of rotteness, to season their pots with." Luffman remarked that one could smell "the fragrance of this place" a quarter of a mile downwind. About three in the afternoon activity in the market began to subside "when the hucksters shops are filled, and their doors crouded, and new rum grog is swilled in large quantities to the benefit of retailers and destruction of the negroes." Many slaves hung about town diverting themselves by dancing, playing dice and staging fights in Otto's Pasture. "They are punishable by law for fighting," Luffman noted, "but the law seldom interferes." However, the "sight of a gun, or a white man, laying about him with a whip, will disperse them immediately; and a negroe durst not return a blow, under the forfeiture of their right hand."[46] At the end of the day the slaves straggled home.

We must remember that Luffman wrote during the 1780s, by which time many laws passed earlier for controlling slaves were not enforced. This was certainly the case with those governing slaves' activities on Sundays. The slave act of 1702 had outlawed fighting, for example, and drinking in grogshops, but these obviously went on in Luffman's time. It would seem, further, that in the early eighteenth century the Sunday market was to end by ten in the morning at the latest. "To the intent that all Opportunities of Idleness and Robbery may be taken away," the act declared, all slaves "though with a Ticket or other Leave from their Owners or Possessors" should not be found trading in any of the Towns after ten o'clock. Slaves caught doing so were to be whipped and redeemed by their owners in the manner prescribed for runaways. Economic restrictions imposed by this early act did little to restrain slaves, for in 1712 the assembly complained that "a very great Evil may Attend the Negros planting Cotton in Such ground as their Masters allow them to plant provisions in." If these industrious slaves continued to grow cotton, whites obviously bought some, breaking the law of 1702 against such trade. But this was not the danger that concerned the assembly; rather, it was because "the said practice not onely Encourages theft, but lessens the price of sd Commodity," according to a complaint that several poor white cultivators lodged. Subsequent legislation would doubtless have had to take into account not simply slave theft but also economic competition between slaves and white cotton growers. The assembly indeed proposed passing new laws to prevent slaves from growing cotton and to fine people purchasing rum, sugar, molasses, and ginger from them.[47]

These laws were later incorporated into the 1723 slave act. A special clause dealt with cotton. It forbade slaveowners to allow their slaves to grow cotton, the fine for infraction being £10. Any white person, free black, or mulatto who sold cotton suspected to have been cultivated by slaves could be arrested and brought before a justice, when they were expected to take an oath that the cotton did not belong to a slave; but if they declined, the goods became the property of the informer. Free persons were prohibited from trading with unlicensed slaves for sugar, cotton, rum, molasses, ginger, and other goods, except logs of wood, firewood, crabs, fresh fish, dunghill fowls, kids, hogs, and ground provisions. Penalties for infringement reflect the legislature's determination that the new laws should be upheld. For a first conviction the fine was from £10 to £30, to be paid immediately, or a maximum jail sentence of three months so long as the fine remained unpaid. A second conviction carried a fine of from £30 to £60 or six months imprisonment, as before. But for a third conviction, the offender was to be "publickly whipped with any Number of Lashes, that the Court think proper, or be set on the Pillory once or more, as the Court shall think fit, and pay also any Fine, not exceeding one hundred Pounds, nor less than sixty Pounds, lawful Money of this Island, and being unable, refusing, and neglecting to pay the Fine immediately, shall be committed to close Custody in the Common Gaol . . . for one whole Year, unless he shall thence sooner redeem himself" by paying the fine and fees. Trading with slaves for stolen goods was also declared a misdemeanor for a first conviction, punishable by a fine of from £20 to £100 and imprisonment for not more than a year. Fines were payable forthwith; if they were not paid, the court could at its discretion order either a whipping or the pillory. A second conviction condemned the offender as a felon to be punished as such. Stolen goods in the possession of any person were presumed to have been supplied by slaves; if it was not possible to identify the slave, the indictment would simply state "from slave unknown."[48] If this law worked, it would have helped prevent thefts by both free persons and slaves, but it was aimed at the latter.

In 1733 the Antigua council drew special attention to slave theft. "Wee are of opinion," the council told the assembly, "that the permitting Negroes and other Slave to sell all manner of live Stock and Guinea Corn in the Ear or in Grain is a very great encouragement to thieving and a very great prejudice to the Planters." The council believed that the only effective remedy would be to authorize persons by law to confiscate "all Live Stock and Guinea Corn in the Ear or in Grain" found in the possession of slaves outside plantations and without ticket from their owners. Some people had objected that such a law would encourage mischievous persons to take away tickets and then rob slaves of their goods, as had often happened in the past before a similar law was repealed in 1723; but the council proposed that the master's sworn statement or that of his overseer that the slave had been issued a ticket should suffice "to prove the Accusation of the Negroe and make the Person accused by the Negroe liable to Restitution and what farther Punishment shall be thought proper." While they were as keenly interested in curbing theft, the assembly interestingly enough would not go along, explaining that "tho' Some inconvenience may attend the Suffering" slaves selling livestock and corn, "Yet we Apprehend many greater would Attend the prohibition proposed."[49] What these were they did not say.

By the second half of the eighteenth century, economic restraints against slaves were steadily evolving into what would become, in Goveia's words, "a comprehensive and restrictive system of economic control" by the end of the century. A law of 1757, for example, in order to obstruct the slaves' traffic in stolen goods, prohibited hawkers and peddlers from selling "Goods, Wares, and Merchandizes of any Sort, in Baskets, Boxes, or Trunks, or otherwise" except "salted Beef and Pork, salt Fish, Bread, and Biscuit, as shall be sold in the Negro-Market on the usual and customary Days." Only special items could be hawked including "cordial Waters or strong Waters (Rum excepted) fresh Provisions, feathered Fowl, Fruits, Roots, and Vegetables of the Earth." Another law of the same year prohibited the employment of slaves "in selling or disposing of any Goods, Wares, or Merchandizes, in Shops or otherwise (Surgeons, Apothecaries, and Druggists excepted, for the making and disposing of their Drugs, and not otherwise)." The fine for infraction was £5.[50]

By the 1760s these regulations and others were part of a legal system that had been developing in Antigua for the systematic control of the slave population since their first introduction into the island. The major slave acts and other statutes, building upon custom and opinion supporting slavery, defined the status and role of slaves and criminal behavior on their part. The law emphasized corporal punishments carried out in public, a presentation of theater for conspicuous display of authority. As in the North American colonies, the "procedural law of slave crimes was designed to expedite the punishment of slaves (or their exoneration if they were found innocent) so as to diminish costs to the whole community, and to assure masters of a fair hearing for their property."[51] Clearly, the law was more concerned with the rights of slaveowners, and not of slaves. In regard to trial procedure, according to the slave act of 1702, slaves accused of minor offenses (misdemeanors) involving damages of less than £6 were to receive summary trial before one justice, and if found guilty were to be punished with a public whipping at the discretion of the justice; "but if the Crime be heinous or the Damage greater than six Pounds" (felonies or capital offenses), the accused would be jailed by a justice, who could take security at his discretion, and later, along with another justice, try the slave. Justices were to pronounce sentence according to the gravity of the crime, "and forthwith issue out their Warrant for executing the said Sentence." In the trial of capital cases the 1723 slave act made one modification: if the two justices "before whom Negroes are tried cannot agree in their Judgement, then they may and shall immediately call a third Justice of the Peace to their Assistance, and the Case shall be determined by the Agreement of any two of them." At all slave trials, slave evidence was permissible and credited only as the Justices "shall think it in conscience deserves."[52] Slave evidence against free persons was inadmissible, and this, of course, worked to the great disadvantage of slaves.

7

Regulating Runaways and Freedmen

Most of the police regulations in the Antigua slave codes dealt with the occasionally disquieting problem of runaways. More than its predecessors of 1697 and 1702, the act of 1723 was passed, as its title implies, because of an alarming increase in the number of runaways and the crimes they allegedly committed. On at least two counts desertion was a menace to be curbed: it deprived slaveowners of their property, and it unquestionably added to the difficulties of maintaining law and order. Many fugitives did not simply take flight never to be heard of again, but also plagued the community by encouraging other slaves to desert, by boldly robbing and assaulting travelers on the highways, and by taking away whatever they needed from the plantation, frequently with the cooperation of resident slaves.

The slave laws encouraged whites to hunt down and capture runaways. According to the act of 1702, anyone capturing runaways was obliged to surrender them to their owners if known or be fined forty shillings; if owners were not known, captives were to be handed over to the marshal. Persons delivering runaways to their rightful owners were entitled to three shillings' reward paid by owners, and nine pence for each mile covered from the place of capture. Owners refusing to pay up were liable to be fined forty shillings plus the fees denied the captor. In order that runaways should be speedily delivered to their rightful owners or the provost marshal, the law imposed a fine of twelve shillings a day for detaining them longer than twenty-four hours; the fine was doubled, however, if the fugitives were tradesmen.[1]

It is not difficult to see that these regulations recognized both property rights in slaves and the pressing need to check running away. Had the law not upheld the sanctity of private property as it did, runaways could have been detained with impunity and put to work, and indeed, slaves who were not runaways could have been easily seized on the pretext that they were, or conniving whites could have found ways of helping slaves to desert. Noting that many people habitually detained slaves "so cunningly and secretly that Evidence of white Persons cannot be had" against them, the act of 1723 sought a solution through reinforcement of regulations passed in 1702 that made it an act of robbery to seize another's legally owned slave who was not a fugitive. To attempt to remove such slaves from Antigua, or to succeed in doing so, or to entice them away from their owners, was considered a felony. The marshal and his deputy were also prohibited from detaining runaways after their owners had settled the required fees.[2]

By law, persons hunting down and killing runaways were not liable to prosecution, neither could they be prosecuted for killing a slave caught stealing. In all cases where slaves were killed or executed by law or banished, owners were compensated out of public funds, as in some of the North American colonies (with the exception of New York, New Jersey and Pennsylvania, where compensation came out of a special fund to which only slaveowners had contributed). In the latter colonies, therefore, the system of compensation did not amount to subsidization of slaveowners and slavery as it did in Antigua and the rest, where, it must be remembered slaveowning legislators themselves had enacted the law regarding compensation. These men did not act against their own best interests by supporting "a severe disciplinary system which included widespread use of capital punishment." Most masters were aware of the relative merits of punishments and rewards in regard to slave discipline and productivity. What they needed, in the words of Robert Fogel and Stanley Engerman, were "devoted, hard-working, responsible slaves who identified their fortunes with the fortunes of their masters." In cases where rewards had clearly not produced compliant behavior and slaves committed serious crimes, masters acquiesced in their trial and execution because of guaranteed compensation, supporting compensation to protect their economic interest while disciplining their slaves. In Antigua, and other slave colonies, compensation may have encouraged some owners "to bring their offending Slaves to Justice, and Concealment of. . .Crimes. . .prevented," but little benefit could be derived if replacements were difficult to find, especially by those badly in need of them.[3] The effectiveness of compensation would therefore depend upon a combination of factors, such as the state of the slave market with respect to number, quality, and price; slaveowners' perception of the seriousness of existing patterns of resistance; or whether they wanted to protect their slaves or go through the trouble of prosecution and later replacement. In Antigua, where planters frequently complained about the irregular arrival of slave cargoes, and where the market in island-slaves was not very lively, they must have often had to struggle against a strong temptation to conceal slave crimes.

During the 1720s, when slave cargoes arrived more regularly, the number of prosecutions for various felonies grew proportionately. The case of runaways is illustrative. Improving on the law of 1702 that had awarded a flat £18 compensation for runaways executed, the act of 1723, no doubt at least partly because of rising slave prices and partly to encourage prosecution of a growing number of offenders, compensated masters at the full value of the slaves appraised by two white freeholders who knew them.[4] Appraisers would have had to take several details into account, including the slave's age, sex, occupation, probable health, and perhaps also ethnic background, in arriving at a valuation. The records show that the number of owners petitioning the legislature for compensation for executed runaways increased from 2 in 1723 and 3 in 1724 to 19 in 1725, when the legislature passed a new act pointing out that compensation had "amounted to Great Sums, and thereby encouraged too frequent and too rigorous Prosecutions."[5] The number of slaves landed from 1723 to 1725 was 2,539 (see table 4.5), with 1,525, or about 60 percent, arriving in 1725 alone; less than 1,000 arrived in 1723 (584) and 1724 (430). Guaranteed full appraised value and supplied with a sizable number of slaves, slaveowners in Antigua chose not to oppose prosecution of rebellious slaves. At the same time the legislature took firm steps for hunting down fugitives. Upon reconsidering compensation in 1725, the legislature now decided upon a payment ceiling: £35 for male and £30 for female runaways. For owners whose slaves carried a higher value such payments disguised a penalty. The legislature also ruled that where runaways deserted in gangs of ten or more and remained at large for ten or more days, any one of them over sixteen years whom the magistrates considered to be "the greatest offender" could be executed, and the owner was entitled to full compensation at appraised value.[6] Clearly another way of reducing compensation expenditure, this provision also restated the clause of the 1723 act that had implied that compensation mounted because of the large number of slaves who ran away "upon slight or no Occasions. . . and absent themselves in Gangs. . .to the ruining and impoverishing of their owners. . .and to the Terror and Danger" of the inhabitants. Authorized payments for individual runaways were close to the average market price of slaves, which in 1726 was about £18 sterling or £28 16s. in the Leeward Islands.[7]

On the subject of runaways, the slave act of 1702 directed the provost marshal to receive all such slaves delivered and, like owners, he was obliged to pay the captor three shillings, and nine pence for every mile covered from the place of capture. He was also responsible for keeping runaways in safe custody and preparing a list showing the slave's name, age, and owner, to be posted on the prison door. If they were not claimed after three months, runaways could be sold at auction, and any money left after the marshal's fees were paid became the property of the slave's owner if known; if unknown, the treasurer retained it until the owner appeared. More than fifty years later, in 1757, the legislature observed in an act that the mere listing of runaways on the prison door was insufficient notification "detrimental to the Owners of new Negroes so run-away, by Reason of the Prison or Gaol being out of the common and ordinary Sight of Owners of Negroes." The act therefore directed that in addition to the lists, the provost marshal or his deputy was to place runaway notices in the public gazette within six days of receiving runaways. In one respect these notices improved on the lists, for if a fugitive's master was not known, a full description of the slave, appearing in the gazette, might help locate him. Gazette notices were to be published every month the slave remained unclaimed.[8]

The entire procedure for advertising imprisoned runaways placed a heavy responsibility on the marshal that he could not easily shirk. Indeed, he could be penalized for allowing fugitives to escape. Some of the responsibility for controlling slaves also fell on all free persons. Through the slave laws and other police measures they, white or black, slaveowners or not, were "coerced as individuals by the popularly elected legislatures toward maintenance of a private tyranny which was conceived to be in the community interest."[9] As for the slaves themselves, they were expected to know what they could and could not do. Obviously, it would have taken newly arrived Africans some time to learn what was expected of them and shape their behavior accordingly if they were so inclined. Partly for this reason, indeed, a law of 1702 described the death penalty prescribed in a 1681 act for runaways absent for three or more months as "too severe, by reason of new ignorant Slaves."[10] The real reason, however, was probably to prevent a drain on treasury funds. In 1688 Lieutenant Governor Edward Powell was quite prepared to repeal the law "as it exhausts the King's revenue." Fourteen years later the repealing act laid down that runaways at large for the same period were to be punished "with Death, Loss of Limb, or Member, or publick Whipping" at the discretion of two justices, who presumably would now take into account how long the fugitives had been in the island.[11]

Desertion reached alarming proportions during the early 1720s. The slave act of 1723, passed just two weeks before Christmas and ordered to be read yearly on the Sunday before Christmas Day in all churches and chapels and also at the head of all militia regiments, was meant to remedy the intolerable situation whereby, as expressed in its preamble, "the Laws now in Force for the better Government of negroes and Slaves, and for punishing such as do withdraw from the Service of their masters have proved too mild and gentle to curb and restrain them." Slaves, the act declared, "have so abused the Lenity of the Laws, that great Numbers of them have deserted the Service of their Masters, and fled to the Mountains and Rocky Parts of this Island, and have armed and assembled themselves in Bands to oppose their Masters, and any that come in pursuit of them." After dark, "when they cannot be easily discovered or taken," these fugitives "do frequently commit divers Thefts and Robberies in the Plantations, . . .to the insupportable Wrong and Damage of many of His Majesty's good Subjects." Fugitives also enticed other slaves to run away and join them, "and it is much to be apprehended their Numbers will greatly increase, without the Aid of some Law to give extraordinary Encouragement for the taking their Chiefs or Ringleaders, and inflicting condign Punishment upon such as shall be taken."[12] The legislature supported naming ring-leaders in the act, but "as we would be tender of the lives of Slaves & not Condemn them in this manner without very good Reasons," they asked that a committee be formed to examine "such persons on oath as desire to have their negroes attainted." Samuel Martin intended to include his slave New Quamina, who, however, returned home before this could be done. Finally, the following slaves were named in the act as having "for a long Time past headed several armed fugitive Slaves, and do all that in them lies to entice other Negroes to desert their Master's Service, and join with them, and have themselves committed, and been the Occasion of committing, many flagrant Thefts and Felonies": Sharper, belonging to Vallentine Morris, Africa, belonging to Henry Lyons, John Gunthorpe's Papa Will, and Francis Carlile's Frank.[13]

The act attainted these four of felony, declaring that if they did not return to their owners within thirty days of its publication, they were to suffer death upon warrant to the provost marshal or his deputy from any two justices. At the same time, rewards were posted for their capture after the period of grace. Any persons, slave or free, who captured and delivered these notorious runaways alive into the custody of the marshals or the gaol keeper, or could prove they had killed them, were entitled to a reward of £20. Other runaways who had spent one year on the island and had deserted for a consecutive three-month period, or a total of six months spread over several absences in two years, were declared felons and were also to suffer death unless they returned to their owners within three months of the act's publication, which would earn them a pardon for "all Crime and Crimes (Murder only excepted) by him or them heretofore committed, or which shall be committed before Notice of this Act by him, her, or them had." Here again, as in 1702, the legislators perhaps recognized that it would take some time (in their estimation one year) before recent arrivals were sufficiently acculturated to understand what constituted correct behavior for slaves. Two runaways, Jack and a female slave Mimba, who had attempted to poison Giles Blizard, an infant, were specifically mentioned as exceptions, ranking with runaway murderers. And because it was partly through their neglect that "the Laws are rendered ineffectual, and Negroes and Slaves grow more insolent and ungovernable," the act ordered justices to take their duties more seriously or be fined.[14]

The act encouraged hunting down fugitives. The rewards for taking a runaway dead or alive after thirty days of the act's posting was £3 and £6 respectively, provided the runaway had been in Antigua for at least a year and had escaped for three or more months; if the slave had been at large for between two and three months, the reward was twenty eight shil-lings.[15] Justices were authorized to use discretion in the number of lashes when ordering a public whipping on the bare back for slaves found guilty of concealing or assisting fugitives in any way. For a first offense of this kind committed by free persons the fine was £10, for a second £20, and for a third £50. Moreover, they were liable to prosecution under the regulations of the act of 1702, which specified certain fines for detaining the slave of another. If they could not pay their fines, they were to be imprisoned for a maximum of two months for the first offense, four months for a second, and six months for a third. Slaveowners were allowed by law to enter slave houses and search for their runaways. Even without a warrant, they could force an entry, provided they first notified the proprietor. If neither the proprietor nor any member of the plantation's white management was present, any white person found on the premises should be notified. The act forbade hindering such a search for runaways. The colonel, lieutenant colonel, major, or captain of the militia, and also the justices, were also authorized, when they received reports of runaway hideouts, "to raise and arm any Number of Men not exceeding twenty, to apprehand alive, or kill such run-away or fugitive Slaves." As usual, whites refusing to join in these raids were fined, but they were permitted to send other well-armed white men in their places. Slaves themselves were often members of these parties, and those killed or maimed were paid for by the public.[16]

These police regulations and others detail part of the network of controls in which the slaves' lives were enmeshed. They emphasized deterrence through harsh punishment, and many slaveowners believed the harsher the better. In 1724 the assembly disagreed with the lieutenant governor and council that the act of 1723 was excessively harsh because justices were not permitted to inflict "less punishment for running away than Death tho the crimes are much greater in some than others." Here again, it must be noted, the burden of compensation expenditure influenced the council's assessment, for they recommended that "the Magistrates have power to take of a Limb or inflict any other punishment they shall judge proper according to the nature of the offence by which means the Publick will be eased of a great charge." But the assembly would not budge, maintaining that "the good effects of that Severity have been plainly seen, & we have great reason to imagine there will be dayly fewer Objects to exercise it on." Moreover, "the amendment now proposed. . .was found a very great defect in the former Negro Act" of 1702.[17] In the end, as we have seen, the two branches of the legislature compromised in 1725 by keeping the death penalty but standardizing runaway compensation.

The assembly had hoped that unwavering application of the death penalty would have at least reduced running away, but they were sorely disappointed, for by 1727 compensation expenditure was still heavy enough to force the council once again to recommend penalties short of execution for slaves at large for at least three months. Of course, to the cost of executing fugitives were added payments for their capture alive or if "killed in pursuit," as well as payments for slaves executed for various felonies. In an address to the assembly in December 1727, the lieutenant governor observed that the "excessive charge the Publick has been at in Executing Negros for running away and other felony's Calls for our Serious Consideration and Redress and in my Opinion 'tis more agreable to Justice that the Magistrates should have a discretionary power to shew mercy to those that are less Culpable by taking of a limb or disabling them some other way." He also felt that "As the Country is at the charge of paying six pounds for taking those [fugitives] that are Convicted 'Tis reasonable the master should refund the money since he has the benefitt of it which otherwise would be of little Value to him." Along similar lines the council advised that "in imitation of our neighbors in the French islands," fugitives deserving execution should be "hamstringed in one legg at the choice of the owner, by which means the slave so hamstringed will be incapable of running away and may be very useful to his owner and a great expense saved to the publick." One "living instance constantly before their Eyes," the council reasoned, "would have a better Effect on the Slaves then many Executed who are no more thought on." In 1728 the council also tried to introduce standard payments of £35 for a male and £30 for a female slave executed for felony, which, if adopted, would have extended to other felonies payments standardized for fugitives in 1725.[18]

That plan recognized the ill consequences of too frequent prosecution of slaves but, perhaps more importantly, prosecution purely for the sake of obtaining compensation. The lieutenant governor and council had mentioned to the assembly in March 1727 that "some persons have made an ill use of the power the law Gives them over the lives of their Slaves, by executing some when they were past their labour and absented themselves without any notice taken thereof by their Master untill the last law [of 1725] was made." Before that law was passed it seems clear that some slaveowners reasoned that it was not worthwhile to prosecute unproductive, old, and decrepit fugitives because not much compensation could be obtained at full appraised value.[19] But when the new law set standard compensations, slaveowners who would have lost money on fugitives of higher appraisable value now tried to profit by vigorously prosecuting even slaves of low value, some of whom were genuine fugitives, while many others had simply wandered off perhaps to be with friends or relatives who were more supportive than masters, or simply to make some kind of life of their own. Prosecution of such alleged fugitives helps throw some light on the precariousness of their lives.

By the 1720s, while slaveowners were compensated for executed runaways according to specific regulations, they were paid by custom for slaves convicted of other serious crimes. The legislature had passed an act in 1669 awarding compensation at appraised value in such cases, but it was repealed in 1682 because it had "been found by Experience to be very prejudicial to the Interest of all the Inhabitants of this Island," in exactly what way there was no mention. Since that time the island had been without an act, until 1730, when the legislature passed a new act awarding compensation for all slaves convicted of felony since 1726, but not yet paid for, at the standard rates for individual runaways. However, slaves executed for "Treasons, or Murders, or other Felonies" would henceforth be compensated for at appraised value. Taking a firm stand, the act also penalized slaveowners for attempting to conceal murders their slaves committed and for neglecting to prosecute them after knowing about such cases for three months. Reinforcing a clause in the act of 1723, the act stipulated that if any other person prosecuted the slave offenders and they were convicted, he, instead of owners, would receive the compensation money, provided prosecution began within thirty days following the three months allowed owners for initiating proceedings of their own. On this point the 1669 act had said that if the owner consented or was accessory to a slave felony, or if he did not make a report twenty-four hours after knowing about it, he would not only forfeit compensation but would also be tried as accessory and suffer the necessary penalties.[20]

Retreating from its firm support of execution for deserving fugitives nine years later, the assembly in 1739 proposed an imaginative and less brutal alternative to the hamstringing of such slaves—that if they were "Condemned to Chains, and Kept upon the Public Works, and the Owner paid for them as if Executed It would not only be of Service to the Country, but a greater Terror to Runaways than by being Executed."[21] As before, when the assembly had inflexibly supported execution, the implication was still that expenditure on fugitives would come down and stay down if slaves were terrorized into not running away. For these men slaves could be cowed only through gross intimidation.

That the lieutenant governor and council could have considered routine mutilation of offenders as a possible deterrent to slave flight and as a less costly form of punishment helps illustrate, perhaps, how the power relationship of slavery brutalized all parties concerned in the long run. This tendency must also have come to the attention of even the imperial authorities, for, in preparing instructions for Christopher Codrington the younger as governor of the Leeward Islands at the end of the seventeenth century, they urged him not only to encourage masters to Christianize their slaves but also to "endeavor to get a law restraining inhuman severities and punishing the wilful killing of Indians and negroes with death." Codrington replied with customary candor that the instruction "I am most inclined I shall be least able to observe." He knew slaveowners would oppose him. "I have always thought it very barbarous that so little care should be taken of the bodies and so much of the souls of our poor slaves," he stated plainly, for truly, few masters were interested in converting their slaves. Their plight "has cost me many a mortifying reflection," observed Codrington, "and yet I know not how I shall be able to mend it in any one respect but feeding my own slaves well. I shall be certainly opposed by all the Planters in general if I should go about to secure their limbs and lives by a law, though I will certainly recommend something of the kind, but much more if I should promote the baptizing of all our slaves."[22] His father, also called Christopher, whom he had succeeded as governor, had been successful only in having a clause inserted in the 1697 slave act that "whosoever shall willfully, inhumanly, or bloodily murder a Slave, shall forfeit for the fact, Ten thousand pounds of sugar to the King, for the public use, besides paying the owner." If unable to pay, the offender was to receive thirty-nine lashes by order of two justices "on the bare back and Six months imprisonment without bail, besides four years Service to the Owner, and if a Servant, (besides whipping and imprisonment) four years Service after free from his master." This was certainly not the death penalty, but one may also wonder if even this law was enforced, because in the new act of 1702 such a clause was conspicuously absent. Codrington the younger, then, had not been able to persuade his slaveowning legislators to impose the death penalty, or even some other, for willfully murdering a slave. Every governor during the first six decades of the eighteenth century also failed. So, severe punishment of slaves continued, and sadistic slaveowners who had reason to defend their conduct could point to a clause in the act of 1702, originally passed in 1697, that "if any Slave lose Life or Limb by Punishment for a Crime, by his master, or the Justice's Order, No Person shall be liable to the law, for the same."[23]

When the slave act of 1723 was being prepared, Governor Hart said, he had used his "utmost Endeavours to make the Murdering a Slave Punishable with Death, but could not gett it past in such a Manner, nor in any other than as It is now sent Your Lordships. . . And I take it as it is to be a great Point gain'd; there being no Law before this, that laid any Penalty on Offenders for the Crimes mention'd." In explaining why the act had been passed, Hart noted that in addition to curbing running away and policing slaves more effectively, the next major reason was "to prevent the Inhumane Murdering, Maiming and Castrating of Slaves by Cruel and Barbarous Persons (as has been too much practiced)."[24] The act stated that "several cruel Persons, to gratify their own Humours, against the Laws of God and Humanity, frequently kill destroy, or dismember their own and other Persons' Slaves, and have hitherto gone unpunished, because it is inconsistent with the Constitution and Government of this Island, and would be too great a Countenance and Encouragement to Slaves to resist White Persons, to set Slaves so far upon an Equality with the free Inhabitants, as to try those that kill them for their Lives." While it was true, the act went on, that slaveowners were not tried for their lives in the British Caribbean, several of these territories had laws inflicting lesser penalties that were "very effectual in deterring Persons from such Crimes." The act then directed that free persons wilfully killing or causing to be killed any slaves "in any such Manner as is not excusable by the Laws of Great Britain, or allowed by the Laws of this Island, whether the same be by excessive Punishment or otherwise, or shall geld or dismember" the slaves, would be prosecuted. And if convicted they could be fined from £100 to £300 for killing the slave, and from £20 to £100 for "Gelding or Dismembering." In both cases, offenders would be "imprisoned till Said Fine paid, and all due Fees, and find Sureties for their good Behaviour for one year" provided they had been prosecuted within a year of committing the offense. They would also have to pay the party wronged (the slaveowner, not the slave) double damages and costs. Persons informing on offenders who were later convicted were entitled to half the imposed fines.[25]

Although the principle of protection of the slave is expressed in the preamble to these provisions, some severe punishments in the 1702 act, such as the slitting of a slave's nose, or dismemberment, or execution by the state for wounding a white person, remained in force. The real intent of the 1723 measures was not so much to prevent the brutal punishment of slaves for their own good but to control situations that could generate slave unrest or hostility. As Goveia has written, "regulations were often intended to control behaviour which was held to be impolitic as well as inhumane."[26]

Into this category of regulations fell those related to slave manumissions. Rowland Ash explained to the absentee Tudway proprietor in 1759 that recent deaths among old and infirm slaves on Parham Plantation "cannot be deem'd any loss, but rather a gain as publick and parish taxes were charg'd on their heads equal with the ablest." The same kind of profit-related reasoning also lay behind the liberation and abandonment of many such slaves by their owners. Some owners cast such bondmen adrift to shift for themselves, thus contributing to the appearance of numbers of black vagrants. In 1757 the legislature passed laws to restrain these manumissions. Now, when slaves were freed, their former owners were obliged to furnish them with shelter and sufficient food or clothing; and if these blacks were found begging or wandering about, such owners could be fined from £5 to £20; so too could any slaveowner whose unfree disabled bondman was found doing the same.[27] It is not clear in what ways these laws affected manumission of slaves without the disabilities mentioned or the size of the free black population. Certainly, however, they extended some protection to slaves who, for one reason or another, were no longer productive, but at the same time it obviously policed them.

These slaves, however, did not pose as many problems to law and order as did runaways, whose activities were so potentially disruptive that by mid-century, indeed in the same act regulating manumission of disabled slaves, new laws or restrictions were passed to prevent detention and employment of fugitives. The old laws of 1702 had been openly flouted. The act of 1757 declared, for example, that "a Custom hath prevailed . . . for permitting slaves to go about the Towns and Country to hire themselves or take their own Liberty and pay their Masters and Mistresses for their Time, by which Means many Negroes, who were actually Runaways, under Pretence of working out, or being at Liberty to hire themselves, have been employed in the Towns or Country unknown to their Masters or Mistresses, and often Robberies are committed by such slaves." In legislation that followed, what may at first glance appear to be efforts to control hiring out and employment of slaves were really meant to make it more difficult for fugitives to remain at large undetected. But obviously, since the two situations were connected, it was possible to get at one only through the other. Slaveowners were prohibited from permitting their slaves "to go at large, and be at Liberty to hire him or herself out, and to seek for Business or Employment of any Kind, either in Town or in the Country." Neither could they lawfully "take or receive from any Slaves or Slave any Sum or Sums of Money, or other Consideration, for allowing or giving up such Slave his or her own Time." The fine for infraction of these laws against slave self-hiring was between £5 and £10. Persons employing or paying slaves without their owners' consent faced a fine of £5 in addition to other penalties "already inflicted by former Laws." Slaves caught wandering about in search of employment or selling goods without their masters' consent could be taken before a justice, who was authorized to have them whipped with not more than fifty lashes, but this provision did not affect slave porters in the towns provided they "do always carry a Badge, made of a broad Piece of Lead, hung around . . . their Necks, with the word PORTER marked or stamped on it, and that they always have a Ticket" signifying their owners' permission to work. Blacks must have dominated this occupation and turned it to their own advantage because the act encouraged free persons to report to any justice slave porters who refused to work "by the Day or by the Job" or who charged exorbitant rates. Offending slaves were to be punished "at Discretion, according to the Heinousness of the Offence."[28] All of these repressive regulations limited slaves' economic maneuverability, making it difficult for many of them to be gainfully employed or to elude the law, if they were runaways.

The numerous laws passed since the seventeenth century dealing with runaways indicate that running away was a persistent problem, serious enough sometimes to alarm authorities, and that some whites who stood to gain often had a hand in it. But these laws delineate principally the control dimension of running away, raising rather than answering questions about it as a form of slave resistance.

Many resourceful fugitives successfully passed as freedmen. Possibilities for success increased during the second half of the eighteenth century when the free nonwhite population had grown much larger than a mere handful, but it was always hazardous in small communities, in which concealment was difficult. Free Negroes and mulattoes, when challenged, had to prove their status. In a society influenced by strong sentiments of race and class, fugitives passing as free quickly discovered they had merely exchanged the rigors of slave life for those of free Negroes and mulattoes, whom whites generally regarded as a step away from slavery, whether free born or freed. In practice they were "slaves without masters,"[29] and because they embodied an implied threat to the social order of masters and slaves, whites believed they should be subordinated along with slaves and in other ways linked with them. This was obviously the intention of provisions in the 1697 and 1702 slave acts for regulating "all Free Negroes, Mulattoes, or Indians." Reports on this intermediate social group often lump those of mixed ancestry and Africans as free Negroes, while at other times the first are differentiated as mulattoes. To avoid confusion in the use of terms, *freedmen* will be used as a general referent to include all free nonwhites, and one must bear in mind that if Indians are taken into account, their percentage probably became negligible quite rapidly after 1700.

From the early decades of colonization to about the middle of the eighteenth century, few slaves appear to have been freed, but, if extracts of wills in Oliver's *History of Antigua* are any guide, attitudes towards manumission may have become more favorable later — perhaps because of the development of a more humane attitude to slaves — the number of freedmen rising from a mere 18 in 1707 (12,892 slaves, 2,892 whites) to 1,230 in 1787 (36,000 slaves) and 3,895 in 1821.[30] In addition to testamentary manumission, there was also manumission through self-purchase, through free gift, or for meritorious service to the state. Freedmen could also be born into that status if their mothers were free.

In Antigua and other sugar islands, the liberty of freedmen was precarious at best. Race and color alone excluded them from the ranks of whites. They held no legal claim to civil or political rights, neither could they hold public or parochial office or serve as jurors. Only against slaves and freedmen was their evidence admissible in court; they could prosecute cases against whites only with white witnesses. Moreover, if unable to show sufficient proof of their freedom, they could slip back into slavery. Equiano talked about a case in which a free mulatto man of St. Kitts, Joseph Clipson, although born free and able to support this with a certificate, was literally kidnapped from the sloop on which he worked, his kidnapper simply telling him "he was not free and that he had orders from his master to bring him to Bermudas." Equiano said such practices were frequent. "I have since often seen in Jamaica and other islands, free men, whom I have known in America, thus villianously trepanned and held in bondage." These experiences sensitized Equiano to the peculiar quality of freedmen's freedom. "Hitherto," he explained, "I had thought slavery only dreadful, but the state of a free negro appeared to me now equally so at least, and in some respects even worse, for they live in constant alarm for their liberty; which is but nominal, for they are universally insulted and plundered, without the possibility of redress." In which case, Equiano asked suggestively, "is it surprising that slaves, when mildly treated, should prefer even the misery of slavery to such a mockery of freedom?"[31]

Still, freedmen everywhere struggled to remain free. Two Antigua cases can be cited. When doubts about her freedom arose, Phyllis, "a Negroe Woman late belonging to Major Kean Osborne deceased," took her case before the legislature in 1707. Claiming in her petition that "her late Master did on his death bed declare her from thence forward to be a free Negroe, which she is now denied of by his Executors," Phyllis asked the governor to interrogate witnesses to her manumission. Major Osborne's widow, and Lieutenant Governor John Yeamans, one of the executors, both testified to the truth of her claim and agreed she should be free. The governor then issued an order that Phyllis be "for ever hereafter manumitted, & sett free, And that she be at Liberty to go at large where she pleases." In 1707 the legislature also heard the case of Ardra, a mulatto man who claimed that, when Leeward Islands forces invaded Guadeloupe in 1703, he had deserted to their side "& came into the said Army, & that by their consent he was to have been freed, & sett at Liberty. And that upon such consideration he was never sold, or accounted for to the said Army. Yet notwithstanding, Collo. Christopher Codrington who was then Captain Generall of these Islands, & commander in Chief on that expedition, doth keep & detain him as a slave." Ardra petitioned the governor to intervene and settle the matter. After examination of evidence, the legislature declared Ardra free but required him to appear before them again, when Codrington would have an opportunity to show why he should not be free.[32]

These two cases show that if freedmen were willing to fight to remain free they could do so before the legislature. No attempt seems to have been made to prevent it. A successful petition secured them the right to freedom and full proof of it; but if unsuccessful, they would be swallowed up again into the slave class. While there is no evidence that freedmen faced forfeiture of freedom as punishment for crimes, still, because each challenge that they prove their status carried a possible threat of enslavement, they must have tried to become invisible or as inconspicuous as possible, particularly perhaps by avoiding open association with slaves. Freedmen's insecurity must have been greatest when they were few in number, and especially among those without property or those who had once been slaves. Yet, secretly, whatever their population size, they could have maintained vital ties with slaves, while working out attachments with influential whites. From the first appearance of freedmen in Antigua society, whites assumed they shared common interests with slaves, and while restricting their liberty through formal and informal controls, they hoped that they would not be driven, as Berlin as noted for free Negroes in the antebellum U.S. south, "into an insurrectionary alliance with slaves."[33]

After sixty-five years of growth and change into a fast maturing slave society, Antigua enacted its first regulations that were meant to limit the liberty of freedmen in the last three clauses of the 1697 "Act for the better Government of Slaves," the title of which, if we were to go by that alone, carried no clue that freedmen were included. White contemporaries, however, would probably have expected their inclusion. In the title of the 1702 "Act for the Better Government of Slaves, and Free Negroes" they received explicit mention for the first time because legislators were eager to pass a more comprehensive act for the control of the rapidly increasing and restless slave population, as well as of freedmen, who had to be kept in their place, even if their number was small at the time, to preserve white supremacy. Henceforth, that act was supposed to apply along with a number of other informal controls woven into the fabric of sanctioned race relations and general conduct.

The new act contained five explicit freedmen clauses. The first, clause 22, provided that "all Free Negroes, Mulattoes, or Indians, not having Land shall be obliged in thirty Days after the Date hereof to choose some Master or Mistress to live with, who shall be owned by them, and with whom they shall live, and take their Abode, to the Intent that their Lives and Conversations may be known to be called to their respective Duties." The wording of the first part of this provision had been different in 1697, referring to freedmen "who have not freehold of their Owne, or who do not live with parents being freeholders." Applicable only to the landless among the few existing freedmen, the law aimed at subordinating them to whites through attachment to surrogate masters with responsibility for their proper surveillance. White patrons therefore found themselves part of the state apparatus for the control of freedmen as well as slaves, but in reality all whites were obligated to uphold the laws that regulated freedmen. Why were landless freedmen so singled out for attention? Perhaps because without such property they could not be expected to behave as responsible, patriotic citizens with a stake in the colony's fortunes, or simply to prevent idleness and mischief. The second was certainly the intent of the provision directed at freedmen "fitt to go out to Trades." They were to be "bound Apprentice to any Person that will receive them for seven Years (unless they choose a Master or Mistress to be bound to) by the next Justice, who shall be informed of such Persons, and who is immediately to cause them to be bound, in ten Days after such Information to any willing to receive them, on Penalty of forfeiting ten Pounds."[34]

The legislature's use of the phrase "who shall be owned by them" to describe landless freedmen's attachment as virtual slaves to patrons or guardians reflected whites' negative perceptions of these people while sanctioning a new order of power relations between whites and nonwhites (alongside that between masters and slaves) that was obviously premised on the master-slave relationship. However, the real difference between freedmen who owned land and those who did not, in relation to the role whites played in their lives, now became the degree and significance of attachment to patrons; for, before 1702, all freedmen would certainly have found it to their advantage to cultivate instrumental friendships with influential whites who could help alleviate some of the burdens of their existence in increasingly race- and class-conscious Antigua. In chapter 3 we saw how the Johnson brothers, who were tried for their lives as accomplices in the 1736 slave plot, used the patronage system to help fight their case. Allowed only limited freedom, shrewd freedmen could have quickly accommodated themselves to their situation and used such friendships to carve out a meaningful life for themselves. Although such attachments would have been lopsided because of freedmen's inferior status to patrons, freedmen could exploit the reciprocal obligations they carried. In return for protection and other useful services, freedmen could reciprocate with other services, loyalty, and deference. Attachments of freedmen to whites, whether they were bound to do so by law or not, helped add another dimension to the developing apparatus for control of nonwhites through the creation of ties of dependence.[35]

Clause 22 of the new act of 1702 also provided that "if any Free Person, not being a White, Shall presume to strike a White Servant, he shall be by Order of the next Justice (on Proof of his striking) severely whipped, at the Discretion of the said Justice." Instead of *white servant* the old 1697 act had stated *white person*. Ruling that even the lowliest, subordinated white servant was the superior of any freedman, that white over black would be preserved in Antigua slave society, the new act tightened the screws of control of freedmen. But perhaps more importantly, the change of wording from *white person* to *white servant* indicated a trend toward a refining of distinctions between social groups, towards a finer tuning of class and race relations. In any case, freedmen, like slaves, were prohibited also by clause 22 from striking whites even in self-defense. According to clause 26, freedmen who were assaulted by whites should be satisfied that "on Proof thereof made to any Justice of the Peace" their attackers would be "bound over to the Sessions, and be punished at the Discretion of the Justices then sitting; any Law or Usage to the contrary notwithstanding."[36]

While all freedmen with land escaped having to find patrons by law after 1702, free Negroes (freedmen of unmixed Negro ancestry) discovered that the legislature had attacked even possession of this important asset that helped define a person's place in society and was a symbol also of independence and liberty. In clear language, clause 23 declared that "for the future no Free Negro shall be Owner or Possessor of more than eight Acres of Land, and in no Case shall be deemed and accounted a Freeholder." Surplus land was to be sold within six months or be forfeited to the crown.[37] It must be noted that these regulations, which did not apply to freedmen of mixed ancestry (mulattoes and other "brown" persons) only limited and did not prohibit altogether free Negroes' ownership of land. That restriction, however, must not have been meant simply to deny them voting rights, which could only be exercised, according to another act passed earlier the same day, by "Owners of at least 10 Acres of Land in the Country, or an House in any of the Towns," for the land restriction law established that free Negroes could not be regarded as freeholders under any circumstances. The real intent behind the restriction could have been to limit opportunities for free Negroes' independence as property owners, and perhaps also to reserve some land with which to attract white migrants to the island to expand the white population, which was not growing as fast as that of blacks. In any case, burdened with additional disabilities in regard to land ownership and voting, free Negroes were prevented from amassing the kind of property that might lead to economic independence and perhaps political influence that might weaken the white stranglehold on life in Antigua slave society.

It would appear that freedmen of mixed ancestry were allowed to own more land than free Negroes. If qualified as freeholders, could they vote? The answer is yes, and there seems to have been no need for covering legislation. In 1728, while settling a dispute over the election of Edward Chester as representative for Falmouth Division, a committee of the legislature replied affirmatively to the question of "whether Mulatto's having ten acres of land have a right to vote for assemblymen."[38] To what extent these people of mixed blood exercised their voting privilege during this early period remains unclear, however. Nor do we know precisely how being able to vote affected their status in society.

The sources do not mention prejudice against freedmen of mixed blood in the island militia; however, if our interpretation is correct, it is evident that free Negroes encountered prejudice and suffered debasement. In 1754 the "Adjutants of the several Regiments of the Militia haveing Summoned the Free Negroes . . . to Appear amongst the white People, many of whom avoid their Personal duty," whites refused to serve, preferring "to pay their Fines rather than Roll with such Negroes." In existence for years, but now for some reason more forcefully expressed, this attitude does help to show that freedmen did some kind of militia service. Indeed, there was no specific law barring them. Whatever the white militiamen's motives, however, the assembly supported them, explaining that so far as they were aware, by "the Militia Act interpreted by the general Policy of this Island, . . . such Free Negroes ought not to be Regimented with white people." Accordingly, they asked the council to join them in recommending that the governor order "all such free Negroes . . . excluded from doing duty in the Several Regiments . . . except in Cases of Alarm when they may attend as Pioneers,"[39] a role that, we have seen, was later given to slaves who accompanied British forces that invaded Guadeloupe and Martinique in the Seven Years' War.

Freedmen endured other limitations to their freedom. "The sociology of the Caribbean plantation, in ideal terms," according to Sidney Mintz, "brooked no interpenetration of the ruling and dominated classes, neither socially, nor culturally, nor genetically." Twelve years after its colonization, Antigua, alone among the British sugar islands so far as can be determined, passed a law "against Carnall coppullation between Christian and Heathen." The law was reissued in 1672. Thirty years later the Antigua slave act, partly to preserve and enforce a clear distinction between free persons and slaves and partly to prevent miscegenation, prohibited marriage between free persons (of whatever color) and slaves. This was also meant to seal off one means of open association with slaves. Ministers performing such banned marriages faced a fine of fifty pounds, while the free party paid "to the Owner of the Slave he hath married, the Sum of twenty Pounds, or be obliged by Order of two Justices to serve four Years."[40] But the ideal of class/race separation these regulations aimed at was never achieved, as the growth in the number of persons of mixed ancestry (slave and free) indicates. Neither, for that matter perhaps, did the intentions of the laws for the control of freedmen always coincide with actual practice.

Whatever the law said about interracial marriage in 1702 did not inhibit interracial sex in later years. John Singleton chastized white men in the sugar colonies for cohabiting with women who were not white. "Shun the false lure of Ethiopic charms," he urged.

> Wherein consists their beauty or their grace?
> Perhaps the dark complexion of the slave
> The eye enjoys, and in an aspect foul
> Wanton delights, enraptur'd to behold
> Deformity of features, shape and soul;
> Detested composition! Made more vile

By th'unsightly fashion of their garbs:
Or does the sable miss then please you most,
When from her tender delicate embrace
A frouzy fragrance all around she fumes?
Can such intice? For Shame! the vice reform

Singleton pleaded with white men to honor their marriage contracts instead
and not

. . .from the nuptial bed, at midnight hour,
With hasty steps depart, and leave forlorn
The pining fair, thro' the long night to sigh,
Torn with heart-rending jealousy and love![41]

But Singleton's was a voice crying in the wilderness. His treasured ideal
remained just that, impossible to achieve in island societies where interracial
sex was openly sanctioned.

Regulations against miscegenation, running away of slaves, and others
we have noted grew out of whites' concern for effective control of nonwhites,
slave and free. While freedmen, few in number compared with the slaves
throughout the slave period and dependent upon whites for advancement
and preservation of freedom, remained powerless as a group and never
directly challenged the social order, the slaves in direct and indirect ways
did pose a threat to white supremacy. Sometimes the threat was serious
enough, as in 1736, to cause great anxiety. If the majority of the restless
mass of coerced workers only outwardly conformed to what was expected
of them most of the time, their resentment was often unmasked to remind
slaveowners that it was not possible to subjugate them completely. This
undoubtedly the slave codes implicitly recognized.

III

Patterns of Slave Resistance

8

"To Make Themselves Masters of the Contry"

The control of slaves, as Frederick Cooper has observed, "was not simply a matter of physical repression, but of creating ties of dependency." Through such bonds slaveowners intended to lead slaves into accepting their moral authority over them, but in reality, dependency for most slaves was never as complete as slaveowners may have wished, since there were areas of the slaves' lives with which masters did not interfere. They simply could not control every facet of the slaves' existence in order to mold abject dependents. Moreover, it was also quite clear to both masters and slaves that masters depended heavily upon their bondmen, without whose cooperation they could not operate their plantations and other businesses. In order to win such cooperation, which many masters perceived sprang from dependency, but which from the slaves' point of view more accurately reflected a shrewd appraisal of the necessary degrees of compliance, masters wielded authority through variable combinations of fear, coercion, and negotiation. These helped determine patterns of master-slave relations and the tone of life in Antigua slave society. Masters were not therefore in control as fully as they would have liked; they were not able to extract slave compliance from a position of complete authority.

One result of this dimension of master-slave relations was that masters failed to stifle the sense of injustice or hostile feelings that slaves could act upon from time to time, in one form or another, in response to specific or more general grievances perpetrated by masters who had thereby broken the unwritten contract of mutual obligations between themselves and their bondmen. Ultimately, whatever techniques of control masters used to establish supremacy over partly dependent slaves did not make slave resistance impossible even among those who may have generally shown marked inclinations to identify with masters' interests. Such identification did not preclude the expression of hostile feelings. Instead of submitting, slaves adapted their responses in most cases to the changing conditions of life around them, struggling to make the best of their situation short of shattering their chains for collective freedom, although under propitious conditions that too would come. Emergent patterns of slave behavior in Antigua, individual and collective, are therefore best studied or illustrated in relation to the changing environment of life and labor as the society and economy developed.[1]

From the early years of emergent slave society in Antigua in the seventeenth century down to emancipation in the nineteenth, slaves engaged in resistance precipitated either by specific grievances or by a generalized disaffection aimed at destroying the system or hampering its effective operation. Most slaves were neither strictly nor unambiguously docile or rebellious. Because of the wide range of responses possible between the poles of abject submission and total resistance that reflected a delicate balance between the slaves' urge to resist and yet at the same time survive, adjustments of most slaves must be seen as infinitely more complex. Slave resistance in this sense was largely accommodative. Accommodation, as an integral part of resistance, allowed slaves to survive, to accept "what could not be helped without falling prey to the pressures for dehumanization, emasculation, and self-hatred," but at the same time it helped camouflage subversive action. Resistance in accommodation and accommodation in resistance, to use Genovese's phrase, were not beyond most slaves, who shrewdly weighed the costs, personal and collective, of different kinds of resistance. "Once the complexities of resistance and survival are aknowledged," writes Mintz, "it becomes obvious that the struggle of the slaves was a subtle, involved and delicate phenomenon." The "house slave who poisoned her master's family by putting ground glass in the food had first to become the family cook," Mintz has cogently observed. "And the slaves who plotted armed revolts in the marketplaces had first to produce for the market, and to gain permission to carry their produce there."

But it has been claimed that what is loosely called slave resistance is not resistance at all, strictly speaking, except perhaps in the case of insurrection, because resistance is a political concept denoting "organized collective action which aims at affecting the distribution of power in a community." Moreover, even though there exists an abundance of evidence on slave behavior that cannot be equated with cooperation with the slave system, it is hazardous to translate these into political resistance. Part of the difficulty, of course, lies in the absence of incontrovertible evidence pointing to the internalized processes behind the acts, the slaves' "subjective disposition" or motivation. Resistance, therefore, may not even be a particularly useful descriptive term for largely undramatic, day-to-day slave activities that harassed the plantation system. Nonetheless, as Genovese has argued, they can with justification still be regarded as a useful foundation from which slaves could develop an edifice of subversion leading to maturation in collective political resistance or insurrection. At the same time it should be understood that there is indeed a big step, a product of slave adaptation, between individual acts of defiance, however frequent, and the emergence of a collective consciousness built around such acts. Along the continuum of resistance, an important qualitative difference does emerge between individual acts of resistance and those that were collective or had collective potential; between small, uncoordinated, yet presistent acts, and collective, organized, unambiguous opposition; between elusive and openly defiant behavior.[2] Slave resistance in Antigua from the seventeenth century to 1763 spanned the continuum.

In the island of Nevis during the second half of the seventeenth century, in the time of Azariah Pinney, founder of a family sugar fortune, Richard Pares noted that the white islanders constituted "a small and close-grained society, surrounded by men of another colour, liable to sudden ruin from hurricanes, fires or French invasions, and concentrated on getting rich quick in a trying climate and a strange landscape." Pares concluded that the community "must necessarily have lived on its nerves." In Antigua and the other Leewards at the time the situation varied only in regard to detail, for the basic outlines were similar, and from an early date in the history of each island slave resistance tested the nerves of the white inhabitants. As early as 1639 whites in St. Christopher were much alarmed when a band of sixty slaves, including women, revolted in the French quarter and fled into the hills in the area then occupied by English settlers.[3]

For a number of years after colonization, Antiguan settlers passed many anxious moments preparing for and fending off Carib attacks from islands to the south, spending more time guarding than planting. The Indian factor in the island's early history made life precarious, but by the time the problem of Carib raids seemed under control, settlers faced a new threat, this time internal, from their rebellious slaves. Under frontier conditions during the first decades of the sugar revolution to the end of the seventeenth century, slavery was harsh as would-be planters raced to acquire land, labor, capital, and profit; and the growing numbers of slaves responded to harsh day-to-day treatment through various forms of resistance, most notably running away, frequently to the Antigua hill country, particularly the Shekerley Hills.

Runaways were probably at large as early as 1666, when it was reported that whites kept "strict guard for fear of the negroes." There were probably fewer than 500 slaves in the island then, but the activities of a number of escapees obviously caused concern. Anxiety increased in ensuing years as growth of the slave population and incidence of running away kept pace with each other. Some slaves reportedly fled south to the Caribs in the islands of Dominica, St. Lucia, and St. Vincent. Slave flight belongs to a category of resistance that Michael Adas has called "avoidance protest," one among a range of responses or ways in which social groups like slaves in the Americas, serfs in medieval Europe, and peasants in Russia or colonial Southeast Asia "seek to attenuate their hardships and express discontent through flight, sectarian withdrawal, or other activities that minimize challenges to or clashes with those whom they view as their oppressors."[4] Many fugitive slaves in parts of the Americas, however, invited clashes with the slavocracy through guerrilla type activities. Their avoidance protest contained an activist element.

Antigua's concern over slave fugitives was reflected in its slave laws, which were largely police regulations dealing with threats to public order, but these laws — and other sources, although scanty — point to other types of resistance. While the island remained relatively underdeveloped and wooded in the seventeenth century, when most of the slaves were Africans old and new, and slavery remained relatively harsh in these formative decades, it is not surprising that running away or escape was the predominant mode of overt resistance.

Such resistance was included among "Divers Treasonable and fellonious acts punishable with death" in 1669, when masters were awarded compensation after the slave's value had been assessed by two "indifferent" men. If, however, the master had consented or was accessory to the crime, or if, having knowledge of it, he did not make a report within twenty-four hours, he not only forfeited compensation but also became liable to trial himself. While this act was not specifically designed to repress runaways, another bearing the same date was. To prevent slaves or indentured servants from making their escape by sea, the act obliged owners or masters of small craft to secure sails, masts, oars, rudders, and other equipment while in port and to guard larger craft carefully. Owners or masters of any craft used for escape were penalized by making "good double damages to the owner of Such Servants Or Slaves So Escapeing or running away, the which damages are to be recovered in the Courts Judicatory of this Island." In 1677 the legislature passed a separate act against runaway servants that recognized a tendency for servants to entice or even force slaves (with whom they shared similar conditions of life and labor and the will to break free) to escape with them. Three years later the legislature passed a comprehensive act against runaways, which can be taken as a clue that a critical point in the evolution of running away and its treatment by the authorities had been reached.[5]

Perhaps for the first time in the short history of the developing slave society, the act of 1680 offered rewards for bringing in fugitive slaves. "Whereas," stated the preamble, "severall Negroes are now Runn away and lurk in the woods to the greate Detriment of their Owners and all the rest of the inhabitants," and "for as much as all other Collonyes have wholesome penale Laws for Restrayneing such Runnawayes," Antigua itself could benefit from similar laws. The act ordered immediate execution by the authority of two justices for all fugitives proved to have been at large for at least three months, and compensation of owners "out of the Common Stocke." Persons who captured and turned in fugitives absent for between one and three months were entitled to a reward of six hundred pounds of sugar or tobacco payable by owners if the captives did not deserve execution. If, however, the justices sentenced the slaves to death the public paid the reward. At the fixed rate of three thousand pounds of sugar or tobacco, the public also compensated owners for fugitives hunted down and killed who had been at large for any length of time. Concealment of fugitives deserving death carried a fine of five thousand pounds weight of either crop. By 1680, therefore, during the first decade or so of the sugar revolution in Antigua, runaways already caused the authorities much concern. Anxieties over fugitives would later become even more intensified before the end of the 1680s.

To understand better running away, we must attempt such minimal differentiation among runaways as the scant seventeenth-century data will allow, based on some of the general circumstances of flight. Some runaways became maroons. As generally understood, a maroon was a runaway who had escaped "the social order of the plantation to live, actually free, but as an outlaw, in areas (generally in the woods or in the mountains) where he could escape the control of the colonial power and the plantocratic establishment." Such runaways had no intention of returning to their owners or intended to stay at large as long as possible. If, as Leslie F. Manigat has pointed out, *maroon* "implies the intention, at least to attempt, to live another life outside of the social order of the plantation as a 'savage,' " then all runaways were not maroons, and all running away was not marronage. Manigat is correct that without "the decision to run wild" there cannot be true marronage. Accordingly, there could be slaves at large who had or had not made that decision for many different reasons. Maroons, far more subversive to the security of slave societies because they stood in direct opposition to the colonial powers, must be distinguished from other runaways at least temporarily motivated by separate criteria not directly threatening to the state, such as a desire to avoid work, to visit friends or relatives, or to defy the master's authority. In Antigua and other slave societies, running away of this kind amounted to a "personal conflict between master and slave," and slaveowners grew to accept it as an inescapable offshoot of slavery, a nuisance if nothing more.[6] But such runaways could become maroons or cause other problems, and legislators were careful to draw the line between running away as misdemeanor and as felony. The 1680 Antigua fugitive slave act, for example, defined a "short" absence as not more than a month; beyond that, running away was a felony.

By 1684 a number of fugitives who had every intention of remaining at large, and had therefore decided to fight rather than submit to enslavement, established a maroon camp in the Shekerley Hills. That year the deputy governor and council called for the quick routing of "Severall Runn away Negroes whoe doe much Mischief in this Island they being all ready in a great body together which may prove of Very ill Consequence to all." This development was particularly unsettling because the runaways encouraged "the Introducing of other Negroes to them upon any Slight occation from their Masters." Taking firm action, the legislature agreed to appoint suitable men to hunt them down and ordered bounties of five hundred pounds of muscovado sugar for any taken alive and two hundred pounds for any killed, payable, however, not by the public but by owners of fugitives so captured. To form a better picture of what it was up against, the legislature also recommended that slaveowners prepare lists of their fugitives.[7] What is particularly important about these developments is not that a sizable number of fugitives lurked in the hills but that these bold slaves, not content simply to remain at large, waged guerrilla warfare against whites, harassed them through their "mischief," and induced other slaves to run away and join them. Such subversive actions openly challenged the plantation order. As in Jamaica and St. Domingue, where for many years the terrain and size of these colonies facilitated formation of bands of maroons, Antigua runaways in the early 1680s, through their success in remaining at large in parts of the uncleared interior, and through direct contact with plantations especially in the island's southwest corner, fomented unrest among other slaves and greatly helped to intensify slaveowners' anxieties in regard to runaways.

The situation had obviously grown steadily more explosive by 1687, when maroons were responsible for what is believed to have been the only genuine slave insurrection in the Leewards in the seventeenth century. On February 14 the council claimed it possessed disturbing information about "a Discourse through the Contry that some Negroes of this Island have plotted and Continued to putt themselves in A bodie, and force their freedom by Destroying their Masters, and other Christian people and... hath filled the Ears and minds of the negroes in Generall wch may bee A means to putt them upon practizes not before Intended by any." For "the Better findeing outh the Truth of what hath allready past, and To prevent the Increase of further mischiefe" the governor commissioned Colonel Rowland Williams, Captain John Frye, Captain Henry Simes, and Henry Winthrop "to Enquire and Make due Inspection into the plott and Contrivance said to bee now on foote Amongst the Negroes on the south seid the Island or Elsewhere and to Cause all such Negroes as they shall finde Worthy to be Aprehended and putt into safe Custody It being absolute necessity that Severitie be used Amongst such as shall be found to have done noe more but to have Discoursed of ariseing or Anything Else Tending To such practices." The commissioners were expected to prepare weekly reports of their proceedings and findings.[8]

It is significant that the plot for a general revolt originated in the south of the island, where runaways, taking full advantage of the uneven and elevated terrain of the volcanic district still not cleared of forest cover, were most numerous and active in harassing and killing whites. Many of the first plantations and villages were established in this general area, the leeward south, and further west, where sheltered bays "offered easy access and secure anchorage for sailing ships." Settlers had first penetrated the forested lands of the volcanic district and central plain behind these inlets, and the 1678 census shows that Carlile Road or Old Road Division in the heart of the volcanic belt, one of the island's ten political divisions, contained 323 slaves or 14.9 percent of the island's total, the second largest number. Commissioners Rowland Williams and John Frye owned 74 and 26 slaves respectively in this region.[9] With the overall expansion of sugar cultivation in the island, the number of slaves in the south also increased. Growth of slave population, the existence of uncleared areas, the harsh conditions of early plantation slavery, and the slaves' will to resist when most were probably recent arrivals, helped generate conditions conducive to unrest and conspiracy to rebel.

To the authorities, runaways who had taken to the hills in the south were already in revolt, and they feared that there might really be a plot afoot for a general uprising led by these rebels. The flight of more slaves at this time only increased their fears. Haunted by visions of anarchy, they moved decisively to intercept whatever was going on. Having already made arrangements to investigate the alleged plot, the legislature next ordered Captain Carden "To take Two or Three pties of men, such as he shall make Choyce of Well fitted with Arms and Ammunition to March under his Command in psuite of the runn away Negroes that are gathered Together Toward the Mountains on the South Seide. . . and them to follow and psue to Death In Case they cannot bee Taken alive." Hunting parties were guaranteed rewards for any success against the fugitives: one thousand pounds of sugar for any taken alive, "then they may Keepe such Negroes until they shall bee sattisfyed the same." The bounty for killing a fugitive was six hundred pounds of sugar. Meanwhile, slaveowners themselves were made responsible for restraining slaves from leaving plantations on Saturdays and Sundays unless they carried a pass and were on the owner's business. In addition, owners were to prevent slaves from beating drums or making "such like Noyse," which they might use to communicate with their brethren in the hills or elsewhere. Slaveowners failing to follow these instructions faced court proceedings.[10]

While no reports of the authorized investigations into the alleged plot have come to light, it nevertheless appears that the maroons persisted in resisting and harassing whites and fomenting slave rebellion. On March 9, 1687 the governor and council again drew attention to the revolt of runaways, saying that they were informed "Divers Runnaway Negroes are gathered Together on the Mountains. . .to ye Numbers of betweene Forty or Fiftie Sume of them being Armed with gunns, and furniched with Ammunition and have sent their Emissaries and Agents to severall

Plantacons, To Excite and stirr up the Negroes To forsake their Masters, and to Come and Joyne with them To the End they may Enable themselves to wth stand the power of the Christain Inhabitants and to Cutt of and Destroy them by firing the plantacons To amuse them and withe Hurry to fall on them To make themselves Masters of the Contry." The governor issued immediate orders for a number of men from each militia company to "March to the Mountains To search the woods and all places, and by force of Armes" to rout the rebels and take them dead or alive. At the same time he ordered mounted patrols on Saturday afternoons and Sundays and the arrest of slaves found outside plantations without passes.[11]

On March 17 the legislature received heartening news that Captain Carden and his men had attacked a maroon village fortified with "Bull Works and Pallysadoes." According to the official account, as the men approached the village "One of the said Negroes bid Defyance to the said Capt. Carden Whoe Led a fyle of men, and Imediately fired att him and wounded him in several places of his Body and wth that or other shots, others of our men were wounded, Nevertheless ye rest of the pty fired at the Negroes and Killed their Leader and fell into their said fortificacon where they found about Twentie houses and the said Negroe Dead, and being two weake to psue soe great a Parttie, they wthdrew, and Immediately Another parttie of our Men met some of the rooted Negroes and slew some of them; the rest fledd." Determined to follow up this success, the legislature quickly sent more men into the hills to pursue the fugitives, but they must have achieved little, for on March 24 the council minutes recorded: "It appears this day that the fugitive Negroes on the Mountaines doe still persist in their Villainy, and sending about their Agents to Encrease theire Numbers and doe by force of Armes Defend themselves haveing opposed themselves against our men and have bid Defiance to the Kings Authority, and all under wch putts the Inhabitants that borders upon the mountains in greate feare of their Lives, being threatened that their plantacions shall bee burned and themselves Destroyed if some speedy course be not taken."[12]

Carden's successful raid and the authorities' determination to continue combing the woods, sometimes with the help of black guides, disrupted the maroons' pattern of existence. Now, instead of establishing semipermanent communities, they adopted a more appropriate guerrilla style, keeping on the move, fighting hunting parties if they wanted to, raiding plantations, and so on. Such a precarious existence could continue to appeal to ideologically committed fugitives, but others could have decided to return to the plantations. Those who came down out of the hills found, however, that orders for their arrest had been issued. Meanwhile, attacking the fugitive troubles from another angle, the legislature ordered the arrest of a number of other slaves suspected of being either in league with the fugitives or involved in the alleged plot to revolt.

Painstaking research has uncovered neither written reports of the commissioners investigating the plot nor references to reports, written or verbal, but this, however, does not mean there was no plot. Here we run again into the familiar difficulties of authenticating slave plots. Nevertheless, the fate of Major Borraston's Pawpaw slave George may help show that something may have been in the making. Remanded in custody on suspicion of being in the plot, George was alleged to have called together one Saturday afternoon neighboring slaves in Falmouth Division in the south, where he lived, to instate him as "governor" over them. Three witnesses gave evidence against him. Joseph Borraston, the major's sixteen-year-old son, testified on March 19, 1687 that, about twelve months before, George had tried to throw him into a boiling sugar copper but that his mother had advised against telling the major. Young Borraston added that a few days before that, while he was in the boiling house, Bese, George's wife, blocked his way and he slapped her. George intervened, striking Joseph Borraston in the chest. "It was not for strength hee knocked his wife Bes," George told the youth. Whatever the cause of the hostility George harbored against his master's son, he obviously would not submit to certain indignities. The legislature no doubt interpreted the testimony to mean that George was a high-spirited slave quite capable of challenging authority. Joseph Borraston in effect had appeared as a character witness against George. So too did Richard Lynch, a man "of full Age," who testified that sometime in 1684, while he was on his way to Rendezvous Bay, on the northeast coast, he had cause to strike George, who drew his knife in retaliation and slashed at him before being restrained by two other slaves.

Another witness, Thomas Smith, aged thirty-six years, stated that around December 28, 1686 he saw George riding on the shoulder of another slave. Smith asked Robin, a Pawpaw slave, what this meant, and Robin replied that George had been made "a grandy Man thatt he was to bee their Govr." Smith then, pipe in mouth, went up and asked George if this was true. George's response was unexpected. He "struck my peip, out of my mouth," related Smith, "and tould me that I might goe about my Business." Smith, however, surprised and angered by this show of hostility and disrespect from a slave, immediately "took up a stick and Broake his head, in soe much yt hee went and made his Complaint to his Master." Later, after George had his head attended to, Smith reported "hee Told mee that by and by for mee and shaked his fist." Smith also claimed that some months later, about the beginning of March 1687, George had threatened him, saying "I should not bee safe in my house but yt a Little stick of fire would burne my house and I should bee the first yt should bee killed." Slave hostility against whites either individually or collectively, or their opposition to slavery itself, conceivably often found expression in threats of violence or misfortune against their oppressors. Sometimes such threats were idle, mere outbursts that were not acted upon, but in George's case the legislature believed the opposite. Even if it could not be proved beyond doubt that George was involved in a plot for a slave revolt, the presumption of guilt seemed strong enough to the legislature, which condemned him to be "burned to ashes" for "all the outrages" at least as a deterrent against conspiracy and collaboration between slaves and maroons.

In custody along with George was Governor Nathaniel Johnson's slave Phillip, who was accused of aiding and entertaining runaways at his house. Phillip allegedly intended to run away himself. Condemned as a collaborator, he was sentenced to have "one of his legs. . .Cutt of, and that if the governor should afterwards see Cause he should Cause his Toung to be cutt out and that hee might remaine as a Living Example to ye rest." Some of the other slaves arrested were more fortunate. They were discharged for lack of evidence. But a few, such as Robin, belonging to Mr. John Sampson, were kept confined. Another of Sampson's slaves was also ordered to be "kept safe as being one of the Mountain Company." Robin later earned a pardon for agreeing to serve as guide and informer against the maroons, who continued to defend themselves against all parties sent after them.[13] If other slaves later shared the fate of George and Phillip, the records do not show it.

Although maroon activity, centered in the south, mainly endangered the lives and property of whites who lived on plantations bordering the Shekerley Hills, the legislature believed it posed a serious enough threat to the rest of the island. Fearing the worst consequences if the number of maroons continued to grow, the legislature routinely sent patrols out after the rebels and increased surveillance of other slaves to prevent collaboration between them. It agreed on March 24, 1687 that all maroons should be condemned to death when captured "unless the Governor and Council shall upon due Examination Thinke any of them fitt objects of Mercy"; that slaves who collaborated with maroons would be treated as accomplices; that whites doing the same became enemies of the country and should be prosecuted; and finally, that slaveowners should seize any fugitives they met and hand them over to the magistrates, even it they were their own property.[14]

In 1684 the governor and council had asked slaveowners to submit lists of their fugitives, and it is probably from these that the legislature drew up its own list of fugitives still in the hills on March 24, 1687, which recorded 27 identified by name, owner, and ethnic group or place of origin (table 8.1). The list, which should not be interpreted to refer to a maroon community, is of limited usefulness in analyzing marronage or running away in the

TABLE 8.1. Runaways in the Antigua Hills, March 24, 1687

Name	Ethnic Group or Place of Origin	Owner
Tony, Tom, Joane	Mallegascos	Jonas Langford
Will, Phillip	Mallegascos	—
Robin, Garret, Nany, Sarah, Mare, One More	Collomantee and Lampo	Lynch
Sarah	Lampoe	Lucas
Will	Magasco	Governor
Joan	Ibbo	Lingham
Betty & her husband	Collomantee & Angola	—
Four Negro Men & One woman	Angola	—
Sham	Ibbo	Bushway
John Premeer	A free man	—
Abraham & Molly	—	Belchamber
Mary	Papa.	Bramble
Robin	Ibbo	—

SOURCE: Council Minutes, Mar. 24, 1687, fol. 63, CO 155/1.

seventeenth century; it does not indicate, for example, any pattern of flight, a major consideration in such analyses, and we simply do not have any direct evidence that touches on it.

Names and sexes of fugitives listed show that the number of males (seventeen) was almost double that of females (ten), but we do not know their ages or how long they had been at large, although some may have been fugitives since 1684 or before that. While the sex ratio is interesting, we are still in the dark about its connection with the sex composition of the slave population, and sex-specific patterns of marronage; in the absence of supporting evidence, questions remain about such things as whether men ran away more frequently than women, whether women fled on their own, or with men, or were simply carried off in raids on plantations. "During the early colonial period throughout the Americas," writes Richard Price, "there was a severe imbalance of male to female slaves, and this proportion was further increased among the original bands of runaways because a disproportionatly large number of men successfully escaped from plantation life."[15] Plantations were often raided for women. While the situation was probably broadly similar in Antigua, it is difficult to determine precise patterns. The presence of "Betty and her husband," one a Coromantee, the other an Angola, in the list of fugitives is intriguing. Could they have run away together, or did they develop ties as fugitives? Perhaps even more interesting, for other reasons, was the inclusion of the freedman John Premeer. How did he come to be classified among fugitive slaves? Although in 1687 a specific law had not yet been passed in Antigua that defined the place of freedmen in society, custom and opinion had probably already gone a long way in limiting their freedom. As we have seen, a decade later the slave act of 1697 spelled out these limits. If already attached to or "owned" by a white patron in 1687, as the later law required of some freedmen, Premeer was virtually a slave, and for whatever reason, perhaps ideological, he could have cast his lot with runaways. It is possible that Premeer had fled from justice, but there is no supporting evidence.

Ethnic identification in the fugitives list throws light also on African groups in the slave population during this early period. It shows a mixture of 6 Mallegasco or Magasco fugitives, 6 Collomantee and Lampo, 1 Lampoe, 3 Ibbo, 1 Collomantee, 1 Papa, and 6 Angola. Two runaways were not designated. Mallegasco or Magasco slaves were from Madagascar. Southeast Africa and Madagascar supplied some slaves to the English plantation colonies especially between 1675 and 1690. Collomantees (Coromantees, Kormantyns), and Papas or Pawpaws, we have already noted, referred respectively to natives of the Gold Coast and hinterland in West Africa, and Dahomey or Whydah on the Slave Coast. Lampo slaves were from Allampo or Lampi, just east of the Volta River. Barbados planters regarded them as the worst of all their slaves in the seventeenth century. From the Bight of Biafra came Ibbo or Ibo slaves, and Angolans were from south-central Africa. From all these areas at least, Antigua received slave imports directly or indirectly in the seventeenth century; some of them fled to the hills, preferring freedom, however precarious, to enslavement. A wide range of values and perceptions related to flight influenced both by tribal affiliations and by adaptation as slaves must have been represented among these early rebels, the majority of whom would have been African, during these first years of the sugar colony.[16]

Detailed lists of fugitives captured or killed in the 1680s have not turned up, but there are isolated references to captives in the few surviving records. One fugitive woman called Jacke, property of Mr. Burrowes, was brought in by John Atkinson. There was also the interesting case of another captured woman slave of Mr. Charles Gosse. The legislature agreed to spare her life after she promised to assist it, and made her a guide. One day, after returning from patrol, she managed to escape back to the maroons. For this, and also for allegedly threatening to kill her master, the legislature quickly condemned her to death if caught. Beyond mention of compensation for fugitives killed or executed in the legislature's minutes of April 7, 1687, and also some concern expressed in 1688 over increases in such expenditure, maroons are no longer referred to in later accounts, which probably means they had been effectively destroyed.[17] In any case, official anxiety seems to have subsided. The burgeoning master class had weathered the first significant challenge from the enemy within.

The Antigua maroon type revolt we have discussed, of which the series of upheavals in Jamaica, especially between the 1720s and 1739, is perhaps the best example for the British islands, centered on the activities of maroons, who did not intend to surrender the freedom they had seized but instead fomented unrest on plantations and encouraged other slaves to escape and join them.[18] Alarmed at such palpable demonstration of slave rebellion and its potential to escalate into something bigger and more threatening, slaveowners and the Antigua authorities understandably took precautions to prevent the development of an islandwide revolt that they believed was the ultimate objective of the rebels, although there is no evidence that such a plan existed. From the marked incidence of slave unrest tied to the exploits of maroons, the slavocracy had derived the existence of a collective consciousness among slaves for large-scale revolt. While it can be argued that such political consciousness was probably fast emerging, shaped by the evolving environment of slavery and the demands made on slaves, there is also every reason why the slave fugitives of the seventeenth century should be regarded as insurrectionists. Slave flight in still-forested Antigua during the 1680s was at the very center of early slave resistance, when the rebels seemed not to have been content with their precarious freedom but to have tried to push the island into the flames of internal war, being aware that on the small and by no means rugged island, it was only a matter of time before patrols caught up with them.

During the final decade of the seventeenth century, Antiguan authorities still regarded runaways as a dangerous nuisance. Some fugitives, sometimes heading for French territory, left the island altogether, starting a pattern of flight that would continue into the eighteenth century. In 1692 the legislature's attention was for a time focused on "the danger of Negroes riseing." This was in reference to French slaves in the island who, it was believed, might seize the opportunity, in the war (1689–97) then in progress between England and France, to foment a general slave revolt. Many of these slaves either had been captured from the neighboring French islands or were fugitives from those places. Warning in 1694 that "Wee may reasonably expect the Enemie Spedily to attack us," the Antigua assembly prepared to find "Some Effectual way" to keep "French Negroes from doing any Mischief upon any Attack ye French may make on this Island." The governor and council were at first slow to agree, believing that no harm would come from the slaves if the islanders behaved like men and prevented a French landing; later, however, alarmed by reports that French Slaves, for their own reasons, were deserting to the enemy, most likely at Guadeloupe, or even St. Christopher, they supported the assembly. The first report came from Captain Samuel Horne, who, complaining that he had lost several such slaves, introduced a motion in the assembly: "That of late hath been Severall plotts contrivances & Combinations of the French Negroes to run from this Island to ye French some have made Escape others been discovered and the masters of said Negroes therein concerned takeing no notice to have them made Examples, it is necessary that some course be taken that Examples may be made to deterr the sd Negroes from the like for the future." Horne strongly recommended "that the Inhabitants of this Island kee[p]ing any boats Perriagoe or Cannoe may be oblidged to bring them under the care of the next guard whenever they have them not in actual use or that they be stowed to peires." The motion was carried, and the governor and council supported passing a special act.[19]

Other runaways of the 1690s never left Antigua. Compensation claims that register their existence throw only a glimmer of light on these rebels, yielding information only about owners' names, compensation awarded, and the nature of the crime. Only four claims have been found for the 1690s and none for earlier years, but this undoubtedly is because of scarcity of sources as well as unsystematic reporting, and not because few runaways were executed. The legislature awarded three thousand pounds of sugar to Captain John Roe in 1695, Alexander Cranford in 1696, and Walter Sampson in 1697 for runaways caught and executed; Dennis Macklemore got a similar award in 1697, but his slave had been killed in the hills. Nathaniel Sampson's overseer killed a "Mounteneer Runaway Negroe" in 1694, for which he got a reward of six hundred pounds of sugar, but compensation to the fugitive's owner is not recorded. Other compensation orders recorded in fragmentary minutes of the legislature indicate that at least 10 slaves were executed for various crimes in the period 1694–99. Two of these slaves had killed an overseer.[20]

After many years of piecemeal legislation to control rebellious slaves, Antigua followed the example of Barbados (1661, 1676, 1682, 1688), Jamaica (1664, 1696), and South Carolina (1696) and finally enacted a comprehensive slave act in 1697, superseded in 1702, that, as we have seen, contained many provisions against various types of slave resistance but obviously concentrated on running away, reflecting the legislators' perception of the grave problems inherent in such resistance.[21] The act itself, however, and others that followed in the eighteenth century, had only limited success against slave resistance broadly interpreted, partly because regulations were not uniformly well enforced, and partly because of the slaves' own determination to resist however and whenever possible, shifting when it seemed wise from openly defiant behavior, which could be suicidal, especially during moments of intensified white vigilance, to less easily detectable strategies that nonetheless kept the spirit of resistance flickering.

9

"However They May Disguise It, They Hate Their Masters"

In the seventeenth century a maroon dimension had heavily influenced patterns of slave resistance in Antigua. Runaways, mostly African-born, fled to the hill country, established at least one maroon village, but after its destruction in 1687, marronage, as we have defined the term, steadily lost much of its force as the area of settlement and cultivation expanded, leaving no room for effective maroon occupation. Henceforth slaves might continue to run away, but because conditions had changed, they had to call upon new strategies for remaining at large or avoiding capture.

Whereas the maroon dimension of resistance weakened in Antigua in the years surrounding 1700, it remained powerful in Jamaica. Eighteenth-century resistance in the smaller island became qualitatively different from that in Jamaica, where the maroon war intensified in the 1720s and threatened to turn the colony upside down.[1] Nothing of the kind seemed possible in Antigua. However, while Antigua slaves may not have run away as frequently and threatened life and property in a long war against whites, in less dramatic but no less significant ways, they expressed opposition to slavery. Where large numbers of Jamaica slaves could grasp freedom and defend it by joining maroons, Antigua slaves, largely because of the island's limitations of size and topography, could not; the only way to achieve freedom collectively was to seize the whole island, a scheme that obviously demanded careful planning and that indeed was attempted in 1736, when a particularly propitious concatenation of circumstances helped motivate the slaves. But until the time seemed ripe for such a gigantic and complex undertaking, how was slave resistance organized?

The 1700s opened with a slave rebellion. The first well-recorded rebellion in the island, it was a small-scale and highly localized affair. It occurred December 27, 1701 at about eight o'clock in the morning, when fifteen Coromantees belonging to Major Samuel Martin of Greencastle Plantation, situated on the northern fringe of the Shekerley Hills in New Division of St. Mary's Parish, attacked and killed their master, who was also speaker of the assembly. "We have lost a very useful Man in Major Martin," Governor Codrington later reported; "next to [lieutenant] Governor Yeomans I think truly he was willing to take the most pains in public busnes; and was best fitted for it of any Man in the 4 Islands."[2] While the official report about the incident did not specify why the slaves had rebelled, it could have been, according to other sources, because Martin "had for some reason or the other refused his slaves their usual Christmas holiday, and compelled them to work throughout the day," in order "to take a crop he thought wd perish if not got in," a plausible enough explanation. Could Martin have denied them their holiday as punishment for something that had happened earlier — a punishment, however, so drastic as to drive the slaves over the brink and kill him? Whatever the circumstances leading up to the planter's violent end, all Codrington mentioned by way of explanation was "I'm afraid he was guilty of some unusual act of Severity, or rather Some indignity towards the Coromantees." The Board of Trade replied that because the reason for Martin's slaying "seems probably to have been some extraordinary Severity towards his Negroes we are the more Sensible of the expediency of a Law for restraining inhumane Severity not only towards Christian Servants but Slaves, which you are directed in your Instructions to endeavour to procure, And we therefore recommend it to your particular care."[3]

Two days after Martin's untimely end, his friend George Gamble wrote the governor a detailed report of what had happened. "The relation I am about to give your Excellency is soe Surprising and Strikes soe deepe into my Soul," Gamble began dramatically, "that [I] am Scarce capable of proceeding further." He explained how the slaves attacked Martin in the presence of his wife and other whites at Greencastle, "and with theyr Knives and bills most barbarously murtherd him; first stabing him with theyr Knives betweene the throat and breast, but by the interposition of the wife; (none else by what I understand having any resolution on the Occasion, if that may be tearmed soe) were diverted from proceeding further; upon which coming back in the Chamber lockd himself in with his wife; who immediately going out of a back doore, in order to come round to the front doore, to passifie the negroes, finding her passage interrupted forthwith returned, but noe Sooner had entered the Chamber againe but found them there forc'd through the Windows, most inhumanly perfecting theyr designes." Gamble then went on to relate the gruesome details of how the slaves cut off Martin's head, and "then they attempted cutting off the armes and shoulders from the trunk, as also his feete having cutt round the Ankles Butt the bones preventing was left in that condition reeking in his blood on the floor." That was the state in which the body was later discovered, "only the head wanting, which wee afterward tooke up in the grass, where they had washed it with rum and triumphed Over it."

Gamble himself had not witnessed the attack, but when the news reached him he "posted away immediately. . .with a few men on horseback, and foot, to prevent further mischiefe if possible, but on our arrival found all the whites were preserved by a Sort of miraculous Escape, but the negroes all in Arms with the Major's gunns, and on theyr defence." One of them was promptly shot dead. The others fled, hotly pursued by Gamble and his men. Only two of the rebels had been captured by December 29. Some other slaves were arrested, but there was doubt about their involvement in the affair.[4]

From Gamble's account it would appear that the episode was nothing more than a hostile outburst directed at Major Martin alone, because apparently the slaves ignored his wife and other whites who were present. It was no miracle that they escaped unharmed if the object of the slaves' wrath was Martin. "I think 'tis plain the Negroes had noe design on their Mistress or ye rest of the family," was Codrington's comment, "or else they would soon have chopt them to pieces." Nonetheless, other whites in the area and beyond, who had only recently got news of a slave plot in Barbados, were understandably much alarmed when they learned of Martin's fate and were on their guard. Were "I to acquaint your Excellency the Comosion this action had made in the Country" declared Gamble, "& the unprovidedness of almost every one on this Occasion of Surprize, you would be astonished at it; in Short there was Scarce a Man would find a gunn, and hee that could had neither powder nor ball nor Sword."[5]

Codrington, however, kept a cool head, mentioning in his report that "Mr. Gamble, from a concern for his friend I believe was in a maze when he writ his letter." The governor, who owned many Coromantee slaves himself, believed, moreover, that the Coromantees could have been driven to kill Martin only after strong provocation, "for they are not only the best and most faithful of our Slaves, but are really all born Heroes." These interesting remarks prefaced a commendation of their outstanding qualities as he saw them.

There is a difference between them and all other Negroes beyond what 'tis possible for your Lordships to conceive. There never was a Raskal or Coward of yt. nation, Intrepid to the last degree, not a Man of them but will stand to be cut in pieces without a Sigh or groan, gratefull and Obedient to a kind Master, but implacably revengefull when ill-treated. My father, who had studyd the genius and temper of all kinds of Negroes 45 years with a very nice observation, would say, Noe Man deserv'd a Corramante that would not treat Him like A Friend rather than a Slave, and All my Corramantes preserve that love and veneration for Him that they constantly visit his grave, make their libations upon it, hold up their hands to Heaven with violent lamentations, and promise When they have done working for His Son they will come to Him and be his faithfull slaves in the other world.[6]

Codrington's observations on loyalty of Coromantees should, however, not be taken too seriously except perhaps as they reflect a ruling class maneuver to make Codrington feel better about owning slaves. In any case, not all slaveowners were as humane or as fortunate as Codrington claimed of his father, compared to whom Major Martin must appear a true villain. Fully aware that many Antigua slaveowners treated their slaves cruelly, and that such treatment could drive slaves to rebellion, Codrington was not surprised at Martin's fate, confessing, "I often wonder there are not attempts of the same Nature every day." Francis Le Jau the missionary commented in 1700 on the "barbarous usage" of slaves in the Leewards, few slaveowners "allowing to their poor Creatures either victuals or cloaths or rest but blows and that most cruelly, whereas the most common crime they are guilty of is that of stealing victuals without which they cannot live." Slaves, in short, were used "worse than beasts."[7]

By the turn of the century, Antigua was enveloped in an accelerating transition from a tobacco- to a sugar-based economy marked by a steadily increasing demand for slaves, land, and capital. In this hectic environment of economic expansion and change, slavery must have been very harsh. Writing about slavery in the United States, Kenneth Stampp has noted that although "cruelty was endemic in all slaveholding communities, it was always most common in newly settled regions. Along the rough southern frontier thousands of ambitious men were trying swiftly to make their fortunes. They operated in a frantically competitive society which provided few rewards for the virtues of gentility and almost put a premium on ruthlessness."[8] The profitability of sugar production with slave labor generated broadly similar tendencies in early eighteenth-century Antigua. Yet there was only one recorded rebellion in those years. This suggests that harsh conditions need not give rise to frequent rebellion, premeditated or spontaneous. Other conducive elements must also be at work to make rebellion possible, such as a favorable geographical environment and a high density of the slave population generally or on several plantations, together with suitable ethnic concentrations.[9] But in the case of the Coromantee rebellion at Greencastle in 1701, the records remain silent about its deeper origins. For some combination of reasons, anyway, this incident flared up suddenly, probably with little or no planning by the slaves, and when they had killed Martin, the prime object of their wrath, they simply ran away. But where to? In Jamaica, where the topography favored a revolt-followed-by-flight sequence of collective rebellion, rebels such as those at Greencastle stood an excellent chance of crowning their efforts with a secure enough existence in the interior. Not so in Antigua, where by 1700 there was really no place left where rebels might be safe from white patrols. The absence of mountain or jungle havens from about the late seventeenth century, it can be argued, goes a long way in helping to explain why, if slavery was so harsh in Antigua, slaves did not rebel more frequently.

The Greencastle incident resembles only slightly what Marion Kilson has called the vandalistic revolt, characterized, as with Nat Turner's in 1831 in Virginia, by "a haphazard expression of opposition to the slave system aimed at the destruction of slave holders and their property." Such revolts, according to Kilson, lack systematic preparation, may be conceived quite suddenly or over a short period, and, unlike long-planned, systematic revolts, which run the risk of discovery, they are more likely to reach fruition. If recruits are to be gathered, this happens as the revolt continues. Revolts of this type also tend to be localized, rural rather than urban oriented, and because there are no "well-defined goals beyond the immediate destruction of life and property of the slaveholder," the rebels implicitly accept "ultimate capitulation to the power of the slavocracy."[10] The Coromantee killing of Major Martin departs from this overly neat category of revolt particularly in that it was not a haphazard demonstration of slave hostility but a discriminating act, suggestive of premeditation, aimed, it is true, not against slavery itself but against a particular master who aroused the slaves' sense of outrage when he most likely broke the "moral" accommodation mediated between masters and slaves.

The general trend of Antigua slave resistance in the eighteenth century was not as dramatic as the rebellion at Greencastle. Slave resistance was instead dominated by the day-to-day or more subtle and indirect variety, effective "protest techniques" nonetheless that caused slaveowners some concern; but there were other forms of retaliation that caused them greater anxiety because they were open and direct, acts such as arson and running away, the latter being still the main type of resistance although now shaped by changing environmental conditions from what it had been in the seventeenth century.

In the 1720s slaveowner Robert Robertson, who had ample opportunity to observe how slaves in the Leewards responded to slavery, commented that in the British sugar islands generally, the slaves' "Sense of their Slavery seems to lie deep in the Minds of many of them, and improves (as some conceive) to a very great Degree their Love of Laziness, Stealing, Stubborness, Murmuring, Treachery, Lying, Drunkenness, and the like." Robertson added that many slaves ran away "upon slight and trifling Pretences, and very often without pretending to have had any Cause or Provocation given tham at all, and generally when their Labour, or Attendance is most wanted." Some, he claimed, escaped to more mountainous parts of islands and remained at large "for whole Years, which is easy in Countries where it is always Summer." Moreover, slaves seldom lost an opportunity to desert to the enemy during invasion. He believed there was an ever-present danger of slave uprisings and conspiracies because "however they may disguise it, they hate their Masters, and wish them destroyed." In short, Robertson concluded, slaveowners had good reason to "keep a strict Eye over" their slaves, "and are often oblig'd to treat some of them with great Severity." Walter Tullideph would have easily recognized this general portrait of slaveowners' "troublesome property." In 1748 Tullideph lost patience with some slaves leased to him. One of these was Fryday "who hath been a very great Rogge and a burden on the Estate" but whose behavior had begun to improve. "I should be very Glad these negroes were out of my Custody," wrote Tullideph; "the Men are tolerable, altho' one of them named Quamina chose rather to Stabb himself rather than worke, abot three months agone, however he is now well and I hope Reclaimed, but as for the women they are hardly worth their food." One of these women "hath a Canker in her head or Pretends So," added Tullideph, "three of the best have Sucking Children which looses One half of their Labour, the rest very lazy." Tullideph wanted the slaves taken off his hands rather than continue to pay unreasonable rates for their use. [11]

Robertson's perceptive observations refer to open forms of resistance as well as others more subtle or elusive and suggest a definite link between slavery, slave resistance, and slave crime. In the case of covert resistance, laziness, theft, lying, and drunkenness were all part of what one scholar has called the psychic warfare that pervaded the master-slave relationship; if slaves were to retain their dignity, they had simultaneously to protect their minds and bodies from the effects of abuse and the master's power otherwise applied, and somehow retaliate. Slave resistance in the Americas and elsewhere included other subtle styles such as carelessness, feigned stupidity, insolence, satire, deliberate evasion, and refusal to work. Largely subversive, they were aimed at harassing the slave system, at hampering its more efficient operation in ways that left the final aim of resistance open to any possibility that might emerge. Slaves handled some of these forms of resistance with such finesse that whites, even those who should have known better, tended to accept them as part of the black stereotype, which can stand as evidence of blacks' effective use of a web of deception for self-preservation and resistance. [12]

Open acts of resistance could, however, be more easily identified and dealt with. How widespread and frequent was such resistance in Antigua? While the slave laws, which "legitimized a state of war between blacks and whites," are a useful source for analyzing resistance because they outlawed certain activities and prescribed penalties, court records would be even more useful because they would give some idea of the frequency with which offenses were committed and how seriously the courts viewed them. [13] No court records for Antigua have been found, but slaveowners' petitions claiming compensation for executed slaves at least indicate how many slaves were executed and for what offenses. These claims are to be found scattered about in the extensive minutes of the legislature, recording unfortunately only the estimated value of slave offenders, their names, owners' names, and offenses. There are obvious limitations to the use of claims that do not supply the wealth of data that newspaper advertisements for runaways did in the mainland colonies for example, data on observable physical and psychological traits, occupation, ethnic origin, probable destination, and familiarity with English, which scholars have used to study runaways. Also, sadly missing from Antigua compensation claims are references to motives behind offenses, and this further limits their utility; yet elsewhere in the legislature's minutes motives of especially troublesome runaways are mentioned. One aspect of resistance deduced through advertisements or compensation claims relates to how often certain owner's names appeared. Close study of these proprietors' operations and relationships with their slaves, if that were possible, might help answer a number of questions about overt resistance.[14]

Antigua compensation claims reveal executions for a range of offenses that might perhaps be regarded as simply crimes, but as Winthrop Jordan has remarked, it is not possible to separate slave crime from resistance to slavery partly because these crimes could and were often meant to undermine the slave system. If objective was important, so too were the circumstances of resistance. Such crimes could represent open expression of a long-concealed inclination to insubordination or rebellion in a critical moment of anger or loss of self-control, or, less spontaneously, after some premeditation. The slavocracy lumped all potential slave threats to the social and political order together as criminal action, not differentiating political crime from common law crime. Emphasizing always the potential criminality of slaves in order to divest slave unrest of moral legitimacy and to avoid ideologically justifying slave subordination, the authorities categorized and punished all slave offenses as common law crime.[15] But slaves conceived in political and ideological terms much of this so-called crime that expressed resistance. It happened on the individual level, among small groups, but was most evident in large-scale attempts at planned rebellion, as my analysis of the origins and organization of the 1736 slave plot will show.

Compensation claims, however useful they might be for studying features of slave crime and resistance, represent only cases that came before magistrates and the legislature and therefore quantitatively underrepresent the level of such activity. It is undeniable that many more cases went unrecorded because masters chose not to prosecute. Similarly, in the mainland colonies, for one reason or another, some runaways were not advertised for, and existing advertisements underrepresent the incidence of running away. In Antigua, compensation claims for the period 1722–63 show that slaves were executed for running away (152), burglary (6), theft (12), highway robbery (4), assaulting whites (9), murdering other slaves (27), felony (56), burglary and felony (12), poisoning (8), robbery (3), rape (1), arson (5), unspecified murders (14), and undisclosed offenses (31), while 41 runaways were hunted down and killed or died of wounds received; altogether 381 slaves killed or lawfully executed over a forty-year period, omitting the years 1751 and 1752, for which data have not been found (table 9.1).

To judge from the slave codes, which give the impression that theft was among the most common of slave crimes, many more slaves should have been executed for it, unless magistrates could award lesser punishment at their discretion, such as severe whipping in public. While most thefts were done with cunning and secrecy, sometimes as underfed slaves sought to satisfy their hunger, burglary and highway robbery were openly defiant; but as with banditry in peasant protest in precolonial Southeast Asia, for example, it is difficult to decide how often and to what extent highway robbery could be termed social banditry as a "genuine vehicle of social protest," or was simply criminal. In 1713 a group of slaves broke into George Pullen's house and, according to Captain Horsford, would most likely have killed Pullen's wife had she not fled into the woods nearby.[16] Runaways, predictably, were responsible for many burglaries and highway robberies, but they would have had to be caught and convicted for their cases to be recorded. This helps to explain why there were only ten executions for those crimes in 1722–63, while there were obviously many more runaways at large. Conceivably, many runaways, before they took flight, stole what they needed from their masters or other whites.

One incident of highway robbery in 1737 vividly illustrates slave defiance of whites and their authority. Thomas Woodyatt, aged twenty-seven years, an indentured servant of Vallentine Morris, made a deposition before Morris that four slaves had robbed and roughed him up on the public highway. On Monday, June 20, 1737, recounted Woodyatt

> as he was coming from St. Johns about Ten O'Clock at Night, about Three or four Hundred yards to the Eastward of Judge Watkins's Windmill formely Monteyro's he met four Negroe Men all Armed with Cutlasses, One of them having a Pistol beside; that they came up. . . and told him, that they were Lynch's Negroes, that they must have that Something he had got there; that they held up their Cutlasses. . . and Swore they would kill him Dead if he did not Deliver what he had got, and all the money he had [.] That. . . being unarm'd, but on

the Horseback, they took from him Six yards of Ozenbriggs,
and a New Pair of Shoes which he had bot in Town, and one
of them Thrust his hand into. . .[his] Pocket with such
Violence that he broke out the Bottom of the Pocket and
Drove the Keys down to the Knees of his Britches and took
one Pistole and an half. . .the same Person Saying at the same
time, let us kill him. . .[Woodyatt] told them he belonged to
Col. Morris, they said God Damn Col. Morris we will have
his hearts blood out by and by. One of them Clapp'd the Pis-
tol to. . .[Woodyatt's] breast, while another took the Mony out
of his Pocket, and another Cut the Knee of his Britches with
his Cutlass, they Pulld. . .[him] three times Off his Horse, as
Oft as he got up, between the Place they first met him and
Pearn's Gut, Over Which they followed him when he Rid as
fast as he Could up to Doc. Dunbar's; they tore. . .[his] Shirt
all to Pieces, and Threatned Several times they would have
Col. Morris's heart blood; and. . .if he had not been on
Horseback,. . .they wou'd have Murder'd him. [17]

It is of particular note that Woodyatt's attackers were not runaways,
admitting themselves that they belonged to Lynch. Moreover they openly
expressed hostility toward Morris himself. The case later came up before
the lieutenant governor and council, who questioned three persons, but
what eventually came of the whole affair we do not know; careful sifting
of compensation claims reveals none from Lynch for slaves executed for
highway robbery. [18]

From time to time and for one reason or another, slaves committed the
most serious crime of physical assault upon whites. An isolated and
unenlightening case of assault involving rape occured in 1722. The only
information found was that William Yeamans was entitled to £35 for his
male slave Nero, "Executed for a Rape." There was also the rare case in
1714 when an assault resulted in the death of a white person: John Roe
claimed compensation for his slaves Richard and Baptist, who were
executed for killing John Haynes. The same year Humphrey Davis petitioned for Mingo, executed for "laying violent hands" on his master "and
almost strangling him." In the provost marshal's accounts for 1729 was the
following entry: "To whipping 8 Negroes 100 Lashes each and cutting of
the Ears of two for attempting to kill a white Man = £2 16s." Jane Hamilton
petitioned for her slave Daniel in 1735, executed for "Attempting and
Endangering the life of Morgan Marawee." Ebo Ned was executed for an
attempt on the life of Nathaniel Sampson Webb, a white overseer.
Somerset's owner claimed compensation in 1755 after the slave had been
executed for stabbing a white man; so too did the owners of Waterford

TABLE 9.1. Slave Crime and Compensation in Antigua, 1722–1763

	Claims	Runaways	Runaways Killed in Hunt	Burglary	Theft	Highway Robbery	Assault on White
1722–29[a]	93	38[8f]	5[1f]	—	6	1	1
1730–39[b]	111	53[1f]	12[1f]	—	1	—	1
1740–49[c]	107	48[2f]	18[3f]	1	—	1	—
1750–59[d]	41	10	5	—	4	1	5
1760–63	29	3	1	5	1	1	2[1f]
Total	381	152[11f]	41[5f]	6	12	4	9[1f]

SOURCE: Antigua Legislature Minutes 1722–1763, CO 9/5–26.
[a]Petitions do not include (14) claims for slaves in 1728-9 plot.
[b]Petitions do not include claims for slaves in 1736 plot.
[c]Petitions do not include claims for slaves in 1736 plot.
[d]Petitions for 1751 & 1752 not found.
[f]Slave women.

in 1756 and Davy in 1762, both of whom made attempts on the lives of whites. The petition for the slave Ralph in 1760 stated that he had assaulted, wounded, and robbed Thomas Nugent. Four years later Thomas Jarvis sought compensation for his slave Frank, who had stabbed Jarvis's servant, John Mash, in the back with a knife. Women slaves were also involved in such acts of violent rebellion. Gemima, John Seaycraft's slave, was burnt for assaulting Elizabeth Coxan, a white infant, while Mimba tried to kill her master, John Watkins.[19] It would help a great deal in interpreting such resistance if we knew the circumstances under which it occurred; whether, for example, these slaves rebelled because of intolerable abuse, suddenly, responding in an unexpected way because they were not known to be particularly rebellious in their day-to-day behavior. By what process were such slaves pushed beyond the limit of their tolerance to strike out at individual whites?

Compensation claims show up more cases where slaves killed other slaves then assaults on whites, and this can be explained in terms of the common response of long-oppressed groups in striking out not only at their tormentors but at themselves. "Because so many of the slaves' attempts were frustrated," explains Leslie Howard Owens, writing of slave resistance in the Old South, "it is no surprise that their aggression spilled over onto themselves as well." Such an interpretation of the meaning behind slave versus slave draws attention to the damage inflicted upon slaves,[20] but it is also true that vicious-minded people exist everywhere and act out of different sets of inclinations. In the 1730s drought, economic recession and other conditions generally worsened the quality of life of most of Antigua's slaves, whose frustrations were conspicuously demonstrated partly in attacks on other slaves, 12 slaves being executed for murder in that decade,

Murder of Slave	Felony	Burglary and Felony	Poisoning	Robbery	Rape	Arson	Not Stated	Unspecified Murder
4	$8^{(1f)}$	—	—	—	1	—	$26^{(2f)}$	3
12	21	4	—	—	—	$2^{(1f)}$	3	2
1	18	3	6	1	—	2	2	6
4	6	1	—	1	—	1	—	3
6	3	4	2	1	—	—	—	—
27	$56^{(1f)}$	12	8	3	1	$5^{(1f)}$	$31^{(2f)}$	14

close to half of all such executions for 1722–63. That 27 slaves were executed for killing other slaves over this long period compared with 9 for assaults on whites (none were killed) should give us pause in interpreting the impact of slavery on slaves and their community.[21]

Throughout the Americas slaves tried to destroy their masters by poison. Authorities in South Carolina were particularly concerned about such resistance in the first half of the eighteenth century. After the Stono Rebellion the slave act of 1740 made it a felony for a slave to administer poison (or to commit arson). And in St. George's Parish of that colony in 1751, "a horrid practice of poisoning their Masters" led to the death penalty for 5 or 6 slaves, "altho 40 to 50 more were privy to it." In 1761 "the hellish practice of poisoning" resurfaced.[22] Here as elsewhere slaves most often made attempts on individual masters and their families, or on other whites such as overseers, who supervised slave labor, but the slave Mackandal in the French sugar colony of St. Domingue planned a revolt in the eighteenth century that centered on mass poisoning of whites through their drinking water.[23] Antigua slaves never attempted anything so imposing, but because many cases may have been difficult for whites to detect, slaves may have resorted to poison more frequently than the few claims for executed poisoners would indicate. In the slave act of 1723, we will recall, the fugitives "Jack a Negro Man, belonging to Giles Blizard an Infant, and Mimba a Negro Woman, belonging to Mary Blizard Widow" were outlawed for "attempting to poison" the young Blizard. Nathaniel Gilbert and John Lightfoot claimed compensation for the slave Greenwich executed for poisoning Phillip Ruddock in 1746. In 1749 Jemmy and Quacko, belonging to Colonel Tomlinson, and William McKinnen's Tony tried to poison Frederick Nicholas and Mr. Chrisman, who were in Tomlinson's employ as sugar refiners. "They were found guilty," reported the *Philadelphia Gazette,* "on the confession of one Toby, who served about the house, and who was employed by Jemmy and Quacko, to put the poison into the tea-water, which was prepared by Tony, a noted negroe doctor." Tony could have been of advanced age, for he was valued at only £10; between them Quacko and Jemmy fetched £260 compensation, a large sum, which probably means these slaves were grown adults of great value. Cato attempted to poison John Harden, an underoverseer, in 1763. Dick and Dublin made an attempt on a white servant of Walter Nugent in 1748. In 1763 Lewis was executed for poisoning a slave woman belonging to his master, Edward Williams; the legislature also moved to punish a male slave on the deceased Benjamin King's plantation after it was determined he had supplied Lewis with the poison.[24] Poisoning was obviously a serious crime, and Antigua authorities tried to detect and punish accomplices.

How some slaves could be driven to dispatch whites in this way came out at the trial of the rebels of the 1736 plot. At the trial of Quawcoo, an old Coromantee belonging to John Pare, Mr. Martin's Quamina testified that Quawcoo and Johnny "had a Design of Poisoning Pares overseer, but that it was Discover'd and Prevented" by someone called Rattle Hall. "And I heard Quawcoo Say," Quamina added, "that same Sunday at Johny's House Speaking of Overseers Ill usage breaking and Starving them, that if it had not been for the little bawling bastard Rattle Hall, his business had been Done Before, We should not have been ill used any longer By the Overseer. We should have put him to Death."[25] Overwork and underfeeding during the hard times of the 1730s pushed Quawcoo and Johnny to conspire to poison.

Other slaves chose arson, as difficult to detect as poisoning, and were executed for it. In 1706 an assembly report said there was a runaway "Negro Man by Name Franck belonging to Dr. Arthur Freeman who wee have a great deal of reason to believe has attempted to burn this town [St. John's] twice, tho providentially prevented." The fires were probably detected before they had done much damage. Urgently, the legislature recommended that Franck be taken dead or alive for attempting one of the catastrophes they most dreaded at the hands of slaves besides insurrection or burning of cane fields. When Franck finally fell into their hands, they ordered his execution for "diverse Villianies, Thefts, Robberies and outrages." Sharper, in 1738, burned down not his master's house but the slave huts, conceivably a case here of a slave's rage or frustration turned in upon the slave community itself and only indirectly against the master. The following year Omer, a slave woman, was executed for "Willingfully setting fire to a dwelling House" of Margaret Gillyatt. Among slaves executed for setting fire to cane fields was Nathaniel Gilbert's Sacky (1745), Walter Tullideph's Pompey (1747), and another of Nathaniel Gilbert's slaves, Little Harry (1754). These slaves and others were executed for crimes specified in the records, but many compensation claims were for slaves executed for a range of offenses vaguely labeled felonies, or in some cases with no designation whatever; in the case of Vallentine Morris's slave Fortune in 1736, his many offenses were lumped together as "Diverse heinous Crimes."[26] This category of slave crime, however imprecise, adds to the picture of slave resistance.

———————————•-•———————————

Runaways. Every year runaways would be captured and executed or killed, as the records so graphically put it, "in pursuit." Some idea of the difficult existence Antigua runaways and others in the Americas led can be obtained from the autobiography of Esteban Montejo, who lived as a fugitive in Cuba in the nineteenth century. Conditions of course varied from territory to territory, but everywhere fugitives emphatically declared their intention not to live as slaves. Probably one of the more dramatic statements made in this regard in Antigua came from the escape of two black men held aboard the sloop *Two Brothers* in St. John's harbor in 1724, who, in what amounted to a jailbreak, swam a quarter of a mile away in a bid for freedom "tho chained by the Leggs to each other."[27] Antigua slaves ran away singly and sometimes in small groups. After the late seventeenth century, the rapidly vanishing forest cover greatly influenced their style of existence. Unable to live undetected in the island's interior, they found new ways to avoid capture. Some of their activities are recorded in the slave codes, compensation claims, and frequently also in the legislature's deliberations whenever they gave particular cause for alarm. Of 381 compensation claims made in 1722–63, 193, or 50.68 percent, were for runaways executed or killed in flight (see table 9.1). Over this long period close to 5 (4.59) runaways a year forfeited their lives. Whether fugitives stayed at large for long or short periods, running away remained the most common form of overt resistance in the eighteenth century.

By the end of the seventeenth century, as we have seen, runaways caused enough trouble that special acts were passed in 1680 and 1697 placing penalties on them and offering rewards for their capture. In spite of similar provisions in the 1702 slave act, slave flight persisted as slaves desperately eluded their pursuers or sometimes boldly formed bands to harass whites in certain areas. In 1706 the lieutenant governor and council drew attention to the existence of "diverse Negroes now runaway from severall Persons in this Island, & [who] committt frequent notorious Robberies, and outrages by stealing, and doing other fellonious Actions." "Wee believe it proper," they told the assembly, "there be an encouragement, or Reward given to any Person or Persons whatsoever who shall take or kill any of them." Observing that the proposed measure was too general, "that it may be of evil consequence," the assembly asked for the names of the principal fugitives. One of these, Caesar, guilty of "Several barbarous Crimes," belonged to Captain Ash and had been at large for about three years. The assembly asked the governor to offer by proclamation twenty pieces of eight for Caesar's capture dead or alive, but the governor hesitated, believing that such action would be "a Means of making him desperate, and causing him to do things that otherwise he would not." While it was imperative in the interest of public tranquility and general slave control that Caesar be brought in or killed, the governor was obviously careful how this should be done and finally decided to issue the proclamation only if Caesar's crimes were "very great, and oath be made thereof."[28]

Six years later, in 1712, at a time when Antiguans feared a French invasion, the assembly anxiously drew attention to runaways as another source of worry. "The Insolency of the Negroes yt are now run Away from their Masters is very Much Complained off," the assembly submitted, and it asked the governor to offer by proclamation rewards of ten pieces of eight for their capture within thirty days if such fugitives had been at large for more than fifteen days. The assembly obviously distinguished between temporary, short-term absences and long-term absences over fifteen days. The former, although a nuisance, could be tolerated, but longer absences could not, because the authorities believed fugitives in this category had every intention of remaining at large for as long as possible, doing much disquieting mischief in the process. These were the ones who had to be wiped out. The assembly therefore, in addition to taking firm action against such fugitives, recommended that "church Wardens and Constables May be ordered to drive all Negroes yt shal be found in town on Sundays after 9 a clock in the Morning Except such who have Tickett or other lycence from their Masters." The assembly also recommended rewards for blacks who might take up runaways.

Among the notorious slaves then at large was Barry Tankard's Jo, who allegedly not only threatened his master's life, but also "declar'd he will do other Mischief, and in order to enable himselfe has gott arms and is confederated with other notorious rouges." Pointing to the "ill consequence" of Jo as fugitive, the assembly recommended a reward of £30 for his capture dead or alive. When the governor and council demurred at the amount offered, the assembly quickly and firmly pointed out that "Jo is a fellow that will not be taken without Some Risque which may deserve ye reward." Moreover, they refused to allow rewards of less than £3 or ten pieces of eight for taking up runaways absent now for more than thirty days instead of fifteen, "experience having taught us that so considerable a reward do's answer the designe of bringing them in and we can't be assured of a lesser Gratification producing the same effect." Determined to crush fugitive agitation, the assembly wanted the proclamation authorizing rewards for their capture extended by another sixty days.[29]

Not much headway seems to have been made against fugitives, for in 1713 the lieutenant governor himself noted that the "Number of Negros run away from their Masters is very great and the Insolencys they commit Insupportable And if some timely care be not taken to have them apprehended and brought in, it May be of very Evil Consequence." It was some of these runaways who broke into George Pullen's house, forced his wife to flee to the woods, and stirred up the legislature to send out militia companies to scour the countryside in search of fugitives.[30] In 1714 the runaway problem was still so pressing that the legislature once again gave full support to hunting down escaped slaves, offering a gratuity to "any one that shall take, kill or bring the head of any Negro that has been out." More than that, it gave colonels of the militia special instructions to "Cause the Padrounds to be Road from Plantation to Plantation and on the High Roads, every Saturday from five of the Clock in the afternoon, untill ten at night, and the whole day on Sunday, Vizt. from five in the Morning, untill ten of the Clock at night, in order to suppress the Insolency of the Negroes, and all Negro houses to search for such Negros that are not belonging to the plantation, to punish them according to Discretion (if there be found) the same not to be to Extreamity and hereof fail not this being your sufficient Warrant for so doing." That year also saw the enactment of new legislation "for the better Regulating Negros and Suppressing their Conspiracies and profanation of the Lords day."[31]

These measures had limited success, for the following year the assembly admitted that "great Quantitys of Runaway Negros (and some of them Notorious Offenders) do still Continue so as to Indanger peoples lives and goods Traveling lawfully." One of these fugitives was Jonno "a Fellow but with one hand" belonging to Christopher Knights. Rewards were posted for his capture dead or alive. Another was Quamino, once the slave of Colonel Blackman and Mrs. Weyman, who had been at large for about two years. A report from the governor and council in 1716 claimed that Quamino had "lately killed a Negro Man belonging to Archibald Cochran Esqr." when that slave had tried to capture him. Dangerous and elusive, Quamino was singled out for capture and rewards were posted. Yet another notorious fugitive was Daniel, escaped from John Yeamans, who "had formerly one leg taken off for Some Offence or other."[32] The new slave act of 1723, which was devoted almost exclusively to fugitives, singled out for special mention the infamous ringleaders Frank, Papa Will, Africa, and Sharper. That they had formed well-organized and armed bands in the hills as late as the 1720s to defend themselves against recapture and had frequently raided plantations, to the discomfort of the legislature and other whites, is proof of the lengths to which some slaves might take resistance if given the right opportunity.

As a result of efforts made to enforce the 1723 act, particularly in regard to runaways, many of them were captured or killed on the run. Only 3 (2 men, 1 woman) were petitioned for in 1724, but in 1725 the number climbed to 21 (19 executed and 2 killed in flight); 16 of these were men and 5 women. The largest number of compensation claims for runaways in the 1720s came in 1725, when they were more that 75 percent of all claims (28). Then in the next four years the number of claims dwindled, not passing the highest figure of 8 in 1727. Of 76 fugitives apprehended from 1722 to 1732, 68 were executed (60 men, 8 women), and 8 more (6 men, 2 women) killed in flight (see table 9.1). Compensation claims obviously gobbled up a sizable portion of public revenue, which explains attempts especially in the 1720s to compensate owners at standardized rates rather than through appraisal at full value. Such a move, we have seen, raised more difficulties than it solved.

Among fugitives at large in the 1720s was William Mackenin's Harry, who, on the run for about a year, was hunted down and killed in 1725. Savey, for whom his master George Thomas sought compensation in 1726, had been a runaway for about two years before he was captured. He did not live to be executed but succumbed to "wounds received when apprehended." The fugitive Adjo was executed that same year as a ringleader, and Colonel John Burton's Sharper in 1727 after being a runaway for over eight months.[33] Many runaways were also at large in the other Leeward Islands in the 1720s, but official concern was most acute in St. Christopher and Montserrat. In 1722, eleven years after passing a general act for the better government of slaves, the St. Christopher legislature, like that of Antigua in 1723, passed another, updating former laws and devoting special attention to runaways. In explaining to the Board of Trade why the new act was needed, Governor John Hart observed that "St. Christophers has a ridge of very high and inaccessible mountains that runs east and west through the island, which has encouraged great numbers of the negroes to run away and resort thereto; and these mountains affording no sustenance," he added, "they descend in the night to get provisions which they secretly steal or rob by open violence from the neighboring plantations." Hart noted that such raids had frequently occurred during his recent visit to St. Christopher, "and as the number of slaves is the wealth of the inhabitants, and there being no law to restrain the fugitives, which might endanger the safety of the Island, to prevent which this Act is prepared, which tho' it may seem to contain several severities to those that are not acquainted with the sullen and barbarous temper of the negroes, yet I presume when it is compared with Acts of the same nature provided in Jamaica and Barbados, these severities will be thought excusable and even absolutely necessary."

Three fugitives received special attention in the act: Lieutenant Governor William Mathew's Johnny Congo, William McDowall's Christopher, and Marmaduke Bacheler's Antego Quamina. Alleging that they "have for a long while past, and still do head several armed Bands, or Companies of fugitive Negroes in this Island, and do all that in them lies to entice other Negroes to desert their Masters Service, and join them; and have themselves committed, and been the Occasion of committing many flagrant Thefts and Felonies," the act attainted them of felony and condemned them to death. Lieutenant Governor Mathew tried to buy leniency for his slave, Johnny Congo, who, shortly after the act was passed "sent a strange Negro to me" said Mathew, "In the night time desireing I wou'd permitt him to surrender himself or that I wou'd Interceed with both Houses [of the legislature] to give him his life, & be Mercifull to him." Mathew agreed, and Johnny Congo came in and was locked up. Mathew asked the legislature not to execute the slave because "his surrendering has saved thirty Pounds Intended for a Reward for taking him and I shall very Willingly send him off the Island or Dispose of him as both Houses shall require." The assembly, though willing to pay Mathew "all the Regard Imaginable" could not accede to his request, which it believed sprang mainly from "a Mercifull disposition." "The saving of this Negroes Life We are Apprehensive," they argued, "would in the End Cost us many More, in Rendring ye Law Designed for their Reformation Ineffectual in any one Instance."[34] Over in Montserrat in 1722 the legislature passed an act ordering persons owning canoes to secure them in order to prevent slaves from leaving the island altogether. Nevis does not appear to have passed any special legislation to control slaves in the 1720s but may have relied on enforcement of its comprehensive slave act of 1717, which also paid special attention to fugitives. Runaways appear to have been on the rampage here particularly in 1726, when the manager of the Stapleton plantation reported that the little rum he made had been put aside for plantation use, but he was forced "to give the greatest part to catch run away Negroes that have plagu'd everybody this year."[35] That there was a connection in the Leeward Islands between intensification of running away in the 1720s and regular arrival of large slave cargoes from Africa is possible, but not easy to demonstrate.

Slaves who were allowed to join manhunts in Antigua by the 1730s, if not before, were rewarded just as any free person. The authorities realized they needed all the help they could get against fugitives. An assembly report of 1730 complained that "a great number of Runaway negroes harbour themselves in a Body in the Mountains called Sheckerleys and about the Road Mountains & commit great Insults and Robberes in the Neighbourhood." Determined to stamp them out, the assembly vowed "to pursue them and take in such as can be taken and destroy those that will not Submit and cannot be taken." It recommended rewards for free persons and slaves who captured or killed runaways and recruitment of trusty slaves to be attached to two or three militia units that should be speedily sent out to comb the back country. Runaways continued to plague the country about the hills in 1732. In the 1730s Antigua was striken by drought, economic recession, natural disasters, and insect pests that destroyed crops, and during that decade, which saw slave resistance grow from a persistent flicker into a threatening flame with the 1736 plot, slaveowners claimed compensation for 65 fugitives (53 executed and 12 killed in flight) (table 9.1). One of these was Bayer Otto Bayer's Grigory, killed after being out for more than nine months. Another was Francis Franklyn's Tom, who, after he was caught, strangled himself. Naney, a woman belonging to the same master, was killed. So too was Benn, alias Jack Spudo, belonging to George Lucas. In the 1740s owners claimed compensation for 66 fugitives, and in the 1750s only for 15, one of whom, Jacob, belonging to Timothy Clearkey, "died of wounds and bruises given him by another Negro Man, in endeavouring to apprehend him."[36]

What worried authorities most about fugitives in the Leeward Islands was their threat to law and order through the bad example set for other slaves by their raids on plantations, robberies along the highway, and other "insolencies." By the eighteenth century, because it was difficult to withdraw completely from plantation life in an environment that was not generally conducive to long-term absenteeism, fugitives could not avoid such activities. Unable to establish an alternative to plantation life safely in their own maroon communities on these islands, all of them tiny if not all relatively flat, fugitives were forced back, more so than their brethren in Jamaica, Brazil or Surinam, for example, upon a parasitic, predatory mode of existence, relying greatly for survival on the society they had wished to reject.[37]

Planters' business accounts and correspondence contribute added detail to our representation of slave flight in Antigua. Rarely did plantations not have at least a few slaves at large every year. Some suffered more than others. Accounts of Main Swete's plantation for September 10, 1738 to August 13, 1739 record payment of 6s. to "a white Man for taking up a Negro woman" on January 18, 1739, and 3s. 10½d. for "taking up Colla A runaway boy." An entry for February 22 showed: "To Cash 3s/9d for taking up a Negro Woman and A Collar for Ditto." On May 11 Samuel Northey, "the old Overseer," was paid 4s. 9d. for capturing two runaways. Colla seems to have escaped again, for on July 10 the accounts show 2s. 3d. spent for bringing him in, and 14s. for a collar and spur for him. And there was yet another entry: "To Cash paid for taking Colla A Notorious runaway & for a Padlock to keep him in Chains — 10s." Colla was obviously a troublesome runaway, but his name does not appear in compensation lists. In the early 1740s the plantation overseer paid Mr. Warner's slaves 3s. for taking Cuffy, whose capture cost the plantation an additional 4s. 6d. Parham

Plantation accounts for 1750 contain entries of payments for runaways captured.[38]

The absentee planter Josiah Martin in 1731 maintained a close interest in proper disciplining of his fugitive slaves. To his representative, Barry Anderson, Martin wrote, "I desire yt. Jenny be put in Chains, well whipt for I think the worst of treatment good enough for that wretch that run away for two years." Martin also wanted to know whether "Cubbah be come home, I hope if she be you treated her as her fault deserved." Some slave-owners, like Walter Tullideph in 1756, tried to get rid of incorrigible runaways by selling them to whoever would buy. Tullideph asked his associate in Maryland, Henry Lowes, to do the best he could in disposing of "one negroe man an able fellow, served 5 or 6 years to the trade of a Wind mill Carptr a valuable business," who had been "so guilty of running away that I choose to send him off." Other slaveowners, like Dr. Joseph Buckshorne, did not get rid of their troublesome runaways but crippled them to break them out of the habit and simultaneously tame the rebellious spirit of others. Buckshorne, who had leased a plantation from Samuel Tyssen, had one of Judea's legs amputated for "frequently absenting herself from the Doctors Service." Among plantation "stores" were "Negro Collars" and other instruments of punishment for rebels. In 1747, along with other plantation supplies, Tullideph ordered from England "Six negroe locks with three chains." The 1751 inventory of Codrington's Betty's Hope Plantation listed six collars; six slaves were also identified as runaways including "Ben, able but outlawed for Murder." The other five were all able working men and women of the field gang: Cudjoe, and the "great runaways" Tom Accubah, Little Charlee (males), Nanno Madge, and little Aubah (females). Described in Codrington's Cotton Plantation inventory that same year as "of no service" was "Tarbree very old & Runaway." Little Susanah of the same plantation was a "great Runaway" who had belonged to the field gang.[39] The Codrington accounts show frequent payments for runaways captured. We do not have reliable enough quantitative data to assess the proportion of the slave population who ran away every year in the colony as a whole, but qualitative evidence strongly indicates that running away was a nagging problem that occasionally became alarming.

Most fugitives, relying upon their own resourcefulness and the help of others, explored every possible way of eluding recapture within Antigua. During the early years runaways took advantage of the uncleared interior, but as forest and woodland even in the hills gave way to plantation culti-vation, they sought refuge among the growing black population of the towns, tried to leave the island altogether, or moved from place to place within it. As kinship and friendship networks developed and expanded with the growth of the black population, runaways, denied a hospitable geographical environment, tended to rely more and more upon kin and friends to remain at large. This factor should not be overlooked in efforts to explain why some fugitives were able to remain at large within the island for remarkably long periods extending from six months to more than a year. At the trial of Barton's slave Joe, accused of being in the 1736 plot, Colonel Frye's Quamina said that the ringleader Secundi had himself admitted having hidden Joe for a whole year as a fugitive. Since then, added Quamina, "Joe do's more Service to the Run away Negroes, than he do's to his Master." Joe must have been familiar with the operations of what amounted to an Antigua underground railroad because another slave claimed that he was "almost always run away."[40] Whites as well as blacks could have helped runaways, and the slave laws imposed penalties on persons doing so.

By the eighteenth century, certainly, many Antigua fugitives, weighing the odds against remaining at large, decided to put the island behind them and headed by sea for other territories. Throughout the slave period in the Caribbean, slaves from one territory fled to another, by land or sea as circumstances permitted. This pattern of flight was particularly strong, for example, from French Martinique to British St. Lucia after 1803. In Antigua in the eighteenth century, it was as if fugitives who fled across the sea saw the frontier of maroon or runaway refuge, which had receded further and further until little or none was left, as having itself crossed the sea. But they sought refuge not only in the hills of the other islands but also in large towns. If the gradual disappearance of a frontier haven forced Antigua fugitives to face the hazards of migration to other territories, then by contrast, in a colony such as Jamaica, where that sanctuary remained virtually impenetrable, one would expect to find a comparatively lower incidence of marine flight. Jamaican slaves did not have as strong a reason to leave their island altogether, at least before 1739. Many therefore held out in the island's interior, fomenting slave insurrection and pushing the island to the brink of anarchy before the British authorities sued for peace. The acute tensions that built up in Jamaica, then, could not have done so in Antigua. There, the most desperate of slaves, who might have followed those in Jamaica were conditions as favorable, transported themselves outside the island. Such circumstances also help explain contrasting patterns of resistance in the two territories.[41]

In the seventeenth century, to remove temptation from the path of slaves who might be inclined to leave the island, the Antigua legislature passed laws obliging owners of boats and canoes to secure them properly when not in use. Whether such laws were enforced or not, desperate and resourceful slaves found ways to make away with small craft or to stow away to other territories. In 1708 Samuel Mayers claimed compensation for his slave, whom he had accidentally shot while preventing some slaves from leaving the island. In 1759 John Gatley petitioned for his slave Emanuel, who was executed "for running away with the King's Boat." It is likely that many fugitives who chose to escape by sea had some acquaintance with that environment as fishermen or seamen. Some sought refuge in neighboring Dutch St. Eustatius. Governor Douglas called the Dutch on that island in 1712 "A poor handful of. . . intollerable neighbours by protecting our negroes deserters from the regiment and all malefactors who fly thither from justice." Other fugitives crossed over to Guadeloupe. [42]

By the 1750s, if not before, fugitives from the Leeward Islands made it to the Spanish island of Puerto Rico, a few hundred miles to the west. Between the two territories were scattered several small islands including the British Virgins, and St. Croix, St. Thomas, and St. John belonging to the Danes. Nearest to Puerto Rico, at its eastern end, was Vieques, or Crab Island, as the British called it, an abandoned island in dispute between the Spanish, British, and Danes. In their passage to Puerto Rico, fugitives from the Leewards probably made temporary stops at some of these places, especially Vieques. Leewards governor Walter Hamilton, commenting on that island's suitability for British occupation, observed in 1716 that while the land was very good, Vieques "Lyes so very nigh the Island of Porto Rico that nobody is secure in his property," not only because the Spanish would oppose settlement but also because "the Negroes or other slaves may upon the least disgust get over to that Island where if once they gett among the Cow-killers (which are a sort of Banditti which are settled in the remote parts of that Island) there is no getting them again altho the governor of that Island should be inclinable to make restitutions he'd hardly have it in his power." [43] In Hamilton's view, the problem of slave flight to Puerto Rico (such as the Leewards later experienced) would be greatly magnified at Vieques if the British settled there. While the island remained abandoned, however, it must have been a convenient stepping stone for Leewards fugitives responding to the Puerto Rico magnet.

What was Puerto Rico's attraction? Four fugitives from St. Croix arrived in Puerto Rico as early as 1664, and the governor, backed by the Spanish Council of the Indies, allowed them to remain free because "it does not seem proper that the King should reduce to slavery those who sought his protection." The Council of the Indies also decreed that runaways reaching Puerto Rico would be free so long as they agreed to be baptized and swore allegiance to the king. "By the beginning of the century," according to one historian of Puerto Rico, "so many had arrived that in the year 1714 they were organized as a separate settlement in the neighborhood of San Juan." Through their network of communication, Leewards slaves no doubt got word of the promised land to the west. Spanish royal orders in 1680, 1693, and 1740, and a royal cedula of 1750 extended the promise of freedom to fugitives landing in Puerto Rico. In 1798 a cedula general to all Spanish colonial officials forbade return of fugitives, but this, it would seem, only openly announced what had been general Spanish policy for many years.[44] Along with the Leewards, several other slave colonies close to Spanish territory lost slaves because of this tolerant policy: Dutch St. Eustatius and the Danish islands of St. Thomas, St. John, and St. Croix to Puerto Rico; Jamaica to Cuba; South Carolina to Florida; and Essequibo in Dutch Guiana to Orinoco or Spanish Guiana (Venezuela).[45]

By the 1750s slave flight from the Leewards to Puerto Rico, stimulated by both "push" and "pull" forces, had become "a matter of great importance." Governor Gilbert Fleming, writing to the secretary of state in 1751, reported that slaves often escaped, especially from Tortola, Anguilla, and Spanish Town, smaller islands in the general Leewards government. From these the flow was apparently heavy enough that Fleming feared white settlers might be forced to abandon their holdings. What Hamilton in 1716 had feared might have happened if Englishmen settled on Vieques began to materialize therefore several years later in other islands close enough to Puerto Rico. Fleming wrote to the Spanish governor Don Augustine De Pareja seeking to recover the runaways, but, Pareja having died, his successor, Don Estivan Bravo de Rivero, responded that he could "say nothing to this point" and supposed that Fleming had "full information" already from Pareja. "The truth is, that the Preists in that Island have the direction of all affairs," Fleming told the secretary of state, "and every Runaway Criminal they Christen serves to swell their account of Conversions. It must be own'd they treat all Nations in this particular with impartiality, and the Dutch at Curacao have demanded a restitution of their Slaves with no more success than we, They therefore on the reception of Deserters at Porto Rico, find means to lay hold of a Priest, and detain him till they are restor'd." Whether Fleming was here advising that the English try to get their hands on Spanish priests is not clear; but that he could not secure the return of runaways from his government certainly irritated him.

To Rivero's claim that fugitives arrived in Puerto Rico "in search of the Catholick Religion" and under royal orders became free, Fleming had a ready response. "I pray leave to assure you," he wrote, "that not a single slave has deserted us in search of the Catholick Religion, or of Christianity of any Denomination whatsoever. If it is imagin'd that their suffering themselves to be Christn'd makes converts of them, and justifys the encouraging their Desertion, this furnishes us with a reason for inviting Your Slaves into the Reform'd Religion in the same manner." On such grounds, said Fleming, "we can neither of us exact their Servitude, and we injure the other, to give Spiritual advantage to Slaves, who are quite insensible of them, except as procuring their manumissions, and a Sacrament, instituted for Penitents only, is of no use to them, but as an Indempnity for their Crimes; and, in their sence, to make their Repentence unnecessary." Fleming hastened to add that if Rivero seriously believed that Puerto Rico's location to leeward gave it the advantage "of laying hold of more of our Slaves than we can of yours," there was no reason why British satisfaction for Spanish wrongs should be confined to Puerto Rico or in respect of slaves alone.[46]

Fleming never secured return of fugitives, whom he called a bunch of "irreligious Criminals." Neither did Governor George Thomas, who reported in 1754 that Tortola and Anguilla were losing slaves, while others from St. Christopher had "lately made some bold and dangerous Attempts" to reach the Spanish island. Unable to curb such flight by attacking its source in the Leewards or securing the cooperation of Spanish authorities, Thomas commented with some exaggeration that the whole affair "will in time prove a more effectual Method of ruining His Majesties Sugar Colonies" than if the king of Spain declared perpetual war; "for in that case," Thomas added, "the Inhabitants of the Leeward Islands would be constantly upon their Guard, and at Liberty to make Reprisals." Evidence from the last quarter of the eighteenth century shows that fugitives continued to arrive in Puerto Rico, where a plantation economy would begin to develop significantly near the end of the century. For years during that century the fugitives issue remained a source of friction in the Caribbean between the British and the Spanish.[47]

Whether runaways remained in Antigua or crossed over to other territories, there are two other important issues about them that deserve attention. Who were they, and what caused them to run away? These questions are obviously related because slaves were largely defined by their roles and occupations in slave society. Many resorted to flight in response to intolerable changes in their environment or changes that made flight a plausible alternative to enslavement. Others were rejecting slavery itself. A number of slaves were habitually absent, whatever their occupation, visiting relatives and friends. The motives of most other fugitives were often more complex. For South Carolina before 1740 Peter Wood found at least three distinct patterns of flight and their causes. One pattern related to fugitives with clear family links, another to newly arrived Africans, and the last to slaves who had recently acquired new masters. These slaves were most likely to use escape in response to various grievances. In South Carolina and Virginia in the eighteenth century it has been shown that most fugitives were likely to be acculturated or native born, while the style of flight, individual, group, or truant, varied between these and new Africans. These conclusions are based on careful analysis of data in slave advertisements especially.[48] The Antigua source material does not permit such treatment of runaways. Compensation lists for 1722–63 indicate, however, that most fugitives were males. There were 193 males executed, or 92.4 percent of the total number of runaways, and only 16 females, 7.66 percent (table 9.1). Ties to offspring probably deterred women from running away in larger numbers. We do not yet know the occupations of these people, whether they were Creoles, acculturated Africans, or new Africans, or specifically why they ran away.

In regard to fugitives' motives there are nevertheless some general contemporary observations to work from. Many "Negroes sometimes upon slight or no Occasions runaway and absent themselves in Gangs," the 1723 slave act stated. The Reverend Robert Robertson, we will recall, also claimed in 1729 that slaves ran away "upon slight and trifling Pretences, and very often without pretending to have had any Cause or Provocation given to them at all, and generally, when their Labour, or Attendance is most wanted." Expressing a similar interpretation in 1783, the Antigua legislature complained about "the late frequent running away of. . .Slaves who generally without any other Reason, than the Dictates of their own Vicious Inclinations, absent themselves from their Duty, and till they are apprehended and Compelled will not return thereto." It was not that slaves ran away without cause, which is nonsense, but that slaveowners could not readily find any that satisfied them. What they failed to appreciate fully, as Jean Fouchard has recently shown in his study of St. Domingue, was that slaves fled to freedom, that is, away from their masters,[49] preferring this status, however precarious, to enslavement. Implied here is a certain level of political consciousness among fugitives who escaped without apparent cause, especially if, according to Robertson, they fled when their services were most needed. We might therefore also expect seasonal variation in patterns of slave flight, with an increase of flight during the crop season. Compensation claims for executed or killed fugitives, however, are not a good source to evaluate this supposition quantitatively since they bear no direct relationship to the specific time of flight. In any case, such well-timed escapes allowed slaves to make very effective use of flight as resistance and greatly inconvenience masters.

Many slaves escaped because of harsh day-to-day treatment, which might make life intolerable especially during periods of subsistence crisis or deprivation brought on by drought or famine, as during the 1720s and 1730s. In 1731 the lieutenant governor and council explained that Antigua slaves "are very frequently put under a Necessity of absenting themselves from their Masters Service by Extraordinary Severities and their not being allowed a Sufficient Quantity of Provisions to enable them to go through the Labour required of them." These gentlemen wanted to reduce the penalties placed on fugitives, many of whom, they felt, were forced into flight by overwork and undernourishment. Under such conditions slaves who might otherwise not have escaped would indeed do so "upon the slightest pretense" such as fear of punishment or possible sale.[50] Slaves who fled, however, when food supplies were generally low all over the island, risked starvation. Runaways plagued Nevis during the critical drought of the mid 1720s and the Stapleton Plantation lost many stock as well as slaves, most of whom had run away. The drought that affected Antigua at the same time might also help explain why so many runaways were apprehended in 1725, to say nothing about those still at large. Of at least 28 compensation claims for executed slaves in that year, 21 were for runaways. We will recall too that vigorous prosecution of slave offenders, mostly runaways, so staggered the Antigua treasury that the legislature ruled on standardized compensation to replace compensation by appraisal. And it is perhaps not surprising that during the season of drought and runaway problems, Nevis had a slave conspiracy in 1725. On the origins of this episode of collective slave resistance there is no hard evidence, but they might be traced to unrest and suffering during these hard times. The incident caused a stir in Nevis, but, after two slaves were found guilty and burned, the alarm rapidly died down.[51]

Four years later it was the Antiguans' turn to feel uneasy. Of twenty-six claims for compensation submitted in 1729, fourteen were for slaves convicted for involvement in a conspiracy to revolt. As in Nevis earlier, there is not a shred of evidence to show what prompted the plot, and as with many other such incidents, it is difficult to tell whether it was real or imagined. Antiguan authorities, for their part, however, believed that it was real enough, and that it had originated among the slaves of a council member, Colonel Nathaniel Crump. The legislature alleged that Crump's slaves planned to kill him and his family "and Cutt off every White Inhabitant." After some preliminary inquiries the attorney general concluded that "the design laid much deeper than is yet imagined," and the assembly concurred, describing the affair as "too Momentous to be given in Charge to Two or three Magistrates," the procedure laid down in the 1723 slave act when slaves faced trial for capital crimes.

Examined before the lieutenant governor and council and tried by three magistrates, five slaves were found guilty and condemned to die. Three (Boquin, Prurry, and Hanniball) belonging to Colonel Crump were burned alive after spending seven days in prison, while another, Hercules, was hanged, drawn and quartered and his head struck up on a pike; the other escaped with banishment. Also sentenced to transportation by a special act were nine others against whom the evidence was not strong enough to bring the death penalty. The assembly's firm recommendation was that they be banished "to some place from whence they cannot carry on a Correspondence with the Negros of this Island," preferably the Spanish coast; "but as Such Traders are Not to be found in a short time," they settled for Virginia or Maryland.[52] These slaves never reached either of those mainland colonies. In 1737, when Antiguans were only just recovering from the sharp shock of the islandwide plot discovered the year before, word reached the governor that the banished slaves had never left the Leewards and were still in the "custody" of Colonel Jessup on his plantation in St. Christopher.

For informing on the plotters, Tom, belonging to Robert Tuitt, was set free and his master paid his full appraised value. Tom was also granted "during Life by the Publick of this Island Ten pounds per Annum to be paid by the Treasurer at two equal payments the first to commence" on March 25, 1729. In all more than £662 was paid out in compensation to owners whose slaves were either executed or banished, an outlay the treasury could ill afford because the governor reported that while many more slaves were obviously involved, "a further Examination is declined as well because everything is perfectly quiet, as upon account of the great Expence it would bring on the country."[53] Public cost, of course, was one thing, but individual slaveowners would have had to consider availability of replacements if they lost slaves. With the conspiracies of both 1729 and 1736, while individual self-interest in relation to the state of the slave market should not be forgotten, it is clear that limited funds primarily helped determine the extent of government retaliation.

Antiguan slaves continued restless in the 1730s, and the general plot of 1736 emerged from such a background, precipitated by a number of developments that deserve separate detailed discussion in the next chapter. But it must be observed here that what happened in Antigua seemed to have been part of a general unrest that swept through several slave societies in the Americas. Slave disturbances of major importance that we know about surged through St. John in the Danish Virgin Islands (1733), Antigua (1736), Guadeloupe (1736–38), Jamaica (1730s), and South Carolina (1739). And there were also other, smaller incidents.[54] While the specific sets of conditions that precipitated rebellion in these cases may vary, one cannot help wondering whether, especially in relation to the Caribbean, the rebellions were interrelated. The geographical proximity of St. John, Antigua, and Guadeloupe invites some intriguing questions about the "dangerous spirit of liberty" that a report from Jamaica observed had seized slaves in several sugar islands. It was not impossible for slaves in one territory to follow the example of others elsewhere into rebellion, as Governor Gilbert Fleming and the St. Christopher legislature obviously knew. In 1750 Fleming reported that the legislature was gravely concerned that the chief fortress, Brimstone Hill, might be "surpriz'd by Runaway Negros," and that the "Genrall insurrection of Negroes at Curacao [off Venezuela] might have a dangerous influence upon Our own Slaves." The

St. Christopher legislature took the wise course, so far as they were concerned, of seeking to strengthen the island's internal defense. If Leeward slaveowners feared contamination from slave behavior in Curaçao, several hundred miles to the south across the wide stretch of the Caribbean Sea, they must have been much more apprehensive when rebellions broke out close to home. That insurrection could be influenced by external upheavals is adequately demonstrated in the case of French St. Domingue during the Revolutionary period, when slaves, fired by events in France, redoubled and redirected their efforts to topple the slave system and eventually set in its place Haiti, the black republic. Just as information about a faraway European event such as the Revolution in France seeped back to the slaves in St. Domingue, who then interpreted events to fit their own objectives,[55] so too did island slaves receive and interpret and act upon similarly (to them) significant upheavals led by slaves elsewhere. This was especially so since these places were within sight and easy reach and therefore figured in their imagination of a wider world of slavery in which they shared a plight with others only a few miles away.

Precisely what caused the Montserrat conspiracy, which was discovered in March 1768, is not known, but Governor William Woodley wrote that the island was "threatened with a Very Dangerous Insurrection of the Negroes, which was however Happily prevented by the Hand of Providence." Woodley, reporting to the secretary of state on April 22, 1768, indicated that he had arrived in the Leewards on April 10 to find Montserrat "in the Utmost Consternation." Upon discovery of the plot Admiral Pye at Antigua dispatched two ships from the Leeward Islands Station at English Harbour to Montserrat, while the president of the St. Christopher council, then in command of the Leewards until Woodley's arrival, sent over fifty men from the 68th Regiment. "The Plot of these Miserable Wretches was deep laid," Woodley explained, "& must have been long projected as they had furnished themselves with Great store of Arms & Ammunition they had concealed in the Mountains." The affair was to have been put into effect on St. Patrick's Day (March 17) "which the Principal of the White Inhabitants, chiefly Irish, usually assemble together to commemorate. Those Negroes that attended within Doors were to have secured the swords of the Gentlemen, and upon a Signal given, Those that were without were to fire into the Room, and put every Man to Death, as he endeavored to escape. Tho Savages, they were not insensible to the Power of Beauty, but had cast lots for the Ladies who they intended to carry off the Island to Porto Rico in the Ships which then lay in the Harbour, and were to have been secured upon the Same Signal." By chance, a few days before the scheme was carried out, a woman (presumably white) overheard two slaves talking about arms and made a report. Her "Evidence was scarcely credited, as she was much in Liquor when she gave it." The authorities checked the story, and, at the time of Woodley's writing from Antigua, five ringleaders had been executed. The governor feared there would be many more. He also hoped that the plot was "entirely crushed," however, and proposed to visit Montserrat himself shortly.

He did so on April 26. The island was under martial law, but the inhabitants' "Fears were. . .a good deal abated, as they had taken and executed seven of the Ring leaders, and two others destroyed themselves in prison, but without making any confession." Woodley noted that he had been in error in his earlier report about slave caches of arms in the mountains. That information "was without Foundation, there being none to be found." When he left, a detachment of soldiers stayed behind, and Admiral Pye kept the man-of-war *Squirrell* stationed there "to be a check upon any farther Views they may entertain against the White people." By the time Woodley got back to Antigua, having visited the other Leewards, martial law had been lifted in Montserrat and "the Inhabitants gone to their several Habitations in the Country." The conspiracy must have given them a good scare if, fearing the worst or a general revolt, they had abandoned their rural plantations. A letter from Pye written on October 6, 1768 reported nine ringleaders executed and more than thirty still confined awaiting transportation at the first opportunity. Responding to news about the plot, the secretary of state communicated to Woodley the king's compassion "for the ignorant and misled Wretches who must suffer," and his wish that "your Humanity will not allow the Punishment to exceed, what future Security renders absolutely necessary."[56]

The next major scare of collective slave violence took place in St. Christopher in 1770, before memories of the Montserrat incident of two years earlier had dimmed. Woodley, writing from St. Christopher, reported that in March the inhabitants had been much alarmed when they believed a plot to revolt was discovered. As it turned out, the authorities were mistaken, but, taking no chances, Woodley ordered the arrest of sixteen alleged ringleaders, who were confined separately aboard several ships in the harbor. After careful inquiry the supposed plot proved to be "nothing more than a Meeting every Saturday night of the Principle Negroes belonging to Several Estates in One quarter of the Island called Palmetto Point, at which they affected to imitate their Masters and had appointed a General, Lieutenant General, a Council and Assembly and the other Officers of Government, and after holding Council and Assembly they Concluded the night with a Dance." Woodley observed further that these goings on, as innocent as they seemed, could have led to a plot, had they not been discovered in time.[57]

It is not certain whether this was the very first time St. Christopher slaves had put on such rituals or ceremonies, whose surface significance may have been that of role reversal or status inversion. In any case, at a deeper level, they call attention to the complex evolution of the slaves' culture as slaves, Africans and Creoles, carved out worlds of meaning for themselves within the larger world established by slavery. These ceremonies bring to mind the "Negro election day" ritual festivals held by the slaves in New England and parts of the middle colonies of the mainland during the second half of the eighteenth century. They had African roots, and it has been argued that, in the colonies where they were permitted, they did not challenge the existing order but confirmed it. In such places on "Negro election day," ritual performance might vary, but characteristically there was great festivity followed by selection of black officials in imitation of white hierarchy. "These officers," according to Ira Berlin, "sometimes held symbolic power over the whole community and real power over the black community. While the black governors held court, adjudicating minor disputes, other slaves paraded and partied dressed in their master's clothes and mounted on their master's horse." The slaves found some respite, some release from slavery through these ceremonies, "an opportunity to express themselves more fully than the narrow boundaries of slavery ordinarily allowed." Perhaps the most meaningful form of expression was recognition of leading or highly respected figures within their community, which helped establish part of the rudiments of emerging black politics.[58] Whites in St. Christopher and other colonies in which slavery was deeply entrenched most feared the political dimensions of role reversal and could not allow such observances even symbolically. By honoring their leaders and organizing legislative sessions, the St. Christopher slaves involved in the supposed plot of 1770 obviously raised the fearful specter of possible subversive action before the eyes of whites who could think only of projected rebellion. Hence, then, Governor Woodley's considered opinion that if the slaves' activities had gone undiscovered they "probably would have ended in what was apprehended."

Slaves in Antigua, women and men, resisted slavery as best they could in countless ways, carefully calculating most of the time how much they could get away with, and when necessary putting their lives on the line by openly challenging the slave system. Data on resistance shows that, while slave women also engaged in resistance, they did not do so openly, in ways comprehended by the law, as often as men. In the case of running away, if it is true that the typical fugitive in New World slave societies was a young unattached male slave, then it should not be surprising that many more males than females were fugitives in Antigua, although it would be extremely useful to know what motivated these few women. When specific grievances and the wider range of possible resistance to slavery in general are taken into account, it might simply mean that Antigua slave women figured more prominently in less overt acts such as "insolence," which says so little and yet so much, and which whites constantly referred to. There were ways in which whites dealt with such behavior, when it was perceived as disrespectful or challenging to the master's authority, that kept offenders off the standard documentary sources. Slave womens' style of resistance probably focused on the day-to-day variety, in which might be included various inventive ways of obstructing sexual exploitation by white males, a form of resistance with strong economic and political implications. Cultural resistance or the slaves' inventive efforts to create their own community and culture underlay, as deeper currents of response, individual and collective resistance by slave men and women. Conditions of slavery, of course, set limits upon the process of community formation; but in all New World slave societies slaves responded creatively to the challenge of shaping their own institutions and values. They drew upon the African reservoir, sometimes replenished by the arrival of new Africans, adapting and responding in ways that suggested a collective awareness that resistance and survival came with not succumbing completely to the master's ideal of fully manipulable property.[59] Elements of the culture of the Antiguan slaves would play prominent roles in the development of the 1736 slave plot.

10

"A Conspiracy Deeply Laid & Extended Wide"

Provoked by a blend of anxiety and curiosity, the burning questions on the minds of the authorities and other whites in every New World slave society after a major slave revolt or conspiracy were, Why and how had it happened? Slaveowners outside afflicted territories, contemplating their own situation, probably also sought answers to these same questions from accounts that reached them. While there is not much in the trial record of the Antigua conspirators of 1736 by which to trace the roots of the plot, the conscientious judges did attempt an explanation, unsystematically framed, however, and based less upon slave testimony directly than upon their own informed understanding of what must have motivated the rebels.[1]

"As it seems to us, agreeable to the Intent of the last Order of your Excellency and Council that we Should Report What Our Opinion is, as to the safety of this Island," they wrote, "we think, it will not be impertinent to touch as introductory to it, upon what we think Encouraged our Slaves to Attempt our ruin and Distruction." Evidently taking island conditions into account and interpreting slave motivation against that background, the judges recorded that "tho' we cannot be very certain, by what Particular Inducement the Slaves might be brought to set on foot this Inhuman Plot[,] Yet we may Say with some Certainty, that next to hopes of freedom, the greatest was the inequality of numbers of White and Blacks neither can we lay down rules to remedy this evil; but think it would be greatly helpt: if gentlemen resided on their estates here, and that men of the best figure and fortune, would not so generally put slights upon the commission of the Peace and Militia"; moreover, "that slaves were disabled from being handicraft tradesmen, overseers, drivers, or distillers, shop keepers, or hawkers and pedlors or saylors; not suffered to keep horses or work out for themselves and that more of our menial servants, and our wet and dry nurses were to be whites and no fiddlers for gain, but whites to be suffered; and that generally more encouragement should be given to whites by our laws and practices and less to slaves." And finally, they added, "our present wholesome laws for government of our slaves [should be] vigorously executed."

Bearing in mind the observation of Sidney W. Mintz that "summaries of possible reasons why slaves revolted . . . are rather more neat than verifiable," and "tend to obscure the daily realities of plantation life,"[2] we may use the judges' summary as a convenient starting point and try to determine, as far as possible, the plausibility of their set of causes, while at the same time identifying others that, taken together, may have had a decisive influence in motivating Antigua slaves to plot whites' "ruin and Distruction."

Apart from the slaves' desire for freedom, the judges also stressed the role of a high ratio of blacks to whites, and we are left to determine its causal significance from their several recommendations to reduce the racial imbalance. These various remedies should therefore be carefully considered because they were meant to refer to existing "situations" within the colony that presumably together helped develop such a striking imbalance. A close reading of the sources suggests that each "remedy," along with the slaves' desire for freedom and their large numbers, may best be discussed as preconditions or underlying, long-run causes that combined to create an environment conducive to slave revolt.

Of the plot's underlying causes, the slaves' desire for freedom seemed so obvious to the judges that they did not bother to elaborate, except to state that "Freedom and the Possession of their Master's Estates were to be the Rewards of their Perfidy & Treachery," and that "a New government was to be Established, when the white Inhabitants were Intirely extirpated."[3] The longing for freedom, universal among slaves in the Americas, helped develop a persistent potential for revolt. But slaves, it can be argued, did not all perceive freedom in the same way; and when historians themselves talk about freedom as an objective of slaves, they fail to define what that freedom meant to slaves, who could be ideologically divided. It is important, for example, to determine whether Africans held certain ideas about freedom that might yet mean binding attachments to others that did not accord with whites' or even Creole blacks' understanding of the term. When some slaves, particularly Africans, sought freedom, they may have wanted above all to sever attachments to white masters, but these same slaves might have considered it perfectly natural, in accordance with homeland practice, to attach themselves to other Africans in some dependent relationship.[4]

What, then, did the Antigua rebels want? We can say with certainty that they aimed at securing freedom from bondage to white slaveowners, although it is not certain, once they were successful, how they would preserve it. There is nothing to show how they planned to consolidate their possession of the island once they had taken it, or what kind of state they intended to establish. A utopia, a "new government," yes, but of what type? Would freedom from enslavement to whites, having been achieved, be extended to all blacks regardless of status, occupation, or ethnic origin, or would other patterns of dependence or social oppression have been introduced? These are intriguing questions, all the more so because the judges claimed that the Creoles, island-born and presumably more fully acculturated slaves, had secretly planned among themselves "to settle a Commonwealth, and to make Slaves of the Coromantees, and Negroes of all other Nations, and to destroy Court, and all such who should refuse to submit to the Terms the Creoles should please to prescribe or impose."[5] If this is true, we must reflect on possible Creole ideas of oppression and their perception of how different they were from Africans and of who should be prime candidates for subordination within their conception of society. One reading of the judges' claim would be that Creoles were not necessarily opposed to servitude so long as they themselves would not become victims. It is certainly not easy to tell from the evidence what kinds of new states or social formations the rebels had in mind when they planned to overthrow whites, and this may be because they had not fully worked this out among themselves. Both Creoles and Coromantees, on the other hand, could have had a secret plan, but the judges probably took note of the Creoles' plan because it emerged more easily out of the evidence they heard and accorded with their belief in divisions within black community along ethnic lines, particularly between Africans, lumped together, and Creoles, whom they saw as the most "sensible" slaves.

Slave resistance in its many forms in the island and elsewhere forced Antigua slaveowners to recognize the potential for slave revolt in their society for, as the judges asserted, the ramifications of sugar and slavery were tightly interwoven. The Reverend Robert Robertson confessed earlier, in 1729, that it was "plain to all that know what sort of Creatures" slaves were, "how they happen to be brought here, & c. that the Planter would purchase none of them, if he could help it; He buys them because, as things stand, they are absolutely necessary to Sugar-making, and the other Business of the Colonies." In their general report on the slave plot the judges declared in similar vein that while holding blacks in bondage gave masters "many Reflections, highly disagreeable and uneasy," they would yet cling to slavery "not of Choice but of necessity," for "unless (as it is not to be imagined) our Mother Countrey should quit that valuable part of its Trade arising from the Sugar Colonies, which its Laws have given So much Encouragement to, Englishmen must continue to be Masters of Slaves, and will be under a necessity of using them as such; even for self preservation." But, the judges added, slaveowners had not established that essential mastery and control over slaves proper to their servile condition; as a result, "having admitted them to the Occupations, truly proper only for Free men, It had like to have been our Ruin."[6] The corollary to continued use of slavery was that slaves would also persistently outnumber slaveowners, who would increasingly put great faith in their system of control to maintain the slave system and the slaves' subordinate position within it.

Next to "Hopes of lawless Liberty," the judges had stated, "the vast superiority in number" of blacks to whites was the other major precondition for the plot. And they believed it was true, for when they asked the legislature to reward cooperative slaves whose evidence had helped at the rebels' trials as a way to plant distrust among slaves, they strengthened their argument by pointing out that "there must of necessity always be a number of Slaves among us, vastly superior to the Whites, which will be a lasting Temptation to the former to enter into Conspiracies."[7] To the judges, then, the slaves' numerical superiority appreciably enhanced the potential for revolt. As we have seen, disease, drought, inability to pay taxes, indebtedness, land engrossment by the wealthy few, fear of war, and the hiring out and training of black tradesmen, together banished all prospect of steady white population growth, which ceased after 1724. In the period 1724–34 the ratio of blacks to whites increased from more than 4, to more than 6 to 1. In 1736 the population of Antigua was estimated at not more than 3,000 whites, and roughly 24,000 slaves, who therefore made up more than 80 percent of the inhabitants. Regardless of high mortality, steady importation of sizable numbers of Africans in the 1720s contributed significantly to slave population growth. If the distribution of population is taken into account, slaves outnumbered whites by larger margins than total population figures would suggest in rural districts with many sugar plantations. And if we remember that Antigua was only 108 square miles in area and studded with sugar plantations from coast to coast, then the large size of the slave population takes on added significance. The density of slaves per square mile was about 222 compared with 28 for whites in 1736, and the sugar plantations huddled together on the small island, often not bounded by fences, were not isolated. Both conditions facilitated communication among slaves.[8] The size of slave colonies and the number, location, and distribution of economic units, among other things, should help to explain varying patterns of collective resistance. A planned islandwide revolt, for example, was far more conceivable in Antigua or Barbados than in Jamaica, which was much larger and where plantations were more isolated, even if the geography of that island made slave resistance more strikingly overt. In mainland colonies such as Virginia, Maryland, and South Carolina, although plantation units were also isolated, other factors militated against frequent rebellion.[9]

Absentee ownership itself, according to the judges, contributed to the small size of the white population and overall population imbalance, but the strength of its role is difficult to assess, although we know there were Antigua absentees in the eighteenth century, at least seven acts being passed against them in the first fifty years. We do not know how many proprietors were absent in 1736, or during the 1730s, a decade when, significantly, no anti-absentee legislation was passed. The lack of convincing evidence linking absentee ownership with the plot, and the judges' own indirect reference to it as a cause, leads to the tentative conclusion that its role was more likely minor. We would like to know much more about the general treatment and behavior of slaves on absentees' plantations, during the economic recession of the 1730s particularly, to discover whether they fared especially badly and played prominent roles in the plot.[10]

While it is admittedly tricky to demonstrate a direct causal link between a favorable ratio of blacks to whites and the development of slave unrest, particularly in regard to revolts and conspiracies, historians have often associated the two, especially when the slave population increased dramatically shortly before the collective effort.[11] Such a striking development did not take place in Antigua, where, in the early 1730s, black population growth was a more gradual, if steady, affair; but the judges and many other slaveowners were aware that the existence of a black majority could lead to internal disorder. What was more important than its growth, however, was the behavior of the slave population. While blacks continued to outnumber whites after 1724 in Antigua, they did not mount any serious concerted challenge to the supremacy of slaveowners, who therefore had just reason, while conscious of its subversive potential, not to be overly worried about population imbalance. The role therefore that the ratio of blacks to whites played in pushing the slaves into rebellion is elusive and should perhaps be examined from the slaves' standpoint.

Did the slave leaders have a clear sense that slaves outnumbered whites? And if they did, was this imbalance one of the first things they considered when planning the revolt? Or did they take it into account later as planning proceeded, as they developed and refined strategy based on assessment of conditions both in their favor and against them? The Antigua plot went through a long gestation of planning and careful organization, during which, it can be argued, slave leaders had ample opportunity to evaluate conditions in the island and their chance for success. Even if they had not taken into account from the beginning that a large slave majority could be advantageous, they would certainly have had to consider slave numbers once they decided that taking the whole island was the most sensible approach to revolt. Such an objective required recruitment of a number of immediate followers from many sections of the island whose efforts would be closely coordinated and who would be privy to the details of the plot. And at the same time, leaders would have had to calculate the extent of rank and file following once the revolt got off the ground. The Coromantee leaders staged a ceremony to determine exactly that, while Court, aware of the immensity and complexity of an islandwide revolt, and that there were not enough of his Coromantee countrymen to pull it off as a purely ethnic affair, brought Tomboy and the Creoles in on the plans. In weighing the chances of success, Court, Tomboy, and other leaders relied on a large enough number of slaves being available to stage the revolt and devised strategy on the basis of (a) a surprise attack, (b) seizure of the main town by several large bands of armed slaves acting in a coordinated assault, (c) seizure of shipping in the harbor, as well as of fortifications, and (d) the march through the countryside toward town by other armed slaves who would leave terrible scenes of destruction in their wake. All of these maneuvers or intermediate objectives involved deployment of slaves in St. John's town and in the countryside.

It is therefore extremely likely that slave leaders in particular were aware of the critical role the existence of a slave majority could play to help a well-coordinated revolt succeed. When these driven rebel leaders went about recruiting other slaves, that could have been one of the points they stressed, especially to those who needed much persuading. Once it was pointed out to more willing slaves, these rebels would have recognized a good opportunity to strike back at slaveowners, particularly if, as we shall see, other conditions in the island nurtured a restless mood. The slaves' numerical superiority and their recognition of it, while not sufficient to cause revolt, were nevertheless important preconditions for the intensification of a predictably explosive situation.

In working out their plans, even with numbers on their side, slave leaders also had to consider the military strength of the white minority. If whites were well equipped, the militia well manned, and morale high, if fortifications were in good repair, if overall the island was in a state of sound military preparedness, then the rebels would need in their favor a great deal more than mere numbers. Generally, however, whites were at a distinct disadvantage. As we have seen, the quality of the militia corps was generally poor, and in 1736 it continued so. In 1734 the force for local defense consisted of 1,373 men: 1,223 militiamen and 150 soldiers stationed in the island. At the same time, the slave population was 24,408. The situation had changed little by 1736, when the governor complained, for example, that the troops in the island, consisting of 5 companies of 31 men each, were "much too small a force for security." When we turn to consider military opposition to the slaves' designs, the real basis of comparison should be not between slaves and fighting white males, but between active adult male slaves and fighting white males. Census data for slaves are of no help because they were usually not broken down by sex and age. However, in such a large slave population, suitable males must still have outnumbered the militia and soldiers, who, it should be noted, would also have had to oppose large numbers of slave women, who "by their Insolent behavior and Expressions," Vallentine Morris believed, "had the utter Extirpation of the White as much at heart, as the Men, and would undoubtedly have done as much Mischief by Butchering all the Women and children."[12]

The situation of the whites was even weaker than the poor quality and small size of the island defense force would suggest because, in addition, the fortifications were in a very bad state of disrepair. Monk's Hill fortification was for months without gates in 1736, and, perhaps not surprisingly, no one stood guard. Gates and guards were quickly provided during the heat of the conspiracy's discovery. Having duly considered military opposition within the colony, slave leaders understood the tactical importance of capturing the forts and shipping and made them primary objectives, keeping the forts meanwhile under especially close observation. At the same time, needing as many arms as they could lay their hands upon, the rebels tried to steal them. Not long before the plot was discovered "two or three Negroes were caught in the night coming into the Fort [Monk's Hill] armed with Cutlaces, and this where is the Grand Magazine of the Island now almost full of Powder, and the only Arsenal of small Armes."[13] How well-armed the slaves were by October 1736, when their long-laid plans would be put into action, it is not possible to say; yet their projected maneuvers suggest that leaders had obviously taken island opposition into account, and, finding it not intimidatingly strong and organized, they continued to develop their scheme for revolt. Governor Mathew, for his part, believed that the size of the slave majority offered sufficient inducement to slaves to plan rebellion. Drawing the attention of the Board of Trade to the contents of the judges' report in 1737, Mathew asked that "Your Lordships will please to Regard the Methods proposd for the Future Safety of this & other His Majestys Colonys, where so great Numbers of Negros Encourage such dangerous Attempts.[14]

Probably much more significant than the slaves' numerical strength was the ground swell of slave resistance that preceded and accompanied the planning stages of the revolt. One writer has contended that in 1736 the slaves were simply building upon the experience of the earlier abortive plot of 1728–29, but the judges did not make that connection. While the precise link between the two plots may not be clear, it is nonetheless obvious that more general slave resistance, particularly if for some reason intensified, could furnish fertile ground for the growth and maturation of more ambitious schemes just when other conditions seemed to favor slave revolt. It is easy, perhaps, to see the plot as the "highest stage" of slave resistance in Antigua up to that time and to make a case for continuity between the two, but the plot undeniably broke sharply with more common types of resistance in many ways. Slave resistance had not been escalating perceptibly before the 1730s, pushing slaves towards more ambitious objectives. Instead, resistance intensified in the 1730s largely because of the deterioration in the quality of slave life that accompanied economic recession and natural disasters, and also because of extremely lax enforcement of slave controls. At the same time Antigua slaves may have been infuenced by news of the major slave revolt in Danish St. John, only a few miles away, where, in 1733, forty whites lost their lives. That event caused great excitement among the islands before order was finally restored, after nearly ten months, with help from the French at Martinique.[15] Court, Tomboy, and other rebel leaders in Antigua probably turned over in their minds all they knew about this revolt and why it failed and resolved to work out their own plans very carefully.

Lax enforcement of slave controls, enhancing opportunities for slave resistance, was perhaps the single most important precondition of the Antigua plot. Over the period 1730–35, 46 fugitives were reported executed or hunted down and killed; 8 slaves murdered other slaves, 13 were executed for felony, 1 for assault on a white person, and 2 more for unspecified murders. Such slave crime was accompanied by a wave of widespread slave insubordination encouraged by negligent supervision, notably in St. John's town. Testimony from justice Robert Arbuthnot, Edward Gregory's slave Emanuel, several town constables, and slave witnesses and others, indicate that overt and covert slave resistance had intensified. Slaves exploited fully the laxness of the police system of control to travel about day and night, ride horses, play dice in pastures, linger about town, and blow conch shells in the night calling comrades to meetings. They were able to have frequent unlawful assemblies, some of which, held openly even in daytime, were attended by large crowds. Most meetings, however, were much smaller affairs held in slaves' huts, at slave grave sites, and elsewhere at night, and rebels were recruited, inducted into the plot through special rituals, and the revolt discussed. Part of the blame for the slaves' mounting unruliness must surely fall upon justices of the peace, who were responsible for punishing offenders in their districts but who shirked their duties. Moreover, it could hardly be expected that a handful of constables could effectively by themselves police the slaves if masters were also negligent. Those whites upon whom much of the weight of responsibility for slave control fell, therefore, through gross negligence, contributed to conditions propitious for slave revolt. Ultimately, general nonenforcement of slave laws and other controls built up the confidence of countless slaves that they could continue to challenge authority without much fear of punishment. As they exploited such permissiveness, their confidence climbed to greater and greater heights, making them in the process more receptive to ideas for a major revolt, the ultimate challenge to the slavocracy.

The plot's timing can be explained not by any set of general underlying causes alone but in conjunction with others more immediate and incidental. When preconditions merged with these precipitants or triggering factors, the plot that was only a possibility was pushed into the realm of probability.[16] The most easily identifiable precipitants were unfavorable economic conditions in the 1730s and the emergence of charismatic slave leadership from among the slave elite.

During the 1730s the British sugar market experienced a recession that adversely affected the sugar islands. In this decade of bad times, the home government passed the Molasses Act (1733) in favor of the sugar islands after planters and their supporters had agitated, among other things, against mainland trade with the French islands for sugar, much of which ended up on the British market and helped create a glut. Because import prices did not decline when sugar prices did, planters faced the unwelcome consequences of unfavorable terms of trade. Antigua's sugar trade was in trouble, and many were the complaints and lamentations that came from the island. By 1734 trade was reported to have sunk to discouraging depths. The assembly, made up of merchants and planters, observed gravely that the "miserable circumstances. . .the Sugar Colonys in General labour under by the low Marketts for Sugar in England with the great Dutys that are there paid for them on Importation has already reduced most of them to the lowest ebb, Especially this Island." As "we can think of no Methods that can be taken which will so Effectually relieve us as Liberty of Exporting our improved Sugars to foreign Markets directly," these burdened gentlemen decided to petition Parliament "setting forth our Circumstances and pray a Relief in that Particular." The following year the Speaker of the assembly advised agent John Yeamans in London that Antiguans were hoping that the Board of Trade would "particularly at this juncture employ their best endeavours to relieve us from the miseries that we now lie under by the prices of our commodities" in Britain. According to Governor Mathew, writing in 1734, "the discouragements the planters have mett with from the low price of sugars have most effectively cur'd them of their former generous ways of living." Island merchants in particular were "frightened to find themselves so much at stake upon two or three bad cropps, no vent at home, or but little for what was made, and a narrow standing between two precipices, breaking debtors on one side, and a threatened warr on the other." Mathew concluded that the economic pinch "brought among us an oeconomy that calls for few supplies from home for our pleasure than heretofore, and this year indeed we have almost wanted necessary's for our familys or estates." Lower down the social scale were poor whites and slaves, who suffered severely. [17]

Other misfortunes only aggravated the island's plight during the decade. Governor Mathew also reported in 1734 on an aphis disease, called "the blast," that for five years had wreaked havoc among the canes, destroying them "in a most extraordinary manner. . .gaining ground even upon the provisions, both roots and vegetables above ground." The distressed islanders had been unable to find a remedy. " 'Tis a publick calamity the Almighty Power that permits it to afflict us can only relieve us from," the governor concluded resignedly. Drought of variable severity accompanied the blast in 1730–32, in parts of 1733 and 1734, and during the whole of

1736, helping to reduce sugar harvests and food production. From "a year of great cropp" measured in tons of sugar produced in 1728 (9,362), and again in 1729 (10,276), output showed the impact of blast and drought especially in 1731 (6,221), 1732 (6,533), 1734 (4,233), and worst of all 1737 (1,732), when Governor Mathew drew attention to the calamitous loss of nine-tenths of the crop. Although better harvests were achieved in 1733 (9,413), 1735 (9,202), and 1736 (7,455), general economic prospects in Antigua were not very heartening during the early and mid-1730s. Also contributing considerably to this state of affairs was soil depletion. According to a report from the legislature in 1731, Antigua lands were "much worn and Impoverished" and required "a more Expencive and Chargeable Cultivation and consequently the Profitts thereby [were] diminished."[18]

When the bout of drought in 1735 seemed to be fading, Walter Tullideph, anticipating better days, wrote home that "we have fine rains and the prospect of a large forward crope for next year, altho' ye blast does much damadge in ye poor land." But Tullideph had spoken too soon, for dry weather was back stalking the land again in 1736. One Antiguan, writing in August of that year, at the end of a respectable crop season in spite of hazards, vividly described the island's "calamitous times" that stretched back five years. "We are almost burnt up," declared the writer, "have had little Rain since January last, Provision is scarce, so that Bread, flour and Corn bears a good Price. The Island is tolerably healthy, but had been otherwise of late, tho' chiefly to transient people." The islanders wanted limes so badly that "they are a Merchandize from other Islands: And indeed good Water is scarce to make a Bowl; most of the Taverns pay from 1/6 to 2/0 per Pail. It is very hard with the Poor, who are daily begging for a Drink of Water. Many of the Ships are obliged to give Six Shillings per Hogshead for Pond Water." As was customary in times of such acts of God, Governor Mathew ordered a general fast for July 21, 1736, "to deprecate God's Anger from whence this Island has been Afflicted with the blast and Dry Weather." The "like instance of dry weather," Josiah Martin solemnly observed, "has not been known in ye memory of the oldest Men here."[19]

On top of the effects of economic recession, soil depletion, drought, and the blast came an epidemic of "black leprosy" (scurvy) and "joint evil." It appears that it began in about 1732, when the lieutenant governor and council observed "with very great concern that a Contageous disease called Black Scurvy has spread over Severall White Familys in some parts of this Island and that many Negroes infected...are daily Travelling about...to the great danger and Terror of the Inhabitants." On October 21, 1734 Walter Tullideph recorded that it had been "very sickly and mortal...Mr. John Morrice, Collo. Wm. Painter's wife, and a great many of inferior note are dead." Cases of infection among both whites and blacks were reportedly increasing in 1735. On Parham Plantation Hanniball, Great Cudjoe,

Montero Quaw, and Maria were on the sick list with joint evil in February 1737. Jackson, Frank, and Green, at the same time were down with black scurvy. Frank finally succumbed to the disease in May.[20] A hurricane in 1733 and severe earthquakes in 1735 compounded the island's miseries. When, after all this, the slave conspiracy suddenly appeared full-blown and menacing in October 1736, Josiah Martin succinctly but forcefully summarized the island's long string of woes. "Misfortunes," he wrote in December 1736, "seems to load the West India Estates, but particulary this Island." Some white families, understandably, quit the island during these years of trial; debtors too left their troubles behind as they moved out.[21]

How did the slaves fare admist all these developments? They too felt the effects of the recession, and there is good reason to believe that their living conditions deteriorated and intensified their restlessness and discontent. Frank Wesley Pitman noted a mounting threat of slave rebellion in Jamaica during the 1730s because, possibly, "the conditions of both the sugar and provision markets, at this time inclined overseers to make greater demands upon the slaves for labor and cut down their supplies of food and clothing." Not only were sugar prices low, but prices of food and other supplies from North America, when they reached the Leeward Islands at all, had increased as the French islands became competing markets. While Jamaican slaves produced much of their own food, Antiguan slaves were more dependent on North American supplies, and drought and blast, which nearly wiped out food production in the island, increased the burden on slaveowners to import food just when prices were high and could not easily be afforded. Walter Tullideph complained in June 1737 that "the long continuance of the dry weather brot such a charge on me to keep my Negroes alive, and my crops next to nothing" that he could not pay certain debts, and he was sure this was also "the case of every planter." Writing to his brother David in May, Tullideph said that "nobody can be sensible of our Calamitous times but those who have been eye witnesses of them, great expences in feeding our negroes all for ready money corn 6/ p bushell & nothing made, many good estates make nothing, & where any is made they reckon 20 hhds a great Crope, all our Division wont made [sic] 30 hhds Sugar." Tullideph believed that most planters had more slaves than "they well can feed." In all likelihood therefore Antigua slaves were fed less, and the lieutenant governor and council hinted as much in 1731 when they observed that numerous fugitives fled simply because they were treated cruelly and underfed. We will also recall that one of the slaves accused of being in the plot, angered by the unjust punishment of some of his comrades (before the plot was discovered), wanted to know by what right did whites punish slaves who were so unreasonably forced to live "upon a Bit and Six herrings a Week."[22] Slaves were also affected in another very important way. Drought undeniably must have also drastically reduced opportunities for them to better themselves through trade at the local Sunday provision market, a crucial part of the island's internal economy that slaves controlled. Some slaves, especially perhaps those belonging to marginal planters who could not clothe and feed them properly, must have had much to complain about.

These were unsettled and unsettling times of economic stress when, unable to cope, some proprietors sold out and slaves changed hands and experienced some disruption of their lives. Herbert Aptheker has pointed to a similar connection between slave unrest and economic depression in the United States.[23] Changes in the external market for sugar, on which island planters depended, reached out to affect the lives of planters as well as slaves, who were important cogs in a complex machinery of production, distribution, and profit making. In Antigua during the 1730s the effects of economic recession on slaves merged with other adverse changes to intensify slave discontent, which was reflected in mounting insubordination, overt slave resistance in various forms, and a plot to revolt. A conjunction of adversity pushed slaves' exasperation and sense of injustice to a high point and made them more receptive to Court and Tomboy's grandiose scheme to topple the mighty from their seat and initiate conditions for a better life. Overworked, ill-treated, and underfed, anxious and restless slaves responded to the urge to rid themselves of white slaveowners if not as a completely practical solution to their predicament, then at least as a means of psychological release. Indeed, struggling with suppressed feelings of anticipation, many slaves must have found it extremely difficult not to behave, act, or speak in ways that might arouse the suspicion of observant whites before the time for the revolt arrived. Mounting insubordination, then, was as much a product of relaxation of slave controls and hard times as an anticipatory projection of a successful revolt. Simply being part of the plot made many slaves cocky and confident, unruly, openly insubordinate. Slave leaders, drawing fully upon the material and spiritual resources of the slave community, shrewdly played upon their comrades' feelings of alienation to convince them that a well-coordinated revolt at this particular juncture in the affairs of Antigua could succeed. Meanwhile slaveowners, preoccupied with other things, were oblivious to signs of the coming crisis.

11

"Daring Spirits to Lead Them On"

The Antigua slave plot of 1736 differed from the earlier plot of 1728-29 in its scale of organization, its objectives, and the roles played by committed and able leaders whose immense responsibilities included the delicate operation of recruitment. Along with other strategies, they interpreted whites' weakness or unpreparedness to their comrades in order to convince them of their own relative strengths and secure their cooperation. To succeed at this, the leaders operated with extreme caution and patience, but the demands of secretly organizing such an elaborate plot taxed the ingenuity of everyone concerned. That the plot came so close to fruition after months of preparation attests to the effectiveness with which slave leaders played their roles, especially in maintaining solidarity among their coconspirators.

The leaders of the plot included many drivers who helped supervise field work, but most of them were privileged Creole slaves who were not normally connected with the field. Table 11.1 lists the 10 main ringleaders, who were executed: 7 had nonfield occupations, and at least 8 were Creoles. The complete list of executed slaves (table 2.1) furnishes even more impressive evidence of the participation of nonfield slaves. There were 13 carpenters, 8 coopers, 1 coppersmith, 2 masons, 1 millwright, 1 wheelwright, 3 waiting men, 1 sugar boiler, 1 butcher, 3 coachmen, 1 head field Negro, 3 fishermen, 1 drummer, 1 wheelwright/carpenter/mason, 3 fiddlers, and 26 drivers; 1 *obeah* man was also listed. The occupations of 18 others were not listed. Among the 49 banished slaves there were only 6 field workers; but there were 8 carpenters, 6 drivers, 1 sugar boiler, 1 carpenter/caulker, 1 driver/ carter, 2 carters, 1 mason, 1 carpenter/fiddler, 2 coopers, 1 carpenter/ boiler/"Succo Negro," 1 mill boatswain, and 1 "Plummer"; another *obeah* man was banished, but the occupations of the other banished slaves were not listed.[1]

The judges expressed outrage in their report that the large number of privileged slaves among the rebels "had hearts and minds capable of conceiving, heads fit for Contriving, and hands and Courage for executing the deepest and most bloody Crimes, even that unparalleled Hellish Plot formed by them," because, as they explained, "none of them [could] justly complain of the hardship of Slavery; their lives being as easy as those of our White Tradesmen and Overseers, and their manner of living much

TABLE 11.1. Principal Slave Leaders of the 1736 Plot in Antigua

Slave	Owner	Ethnic Group	Occupation	Execution
Court	Thomas Kerby	Coromantee	waiting man	broken on wheel
Tomboy	Thomas Hanson	Creole	carpenter	broken on wheel
Hercules	John Christophers	Creole	carpenter	broken on wheel
Jack	Philip Darby	Creole	cooper	burned
Scipio	Philip Darby	Creole	waiting man	burned
Ned	Col Jacob Morgan	Creole	mason	gibbeted
Fortune	Mrs. Johanna Lodge	Creole, or arrived as child	carpenter/fiddler	burned
Tony	Col. Samuel Martin	Creole	—	broken on wheel
Secundi	Estate of Thomas Freeman	Creole	driver	gibbeted
Jacko	Sr. William Codrington	Creole	driver	gibbeted

SOURCES: General Report, CO 152/22, W94; Mathew to BT, May 26, 1737, CO 152/23, X7.

more Plentiful, than that of our Common Whites, who were looked upon by some of them, for their Poverty and Distress with Contempt." These treacherous wretches, whom the judges thought should have know better than to plan a revolt, were employed in "handycraft Trades, Overseeing or as house Servants."[2] These remarks from the court imply a justification of slavery: that there was nothing wrong about enslaving blacks so long as their day-to-day living conditions removed cause for just complaint or protest; but more importantly, the court's comments reflect profound puzzlement tinged with a distinct sense of injury over the unexpected behavior of the slave elite — behavior that could not be "explained" by the ideology of slavery. That these slaves should spearhead a large-scale plot to revolt (a new dimension to slave resistance in the island) must have appeared utterly contradictory to much of what the judges and other whites believed about the character of slaves and the institution of slavery itself. Nothing remotely approaching the scope and organization of the plot had occurred in recent years to prepare whites for what they faced so suddenly in 1736. Confronted with evidence establishing that his slave Court was at the head of the whole affair, Thomas Kerby was incredulous, believing that Court was "incapable of any bad Design, for that he was an Elderly Distemper'd Fellow and had Always behaved like a Faithful Slave and lived very well besides which he was under no Temptation, for that he had offer'd him his Freedom." But, as many studies have shown, there was hardly a New World slave revolt or conspiracy that was not led by slaveowners' "most-trusted slaves."[3] What, Kerby, must have asked himself, had Court to gain by being involved in or even leader of the conspiracy? Many other whites, including nonslaveowners, were as perplexed as Kerby when the full meaning of the averted disaster hit them. Why had the slave elite, contrary to expectation, combined against them? The motivation of these slaves deserves careful attention.

Using his experiences in the Leeward Islands as a basis, the Reverend Robert Robertson offered some shrewd observations in 1729 on leaders of slave insurrections. "One indeed would be apt to think," he wrote, "that none of them but such as are some way or other ravish'd from their Native Land, or injuriously treated by us, could seek our Destruction; but Facts (as one says) are stubborn Things, and there is no reasoning them away." These facts showed that "in all their Plots and Conspiracies in the Sugar-Colonies, the Creole-Negroes, i.e. the Slaves born among us, and some of those from Africa that were most favour'd and whose Masters thought they could have intrusted them with their Lives, have been found deepest in the Design, and the prime Directors and Actors of all the mischief." The Antigua slave plot and most slave rebellions that occurred later in the Americas confirm Robertson's observations, which implied that the slave societies harbored a constant potential for slave revolt. Robertson himself believed that probably one of the best ways to control that potential was to sow division among the slaves so as to inhibit the development of cooperation and solidarity among them — a strategy that, interestingly enough, Barbados slaveowners had reportedly put into practice in the seventeenth century and Brazilian slaveowners also tried in the nineteenth century.[4] To Robertson the process by which ordinary slaves became rebels was far less difficult to comprehend than that for the slave elite, whose behavior might be profitably analyzed with respect to level of acculturation to island culture, general day-to-day treatment, occupational status, and the impact that these had on master-slave relations. The interaction of these determinants of elite slave behavior suggest that some analytical distinction may be made between the motivation of the slave elite and that of all others involved in the Antigua slave plot and other similar episodes of collective slave action.

Both among the plot's upper echelon of leadership and in the secondary ranks, nonfield slaves predominated, and their elevation to positions of higher status with considerable independence and intimate contact with whites was another underlying cause of the plot, because it helped nurture the personalities of those slaves with leadership potential who later developed the whole scheme. This the judges must have recognized upon reflection. While their reference to such a connection was admittedly indirect, they had conducted several weeks of trials, cross-examined witnesses, and listened to lengthy testimony, and therefore they were well aware that the conspirators whom they considered to be the most culpable represented a cross-section of skills. To troubling questions about the origins of slave leadership from which revolts and conspiracies might emerge, the judges sought answers in the reliance of slaveowners on the skills of slaves that "the inequality of numbers of White and Blacks" made inescapable. Thus among their solutions to this immediate situation of "imbalance" was that "slaves [were to be] disabled from being handicraft tradesmen, overseers, drivers, or distillers, shopkeepers, or hawkers and pedlors or saylors; not suffered to keep horses or work out for themselves and that more of our menial servants, and our wet and dry nurses were to be whites and no fiddlers for gain, but whites."[5] The Antigua plot's leadership originated in the ranks of slaves with such skills and associated life styles, trusted slaves who profited from a great deal of social space and freedom from surveillance. Indeed, they were the only slaves with leadership potential, mobility, and the trust of their masters who could have hatched such a well-concealed and elaborate plot. The vast majority of recruited field hands seem to have formed the rank and file following, who were not necessarily privy to the plot's details. There were, of course, many unrecruited field hands, but the leadership of the plot believed that these slaves would fall in line or could be persuaded to do so once the revolt got off the ground.

In a perceptive study of slave resistance in eighteenth-century Virginia,

Gerald W. Mullin contended that the slaves' adjustment to slavery was dependent on at least three factors: for "outlandish" or recently imported Africans, the influence of their African cultural heritage was decisive, while for seasoned slaves and those born and raised in the slave society, work and acculturation were more critical.[6] The African heritage, work experiences, and degree of acculturation also helped differentiate slave responses in Antigua between new Africans and island-born slaves, but, as we will show, attachment to Africa could still greatly influence the behavior of seasoned Africans.

The interdependent relations of work and acculturation can be used to explain the characterization of the Antigua rebels and their leadership. Clearly a collective effort to seize control of the whole island, the plot, with all its distinctive features, could have been developed only by slaves (African or Creole) who, in addition to having lived in Antigua for many years, earned their master's trust, and enjoyed considerable freedom of movement or other privileges, also understood the weaknesses of the white minority and felt reasonably confident of their ability to mobilize a sufficient number of highly motivated followers who would not prematurely give away the secret of the planned revolt. Above all, perhaps, the slaves who organized the plot, as the plans show clearly, had to have been ones who could grasp the absolute necessity for careful planning and act accordingly. What slaves then might have been regarded as risks in the planning of the revolt? These included recently arrived Africans, who were unfamiliar with the Antigua world of slavery and had not yet learned to live in it, especially non-Coromantees; we will recall that the plot originated among the Coromantees. But the leaders of the plot still counted on these slaves, most of whom would have been common plantation field hands, to lend their weight when the revolt, which would have begun in St. John's town, spread into the surrounding countryside and the plantations beyond. Unlike these slaves, who were not specifically recruited into the plot, Creoles, on the basis of the importance of work experience and acculturation in shaping motivation, were prime candidates to participate in a systematically organized revolt. One slave testified that "Court and Tomboy [both of whom lived in St. John's] often told me that all the Town Negroes were let into the Secret both Men and boys except New Negroes All the Creoles and Coromantees."[7] To add to this core group of rebels, Court, Tomboy, and other leaders exerted themselves to recruit more Creoles and Coromantees from outlying plantations.

The evidence available makes it easier to explain the roles of Creoles, who were assimilated blacks, proficient in English or the local patois, sometimes literate, and usually skilled. Table 11.1 shows the distribution of skills among the Creole leadership, which may be taken to represent a similar pattern among slaves executed or banished, for whom the official lists do not differentiate between Africans and Creoles.[8] Tomboy, Hercules, Jack, Scipio, Ned, and Toney, all Creole ringleaders, according to the judge's report had been "lately baptized and several of them could read and write." Secundi and Jacko, also Creoles, who were "the most active Incendiaries under Tomboy," were reportedly of "French Parentage, and initiated into Christianity according to the Romish Church." One banished Creole, Tilgarth Penezar, alias Targut, who belonged to the widow Roach, was "a Carpenter and Caulker and a very Stout Resolute Sensible fellow that has been to Northward and Can read and write Say Prayers and ca. He directed us for his name," the judges said, "to the 1st Book of Chronicles 5th Chapter 2d Verse." Judge John Vernon's slave Cudjoe, a carpenter and fiddler, who was executed, had been to Boston. Antigua whites regarded such Creoles as less alien or outlandish than Africans and believed they understood them better. The judges stated flatly that Creoles were the most "sensible and able" of the island's slaves.[9]

Because of their special occupations and status as members of the slave elite — a classification imposed by whites and to some extent probably discriminatingly used by slaves themselves — Creole artisans, boilers, stewards, drivers, and so on received preferential treatment, although on some small to middling plantations they alternated between skilled functions and common field labor. They enjoyed their masters' trust and had much latitude to exercise initiative and engage in multiple role playing that fortified their self-awareness. Often assigned leadership roles among the slaves by whites, these privileged slaves mediated "between the oppressor and the oppressed...transmitted the directives of the white master, supervised their implementation, disciplined, absorbed slave discontent, and curbed unrest." Particularly well situated to play such roles were slave drivers who, by the very nature of their work, stood astride the worlds of slaves and slaveowners. Drivers must have become "first-rate economic managers and skilled defenders of their people through the art of compromise and the juggling of contradictory demands from above and below" or from both worlds. They were, in the words of Eugene D. Genovese, "the men between."[10] But if they and other Creole leaders could accomplish as much, they could also shrewdly foment or capitalize upon slave discontent.

The acculturative process whereby Creole slaves were socialized into the mores of slave society from birth did not necessarily hamper their ability to undermine the slave system, although their patterns of resistance might be more discriminating, more circumspect, than those of new or even seasoned Africans. In the 1730s the expectations of Antiguan Creoles in regard to the quality of their lives may have been so frustrated by the economic recession, when probably many were ordered to work in the field alongside common field hands to help salvage planters' fortunes and investments, that they contemplated the possibility of capsizing the whole slave system, as many Africans of the slave elite also did. In this sense status deprivation and unfulfilled expectations of continued privileges, along with an intensified consciousness of their plight as victims of the slave system, may have played key roles in the process through which Creoles could identify with a movement to overthrow whites, in spite of psychological handicaps with which slavery may have burdened slaves born and socialized in the system.[11] Powerfully reinforcing that process were tensions that the slave elite experienced in trying to maintain a hold on their self-respect while acting out whites' model of the ideal, submissive slave. Behind Sambo's mask, behind Quashee's dissembling, there lurked a discerning intelligence nourished on an ambiguity-packed existence.

The psychological and sociopolitical base for a large-scale plot was perhaps strongest among the numerous artisans, especially in the towns, who regularly paid their owners a part of their earnings obtained either by being hired out or by working on their own. As the judges indicated in their report, slaves had established themselves in such pursuits in competition with white tradesmen. Masters obviously relied upon the productive capabilities of such slaves, who, recognizing this, exploited the latitude of existence allowed them that ultimately nurtured a spirit of independence and made them difficult to control. As the complexity of slavery developed, problems of slave control became correspondingly more intricate and difficult to handle. Skilled slaves like the Creole leaders Tomboy and Hercules, for example, presented certain problems of control. Tomboy was a master carpenter. Like Court, he was "very kindly used by his Master, being admitted for his own Advantage to take Negroe Apprentices, and to make all the Profits he could of his own, and their Labour, paying his Master only a monthly Sum, far short of his usual Earnings." According to the judges' report, Tomboy was "generally Master of much Money, and [he] did not fail applying it upon all Occasions to the Promotion of his vile Purposes among the Creoles." Tomboy was such a well-known and trusted tradesman that the leaders of the plot believed he would have been able to "procure the making of the Seats" for the governor's ball, which would have made it possible for him to plant gunpowder in the building with which to blow up "all the People of Distinction in the Island" and start off the slave revolt. Hercules himself was an "excellent tradesman [carpenter] and allmost the Support of the poor family that owned him."[12]

Both of these men, and many others like them, were acculturated blacks, and mobile and unsupervised because of the circumstances of their employment. Mobility offered them, especially those who lived in town, access to a wider world óf values, ideas, and experiences as they mixed with whites and blacks from town and country, visitors from abroad, or sailors who had seen the larger world beyond Antigua. Such regular exposure to a more varied and extensive web of experience than would have been ordinarily accessible to plantation slaves, such opportunities for self-education and multiple role playing, shaped the consciousness and personalities of these slaves and facilitated their organization of the plot. Of higher status than ordinary slaves, employed at skilled occupations, and in regular contact with the extraplantation world, highly motivated privileged slaves in Antigua could more readily conceive of, and act upon, the realization of a different order of things without "white masters" in which they might control their own destinies. With the latitude that acculturation, job allotment, and lax enforcement of the slave laws made possible, many Creoles were more than psychologically equipped to participate in the plot or to be in its vanguard. It should come as no surprise that the Creoles of St. John's town were deeply involved in the planned revolt of 1736, which would have started not on a plantation but in the town.

Though outnumbered by the Creoles, the Coromantees were a sizable minority of the Antigua slave population in 1736; and while many of these Africans were acculturated and skilled, the majority seem to have been unacculturated and field hands. Like most Creoles, acculturated and skilled Coromantees could often manipulate their privileged status in the interest of resistance, but ultimately, and more than any other factor, perhaps, it was Court's charismatic influence and the memory and image of Africa that drew them into the plot, along with common Coromantee field hands.[13] It is not certain what role recent Coromantee arrivals played in the plot's development, but we should remember that large numbers of them arrived from the Gold Coast in the 1720s.

Coromantee Court, alias Tackey, reportedly arrived in Antigua as a boy of ten years and lived there until his execution at the age of about forty-five years. A slave in the island since 1701,[14] Court had therefore lived through the restless 1720s, when slave resistance demanded much more attention from the authorities, when the exploits of the social rebels/bandits Africa, Sharper, Frank, and Papa Will precipitated the passage of a special act against them and other fugitives in 1723, when slaves belonging to Colonel Nathaniel Crump hatched their abortive plot to revolt (1728–29). All of these developments, which made quite an impression in Antigua, were part of Court's experience and acculturation. If he arrived in the island at the young age of ten, his adaptation to slave life was probably not as difficult as it might have been had he come as an adult. It may be argued that by 1736 Court had had adequate time to become sufficiently accul- turated or creolized to pass for a Creole, but he apparently self-consciously preferred to be known as an African and had "for many Years covertly as- sumed among his Countrymen here, the Title of King, and had been by them address'd and treated as such." The judges claimed that, as they were informed, he was "of a considerable Family in his own Country, but not as was commonly thought of Royal-Blood" by the other slaves. Even if Court was descended from only a leading family, Coromantees older than he in Antigua, who were knowledgeable about Coromantee or Akan institutions, could have pushed him forward as king as one vital way of proceeding to reknit the cultural tapestry of the homeland that would give familiar meaning to their lives. In Asante and other Akan states in Africa, rulers were elected by "a combination of hereditary eligibility and popular selection." It is entirely likely therefore that Court did not take on by himself the title of king and then proceed to impose his will on the other Coromantees, but that instead they made him king or chief, a position that carried with it certain important responsibilities.[15] An appreciation of this and other Coromantee dimensions of the Antigua slave plot can best be achieved in relation to their links to Akan society and culture, as we shall see.

Living in St. John's town with his master and employed primarily as a valet or waiting man, Court was among the island's slave elite. His master, Thomas Kerby, reportedly allowed him "to carry on a Trade and many other greater Indulgencies than were allowed to any Slave in the Island." The judges' report claimed that his "Indulgences from his master were great and uncommon which gave him an Opportunity of acquiring much more money than Slaves are usually Masters of."[16] These opportunities and the life style of a privileged town slave, as much as the strategic importance of blowing up the governor's ball in town to start the revolt, greatly help to explain why, unlike most other slave revolts and conspiracies in the Caribbean, the Antigua plot began with a town and not a plantation focus. Court and Tomboy, who knew each other but were not friends, both lived in St. John's town and recruited heavily from among the slaves there, most of whom were, most likely, Creoles.

Both men were also well-known island figures. "The Persons and Characters of these two Chiefs were so well known to your Excellency, and to this Island in general," the judges reported, "that little need be said of either"; nonetheless they did add much more, especially about the African Court, whose role in the plot captured their curiosity. Over several years Court had succeeded in establishing himself as a highly respected figure among all ranks of slaves, especially, however, among his Coromantee countrymen, "who all paid him great Homage and Respect and Stood in great awe of him" as their king or chief. To the judges, Court seemed "artful and Ambitious, very proud and of few words," characteristics that obviously, to them, did not speak in his favor. Court's did not exemplify the ideal, required slavish personality, the Sambo, the Quashee. Worse, at his execution, the judges said, Court "endeavoured to put on a Port and Mien suitable to his affected Dignity of King." Some of the slave leader's detractors characterized him disparagingly as a "Dark Designing, Ambitious, Insolent Fellow." Whatever the picture whites may have had of Court, with the help of the slaves he emerged as one of their leaders; but although (as a

Coromantee) he had won the respect of Creoles, these island-born slaves reportedly had a stronger allegiance to Tomboy, who was one of them. A "Fellow of Robust Strong body, and resolute Temper," Tomboy had "a great Awe and Influence" over the Creoles, and a "Genius adapted to Caballing." Neither leader can be said to have risen from obscurity to the leadership of the plot. Both were already figures of respect and authority among the slaves. They therefore had good reason to believe that they could mobilize slave support. While we have more information about the personality and social origins of Court, Tomboy too was obviously a charismatic figure. He, like Court, can be placed alongside the slave leaders Gabriel Prosser, Denmark Vesey, Nat Turner, or Sam Sharpe in the leadership of internal wars in agrarian, preindustrial societies of the eighteenth and nineteenth centuries.[17]

In the Akan country of the Gold Coast, the period from the late seventeenth to about the middle of the eighteenth century was extremely unsettled. A series of wars associated with the rise and expansion of the state of Asante characterized those years, and as a result large numbers of Akan captives reached the coast and were sold into slavery through European traders.[18] Many, including high-born Court, reached the shores of Antigua, where they proceeded to refashion something of their Akan world within the interstices of the Antigua slave system. That they were of Akan origin is also indicated by their typically Akan day-names, as well as by fragments of vernacular and other details of Akan culture that turned up during inquiries into the plot. At several levels of the plot's development, Akan culture played a very prominent role in relation to the Coromantees' participation.

Long recognized by the Antigua Coromantees as their leader, Court already had a solid base from which to build the structure for revolt. We can better understand the Coromantee dimensions of the plot as they centered on Court's role — from his emergence as Coromantee leader many years before the plot up to his execution — in relation to the role of rulers in Akan states. Madeline Manoukian wrote that in the traditional Akan social system, the chief served "as the central point round which the community was held together as a unit in defending itself from destruction by enemies, in the maintenance of law and order and the rule of custom, in obedience to the ancestors and gods." Among the Asante, according to Kofi A. Busia, the chief is "important not only as a civil ruler who is the axis of the political relations of his people and the one in whom the various lineages that compose the tribe find their unity; he is also the symbol of their identity and continuity as a tribe and the embodiment of their spiritual values. An Ashanti chief fills a sacred role as the 'one who sits upon the

stool of the ancestors.' " Court may have played similar roles among the
Antigua Coromantees. As "intermediary between the living and the dead,"
between "the community and the royal ancestor spirits," Court was recognized as civil and religious ruler of his people long before 1736, and he
developed the slave plot from that crucial base.[19]

Tutored by Coromantee "elders" in the island about the customs of his
ancestors, Court shouldered some heavy responsibilities, which must have
made it impossible for him to accept the gift of emancipation that his owner
had offered him; if his freedom had originally been taken away by force,
then perhaps as "leader of the people in war" the only "honorable" way to
regain freedom for himself and his countrymen was to take it through a
revolt. Coromantee ethnic pride thus became in Court's hands a "coor-
dinating agency capable of concentrating the diffuse energy of general
discontent [of the 1730s] into a powerful and concentrated thrust" against
the whites. Recognizing the real complexities of the projected revolt, Court
realized that he had to throw a wider net, the judges said, and he moved
to include the Creoles, the most numerous, if not the most easily disaffected
slaves. By forming an alliance with the Creole leader Tomboy from the
town, Court tried to ensure success through recruitment of a larger number
of slaves and through concentration on the initial strategic attack on St.
John's, where there was a large concentration of Creoles. To achieve his
goal the Coromantee leader reportedly overcame "a long Coldness between
him and Tomboy," whom he befriended "and found him every way ready
for, and equal to his Purposes."[20] Let us remember that this information
about the recruitment of the Creoles and the origination of the plot among
the Coromantees, led by Court, was supplied by the trial judges. Most
Antigua whites probably believed them, seeing the logic in what they said.

If we set aside the judges' report on the plot for the moment, it may be
argued that the Coromantee-Creole coalition was, strictly speaking, not
a triumph over divisive ethnic differences (although Antigua whites may
have seen it in those terms) but represented instead the fusion of two
social groups of different status within the slave community. While the
Coromantees were born in Africa and the Creoles in the Caribbean, large
numbers of the latter had African parents, and, for this reason at least,
ethnicity within the Antigua slave population, which by the 1730s had a
sizable Creole minority (if not yet a majority), was less important as a factor
of internal division, even if, at the same time, Coromantees adhered to
their ethnic pride. Coromantees and Creoles in this regard therefore were
different segments of the same population, and not, as the judges would
lead us to believe, two ethnically distinct groups who were forced together
out of common interest. Along the lines of status differentiation in Akan
society, the Coromantees may well have been regarded as *elders,* the wise
ones, because they had had direct experience of the African homeland,

while the Creoles, who had not had that experience, may have been regarded as the *young men,* who represented the strength, energy, and backbone of the community. In Akan society the young men are regarded as a distinct social group called *mmrantie* (plural of *abrantie*). They may chose their own leader, but they owe allegiance to the state ruler and can be called upon by the elders for various services of importance to the state; the elders, however, maintain their distance from the young men, who have frequently posed a political threat to traditional Akan rulers.[21]

The striking resemblance between these facets of Akan social organization and institutions and the way in which the slave plot was reportedly organized in Antigua suggests that the Coromantee-Creole coalition may have been naturally linked to Akan practices, which the judges and other whites did not understand. By this reading therefore, the plot originated among the Coromantees not as a particularly ethnic affair but instead because these Africans were the wise elders who made the major decisions about the future of a much larger body of slaves to whom they were attached. The "long coldness" between Court and Tomboy, which the judges alluded to, could have been (for some unknown reason, if they were right) an exacerbation of normal social distance.[22] This, however, Court tactfully bridged, as the young men (Creoles), or the sinews of the slave community, had to be brought in as the troops; it was not simply to increase the number of rebel slaves who could take the field, as the judges claimed, although that would undoubtedly have been the result. The participation of the Creoles, then, according to Akan principles, perhaps explains why among the ten main ringleaders of the plot (table 11.1) Court was a Coromantee, while eight were Creole and one was either a Creole or had arrived in Antigua as a child. These Creoles became Court's generals. Tomboy, as leader of the Creole slaves, was the most important of them all. While imperceptible to whites, traditional Akan practices operated in the organization of the slave plot, and we have an interpretation of collective slave rebellion that takes into serious account the cultural background of the Africans involved. This interpretation also suggests that African culture continued to play an important role in the shaping of the Antigua slave community even while the proportion of Creoles mounted, and that up to the 1730s at least the Akan were a dominant group among the island's slaves. Much that scholars may never be able to uncover must have lain beneath the surface of slave life and action.

For Court and Tomboy it was no simple matter recruiting into their scheme a considerable number of slaves of diverse social and occupational, if not ethnic origins. How did they achieve this? First, Court, assisted by Coromantee deputies, accepted special responsibility for recruiting and mobilizing Coromantees, while Tomboy and his men did the same for the Creoles. Valuable testimony from the trial record shows how rebels were recruited. Not only did recruiters play upon the slaves' discontent and sense of frustration brought on by hard times, but they also employed the psychological tactic, as with the recruitment procedure of Gabriel Prosser's Virginia revolt, of questioning slaves' manhood or toughness. The Creole slave Quashee (his mother was a Coromantee) who, like Tomboy, belonged to Thomas Hanson, confessed his involvement in the plot, but said that Tomboy forced him into it using threats. It is interesting that, although not born in the Gold Coast, Quashee had an anglicized Akan day-name (Kwasi, in Akan). Partially "Akanized," Quashee was recruited by force into the plot as a Creole. Trebling, another slave giving evidence, said "Tomboy Often Affronted Quashee by calling him Miss Betty." Not that recruiting from among the Coromantees did not pose its own problems; one slave testified that "Court said he had a Great Deal of money & if he Could not get his Country Men by any Other Means he would give them money."[23]

While threats were often used against individual slaves to persuade them to join the plot, groups of slaves also received similar treatment, especially at feasts and other gatherings. At one such meeting, testified Billy, "it was Mentioned there, that those who Could not appear at the Next Feast at Jacko's to Windward must have their heads Cutt Off." Such tactics were often used to win over unwilling slaves. Even the less hesitant had to be persuaded, and recruiters used flattery and praise to secure them. Jemmy testified that at a feast at Wavell Smith's plantation at which "Quashee, Morgans Ned, Jack, Billy, Hercules, Stephen's Cuffey, Budinots Dick and my Self & many more that I Cannot Recollect" were present, Morgan's Ned said: "Court and Tomboy have been talking a long time of rising and Destroying the White People. Which of you have not heard of it?" The company replied that they had heard. Ned called Dick "a Cleaver Lusty Fellow." "All Creoles that have Promised to Assist," he said, "are Cleaver Lusty Fellows." Getting Ned's drift, Dick observed that he had had "a great fit of Sickness, but thank God, I am pretty hearty now, and begin to pick up flesh . . . I have promised Tomboy already," he added when Ned pointedly asked him whether he would join the conspiracy, "and as I live in Town, I shall be ready to Assist whenever I am Called upon."[24] Pare's slave Cudjoe, a boiler, was recruited in like fashion. Stephen's slave Dick, testified

> that he saw Cudjoe take the Oath at Secundo's great Feast
> that Secundo Drank to him in Dram Mixed with Grave Dirt
> Strained, Saying here is to all true Men and Damnation and
> Confusion to them who will be false, and will not Stand by
> and help kill the White People; that Cudjoe Pleged him
> repeating the same Words; that Secundo Clapp'd him on the
> Shoulders and Said he was a Cleaver Fellow, it was Such

Fellows as he, that he Wanted; that Cudjoe Drank the Same
Damnation Oath to Yeaman's Quashee Cumma repeating the
same Words; that he was almost always with Secundo, and
has a wife at the next Door; that Secundo said to Cudjoe, you
are a Damn'd Fellow at killing People, You have killed one
already, Oh Says Cudjoe that's but a Wind blow; that he has
Seen Cudjoe Among the Conspirators at Parham Plantation,
and that Secundo told Dick that he had bought three Jarrs of
Rum of Cudjoe for that very Feast.[25]

Recruiters often used such subtle persuasion, but slaves like John Pare's
old Coromantee Quawcoo, required little nudging. At Quawcoo's trial the
slave Quamino deposed: "The first Sunday that Secundi was at Johny's
Quawcoo Came after the Oath was Drank, Secundi and Johny both told
him, that they had been talking of heading the White People and he said
he would Join with all his heart. Secundi also Spoke to him in Cormantee;
Drank to him and Said, Here Country Man (Chawa Worra Terry) i.e. Cutt
your Masters head Off,[26] he answer'd with all my heart, and I am not so
well Used now as I was in my Old Masters time and if I Cant Do much
my Self, I have a Son that Can, and I have a Gun of my Own." Quamino
said he had heard Quawcoo "Complain thus Several times." When Caesar,
a driver belonging to Colonel Lucas, was initiated into the plot he reportedly cursed whites: "the Devil Damn the White People, they abused him
very much." But Caesar had another painful grievance. He told the slave
leader Secundi that "his Master had sold his Father and his Mother, and
that he did not care how soon he went to fight against the White People."
Another Coromantee slave, Troilus, "commonly called Yabby," a carpenter
on the plantation of Thomas Freeman, did not need to be persuaded to
join the plot. The slave Jack testified, "This Troilus took the Oath with
me at Secundi's the Sunday Night and Said he Did so much Work in his
Masters Plantation, that he Did not Care he would Join, for they gave the
Negro's Six herrings a Week and gave him no more; he promised to be
true to Secundi." The judges noted that Troilus admitted his guilt in jail.[27]
Overwork and underfeeding must have similarly influenced many other
slaves besides Troilus.

Sometimes recruiters implicitly or explicitly asked others to join them in
recognition of services or favors rendered in the past. At the trial of Barton's
slave Joe, Quamina's deposition was recorded.

he saw Joe take the Damnation oath at Secundo's Great feast,
Secundo Drank it to him in a Bowl of Punch with Grave Dirt,

and said Joe I kept you a whole year when you was run away, and you never did me any Service, Joe said my Master trusts me to Pick Cotton, and I cou'd not Come, but I heard you were going to make a feast and have brought you some Fish (Joe having then brought three large Fish) you are Welcome Says Secundo, you are come in good time, and bid him give the Fish to his Wife;...Says Secundo Joe, I am going to fight against the White People, I hope you'll be one. O Lord Says Joe, before you begin I will come and Stay along with you. Secundo Drank the Damnation Oath to him in Punch with the Oath Ingredients, concluding with the Devil Damn all the Baccarara's [whites]. Jo Pledged him repeating the same Words, and Said with all my heart, I will Stand by you and help kill all the Baccararas. Secundo Said further, Joe when you were run away I was not false to you, Joe replyed never fear, I will never be false to you, I will be your Right hand...Joe said he could not bring any hands, but would bring his Cutlass. Quamina Says he knows Joe had a cutlass, for he has Seen it.[28]

In a number of cases recruiters issued the invitation to join the plot as a challenge, but most often flattery, praise, questioning slaves' manhood and courage, and other techniques of persuasion were mixed together. Mr. Skerret's Creole slave Billy "Confessed his Guilt largely to his Master, how he was Drawn in by Tomboy & how the Plot was to have been Executed." Whatever the approach, Court, Tomboy, and others realized that recruitment could be facilitated if top slaves on plantations were first sounded out and recruited. With influence over others on their plantations, they could be expected to do some successful recruiting themselves. At the trial of Cubbinah, a Creole driver from Henry Osborne's plantation in Popeshead Division, slave witness Jemmy said that Tomboy had told him Cubbinah agreed "to supply him with some of the People of Popes-head." Tomboy spoke of Cubbinah, "as one of the Ablest Men there, that he Could Drive most of the Plantation Negro's before him, that he was so Stout a fellow that 5 or 6 Negro's Could not Stand before him." Jemmy added that Tomboy "placed his great Dependence upon him." Stephen's Dick mentioned that he knew nothing about Cubbinah "but that he is much look'd upon among the Negro's and that one Sigworth's Quamina now Dead was formerly Called Popeshead General."[29] But while head slaves on the plantations were well placed to recruit men, they could be even more valuable if they or their comrades had access to arms. Men and arms were the two key ingredients Court and Tomboy required to explode their revolt and wipe out the whites. The slave Jemmy testified at the trial of Tom, Edward Otto's Creole field slave, that

> Of a Sunday, two or three Sundays before Courts Dance Coming to Town with Ducks, Tomboy & I met him, at the Entrance of the Town. Said Tomboy to Tom hath Jean said anything to you; no said he. Tomboy then said I understand that you have a very good Gunn. Yes said Tom; well said Tomboy to him, You know what we are going about to Attack the White People, & we must get up all the Armes and Cleaver fellows that We Can, I hope your Gunn is good Order. Yes said Tom, it is, & I have both Gunn Powder & Shot. Said Tomboy, I Dont think we have Occasion for Shot, but Powder is Wanting. Tom said my Horn is full of Powder. Said Tomboy to him, Can you get anybody Else? Said Tom, I am not a head Man, Jean is Over us all, but my Self my Gunn, Powder & Shot is at your Service. And he said his Father had a Gunn too, but he Did not know whether it was in good Order or not. Tomboy Desired him to Look Over his fathers Gunn to See it in good Order.[30]

While recruiters might try to persuade slaves to enlist in the plot at any time or place, the most crucial part of the recruitment process was the ritual ceremony or feast at which slaves were formally initiated into the secret undertaking. At these ceremonial feasts of varying elaborateness in regard to numbers present and the amount and variety of food and drink served, first people would be fed, then the purpose of the gathering and the plot would be discussed, and then would-be recruits, many of whom had been previously sounded out, were required to take a solemn "Damnation Oath" to support the plot in whatever way possible and not betray it. Slaves, Coromantees as well as Creoles, did not become true participants or members of the plot with sacred obligations until they had declared themselves by taking the oath of initiation and solidarity before witnesses. So far as the judges who tried the rebels were concerned, taking the oath sealed the guilt of all who did.

In the trial record are some intriguing descriptions of the oath-taking ceremonies and feasts.[31] The Creole slave Tilgarth Penezar, alias Targut, held one at Lyndsey's plantation, with the manager's permission, that deserves quoting at length. According to slave witness Jemmy,

> There was a feast at Lyndsey's — Cant say how long ago — whether before Mr. Carlile went to England or not. All the

Town People almost were there; he invited me and my Wife, and he invited a great many More, half the Town. I went my Self in the afternoon & they had not Yet Dined. Targut was gone to Town to fetch the Towns People to Dinner. The Dinner was Waiting for Court, Tomboy, & the Rest of the Towns People Which Affronted the Company that was there, who were Sitting about in great Numbers & Complained of Targut & the Towns People for having made them stay so long. There were Forty slaves & more waiting when I went: Mulatto Ned & many of Chesters Negroes, many of Doc. Haddons, & Some from the Town, & Some of the Company Set upon the Rocks. At length I saw Targut coming up from the Town, and Several Towns People at a Distance. Targut Arrived first and Others came After Viz. Court, Tomboy, Hercules, Hoskin's Quashee, Wilkerson's Quashee, Morgans Ned and Jack & Others, Creoles & Coromantees. I went into the Old house with Maria and others, & we Drank Cool Drink, the Cloth was laid in his New House & at Length I was Called in. I was very Dirty. Maria Sat at the Table and She looked very Black on Seeing So many Coromantees there, and she and I made Signs of Contempt to Each Other. I think there was a White Man that Dined there with us, & there was a Short White Woman in the little Old House Not in the Room where they Dined.

There was two Tables Joined together & a great number of Creoles and Coromantees that Dined there. A Boiled Course was Served up first & then a Roast Course; there were Two Dishes almost of Every Sort. There were Fowles, Two Sorts of Pies, Turkey's boiled & Roast Porke, boiled & Roast Kid & three Sorts of Puddings—Boiled, Baked, & Custard Puddings.

After Dinner Maria & all the Other Women went away then Targut brought in Punch, Sangaree & Wine & we Drank & the first Discourse was, Tomboy Said some of them were not Men Because they had not Double breasted Jackets. Tomboy, Ned & Morgans Jack were Bantering One Another on that Subject. Targut then went Out & brought in two Bottles of Liquor, & put them on the Table. No White Person was there at that time. There were Glasses, Stone Mugs & ca on the Table & a good Deal of Cool Drink. Tomboy then took up a Bottle & fill'd into a Glass & Said Gentlemen, I am going to Toast a Health, & Damnation to them that wont Pledge it or wont give their Assistance. According to their Pledging the health. Said they what it is? Said he, we are

going to Attack the Town to Kill the Baccararas and Every
Body must Join Court and me to Do it, & provide with
Cutlasses, Guns and what they Can & they that Refuse
Damnation & Confusion Seize them. So they all Drank and
Particularly Targut, & Tomboy Said to Targut, what Do you
Intend to get. Targut Said if this had happen'd some time ago
in his Old Masters Time he Could have got a great many fire
Arms & Pistols & Swords Enough, but now my Young master
is Marry'd & gone to Mrs. Dayly's & Carried them a way, I
can't go there to get them, but to be Sure I will Provide you
with my Self and whatever Else I Can get.[32]

At the feast just described, Tomboy offered a simple toast with liquor
that was meant to bind those present to the conspiracy; but more often
than not, recruits were initiated by drinking liquor with "Oath Ingredients."
In the latter case, according to the judges, the oath was taken "by drinking
a health in Liquor, either rum or some other with Grave Dirt, and sometimes cocksblood, infused; and sometimes the Person Swearing, laid his
hand on a live Cock." Sometimes too, the inducted "Chewd Melageta
Pepper." Slave witnesses Dick and Jemmy swore before the court that both
methods of swearing allegiance, with or without special ingredients in
liquor, were binding; but Jemmy also pointed out that the slaves "did not
Apprehend such terrible consequences from the breaking it, as when
Administered with Grave dirt, or Cock's blood." It was disclosed at the trials
that the Ibo slave Oliver and some others who took the oath swore that
they "would Die first" rather than "betray the Secret" as "they knew what
would befall them after Drinking a grave Dram." The judges believed that
the slaves commonly took the oath "Two, three or four times in a Day,
According as they fell into Different Companys, who were taking it, and
likewise as common for them to repeat the words of the Oath as Oft as
they met together, and Drank in Common without the Oath
Ingredients."[33]

The dirt the rebels used at their solemn initiation rituals came from the
graves of deceased slaves. The ceremony indeed could be conducted at a
grave site. When the slave woman Obbah (Aba in Akan) held a feast, she
brought some "Dirt from her Sisters Grave (for whom this feast was made)
in a Callabash," which Watty mixed with wine. On another occasion
Johnno, a cooper from the Folly plantation, and Secundi "went Down to
a Silk Cotton Tree to the Grave of Secundo's Sister Cicile and talked at
the Grave, about a Quarter of an hour, then they returned to Secundo's
house, Secundo bringing up some of the grave Dirt in his hand; he put
some of it in a Glass, and then poured Rum on it out of a Bottle and Drank
the Damnation Oath to Johnno." Similar rites involving the use of grave

dirt were also part of the Akan-planned St. Croix slave plot of 1759 and the abortive rebellion in Jamaica in 1760.[34]

In various modern and premodern social and political movements, rituals have played prominent roles in enlarging the movements and instilling solidarity. Used also to achieve such an objective, the oath taking of the Antigua rebels was deeply rooted in Akan religious tradition, which illustrates, especially in the context of collective resistance, the important sociological and political role that religion played. Derived from African culture, this religion possessed functions of explanation, prediction, and control, and influenced the beliefs and behavior of both Africans and Creoles, though perhaps to a lesser degree in the case of Creoles. However, they also took the "damnation" oath knowing what it meant. For them as for the Coromantees, taking the oath with grave dirt signified that the world of the living was intertwined with that of the dead, that they were united with their ancestors, by whom they swore to be true to their solemn obligations or incur dreadful sanctions. Among the Akan, Manoukian has written, "the cult of the ancestors is the most prominent aspect of religion. . . . Belief in the ancestral spirits is at the basis of all laws and customs regulating the lives of individuals within the family and clan, and ancestor worship is very closely bound up with the political organization." In accordance with Akan belief, the Antigua rebels, more particularly the Coromantees, recognized that blessings and misfortune came from the gods, the Supreme Being, and the ancestors. The Akan believed that the ancestors are "always watching the behavior of those they have left behind on earth, helping and protecting them, or punishing them if they do not behave. The ancestors are the custodians of the laws and customs of the tribe and will punish with sickness and misfortune those who infringe these rules; this is a very powerful sanction of morality among the Akan." If, then, the Coromantee rebels in Antigua interpreted the hard times of the 1730s partly at least in terms of the ancestors' displeasure with them, through their solemn damnation oath they appealed for the ancestors' help to change things, to bring back good fortune, and also to destroy slavery, which was conceivably the worst misfortune that had befallen them. The intensification of old frustrations and the creation of new ones in the 1730s disposed the slaves to do what they could to break their chains. Religion was at the core of their vision to affect reality, to create a new existence, a new world.[35]

Some sources claim that Creole, baptized slaves swore by the bible, but the judges themselves did not make that distinction between Coromantee and Creole initiations, nor does it appear in the trial record. Summarizing their understanding of the rebels' recruitment procedures in their report, the judges stated that the "chief Measures used by the two Heads to corrupt our Slaves, were, Entertainments of Dancing, Gaming, and Feasting; and some of them very Chargeable ones, always coloured with some innocent pretence; as of commemorating some deceased Friend by throwing water on his Grave, or Christning a House, or the like, according to the Negro Customs; where they were debaucht with Liquor; their Minds imbittered against their Masters, and against their Condition of Slavery, by strong Invectives thrown out against both."[36]

Another feature of the recruitment and initiation of the rebels underscored the critical role that Akan culture and religion played in the organization of the plot. While most induction ceremonies were performed without special functionaries, on at least one occasion the slave leader Secundi used the services of probably the Coromantee Quawcoo (Kwaku in Akan), "an Old Oby Man [obeahman] a Physition" belonging to William Hunt, to perform the ritual in a more imposingly formal manner before a large number of slaves. *Obeah* refers to "a supernatural force given to man to protect and heal him," though the term "also refers to the charms which derive their power from this force." Akan slaves in the Americas were distinguished by their belief in *obeah*. According to Monica Schuler, the *obeah* man, "practitioner of magic, may have been less a magician and more of a priest during most of the eighteenth century. Whatever his role he was definitely in a position to influence and control the slaves — possibly even those outside his own ethnic group, for all the slaves feared his powers. *Obeah* men were at the center of the Akan rebellions in Jamaica" and other Caribbean societies, and their role was "very like the role of priests and magicians in Ashanti military campaigns" who accompanied the army, and among their functions prepared it for battle by appealing to the supernatural powers for victory, advised the military command, administered oaths that soldiers would face the enemy bravely, and issued to the soldiers "protective charms and amulets, some of which were believed to make their wearers invulnerable to bullets." When Quawcoo the Antigua *obeah* man officiated at the oath-taking ceremony, he was preparing those present for war against the whites. Like vodun, which C.L.R. James says was "the medium of the [Boukmann] conspiracy" that in 1791 helped accelerate events leading up to the Haitian Revolution, *obeah* in Antigua and other Caribbean societies helped embolden slaves in their organization of collective rebellions.[37]

Perhaps at least three *obeah* men were involved in the Antigua slave plot: the Coromantee Quawcoo, who was banished; Governor William Mathew's Caesar, who was executed; and another slave John Obiah, at whose house several slaves reportedly took the damnation oath. Secundi, driver on the plantation belonging to Thomas Freeman, who took command of the plot after Court and Tomboy were executed, "called to his Assistance," the judges wrote, "a Negroe Obiaman, or Wizard, who acted his Part before a great number of Slaves, assembled at Secundi's to take the Oath, and assured them of Success."[38] This was Quawcoo, who apparently also performed the rites privately for Secundi one night at his house. This ceremony seems to have been meant to prepare Secundi to lead a revolt to avenge Court and Tomboy's deaths. Colonel Frye's Quamina (Kwamina, in Akan) described Quawcoo's role.

> I saw this Obey Man at Secundi's House after I waked at
> Midnight, I found him and Hunts Cuffy there. Secundi gave
> him a Chequeen, a Bottle of Rum and a Dominique Cock
> and Quawcoo put Obey made of Sheeps Skin upon the
> ground, upon and about the bottle of Rum, and the
> Chequeen upon the bottle, Then took the Cock, cut open his
> Mouth, and one of his Toes, and so poured the Cocks blood
> Over all the Obey, and then Rub'd Secundi's forehead with
> the Cocks bloody Toe, Then took the Bottle and poured Some
> Rum upon the Obey, Drank a Dram, and gave it to Secundi
> and made Secundi Sware not to Discover his Name. Secundi
> Pledged him and Swore not to Discover his name to anybody.
> Secundi then Asked him when he must begin to Rise.
> Quawcoo took a String ty'd knots in it, and told him not to be
> in a hurry, for that he would give him Notice when to Rise
> and all Should go well and that as he tyed those knots so the
> Bacararas should become Arrant fools and have their Mouths
> Stoped, and their hands tyed that they should not Discover
> the Negro's Designs.[39]

"By God," Quamina told the judges, "If you had not Catched me I would have not told you now. I am afraid of this Obey Man now, he is a Bloody fellow, I knew him in Cormantee Country." The judges made the observation in a note to this deposition that "just in the Latter part of this Evidence Quamina seemed to be in a great Consternation at the Sight of the Obey Man."[40] Without the intervention of the *obeah* man at the oath-taking ceremonies the oath was binding, but, for those who were initiated by the *obeah* man, fear of his powers and the disasters that would befall them should they break the oath bound them securely to the planned revolt.

Slave women were frequently present at induction ceremonies, mostly as onlookers, or guests, helping with arrangements and serving food and drink, at which men presided. That there is no direct evidence that any of them took the oath does not mean that they did not do so; and certainly many women knew what was going on even if they may not have been deeply involved.[41] Our attention is drawn, however, to the activities of two women who clearly played much more than peripheral roles. One of them we know simply as Queen. At the trial of Quawcoo, an old Coromantee belonging to Mr. John Pare, slave witness Quamina deposed that "Court used to be very Often at Pares Plantation to go to an Old Womans house Called Queen and Send Butter, Bread, and other things to her to sell for him, and I have bought some of her and this man Quawcoo knew it very well. Court Sent a Boy on a White horse to Old Queen to tell her they were going to put him to Death, and She might keep what things She had of his. Quawcoo was very great with Court and Secundi." The other Antigua slave woman of whom we should take special note was Obbah, who held one of the big initiation feasts at her house and who used grave dirt to make the initiation drink. Many slaves took the oath at her feast.[42]

What was the relationship of these women to Court? If Court himself was cast in the role of Akan ruler, could it be that Queen or Obbah, like Abena the Akan "Queen of Kingston" in Jamaica who was connected with a conspiracy in that city in 1760, was "cast in the role of a traditional Akan Queen-Mother?"[43] In Akan society the queen-mother, who was often really the chief's sister, was constitutionally regarded as his "mother." According to Manoukian, among her state functions "she is expected to advise the Chief about his conduct and may scold and reprimand him in a way not permitted to his councillors. When a Chief's Stool is vacant the Queen-Mother proposes his successor; she is regarded as the authority on kinship relations in the Royal lineage." The queen-mother therefore played a very important role in the Akan state.[44] It seems entirely likely that both Queen and Obbah could have been advisers to Court, especially about Akan tradition, which he had to learn, having left the Gold Coast as a mere boy. That Queen herself was called by that name is most suggestive.[45] She was clearly in frequent contact with Court, and it seems likely that she rather than Obbah was a principal adviser to Court. Obbah herself, however, was not without influence in the Coromantee community. While many more men were involved in the plot than women, we must take note of the possible heavily influential role of Queen and Obbah. That no women appear in the lists of slaves executed or banished for their part in the Antigua plot can be explained by whites' lack of understanding of the working of the slave community, so that, operating from a white-oriented perception of island life, they searched out slave men as the most dangerous slave conspirators. In any case, the trials, we know, were brought to an end because the expenditure on them was heavy and because some legislators believed that enough slaves were executed as an example to the rest. Had such considerations not prevailed, some slave women might also have been executed or banished.

One additional feature of the rebel's confidence- and support-building methods deserves mention, in relation to their range and variety. At some of the recruitment sessions slaves assumed or were given names of proprietors or prominent island whites. Colonel Samuel Martin's Toney told Major William Byam before his trial that "at a Feast of Capt. Kings Dick at Ashes Plantation...he heard several Negros Assume Gentlemens Names, that Mingo was called Majr: Nanton." At another feast at Morgan's plantation, related Thomas Hanson's Quashee, "We Drank healths, Majr. Vernon's, Collo. Gilberts; there were Negro's that went by those Names; Court got upon the table Jumping about, saying he would have St. George's health Drank." At some gatherings Caesar Rodney's Ned Chester, a mulatto carpenter, was called "Capt. Clarke." By assuming and assigning "titles" or proprietors' names, the rebels declared their firm commitment to the revolt through symbols of the rewards that awaited those who carried out their obligations. Indeed, plantations were promised to those who enlisted.[46] These recruiting methods strengthened the slaves' resolve and projected in their minds the Antigua world of slavery turned upside down, with roles reversed to black over white instead of the other way around. Finally, kinship ties were also important, as already committed rebels recruited others from among their relatives. Many slaves followed their kinfolk and joined up.[47]

On Sunday, October 10, 1736, just days before the plot was discovered, the Creole leader Tomboy (whom some slaves called Thomas Boyd) held "a very Sumptuous Publick feast" in St. John's town at his master's house "to which were invited a great Number of Slaves," and "Several White Persons were Spectators of it." This information is included in the report of justice Robert Arbuthnot to the legislature. It was Arbuthnot, we will recall, who initiated investigations that led to the discovery of the plot. Arbuthnot also reported that one week before Tomboy's feast, on Sunday, October 3 Court was "Crown'd King of the Coromantees" in the presence of nearly two thousand slaves. A "Great many White People were present and saw the Coronation." At this ceremony Tomboy stood next to Court in importance. Court was seated under "a Canopy of State, Surrounded by his great officers." He "Walked in Procession as King, and had all the Homage and Respect of a King paid to him." Arbuthnot and others, who had strong reason to believe that Court was deeply involved in some mischief of which, at the time, they could not yet be certain, disagreed with Court's master, who passed the "coronation" off as "Only an Innocent Play of Courts Country, and that no harm Could be meant by it, More Especially as it was Represented before so many White People."[48]

But this "Play" was far from innocent. It was in fact Akan ceremonial that prepared participants for war against the whites. In broad daylight at two o'clock in the afternoon of October 3, 1736, at Mrs. Dunbar Parke's pasture near St. John's, white and black onlookers were treated to a dazzling display of Akan ceremonial when Court staged a military *"ikem"* (in Akan *ekem* or *akyem*, meaning "shield") dance or "one grand Test" to ascertain how many followers he could count on, and to give notice to those who understood the meaning of the performance that he intended to go forward with the planned revolt. The elaborate rites of preparing for war were meant to test and increase solidarity among the slaves. The description of the *ikem* or shield dance in the judges' report deserves careful consideration and quoting in full. "The Evidences of Witnesses and Confessions of many of the Criminal Coromantees make it appear to us," the judges wrote

> That it is the Custom in Africa, when a Coromantee King has resolved upon a War with a Neighbouring State, to give Publick Notice among his Subjects, That the Ikem-dance will be performed at a Certain Time & Place; and there the Prince appears in Royal habit, under an Umbrella or Canopy of State, preceeded by his Officers, called Braffo & His Marshall, attended by his Asseng (or Chamberlain) & Guards, and the Musick of his Company; with his Generals & Chiefs about him. Then he places himself up an advanced Seat, his Generals setting behind him upon a Bench; His Guards on each Side; His Braffo and Marshall clearing the Circle, and his Asseng with an Elephants Tail keeping the flies from him; The Musick playing; and the People forming a Semicircle about him. After some Respite, the Prince arises, distributes Money to the People; Then the Drums beating to the Ikem-beat, he with an Ikem (i.e.) a Shield composed of wicker, Skins and two or three small pieces of thin board upon his left Arm, and a Lance in his Right hand, begins the Dance, representing the defensive Motions of the Shield, those of throwing the Lance, and the several gestures by them used in Battle. When the Prince begins to be fatigued, The Guards run in and Support him; he delivers the Ikem and Lance to the Person who next Dances; then is lead Supported to his Chair, and is seated again in State. Whenever he rises, he is in like manner Supported. Then the Same Dance is performed by Several Others, but without the Ceremony of being Supported. Then the Prince Stepping into the Area of the Semicircle, with his Chief General, and taking a Cutlass in his hand, moves with a Whirling motion of his Body round a Bout, but dancing and leaping up at the same time from one Horn or point of the Semicircle, quite to the other, so as distinctly to be viewed by all; and then returning to the Cen-

ter of the Semicircle, with his General, makes several
flourishes with the Cutlass, gently touching with it the
Generals Forehead; and having at the same time, the Ikems
(the number of which is uncertain) held between his own and
the others Body. He takes an Oath highly reverenced by the
Coromantees, which is to the following purpose. He Swears to
the General, that where he falls, He'll drop by his side, rather
than foresake or desert him in Battle; and that he will behave
as a brave prince ought; but in case he should fail in his Oath
he agrees with and desires his subjects present, to take off his
head, and makes them a Grant of his Houses, Lands, and all
his Substance. This Oath (tho in the first Ceremonial part
directed to the General only) is nevertheless, understood to be
made to the people as well as him. If he is answered by three
Huzzas from those present; By the Custom of their Countrey
it signifies, not only a Declaration of their believing, that he
will Observe his Oath; but it is an actual & Solemn
Engagement on their side to do as he does, and to join and go
forth with him to the Warr: For the breach whereof they are
regarded as Traitors. Braffoo Standing behind Court with a
wooden Cutlace Cryd Tackey, Tackey, Tackey, Conguo: which
Signifies King, King, King, Great King; which words are
used in the Coromantee Countrey Every morning at the
Kings door by Braffoo, and thereupon a Captive taken in the
Course of the Warr is cut to pieces by Braffoo: Then the
Ceremony of this Dance is concluded by Braffoo's cutting to
pieces in the Semicircle a Captive taken by Surprise from the
People the Warr is intended against; Braffoo thro the whole
Ceremony having his face whitend over, to prevent being
known, and dresst with a Cap full of Feathers & a bundle at
his back representing a dead Negro Child, as the badge of his
Office.[49]

This elaborate martial display or "military Dance and Shew," the judges
believed, was the "Masterpiece of the plot and was to be done in open
daylight." Whites, and non-Coromantee slaves or those not yet part of the
plot "might be Spectators, and yet ignorant of the meaning; The Language
and Ceremonys used at it, being all Coromantee." Court took "the oath
and observed all the Ceremonies of it," but there was no umbrella or Akan
ceremonial canopy, Emanuel, Edward Gregory's "faithful" slave, having
failed to make it.[50] In place of the canopy there were two *ikems* or shields,
and "the Cutlaces and Lances were intirely of wood"; and instead of a man,
a drum was cut to pieces "figuring by this last, how they would serve the

Whites, when overcome." At Court's side hung "a good Sabre. . .with a red Scabbard," and his whole appearance was that of a King "having on a particular Cap, proper to the Kings of his Countrey." The cap was made of "green Silk imbroidered with Gold, with a deep border either of black Fur, or black Feathers, and three plumes of Feathers in it."[51] The judges observed that Court had often worn that same cap but without the feathers. "Hawes's Gift was his Braffoo, Gregorys Animoo his Marshall, and Gregorys Quashee was his Asseng; and Tomboy, Hercules, Fortune, and Darbys Jack were his Generals, who at their coming (Court being before there and expecting them) were introduced with much State and Ceremony, and Seated properly behind Court; but Tomboy was the Greatest General, to whom the Ceremony of the Oaths in the Coromantee Language, was performed by Court." At the taking of the oath, according to the judges, the slave crowd "huzzad three times, The Coromantees knowing, but the Creoles not understanding, the Engagement they Entered into by it." To some of the slaves who understood the meaning of the oath rites "nothing appeared so Audacious and terrible," the judges added, "That Some of the Coromantees endeavoured by means of Jumping among the Dancers and Spectators and otherwise, to prevent its being performed, apprehending the meaning of it might be discovered, and being sensible, nothing could be intended by it, less than a Declaration of War, and of necessity against the Whites." Without the oath the dance was often staged "in the Coroman-tee Country, as an Entertainment, and upon other Innocent occasions," but with the oath it is "so certain a Declaration of War, That the neigh-bouring Princes send to know, against whom the War is intended, and according to the answer returned, prepare or not for their Defence." So sacred was the custom that it is "Death for a Subject not licensed by his Prince, to use it with the Ceremony of the oath."[52]

Historians must be grateful to the judges for recording what they regarded as a "very uncommon" part of the plot, so unusual as to deserve that they be "the more particular in it." Brought to the surface only because of the plot, that remarkable piece of ethnography in several ways adds to our understanding of the uses to which the slaves might put their African culture and institutions, as they did the best they could with what they had under the constraints of slavery, seeking not only to survive but also to effect changes in their lives even to the ultimate point of organized revolt.

While the judges claimed that Court was "crowned" at the *ikem* ceremony, in the Gold Coast Akan rulers were not crowned but "enstooled" during elaborate ceremonies.[53] Court was not enstooled at the *ikem* dance but occupied the position of an already installed ruler. It seemed to the judges, as outsiders who were observing the slaves' peculiar activities, that Court's "coronation" was incorporated into the whole affair as he did appear as king, "having on a particular Cap, proper to the Kings of his Countrey."

That Tomboy himself was not crowned at any time shows that he was not a chief. As suggested earlier, he was more likely to have been leader of the *young men*. It is true that Tomboy held his own major feast, but at the *ikem* dance he was only Court's principal general, to whom Court addressed the oaths of the ceremony in Coromantee; Tomboy did not occupy as exalted a position as Court, who, therefore, while sharing leadership of the plot with him, did not relinquish ascendancy over the whole affair, which remained distinctly Coromantee or Akan inspired. So the Coromantee/Creole alliance emerges as an effort made by an Akan ruler in preparation for war and does not necessarily imply that Court would share power with Tomboy in the new state. In this light, the judges' claim that the Creoles had planned to subjugate the Coromantees if the revolt succeeded does not seem far-fetched, although the details of everyday relations between Africans and Creoles remain hidden from view.

If the dance described by the judges is today part of a wider Akan ritual that is not particularly linked with war, as performed in Antigua in 1736 it clearly had military significance. Cast in the role of an Akan ruler, Court was the leader of his people in war, and the *ikem* dance only emphasized this. His generals who attended him—Tomboy, Hercules, Fortune, and Jack—were Creoles (though the judges were not sure about Fortune) and were later executed (see table 11:1). Presumably all Coromantees, Gift, Quashee, and Annimoo, who were also executed, occupied the other three important ceremonial positions of *braffo, asseng,* and marshal respectively. The *braffo* would correspond in Akan to the *abrafo,* who were the ruler's law enforcement officials and who were often called the executioners. The judges reported that the *braffo* had a whitened face throughout the ceremony to conceal his identity, but they could have been grossly mistaken about the reason for this, because among the Akan white symbolizes purity, virtue, virginity, joy, victory, God, and the spirits of the ancestors. It would be in keeping with the essence of the *ikem* dance if the *braffo*'s whitened face symbolized an appeal to the spirits to witness the solemn declaration of war and give victory over the enemy. The *braffo*'s cap of feathers also formed part of the ceremonial dress of particular officials in Akan states. The *asseng* official at the dance would be the Akan *esen,* who, strictly speaking, were the heralds and messengers, though the judges referred to them as chamberlains. There is an Asante myth that the Creator made a herald, a drummer, and an executioner, and these officials take precedence in that order in an Asante court.[54]

The *ikem* dance was above all a formal declaration of war, complete with Akan oath rituals, which conformed with Gold Coast practices and West African conventions of warfare. Among these conventions, writes Robert S. Smith, "the formal declaration of war was perhaps the most important, giving an enemy time to prepare for an attack and an opportunity for parleying and for sending women, children and the elderly to safety." But such "deliberation amounted to a conscious sacrifice of the advantage of surprise in the attack." In any case, even if the Antigua Coromantees staged the *ikem* dance to "inform" whites of their intention to fight against them, whites obviously would not have got the message, so the more important objective of the display was to communicate with and mobilize slaves who knew what was going on. And when, at one point in the proceedings, the *braffo* cried out "Tackey, Tackey, Tackey, Conguo," which the judges translated as "King, King, King, Great King" but which (because Tackey or Takye was a name common in parts of the Gold Coast and may have been Court's "African" name) could really have meant "Takye's stool (or throne)," the overall message of what the *ikem* dance represented would not have been lost on Akan slaves: King Court was ready and willing to lead his people into battle against the whites.[55]

The functional elements of Akan culture that we have uncovered in this chapter in relation to the Antigua slave plot convincingly indicate the possibilities of cultural resistance in New World slave societies and the way in which that resistance might, under propitious conditions, be attached to the chariot wheels of greater revolutionary endeavor. When such conditions emerged, as the Antigua plot demonstrates, potential slave leaders whose sanctions were derived mainly from economic, religious, and ethnic sources were already equipped to organize revolts, although they faced many difficulties.

Conclusion

"By the end of the eighteenth century," Genovese has argued, "the historical content of the slave revolts [in the Americas] shifted decisively from attempts to secure freedom from slavery to attempts to overthrow slavery as a social system." While it is true that the "great black revolution in Saint-Domingue marked the turning point," developments associated with the American and French revolutions and the humanitarian movement in parts of Europe to abolish the slave trade and slavery also played important roles. Genovese is convincing; and when he uses the term *decisively* to describe the shift from "restorationist" revolt to revolutionary overthrow of the slave system, he takes into account that the transition may have begun earlier than at the end of the eighteenth century in some places, and for different reasons.[1] This was certainly true for Antigua and Barbados, whose small size and relatively flat terrain meant that, after the first few decades of the pioneer period, slaves could not successfully escape slavery within those territories. In Jamaica, however, they could, especially before the maroon treaties of 1739–40. With the waning of an effective maroon dimension to slave resistance in Antigua and Barbados in the seventeenth century, a successful slave revolt required taking over the whole of each island. The Barbados slaves planned several revolts in the seventeenth century (none of which got beyond the conspiracy stage), and did not plan another until 1816, this time one that actually took place. Why there were no revolutionary slave attempts to take over the island in the entire eighteenth century after the restorationist period had vanished with the forest is a subject that has not yet received the serious study that it deserves, but an adequate explanation must certainly take into account the immensity of the task Barbados slaves would have faced.[2]

Unlike the Barbados slaves, those in Antigua did try to seize the island in 1736 and overthrow the whites. Here, collective resistance had moved away from a restorationist past to exhibit more revolutionary tendencies, which were determined by circumstances within Antigua itself. A complex manifestation of slave resistance, the conspiracy reflected many dimensions of the slave society within which it gradually crystallized, and it is best understood within that context, especially in relation to the obvious limitations of masters' control over their slaves. After years of resistance that mostly fell short of collective open rebellion, Antigua slaves, prodded by a combination of developments, collectively expressed their intensified frustrations in a plot for an islandwide revolt that involved mainly Coromantees and, for the first time, Creoles. The emergence of Creoles in the forefront of revolt long before the late slave period, when they were unmistakably prominent, suggests the arrival of an important stage in the evolution not only of slave resistance, but of the slave community itself, as both were influenced by demographic and cultural changes associated with the creolization of slave society.[3] The etiology of the 1736 plot itself can be traced back to the slaves' desire to destroy slavery as it existed, to their ideological commitment to resistance short of open rebellion or gaining actual freedom, to population imbalance greatly in their favor, to lax enforcement of slave controls, and to the general character of slavery. These preconditions were the foundation of a volatile situation with a strong potential for collective rebellion, which later merged with the effects of economic recession in the 1730s, natural disasters, sickness, and above all, the emergence of charismatic African and Creole slave leaders to make revolt highly predictable. In the organization of their revolt, moreover, these leaders were able to draw heavily upon functioning resources of African tradition, which is clear evidence of the cultural resistance that was possible under slavery, under certain conditions — resistance that could extend from the individual to the collective level.

Together, these developments in Antigua slave society, insofar as they influenced the experiences and perceptions of the slaves, lend credence to Eric Wolf's observation, made in connection with peasant revolt but applicable also to slave revolt, that "a rebellion cannot start from a situation of complete impotence; the powerless are easy victims." To borrow from Wolf, if the relations of slaves "to the field of power" that surrounds them is ultimately decisive in projecting revolt,[4] then it is quite clear that Antigua slaves by the 1730s, under conditions that sharpened their awareness of the possibilities to change their lives, were far from powerless. Perceiving that there was much in their favor that meant they did not have to be forever victims, they calculatingly risked a great revolt. As a window upon Antigua slave society and master-slave relations, the plot shows that the slaves were able to exploit available social and psychological space that allowed them to develop a world of their own that whites did not penetrate and whose resources could be used to challenge the power of the master class.

The Antigua slave plot also stands as a striking contrast to the predominant modes of resistance in the seventeenth and eighteenth centuries and increases our understanding of some of the forces in slave societies that can influence changes in patterns of slave resistance. In his well-known study of the Haitian Revolution, C.L.R. James observed that "the slaves worked on the land, and like revolutionary peasants everywhere, they aimed at the extermination of their oppressors."[5] It is no doubt true that, from the earliest years of the sugar revolution and slavery's establishment in Antigua, the slaves dreamed of somehow escaping the fate mapped out for them, but it was not at all an easy matter to translate these dreams, particularly that of wiping out their masters, into reality. Conditions in Antigua that were broadly similar to those in the mainland North American colonies inhibited the development of such schemes. In both areas slave revolt was not as sustained as in Jamaica and St. Domingue, where favorable geography, the nakedly exploitive nature of slavery, and the steady importation of Africans direct from the coast were only three among many influential factors that enhanced the potential for revolt. Throughout the slave period in the United States, climate, a relatively weaker reliance on African supplies of slaves, the early appearance of a growing proportion of American-born blacks in the slave population as a result of conditions that favored natural increase, and patterns of settlement and social control all helped determine that styles of resistance would emphasize the day-to-day variety rather than revolt.[6] In Antigua up to 1763 similar resistance patterns were shaped by the early appearance of a significant proportion of Creole slaves, an irregular slave trade, the small size of the island, and the absence of rugged terrain or jungle after the end of the seventeenth century to which slaves could escape and establish their own alternative type of existence.

This last factor was probably the most important. Our evidence indicates that, while areas of forest cover lasted in Antigua in the seventeenth century, particularly in the Shekerley Hills, numerous fugitive slaves sought refuge there, and the opportunities for such maroon resistance increased slave flight and unrest on the plantations. These developments were behind the widespread alarm over the possibility of islandwide revolt in the 1680s. During these frontier days slaveowners relied heavily upon coercion to discipline and control their slaves. By the late seventeenth century, however, the maroon dimension to resistance had all but vanished as sugar plantations expanded aggressively into the interior, and as the authorities moved systematically to scour such areas for fugitives. Deprived of such havens, the slaves were forced back onto patterns of resistance that were accommodative and patently less dramatic than rebellion, flight to the interior, or attacks on whites and plantations. However, some unyielding rebels tried to leave the island altogether, especially for Puerto Rico, while others engaged in sporadic outbursts of the collective maroon type resistance that had been characteristic of the seventeenth century. Resistance-in-accommodation largely on the individual and small group level characterized the patterns of the eighteenth century. But as the slaves settled down to working this out in ways that did not amount to suicidal challenges to white authority, the slave society itself, always unstable, always capable of being split apart by internal discord between masters and slaves, came to rely less upon coercion and more upon a mixture of coercion and consensus to preserve some semblance of order within which masters and slaves might pursue their interdependent and independent interests. The growth of the Creole component within the slave population increasingly reinforced the role of consensus.

The overall history of slave resistance in Antigua, therefore, must be seen against the background of changing environmental conditions that in turn affected the character of slavery in the island and the slaves' adjustments to those realities. Largely because plots and revolts there were not endemic as in Jamaica, some scholars have written as if to suggest that slaves in Antigua and the other Leewards were not rebellious;[7] but realistically to gauge the responses of the slaves in those smaller, more compact territories to slavery, one should ask, What did they do with what they had? How did they use the resources at their disposal? It would be unwise to conclude that they were more contented slaves. A close reading of the Antigua slave experience suggests a different interpretation that has more to do with the slaves' shrewd appraisal of their total environment in regard to the potential for successful revolt, which was reflected in a style of resistance that commonly did not openly challenge the slave system yet persistently subverted it nonetheless without bringing down upon the slaves' heads the full, terrible might of the state. In the 1730s, during a period of profound economic distress, seemingly contented slaves in Antigua seized the chance to break their chains and realize a long-cherished dream. The slave leaders planned that affair very carefully. It was now or never, as they well knew. The opportunity was too good to miss. As for the slaveowners, having barely averted the ultimate disaster of their world turned upside down, they wrestled anew with longstanding, troublesome questions about how to establish supremacy over the restless slave population.

List of Abbreviations

AHR	*American Historical Review*
BELC	*Boletin de Estudios Lationamericanos y del Caribe*
BT	Board of Trade
CO	Colonial Office Series, Public Record Office, London
CQ	*Caribbean Quarterly*
CS	*Caribbean Studies*
CSP	Calendar of State Papers, Colonial Series: America and West Indies
CSSH	*Comparative Studies in Society and History*
EHR	*Economic History Review*
JAH	*Journal of African History*
JCH	*Journal of Caribbean History*
JEH	*Journal of Economic History*
JHR	*Jamaica Historical Review*
JIH	*Journal of Interdisciplinary History*
JNH	*Journal of Negro History*
JSH	*Journal of Southern History*
JSocH	*Journal of Social History*
NWIG	*Nieuwe West-Indische Gids/New West Indian Guide*
NYRB	*New York Review of Books*
PRO	Public Record Office, London
RAC	Royal African Company
SCHM	*South Carolina Historical Magazine*
SES	*Social and Economic Studies*
SS	*Southern Studies*
WMQ	*William and Mary Quarterly*

Notes

Preface

1. Drew Gilpin Faust, "Culture, Conflict, and Community: The Meaning of Power on an Ante-Bellum Plantation," *JSocH* 14 (Fall 1980):83–97.
2. E. J. Hobsbawm, "From Social History to the History of Society," in *Essays in Social History,* ed. M. W. Flinn and T. C. Smout (Oxford: Clarendon Press, 1974), pp. 1–22.
3. When quoting from manuscripts I have adhered to their punctuation and spelling except in cases where small changes were necessary for the sake of clarity. However, proper names are spelled exactly as in the source quoted, and this results in a few inconsistencies where sources differ as to spelling. All dates before 1752 are Old Style, except that the year is taken to begin on January 1.

Chapter 1: "No People Were Ever Rescued from a Danger More Imminent"

1. [Mrs. Flannigan], *Antigua and the Antiguans,* 2 vols. (London, 1844), 1:86; Mathew to BT, Oct. 12, 1727, CO 152/16, S16–22; Nevis Treasurer's Accounts, CO 152/18, T70.
2. A major source of information on the affair is the judges' General Report (hereafter General Report), copies of which can be found in Mathew to BT, Jan. 17, 1737, CO 152/22, W94; in Council Mins., Jan. 24, 1737, CO 9/10; and in Assembly Mins., Jan. 3, 1737, CO 9/12. A printed and slightly edited version entitled *A Genuine Narrative of the Intended Conspiracy of the Negroes at Antigua. . .* (Dublin, 1737) has been reprinted (New York: Arno Press, 1972). For a fictionalized account, see "A Legend of the Ravine" in *Antigua and the Antiguans,* 1:91–107. See also the extensive minutes of the legislature, which contain, among other data, the trial records of slaves banished and some of those executed. CO 9/9–12. The trial record [TR] for banished slaves is in Council Mins., Jan. 12, 1737, CO 9/10, and Feb. 24, 1737, CO 9/11; for the eight executed slaves see Council Mins., Feb. 14, 1738, CO 9/11. Quotations from the General Report are taken from the copy in CO 152/22, W94.
3. "Extract of a Letter from Antigua," Oct. 24, 1736, *Virginia Gazette,* Apr. 18, 1737 (also in *Gentleman's Magazine,* 7 [1737]:59); Antigua letter, Oct. 24, 1736, *South Carolina Gazette,* Dec. 4, 1736.
4. General Report.
5. Letter dated Jan. 15, 1737, Dr. Walter Tullideph Letter Books, in Vere Langford Oliver, *The History of the Island of Antigua,* 3 vols. (London: Mitchell & Hughes,

1894-99), 3:408. Extracts from the letter books in this volume covering 1734-67 are to be found on pp. 156-62, 408-10. The manuscript letters (1731-67), in three volumes, are in the Scottish Record Office, Edinburgh, Scotland. I am indebted to Richard B. Sheridan for lending me a microfilm of these letters (hereafter cited as Tullideph Letter Book, MS). See also General Report; *Virginia Gazette,* Apr. 8, 1737; *South Carolina Gazette,* Dec. 4, 1736.

6. General Report. The governor of the nearby French island of Guadeloupe compared the slave conspiracy to the Gunpowder Plot in seventeenth-century England, which, he said, had perhaps been too often spoken of in the slaves' presence. Oruno D. Lara, "Le Procès de résistance des nègres de Guadeloupe: guérilla et conspirations des nègres cimarrons, 1736-1738," *Cimarrons* 1 (1981):60.

7. One source claims the ball was postponed because of the death of "the General's [governor's] Son at St. Christopher." *Virginia Gazette,* Apr. 8, 1737; *A Genuine Narrative,* p. 10n.

8. General Report; *Virginia Gazette,* Apr. 8, 1737.

9. *South Carolina Gazette,* Dec. 4, 1736; General Report.

10. For the Vesey affair, see John Lofton, *Denmark Vesey's Revolt: The Slave Plot That Lit a Fuse to Fort Sumter* (Kent, Ohio: Kent State University Press, 1983), first published as *Insurrection in South Carolina: The Turbulent World of Denmark Vesey* (Yellow Springs, Ohio: Antioch Press, 1964). See also Eric Foner, "Black Conspiracies," *NYRB* 17 (Nov. 4, 1971):39; Richard C. Wade, "The Vesey Plot: A Reconsideration," *JSH* 30 (May 1964):143-61. For interpretations opposite to Wade's see, for example, Robert S. Starobin, ed., *Denmark Vesey: The Slave Conspiracy of 1822* (Englewood Cliffs, N.J.: Prentice-Hall, 1970); John Oliver Killens, (ed.) *The Trial Record of Denmark Vesey* (Boston: Beacon Press, 1970), introduction; Sterling Stuckey, "Remembering Denmark Vesey—Agitator or Insurrectionist?" *Negro Digest* 15 (Feb. 1966):28-41; William D. Freehling, *Prelude to Civil War* (New York: Harper & Row, 1966), pp. 53-61.

11. Mathew to BT, Jan. 17, 1737, CO 152/22, W88. Among the best-known slave conspiracies in colonial British America is that of New York in 1741. For discussion of difficulties of authenticating and interpreting this affair, see the introduction by Thomas J. Davis in Daniel Hormansden, *The New York Conspiracy* (1810; reprint, Boston: Beacon Press, 1971); Thomas J. Davis, "The New York Slave Conspiracy of 1741 as Black Protest," *JNH* 56 (Jan. 1971):17-30; Leopold S. Launitz-Schurer, Jr., "Slave Resistance in Colonial New York: An Interpretation of Daniel Hormansden's New York Conspiracy," *Phylon* 41 (June 1980):137-52; Ferenc M. Szasz, "The New York Slave Revolt of 1741: A Re-Examination," *New York History* 48 (July 1967):215-30.

12. Foner, "Black Conspiracies," p. 38. Useful illustrative studies include Philip D. Morgan and George D. Terry, "Slavery in Microcosm: A Conspiracy Scare in Colonial South Carolina," *SS* 21 (Summer 1982):121-45; Edwin A. Miles, "The Mississippi Slave Insurrection Scare of 1835," *JNH* 42 (1975):48-60; Laurence Shore, "Making Mississippi Safe for Slavery: The Insurrectionary Panic of 1835," in *Class, Conflict, and Consensus,* ed. Orville Vernon Burton and Robert C. McMath, Jr. (Westport, Conn.: Greenwood Press, 1982), pp. 96-127; John Scott Strickland, "The Great Revival and Insurrectionary Fears in North Carolina: An Examination

of Antebellum Southern Society and Slave Revolt Panics," in Burton and McMath, *Class, Conflict, and Consensus,* pp. 57-95; Charles B. Dew, "Black Ironworkers and the Slave Insurrection Panic of 1856," *JSH* 41 (Aug. 1975):321-38; Dan T. Carter, "The Anatomy of Fear: The Christmas Day Insurrection Scare of 1865," *JSH* 42 (Aug. 1976):345-64; Jeffery T. Crow, "Slave Rebelliousness and Social Conflict in North Carolina, 1775 to 1802," *WMQ*, 3d ser. 37 (Jan. 1980):79-102; Marion D. de B. Kilson, "Towards Freedom: An Analysis of Slave Revolts in the United States," *Phylon* 25 (Summer 1964):186.

13. Council Mins., Jan. 8, 1737, CO 9/10, including "The Substance of the Information given by Robert Arbuthnot Esqr. to the General & Council on Fryday the fifteenth Day of October 1736 of the Discoverys he had made of the Dangerous Designs & behavior of the Slaves" (hereafter Arbuthnot Report). Morris to Gov. and Council, Jan. 24, 1737, Council Mins., Jan. 31, 1737, CO 9/10, arguing against ceasing executions of convicted slaves and further prosecutions.

14. General Report. In regard to the Vesey plot (1822) in South Carolina, the first court similarly justified its decision against public trial of slave conspirators. And in New York City the trials of those involved in the slave plot of 1741 "were in general conducted in a private manner." Killens, *Trial Record,* pp. 3-4.

15. At the trial of the freedmen Johnson brothers on Jan. 19, 1737, the confessions of Court and Tomboy were reportedly read out to the court. Assembly Mins., Jan. 19, 1737, CO 9/12. The first court that tried the slaves also claimed that Tomboy and Court confessed, and there are references to other slave confessions (though no copies of the actual confessions) in the trial record and the legislature's minutes. General Report; see also, for example, "Tryal of John Sabby a Mulatto Carpenter belonging to Mr. Pare 16th December [1736]," "Tryal of Monk's Mingo [Nov. 1736]," "Tryal of Tom a Creole Driver of Francis Delap 8th Decem. [1736]," "Tryal of Robin a Creole Slave of Francis Delap 8th December [1736]," "Tryal of Codrington's Sackey a Creole Carpenter 8th December [1736]," "Tryal of Caesar alais Geddon a Cormantee Field Negro belonging to Mr. Pare 10th Dec. [1736]," "Tryal of Quaw, sone of Old Cormante Tom belonging to the Estate of Edwd. Byam Decd 10th December [1736]," "Tryal of Troilus commonly Called Yabby a Cormantee Carp: belonging to the Estate of Thomas Freeman Decd 10th Dec. [1736]," TR, Council Mins., Jan. 12, 1737, CO 9/10. Weatherill's slave Booty, and George and Attau of Parham Plantation were pardoned and released after confessing their guilt and supplying the court with much useful information. The court recommended the same for Langford's Cuffy, who also "made a full and free Confession, and does not Appear to be a Principle Contriver or Promoter of the Intended Insurrection." Council Mins., Mar. 17, 1737, CO 9/11. For securing of slaves on ships in St. John's harbor, see Council Mins., Nov. 18, 29, Dec. 9, 20, 30, 1736; Jan. 3, 1737, CO 9/10.

16. Council Mins., Feb. 14, 1737, CO 9/11.

17. General Report.

18. Council Mins., Nov. 15, 1737, CO 9/11, Jan. 17, 1737, CO 9/10; "Evidence against Vernons Cudjoe [Jan. 26, 1737]," TR, Council Mins., Feb. 14, 1737, CO 9/11.

19. General Report; Arbuthnot Report.

20. "Examination of Emanuel, a Portuguze Negro Slave belonging to Mr. Edward Gregory a Cooper in the Town of St. John's [Oct. 12, 1736]," Council Mins., Jan. 8, 1737, CO 9/10.

21. Arbuthnot Report.

22. When Martin's Jemmy was brought to town for questioning,

> Mrs. Booth was Sent for who Deposed in Presence of Jemmy and his Brother Toney that Accompanyd him
> That Martin's Jemmy called upon her in the Evening the 12th of October & presented her with a Couple of Roses & told her she was Acquainted with the Soldiers. No she said, She was not, she had left off that Acquaintance. Said he, I wish you would buy some Powder for me. Powder, said she. Yes, Gunn Powder. I wish you would buy as Much for me as you Can get and I will pay you for it, And for [your] Trouble. And another Woman one Mary Vaughan who was Present Confirmed the same thing on her Oath." In his defence Jemmy said that "a Brother in Law of his call'd Mingo, who lived at Turners Plantation had Desired him to buy some Gunn Powder for him to Shoot Ducks in the Flashes, And that he told the Woman So; And Toney Vouched for his Brother that he had no Ill Design; But both Woman Denying that Jemmy had said anything of the kind,

Arbuthnot locked him up. Arbuthnot Report.

23. *Ibid.* There is some confusion in the sources about the date of Court's crowning. Delap said it was "the Sunday Seven night before" Oct. 13; but Oct. 6 was a Wednesday. Delap, however, could have meant to refer to Sunday of the preceding week. The judges' report cited Thursday, Oct. 3, but that date would have been Sunday. At the trial of one of the conspirators (Newport) a slave witness said that "Newport was one of those that met Down at a grave at the Point with Court and Tomboy of a Saturday Night about Six weeks before Courts Dance at Park's which was on Sunday the 3rd of October last," and there took the oath to kill the whites. I have settled for this last reference because the day and date coincide, and because it seems the more likely. See "Tryal of Morgans Newport 9th of November 1736," Council Mins., Jan. 12, 1737, CO 9/10. The ceremony accompanying Court's crowning the judges called an "*ikem* dance." See below, chap. 11.

24. Arbuthnot Report. The date of Tomboy's festivities is cited in "Tryal of Monk's Mingo," Council Mins., Jan. 12, 1737, CO 9/10.

25. Arbuthnot Report; Killens, *Trial Record*, p. 30.

Chapter 2: "Our Island is in Such a Miserable Condition"

1. Arbuthnot Report; Assembly Mins., Oct. 15, 1736, CO 9/12; Council Mins., Oct. 15, 1736, CO 9/9.

2. Assembly Mins., Oct. 19, 1736, CO 9/12; General Report; Council Mins., Feb. 14, 1737, CO 9/11.

3. Assembly Mins., Oct. 22, 23, 1736, CO 9/12; Mathew to Sec. of BT, Jan. 17, 1737, CO 152/22, W89; "An Act for better discovery of Conspiracys Treasons and Rebellions of Slaves," Oct. 23, 1736, CO 8/6; General Report.

4. *Ibid.* Sources do not always agree on precise dates of executions of the 88 slaves so punished, but see the official list: "A List of the Names of Negros that were Executed for the late Conspiracy, Their Trades, To Whom they Belonged, the day and Manner of their Respective Execution," enclosed in Mathew to BT, May 26, 1737, CO 152/23, X7; *New York Weekly Journal,* Apr. 25, 1737.

5. "Extract of a Letter from Antigua," Oct. 24, 1736, *Virginia Gazette,* Apr. 8, 1737; General Report; Execution List.

6. *Virginia Gazette,* Apr. 8, 1737; *New York Weekly Journal,* Apr. 25, 1737; "Extracts of a Letter from Antigua to Mr. Smith Sec. of the Leeward Is." Nov. 10, 1736, CO 152/23, X32; "Extract of a Letter from Antigua," Jan. 15, 1737, *Virginia Gazette,* May 20, 1737; Execution List; *New York Weekly Journal,* Apr. 25, 1737.

7. General Report; Council Mins., Nov. 8, 1736, CO 9/10; *New York Gazette,* Mar. 22, 1737 (from a letter dated Antigua, Dec. 13, 1736). See also General Report on role of Secundi.

8. Council Mins., Nov. 1, 8, 15, 1736; CO 9/10. In England in the eighteenth century gibbeting, according to one scholar, was "a refinement of capital punishment that added infamy to death." Douglas Hay, "Property Authority and the Criminal Law," in Douglas Hay, Peter Linebaugh, John G. Rule, E. P. Thompson, and Cal Winslow, *Albion's Fatal Tree* (New York: Pantheon, 1975), p. 50. See also Negley K. Teeters, *Hang by the Neck* (Springfield, Ill.: Charles C. Thomas, 1967), pp. 19–46; Thorsten Sellin, "The Philadelphia Gibbet-Iron," *Journal of Criminal Law, Criminology and Police Science* 46 (May–June 1955):11–25.

9. The Execution List gives the execution dates of Coley, Cuffey, and Quashey as Nov. 2, but according to a 1737 inventory of Clement Tudway's Parham Plantation, "Cuffie, the Mason was Executed for the plott the 10th Nov. 1736." The latter date seems more likely if the date of the justices' report is taken into account (Nov. 6). Execution List; "A List of all the Negroes, Men, Women & Children on Parham Plantation taken the first day of February 1736/7," Tudway Papers, DD/TD, box 16, Somerset Record Office, Taunton, England; Council Mins., Nov. 8, 1736, CO 9/10; *New York Weekly Journal,* Apr. 25, 1737.

10. The judges recommended a pardon for Jemmy, but the assembly wanted him banished, as he was a "most Dangerous Criminal." Council Mins., Mar. 17, 1737, CO 9/11. See List of Banishments appended to Execution List, and also to be found at end of General Report. For Jemmy's performance as a witness see, for example, trial record of slaves to be banished, TR, Council Mins., Jan. 12, 1737, CO 9/10.

11. List of Banishments; Council Mins., Nov. 8, 1736, CO 9/10; General Report.

12. Execution List; Council Mins., Nov. 15, 1736, CO 9/10; *Virginia Gazette,* May 27, 1737; *New York Weekly Journal,* Apr. 25, 1737; *New York Gazette,* Mar. 28, 1737; Execution List; Council Mins., Nov. 15, 1736, CO 9/10; *New York Weekly Journal,* Apr. 25, 1737; Execution List; *New York Weekly Journal,* Apr. 25, 1737.

13. Execution List; Council Mins., Nov. 18, 1736; Jan. 8, 1737, CO 9/10; *New York Weekly Journal,* Apr. 25, 1737; *Virginia Gazette,* May 20, 27, 1737; General Report. Execution List.

14. Michel Foucault, *Discipline & Punish* (New York: Vintage, 1979), pp. 3–69; Peter H. Wood, *Black Majority: Negroes in Colonial South Carolina from 1670 through the Stono Rebellion* (New York: Norton, 1974), pp. 281–83, and passim; J. Thorsten Sellin, *Slavery and the Penal System* (New York: Elsevier, 1976), pp. 133–38; Anthony Babington, *The Power to Silence* (London: Robert Maxwell, 1968), pp. 6–9, 53–60; Teeters, *Hang by the Neck,* pp. 19–46; Ted Robert Gurr, *Rogues, Rebels, and Reformers* (London: Sage, 1976), pp. 150–52.

15. Teeters, *Hang by the Neck,* p. 92; Herbert Aptheker, *American Negro Slave Revolts* (New York: International, 1974), pp. 172–73, 192–95; Hormansden, *The New York Conspiracy,* p. vii, and pp. 468–73, "A List of Negroes Committed on Account of the Conspiracy;" Wood, *Black Majority,* p. 318.

16. Wood, *Black Majority;* "Summary of Trial Proceedings of Those Accused of Participating in the Slave Uprising of January 9, 1811," *Louisiana History* 17 (Fall 1977):472–73; Winthrop D. Jordan, *White over Black: American Attitudes toward the Negro, 1550–1812* (Chapel Hill: University of North Carolina Press, 1968), p. 112; Newman Graeme, *The Punishment Response* (Philadelphia: J. B. Lippincott, 1978), pp. 55–60, 79–101.

17. "An Act for regulating the Militia of this Island," June 28, 1702, CO 154/3; see also "An Act declaring the Several Articles Martiall laws shall Consist off," June 28, 1702, CO 8/3, acts nos. 131 and 132 of 1702, in *The Laws of the Island of Antigua consisting of the Acts of the Leeward Islands, 1690–1798 and Acts of Antigua 1668–1845* (hereafter *Laws of Antigua*), 4 vols. (London, 1805–46). According to clause 14 of the first act, "Martial law shall be in full Force, and duly executed, in all Time of actual Invasion, Insurrection, Alarms, or whenever the Commander, by and with the Advice and Consent of the Council and Assembly, shall think Guards necessary to prevent the spreading of contagious Distempers, or of any other Publick Benefit whatever." Council Mins., Nov. 15, 1736, CO 9/10.

18. Council Mins., Nov. 8, 1736, CO 9/10.

19. Council Mins., Nov. 15, 1736, CO 9/10.

20. Ibid.

21. Execution List; Council Mins., Dec. 9, 20, 1736, CO 9/10; Mathew to BT, Jan. 17, 1737, CO 152/22, W88; Council Mins., Dec. 20, 1736, CO 9/10.

22. See below, chap. 6; *New York Gazette,* Mar. 22, 1737, *Virginia Gazette,* Apr. 8, 1737; Wood, *Black Majority,* pp. 320–21.

23. General Report.

24. Ibid.; Mathew to BT, Jan. 17, 1737, CO 152/22, W88; *New York Gazette,* Mar. 22, 1737; *Virginia Gazette,* May 27, 1737; *Gentleman's Magazine,* Mar. 1737, pp. 187–88.

25. Execution List; Council Mins., Mar. 8, 1737, CO 9/11. The list of executions cites Mar. 8 for nine executions, with two undated, while the legislature's minutes for that day indicate that the slaves were to be executed on the following afternoon "by five of the Clock at farthest." By Mar. 9 the governor was able to claim that there "remains no further Punishment to be Inflicted on the Conspirators Except Banishment" of forty-five. "All the Slaves . . . who are Designed to be made Examples of in that Manner" had been executed. Three suspects, fled from

justice, were still at large. Major Royall's Quau was "reprieved at the Stake, upon his Promise to make Discoverys of great Moment," said the governor; "till I know how well he has made good those Promises, I can not Say how he is to be Disposed of." Quau was eventually banished. Council Mins., Mar. 9, 17, 1737, CO 9/11; List of Banishments.

26. Council Mins., Mar. 9, Feb. 24, 20, Mar. 7, 17, 1737, CO 9/11; General Report.

27. Council Mins., Feb. 28, Mar. 7, 1737, CO 9/11; "An Act for attainting several slaves who abscond and are fled from Justice and for the Banishment of other[s] concerned in the conspiracy," Apr. 11, 1737, CO 8/6; see also "An Act for Banishing a Negro Man Slave called Parmenio belonging to Henry Kipps," June 25, 1740, CO 8/8; Council Mins., Mar. 9, 1737, CO 9/11; Mathew to BT, May 26, 1737, CO 152/23, X6; Assembly Mins., Jan. 2, Feb. 6, Mar. 7, June 3, Aug. 5, 1740, CO 9/12.

28. Council Mins., Mar. 17, 1737, CO 9/11. The legislature came to an agreement with Arthur Wilkinson to transport the "Criminals" to Hispaniola or the Spanish American mainland "and to sell them to the French or Spaniards, at some of those places, Provided he may have a reward of half of their Gross Proceeds." Later, however, the legislature had difficulty recovering proceeds of the sale from Wilkinson, who had taken the slaves away on an armed sloop. Council Mins., Apr. 12, 13, 25, 1737, CO 9/11; Assembly Mins., Feb. 15, Mar. 16, 1738, CO 9/12.

29. Act for banishing the slaves, Apr. 11, 1737, CO 8/6; Waldemar Westergaard, "Account of the Negro Rebellion on St. Croix, Danish West Indies, 1759," *JNH* 11 (Jan. 1926):50–61.

30. Walter Tullideph to David Tullideph, Antigua, May 25, 1737, Tullideph Letter Book, MS; General Report. For witnesses see list appended to Execution List. See also TR, CO 9/10 and CO 9/11.

31. Council Mins., June 1, 1738, CO 9/13. According to the assembly in regard to Treblin, belonging to Samuel Morgan, "for the Ingenuity and fullness of his Confession and Evidence against the other Conspirators [he] did Deserve some Gratuity from the Publick." Council Mins., Mar. 16, 1738, CO 9/11; Council Mins., Mar. 29, 1739, CO 9/13; "An Act for making Free Two Negroe Men Slaves named Cuffee and Robin and Appointing Each of them a Reward to be Paid out of the Publick Treasury of Antigua for their good and faithfull Services in first Discovering the late Horrid Intended Insurrection of the Slaves of this Island and for paying the Vallues of the said Cuffee and Robin to their Respective Owners, and for appointing a Reward for Manuel another Negroe Man Slave for his good and faithfull Services in the further Discovery of the same horrid intended Insurrection," May 24, 1739, CO 8/7.

32. Assembly Mins., July 31, 1738, CO 9/12. One interesting proposed amendment to the bill was that, when passed, the act "should be read at the head of the Several Militia Companys than in Church." Assembly Mins., May 18, 1739, CO 9/12.

33. Council Mins., Jan. 8, 31, 1737, CO 9/10; Feb. 14, July 13, 1737, CO 9/11; "Some Reasons humbly Offered for Consideration for Stopping the further Execution of Slaves Concern'd in the Barbarous Conspiracy Except Such (if any Actually Remain) as have been grand Promoters and Contrivers thereof, and

Except too the free Negros," Council Mins., Jan. 17, 1737, CO 9/10. Morris responded to these representations in Council Mins., Jan. 31, 1737, CO 9/10. For compensation claims see legislature's minutes in CO 9/11, 12. The large plantation the judges referred to, about which they had information "of half the Negros" being involved in the plot, was most probably Parham Plantation in the northeast Parish of St. Peter, owned by the Tudways. See "Evidence against Parham Cuffey a Driver who can Read and Write," Dec. 15, 1736, TR, Council Mins., Feb. 24, 1737, CO 9/11; "Evidence against Parham Watty," Jan. 14, 1737, Council Mins., Feb. 14, 1737, CO 9/11.

34. Mathew to BT, June 21, 1738, *CSP,* 1738, 44, no. 298, p. 149. "Resolution of the Council and Assembly of Antigua on subject of additional pay to General Dalzell's regiment," enclosed in Mathew to Duke of Bedford, Oct. 25, 1750, CO 152/45. According to Mathew, "The consequences of the Conspiracy formed against us by our Slaves in the Years 1736 and 1737 are at this day too sensibly felt in a large Debt still running at the high Interest of Ten p Cent and contracted to support the Credit of the Island under the unhappy Exigence." There are scattered references to costs incurred through the slave plot: see, for example, Council Mins., Nov. 29, 1736, CO 9/10; March 9, 10, 31, June 3, 1737, CO 9/11; Assembly Mins., Oct. 3, 1738, CO 9/12. Walter Tullideph believed the plot contributed to the drying up of slave imports. Walter Tullideph to David Tullideph, Antigua, May 25, 1737, Tullideph Letter Book, MS.

35. Council Mins., Mar. 31, 1737, CO 9/11. Yeamans to Sec. of State, Mar. 21, 1737, CO 152/44; Order in Council dismissing petition of John Yeamans, agent of Antigua, and others, Apr. 21, 1737, CO 152/22, W103.

36. Council Mins., Mar. 16, 1738, CO 9/11; Assembly Mins., Oct. 3, 1738, CO 9/12; "Copy of an Order in Council directing the Gov. of the Leeward Islands to take care that the Island of Antigua should Provide an Additional Subsistence to the Forces His Majesty should send thither," Dec. 27, 1739, CO 152/24, Y10; "The Representation of Lieut General Robert Dalzell Collonel of his Majestys Regiment of Foot in the Leeward Islands," (St. Christopher) Council Mins., Dec. 2, 1742, CO 241/5; Mathew to Duke of Bedford, Oct. 25, 1750, CO 152/45. In the 1750s and 1760s the Antigua legislature took care to pass acts to support troops stationed in the island, for, as the preamble of the 1755 act stated, "the several conspiracys that have been formed against us by our slaves have taught us the necessity of guarding against the like dangerous designs for the future and there seems to be no means which will more probably discourage such attempts or more effectually disappoint them than the keeping up a body of regular and well disciplined Troops in a condition to act upon the most immediate notice of danger." "An Act for paying an additional subsistence to all of and under the rank of Lieutenants in the Regiment now posted in this Island commanded by Collo. Alexander Duroure and appointing a fund for the same and for the encouragement and support of disabled Soldiers," Jan. 10, 1755, CO 8/11.

37. Mathew to BT, Jan. 17, 1737, CO 152/22, W88; "An Act for the further Restriction of Slaves, by prohibiting them from planting any Indigo, Cotton, Ginger, Coffee, or Cocoa; and from keeping a public Market on Sundays; and for further restraining licentious Meetings of Negroes," act no. 112, 1736, *Montserrat Code of Laws From 1668 to 1788* (London, 1790), pp. 67–69. Gov. Mathew claimed

that restricting slaves' economic activities was "a most reasonable provision, as their Planting Such Commoditys was not only an Injury to the poor but chiefly a Cover to hide their Robberys and Stealing Such Commoditys from those Inhabitants pretending what they Stole was of their own produce." Mathew to BT, May 11, 1737, CO 152/23, X3. See "An Act for establishing, regulating, and disciplining the Militia Forces of the Island of Nevis," act no. 110, 1736; "An Act to amend, explain, and make more effectual an Act made in the Fourth Year of the Reign of King George the First, intituled, An Act for the good Government of Negroes, and other Slaves in this Island," act no. 111, 1737, *Acts of Assembly Passed in the Island of Nevis From 1664 to 1739, inclusive* (London, 1740), pp. 122–30, 131–34. See also Mathew to BT, Aug. 31, 1734, CSP, 1734–35, 41, no. 314, ii, p. 239. (St. Christopher) Assembly Mins., Nov. 29, 1736, CO 241/3.

38. Assembly Mins., Nov. 8, 1736, Jan. 3, 1737, CO 9/12; Council Mins., Mar. 10, 1737, Feb. 15, 1738, CO 9/11, Sept. 13, 1739, CO 9/13.

39. The New York conspiracy (1712) and Stono, South Carolina revolt (1739) are only two examples. Kenneth Scott, "The Slave Insurrection in New York in 1712," *New York Historical Society Quarterly* 45 (Jan. 1961):71; Wood, *Black Majority*, p. 324; Jordan, *White over Black*, p. 116; Kilson, "Towards Freedom," p. 186.

40. *Virginia Gazette*, May 27, 1737; *New England Weekly Journal*, Apr. 12, 1737; see below, chap. 10.

41. Mathew to BT, Jan. 17, 1737, CO 152/22, W88, with enclosures; Lara, "Le Procès de résistance," pp. 38–61.

42. Kilson, "Towards Freedom," pp. 175–78, 186.

Chapter 3: "Not...Bound...by the Ordinary Rules of Law"

1. CSP, 1737, 43, no. 99, p. 50; Council Mins., Jan. 31, 1737, CO 9/10.

2. General Report.

3. Morris, John Vernon, et al. to agent John Yeamans "desiring him to appear for and sollicite the Bill of Attainder of Benjamin and William Johnson." Council Mins., July 13, 1737, CO 9/11; "An Act to attaint of High Treason two freed Negro men named Benjamin Johnson and William alias Billy Johnson," Apr. 12, 1737, in Mathew to BT, May 11, 1737, CO 152/23, X4; "Petition of Benjamin Johnson and William alias Billy Johnson of Antigua against a Bill passed by the Council & Assembly of that Island to attaint them of High Treason," CO, 152/23, X18; Douncker to Duke of Newcastle, Mar. 22, 1738, CO 152/44.

4. Council Mins., Dec. 30, 1736, CO 9/10; Assembly Mins., Jan. 3, 1737, CO 9/12.

5. Assembly Mins., Jan. 12, 1737, CO 9/12; Council Mins., Jan. 12, 1737, CO 9/10.

6. Assembly Mins., Jan. 17, 1737, CO 9/12.

7. Assembly Mins., Jan. 18, 19, 1737, CO 9/12.

8. Assembly Mins., Jan. 24, 1737, CO 9/12.

9. Assembly Mins., Jan. 25, 31, Feb. 1, 5, 1737, CO 9/12; Council Mins., Mar. 31, 1737, CO 9/11.

10. Antigua freedmen who did not meet certain requirements were forced by law (1702) to bind themselves to whites as their virtual possessions. Such conditions also forced upon other freedmen who did not have to seek white "masters" the necessity of at least attaching themselves to white patrons in "patron-client" relationships. See Chap. 7.

11. Council Mins., Feb. 28, Mar. 9, Apr. 25, 1737, CO 9/11.

12. Council Mins., Mar. 10, 17, 1737, CO 9/11.

13. Council Mins., Mar. 31, Apr. 12, 13, 1737, CO 9/11. In regard to the legislation against the Johnsons, the governor promised to lose "no time in Informing myself whether I ought to pass that Bill or no, But if from the Evidence, I find it is fitt to be passed, I shall dispatch it by the first opportunity, with my Observations upon it, to their Lordships of the Board of Trade, to be laid before His Majesty and shall at the same time press the Agent to Loose no time, in Solliciting, for His Majesty's leave for my passing a Bill of so Extra ordinary a Nature." Council Mins., Apr. 13, 1737, CO 9/11. For the case of Mulatto Jack see Council Mins., Apr. 25, 1737, CO 9/11.

14. Mathew to BT, May 11, 1737, CO 152/23, X3. For slave evidence linking the Johnsons with the slave conspiracy, see, for example, "Evidence against Parham Cuffey a Driver [Dec. 15, 1736]," "Evidence against Bartons Joe [Jan. 20, 1737]," TR, slaves to be banished, Council Mins., Feb. 24, "Evidence against Vernons Cudjoe [Jan. 26, 1737]," "Evidence against Parham Watty [Jan. 14, 1737]," TR, slaves to be executed, Council Mins., Feb. 14, 1737, CO 9/11.

15. This "respected gentleman" may have been John Douncker, who wrote the Earl of Newcastle defending the Johnsons and describing some of the circumstances surrounding their prosecution. See Douncker to Newcastle, Mar. 22, 1738, CO 152/44. "You Must Understand," wrote Douncker, "that the said Benja. Johnson sued one James Hanson and Recovered a Sume of Money from him the Year before the Disturbance was in the said Island whome Carryd A Mallato Heathen from the Goal of the Guard house to one and Twenty heathen Evidences that was there for the said Mallato to tell those Heathens" that the Johnson brothers "did take the Cruel oaths with them."

16. "An Act for the Tryal of John Coteen a free Negro Man, and Thomas Winthorp a free Mulatto Man for an intended Insurrection to destroy the white Inhabitants of this Island and declaring the same to be high Treason and Rebellion in the said John Coteen and Thomas Winthorp, and Makeing the Testimony of Slaves Evidence against them but respiting sentence of Death and awarding Execution against them until His Majesty's Pleasure shall be signified and Made Known." Apr. 13, 1737, CO 8/6. For the governor's comments on the act, see Mathew to BT, May 26, 1737, CO 152/23, X6.

17. Council Mins., Apr. 25, 1737, CO 9/11; Assembly Mins., Apr. 25, 1737, CO 9/12.

18. "An Act to attaint of High Treason Benjamin Johnson and William alias Billy Johnson," in Mathew to BT, May 11, 1737, CO 152/23, X4.

19. "An Act for the Tryal of John Coteen and Thomas Winthorp," Apr. 13, 1737, CO 8/8.

20. Council Mins., June 3, 1737, CO 9/11; Morris, Vernon, et al. to Yeamans, Council Mins., July 13, 1737, CO 9/11.

21. BT to Mathew, Aug. 11, 1737, CO 153/16; Mathew to BT, Dec. 10, 1737, CO 152/23, X24, Feb. 23, 1738, CO 152/23, X26 (Blizard's letter to Mathew, Jan. 3, 1737, enclosed); Council Mins., Dec. 9, 1737; Council Mins., Feb. 1, 1738, CO 9/11.

22. Johnsons' Petition, CO 152/23, X18. The Johnsons were allowed to arrange for their defense in England. Council Mins., May 20, 1737, CO 9/11.

23. Douncker to Newcastle, Mar. 22, 1738, CO 152/44.

24. BT to Privy Council, May 11, 1738, CO 153/16.

25. Fane to BT, May 15, 1738, CO 152/23, X28; BT to the king, June 21, 1738, CO 153/16. It should be pointed out here that by an act of 1694, Jewish traders were threatened with the use of slave evidence against them in order to curb their dealings with the slaves, who, the authorities believed, stole much of what they traded. The act was, however, later repealed. See "An Act against Jews ingrossing Commodities imported in the Leeward Islands, and trading with the Slaves belonging to the Inhabitants of the same," Aug. 31, 1694, CO 8/1; "An Act to repeale a certain Act against the Jewes," Dec. 10, 1701, CO 8/1.

26. "Copy of an Order in Council disapproving a Bill passed at Antigua by the Assembly, for attaining the Johnsons of High Treason, and for restoring them to their former State of Liberty as before that Bill passed," July 20, 1738, CO 152/23, X57; "Copy of an Order in Council approving a Representation of the Board of Trade for Repealing an Act of Antigua for the Trial of John Corten a free Negro and Thomas Winthorp a free Mulatto, and ordering that they be bailed if in prison," Nov. 30, 1738, CO 152/23, X59; BT to Mathew, Aug. 10, 1738, CO 153/16; Council Mins., Nov. 29, 1738, CO 9/13.

27. Agent Yeamans had communicated this information in conversation with members of the Board of Trade. BT to Privy Council, Nov. 21, 1738, CO 153/16.

28. Council Mins., Apr. 12, 26, 1739, CO 9/13.

29. Jordan, *White over Black,* pp. 122–23; see below, chap. 7.

Chapter 4: African Recruitment

1. Richard S. Dunn, *Sugar and Slaves: The Rise of the Planter Class in the English West Indies, 1624–1713* (Chapel Hill: University of North Carolina Press, 1972), pp. 118–26. This is by far the best study of the early social history of the British islands, but for the Leeward Islands, especially Nevis, see Richard Pares's excellent study *A West India Fortune* (1950; reprint, New York: Archon, 1968), which traces the long involvement of the Pinney family as plantation owners from the seventeenth to the nineteenth century. Colonization of the Leeward Islands began in 1624 when Sir Thomas Warner of Suffolk, after an unsuccessful attempt to plant in Guiana, founded a colony on the island of St. Christopher (St. Kitts), from which Nevis (1628), Antigua, and Montserrat (1632) were later settled. For settlement and early history of these islands, see, for example, David R. Harris, *Plants, Animals, and Man in the Outer Leeward Islands, West Indies: An Ecological Study of Antigua, Barbuda, and Anguilla* (Berkeley: University of California Press, 1965), pp. 84–89; R. B. Sheridan, *Sugar and Slavery: An Economic History of the British West Indies, 1623–1775* (Baltimore: Johns Hopkins University Press, 1973), pp. 184–85;

James A. Williamson, *The Caribbee Islands under the Proprietary Patents* (London: Oxford University Press, 1926); C.S.S. Higham, *The Development of the Leeward Islands under the Restoration 1660–1688* (Cambridge: Cambridge University Press, 1921); Richard Pares, *Merchants and Planters* (Cambridge: Cambridge University Press, 1960), pp. 20–22; J. H. Bennett, "The English Caribbees in the Period of the Civil War, 1642–1646," *WMQ,* 3d. ser. 24 (July 1967): pp. 359–77. On the question of the introduction of sugar cultivation in the islands see Richard Ligon, *A True and Exact History of the Island of Barbadoes* (1657; reprint, London: Frank Cass, 1976); Dunn, *Sugar and Slaves,* pp. 188–223; F. C. Innes, "The Pre-Sugar Era of European Settlement in Barbados," *JCH* 1 (Nov. 1970):1–22; Robert Carlyle Batie, "Why Sugar?: Economic Cycles and the Changing of Staples on the English and French Antilles, 1624–1654," *JCH* 8 (1976):1–41; Mathew Edel, "The Brazilian Sugar Cycle of the Seventeenth Century and the Rise of West Indian Competition," *CS* 9 (Apr. 1969):24–44; Elsa V. Goveia, *Slave Society in the British Leeward Islands at the End of the Eighteenth Century* (New Haven, Conn.: Yale University Press, 1965), p. vii.

2. Ligon, *A True and Exact History,* p. 85; J. H. Parry and P. M. Sherlock, *A Short History of the West Indies,* 3d ed. (New York: St. Martin's Press, 1971), pp. 64–65; Dunn, *Sugar and Slaves,* pp. 117–26; Noel Deerr, *The History of Sugar,* 2 vols. (London: Chapman & Hall, 1949–50), 1:172; Sheridan, *Sugar and Slavery,* p. 185.

3. Sheridan, *Sugar and Slavery,* pp. 184, 193; Bryan Edwards, *The History Civil and Commercial of the British Colonies in the West Indies,* 3d ed., 3 vols. (London, 1793–1801), 1:474.

4. Plantation inventories, May 15, 1740, Codrington Papers, D1610/E5, Gloucestershire County Record Office, Gloucester, England. Robson Lowe, *Codrington Correspondence 1743–1851* (London, 1951); George C. Simmons, "Towards a Biography of Christopher Codrington the Younger," *CS* 12 (Apr. 1972):32–50; Sheridan, *Sugar and Slavery,* pp. 192–93; Pym Letters, Historical Manuscripts Commission, 10th Report, pt. 6, p. 96, quoted in ibid., p. 191.

5. CSP, 1669–74, no. 680, pp. 290–91, no. 508, p. 205.

6. According to Wheler, "The commodities are sugar chiefly" in the Leewards, but "tobacco in great quantity in Antigua, so much indigo and cotton" too in the islands "that he hopes his Majesty will favour them in the prohibition of Cyprus cotton and East India indigo which rob England of money; no manufactures, nor shall be while he is Governor, unless he has further commands." CSP, 1669–74, no. 680, pp. 288, 290. A report of 1670 expressed a demand for slaves: "A great drought has rendered the crops backward and bad, and brought the planters in debt, and, if the rigour of the law be used, they fear a general desertion of the land, and nothing will stay the planters or increase the settlement but a free trade or supply of slaves, which, if his Majesty would connive at for a time, the island were made, otherwise utterly ruined." CSP, 1669–74, no. 508, pp. 205–6.

7. CSP, 1675–76, no. 1,152, pp. 497–502; Dunn, *Sugar and Slaves,* pp. 110–11.

8. The Antigua census is reprinted in Oliver, *History of Antigua,* 1:58–61. For an analysis of the census see Dunn, *Sugar and Slaves,* pp. 126–31. Data on population change are given in Dunn, *Sugar and Slaves,* p. 122; CSP, 1669–74, no. 896, iv, p. 394, no. 977, p. 441; CSP, 1675–76, no. 861, p. 367. For a study of the Leewards population see Robert V. Wells, *The Population of the British Colonies in America before*

1776: A Survey of Census Data (Princeton, N.J.: Princeton University Press, 1975), pp. 207-36.

9. Hart to BT, July 12, 1724, answer no. 15 to queries from BT, CO 152/14, R101; Dunn, *Sugar and Slaves*, p. 141; Hart to BT, Mar. 1, 1725, CO 152/15, R152; Mathew to BT, Jan. 20, 1728, CO 152/16, S72; Sheridan, *Sugar and Slavery*, p. 195.

10. K. G. Davies, *The Royal African Company* (New York: Atheneum, 1970), p. 311; CSP, 1677-80, no. 1, pp. 441, 573; CSP, 1675-76, no. 1, pp. 152, 500-501; Davies; *Royal African Company*, p. 311; Dunn, *Sugar and Slaves*, p. 235.

11. CSP, 1677-80, no. 1, pp. 441, 573, no. 1, pp. 442, 574-75. As a result of the St. Christopher and Montserrat action, the Board of Trade resolved to advise the king that the company be obliged to "take particular care that Montserrat and St. Christophers (from whence came great complaints) be well provided for in future." CSP, 1677-80, no. 1, pp. 583, 629. For Antigua see "An Act for Encouragement of the Royall Affrican Company in England for the Supplying this Island with Negroes," act no. 31, May 3, 1675, CO 154/3.

12. CSP, 1685-88, no. 1,773, pp. 552-53.

13. Council Mins., Aug. 2, 1708, CO 9/1; Parke to BT, Aug. 23, 1708, CO 152/7, L96-97, enclosures. The accounts are printed in Elizabeth Donnan, ed., *Documents, Illustrative of the History of the Slave Trade to America*, 4 vols. (Washington, D.C.: Carnegie Institution of Washington, 1930-35), vol. 2, nos. 25-26, 33-34; Davies, *Royal African Company*, p. 143, n. 1. Records of the RAC show that at least 2 shipments of slaves arrived in 1689: (1) "203 negroes & 3 small boyes" by the ship *Mary*, Apr. 13, 1689; (2) 81 slaves by the ship *Sherbrow*, Sept. 27, 1689. African Companies, Accounts: Invoice Books, Homeward Bound, PRO, T70/944. One shipment of 80 slaves was sold in 1688 from the ship *Benjamin*, PRO, T70/943. A cargo of 86 arrived by the ship *Experiment* in 1693, PRO, T70/946. For additional data on seventeenth-century trade of the RAC with the Leewards see abstracts of letters to the RAC from the West Indies relating to Committee of Correspondence, PRO, T70/12 (July 28, 1683-Apr. 28, 1698). For a discussion of slave prices and supply in the emergence of the seventeenth century British sugar islands see H. A. Gemery and J. S. Hogendorn, "Elasticity of Slave Labor Supply and the Development of Slave Economies in the British Caribbean: The Seventeenth Century Experience," in *Comparative Perspectives on Slavery in New World Plantation Societies*, ed. Vera Rubin and Arthur Tuden (New York: New York Academy of Sciences, 1977), Annals of the New York Academy of Sciences, 292:72-83. The British-American gravitation to the use of slave labor in the seventeenth century is discussed in Richard N. Bean and Robert P. Thomas, "The Adoption of Slave Labor in British America," in *The Uncommon Market: Essays in the Economic History of the Atlantic Slave Trade*, ed. H. A. Gemery and J. S. Hogendorn, (New York: Academic Press, 1979), pp. 377-98; Richard N. Bean, *The British Trans-Atlantic Slave Trade, 1650-1775* (New York: Arno Press, 1975), pp. 8-19, 103-22. David Galenson, *White Servitude in Colonial America: An Economic Analysis* (Cambridge: Cambridge University Press, 1981), pp. 117-68; Galenson, "White Servitude and the Growth of Black Slavery in Colonial America," *JEH* 41 (Mar. 1981):39-49.

14. Parke to BT, Aug. 23, 1708, CO 152/7, L98. The list is also printed in Donnan, *Documents*, vol. 2, no. 27, pp. 34-43. Donnan, however, omits data for the vessels *Constant Rachel, Regard,* and *Flying Fame.* References in Chester's list but

not Parke's include (1) July 24, 1702, the *Will'm and Jane* (155 slaves); (2) Aug. 17, 1702, the *Canterbury* (94 slaves); (3) Oct. 27, 1703, the *Bridgewater* (218 slaves). For additional information on slave shipments to Antigua over the period see PRO, T70/950-54; see also abstracts of letters received by the RAC relating to Committee of Correspondence, PRO, T70/13 (1702-1704); letters to the RAC from the West Indies, PRO, T70/8 (1706-1719); Antigua Shipping Returns (1704-1720), CO 157/1.

15. Davies, *Royal African Company*, p. 299; Herbert S. Klein, *The Middle Passage: Comparative Studies in the Atlantic Slave Trade* (Princeton, N.J.: Princeton University Press, 1978), pp. 239-42. For the Senegambia region "age and sex distribution in the slave trade... depended on African as well as American conditions." Philip D. Curtin, *Economic Change in Precolonial Africa* (Madison: University of Wisconsin Press, 1975), pp. 175-77; Sheridan, *Sugar and Slavery*, pp. 242-43.

16. David Galenson, "The Slave Trade to the English West Indies, 1673-1724," *EHR*, 2d ser. 32 (May 1979):247; Galenson, "The Atlantic Slave Trade and the Barbados Market, 1673-1723," *JEH* 42 (Sept. 1982):504-10.

17. Davies, *Royal African Company*, pp. 143-44, 313-15, 364; Sheridan, *Sugar and Slavery*, pp. 251-53; Dunn, *Sugar and Slaves*, p. 237; "Reasons offered to prove that it is more for the advantage of the Sugar Colonys to have the Trade to the Coast of Africa for Slaves managed by a Joint Stock under the direction of an United Company than by Separate Adventurers," Mins. of Council in Assembly, Dec. 23, 1724, CO 9/5; RAC to BT, received Jan. 3, 1709, CO 388/11, I81; Perry, secretary RAC, to BT, Nov. 17, 1710, CO 388/3, L57.

18. Separate Traders to BT, undated, CO 388/12, K54, Dec. 11, 1710, CO 388/13, L85. Prices at Barbados 1709-10 were quoted at £25-£28 a head, currency there being the same in relation to Jamaica's. For currency values in the West Indies see John J. McCusker, *Money and Exchange in Europe and America, 1600-1775: A Handbook* (Chapel Hill: University of North Carolina Press, 1978).

19. Separate Traders to BT, Dec. 11, 1710, CO 388/13, L85. For very useful studies of the economics of the slave trade to the British-Caribbean sugar islands (1673-1724), see Galenson, "The Slave Trade to the English West Indies," pp. 241-49; Galenson, "The Atlantic Slave Trade and the Barbados Market," pp. 491-511; Bean, *British Trans-Atlantic Slave Trade*.

20. St. Leger to BT, Aug. 23, 1712, CO 152/10, 04. The slaves were brought in by 4 "Permition Ships."

21. Klein, *Middle Passage*, pp. 191-93; Ralph Davis, *The Rise of the English Shipping Industry* (London: David & Charles, 1972), p. 279; Leslie Imre Rudnyanszky, "The Caribbean Slave Trade: Jamaica and Barbados, 1680-1770." Ph.D. thesis, Notre Dame University, 1973, p. 158.

22. Hart to BT, Feb. 15, 1727, CO 152/15, R190. Over the same period St. Christopher imported 5,600, of which 116 came from Barbados and 38 from Antigua. Hart to BT, Feb. 15, 1727, CO 152/15, R191. Nevis imported 1,267 and Montserrat 1,776 (Dec. 25, 1720-Dec. 25, 1726). Hart to BT, Apr. 10, 1727, CO 152/15, R204-5. For the period Mar. 25, 1721-Dec. 25, 1729 Montserrat imported 3,210, of whom 26 came from Antigua. CO 152/18, T67. St. Christopher is reported to have imported 4,758 slaves from Dec. 25, 1726 to Sept. 25, 1730. CO 152/19, T150.

23. Mathew to BT, Dec. 1, 1727, CO 152/16, S65. Over the same period St. Christopher got 381. CO 152/16, S34. Montserrat imported 192, and these sold at from about £17 to £20 sterling a head. CO 152/16, S70. For Nevis: "In the Sloope Rose from Antigua Avon Ward Master Thirty Five Negroes consigned Mr. John Woodley by Mr. Edwd. Tarleton of Liverpoole of which were sold here but twelve the remaining twenty three being exported which twelve came out at an Average at the Sum of 27.3.6 this money each." Mathew to BT, Nov. 1, 1727. CO 152/16, S27.

24. Mathew to BT, May 28, 1730, CO 152/18, T78; CSP, 1734–35, 41, no. 314 ii, p. 208; Frank Wesley Pitman, *Development of the British West Indies, 1700–1763* (1917; reprint, New York: Archon, 1967), p. 76.

25. Philip D. Curtin, *The Atlantic Slave Trade: A Census* (Madison: University of Wisconsin Press, 1969), p. 62; Pitman, *British West Indies*, pp. 76–77.

26. Deerr, *History of Sugar,* 1:195.

27. Richard Sheridan, "Africa and the Caribbean in the Atlantic Slave Trade," *AHR* 77 (Feb. 1972):29. The mortality rate for 1720–28 was calculated using Sheridan's formula

$$\frac{M = 1 - P}{C \ X \ A + 9 \ x \ P,}, \text{ where}$$

M = slave mortality rate, or annual rate of population decrease.
I = net slave imports during 9-year period
P = increase of slave population during the 9-year period
C = compounding factor, or $1+2+3\ldots 9$, or 45
A = annual net increase in slave population, or P/25
P, = slave population in year one of the 9-year period

For Antigua (1720–29) the solution for M is as follows:

$$M = \frac{11{,}278 - 3{,}425}{\dfrac{45 \times 3425 + 9 \times 19{,}186}{9}} \quad \frac{7853}{189799} = 4.13\%$$

where I=11,278, P=3,425, C=45, A=380.5, and P,=1,9186

28. Ibid., pp. 20–21; Sheridan, *The Development of the Plantations to 1750* (Barbados: Caribbean University Press, 1970), pp. 20–21; Sheridan, "Mortality and the Medical Treatment of Slaves in the British West Indies," in *Race and Slavery in the Western Hemisphere,* ed. Stanley L. Engerman and Eugene D. Genovese, (Princeton, N.J.: Princeton University Press, 1975), pp. 285–310; Pares, *Merchants and Planters,* pp. 38–39; Philip D. Curtin, "Epidemiology and the Slave Trade," *Political Science Quarterly* 83 (June 1968):210–15; Michael Craton, "Death, Disease and Medicine on Jamaican Slave Plantations: The Example of Worthy Park, 1767–1838," *Histoire Sociale/Social History* 9 (Nov. 1976):237–55; Kenneth F. Kiple and Virginia H. Kiple, "Deficiency Diseases in the Caribbean," *JIH* 11 (Autumn 1980):197–215; Kiple and Kiple, "Slave Child Mortality: Some Nutritional Answers to a Perennial Puzzle," *JSocH* 10 (1977):284–309. For a useful study of conditions on the Codrington plantations of the Society for the Propagation of the Gospel in Barbados, see J. Harry Bennett, Jr., *Bondsmen and Bishops: Slavery and Apprenticeship*

on the Codrington Plantations of Barbados 1710–1838 (Berkeley: University of California Press, 1958), pp. 44–62. Bennett, "The Problem of Slave Labor Supply at the Codrington Plantations," *JNH* 36 (Oct. 1951):406–41 and *JNH* 37 (Apr. 1952): 115–41. The history of these plantations is also told in Frank J. Klingberg, ed., *Codrington Chronicle: An Experiment in Anglican Altruism on a Barbados Plantation, 1710–1834* (Berkeley: University of California Press, 1949).

29. For a suggestive study of implications of subsistence crises for slave societies in the West Indies, see Robert Dirks, "Resource Fluctuations and Competitive Transformations in West Indian Slave Societies," in *Extinction and Survival in Human Populations,* ed. Charles D. Laughlin, Jr., and Ivan A. Brady (New York: Columbia University Press, 1978), pp. 122–80. On the hazards experienced by Africans sold into slavery and related features of the slave trade that helped determine levels of morbidity and mortality, see Robert Stein, "Mortality in the Eighteenth-Century French Slave Trade," *JAH* 21 (1980):35–42; Joseph C. Miller, "Mortality in the Atlantic Slave Trade: Statistical Evidence on Causality," *JIH* 11 (Winter 1981): 385–423; comment on same and Miller's reply, *JIH* 13 (Autumn 1982):317–29, 331–36; Curtin, *Atlantic Slave Trade,* pp. 275–86; Curtin, "Epidemiology and the Slave Trade," pp. 190–216; Klein, *Middle Passage,* passim; Johannes Postma, "Mortality in the Dutch Slave Trade, 1675–1795," in Gemery and Hogendorn, *The Uncommon Market,* pp. 239–60; Herbert S. Klein and Stanley L. Engerman, "A Note on Mortality in the French Slave Trade in the Eighteenth Century," in Gemery and Hogendorn, *The Uncommon Market,* pp. 261–72. Colin A. Palmer, *Human Cargoes: The British Slave Trade to Spanish America, 1700–1739* (Urbana: University of Illinois Press, 1981), pp. 42–54. On seasoning in the West Indies, see, for example, F. W. Pitman, "Slavery on the British West India Plantations in the Eighteenth Century," *JNH* 11 (Oct. 1926):632–33; Orlando Patterson, *The Sociology of Slavery: An Analysis of the Origins, Development and Structure of Negro Slave Society in Jamaica* (London: MacGibbon & Kee, 1967), pp. 98–101, 150–51.

30. Robert Robertson, *A Detection of the State and Situation of the Present Sugar Planters of Barbados and the Leeward Islands* (London, 1732), p. 44. Explaining high mortality rates, Robertson noted that "in dry years when Provisions of the Country Growth are scarce, I have known it One in Seven in my Plantations, and the same or worse in sickly Seasons; and when the Small-Pox, which is almost as much dreaded in the Leeward Islands as the Pestilence is any Party of Europe, happens to be imported, it is incredible what Havock it makes among the Blacks." But there was more. Robertson added that while there were slave births, "considering how hard the Negroes are generally kept to work, and that Polygamy (which, whatever it may do in their native Countries, is found among other Mischiefs, to hinder Breeding here) is permitted to them; and allowing for the Numbers of Infants that die, the little Work the Mother can do for three Months before and nine after the Birth, Midwifery, and some other Incidents, and the Maintenance of the Child for six or seven Years at a Penny per Diem, the Gain from thence cannot be great." Ibid., pp. 44–45; Robertson, *A Letter to the Right Reverend the Lord Bishop of London* (London, 1730), p. 11.

31. Wells, *Population of the British Colonies,* p. 214; Pitman, *British West Indies,* pp. 47–50; Hamilton to BT, Aug. 22, 1720, CO 152/12, Q46.

32. Yeamans to BT, May 27, 1734, CO 152/20, C29; Johnson to Sec. of State, May 28, 1706, CO 7/1.

33. Parke to BT, Mar. 8, 1708, CO 152/7, L52; BT to Parke, Oct. 30, 1707, CO 153/10.

34. Hart to BT, Mar. 1, 1725, CO 152/15, R131; "An Act for encouraging the Importation of White Servants to this Island," act no. 153, July 11, 1716, *Laws of Antigua*.

35. Mathew to BT, Oct. 17, 1724, CO 152/24, Y53; CSP, 1734–35, 41, no. 314, p. 217; Assembly Mins., Oct. 4, 1726, CO 9/5. In the end, the white servant acts did not bear the desired fruit. Plans to purchase lands on which to settle voluntary migrants and former servants also achieved little. In 1724, for example, the assembly wanted 200 acres purchased from Henry Martin and parceled out to poor settlers in ten-acre lots. Mins. of Council in Assembly, May 12, 1724, CO 9/5; Hart to BT, Mar. 1, 1725, CO 152/15, R132; Assembly Mins., Nov. 30, 1730, CO 9/7. To encourage the poor and common folk not to leave the island, the authorities often exempted them from annual taxes and, in times of distress, donated relief. In 1722, twenty-nine poor persons in the eastern division of Non-such in the Parish of St. Paul, and twelve others, had their taxes remitted after petitioning the legislature. The following year, twenty-five from Non-such, and twenty-six from Indian Creek and English Harbour in the Parish of St. Paul received similar relief. In all cases, their petitions were granted so long as they agreed to remain in Antigua, but if they left they could be held accountable for the taxes and arrears. Assembly Mins., July 4, Sept. 20, 1722; May 25, 1723; Mar. 10, 1724, CO 9/5. Some parish returns on burials and baptisms from which death and births can be inferred are scattered through island reports to the Board of Trade in CO 152. For analysis of such and other population data, see Pitman, *British West Indies*, pp. 378–87; Wells, *Population of the British Colonies*, pp. 207–36.

36. Byrd to the Earl of Egmont, July 12, 1736, in *Bases of the Plantation Society*, ed. Aubrey C. Land (Columbia: University of South Carolina Press, 1969), pp. 69–71.

37. Parke to RAC, Nov. 10, 1707, PRO, T70/8, 51; RAC to BT, Oct. 2, 1719, CO 388/21; Hamilton to BT, July 20, 1719, CO 152/12, P207; Mins. of Council in Assembly, Dec. 23, 1724, CO 9/5.

38. CSP, 1734–35, 41, no. 314ii, pp. 207–8; Robertson, *A Detection*, p. 82. For the same reason Robertson believed Montserrat needed about 5,000 slaves, Nevis 6,000, St. Kitts 9,000, and Jamaica double its existing slave population. All, added Robertson, would also require "a proportionable Number of White Inhabitants, and a sufficient Strength of other Stock to employ those numbers if they had them."

39. Thomas to BT, Feb. 20, 1756, CO 152/28, Bb75; Mackinen and Blizard to Redwood, June 13, 1755, *Commerce of Rhode Island 1726–1800*, 2 vols. (Boston, Massachusetts Historical Society, 1914–15), 1:511.

40. Pitman, *British West Indies*, pp. 61–90; Memorial of Gov., Council, and Assembly of Antigua to BT, Assembly Mins., Nov. 8, 1750, CO 9/20; Samuel Martin, Sr., to Samuel Martin, Jr. in London, Sept. 24, 1750, Martin Letter Book, 1, fol. 8, Martin Papers, Add. MSS 41,346, British Library.

41. Tullideph to Thomas, Mar. 25, 1752, R. B. Sheridan, "Letters from a Sugar

Plantation in Antigua, 1739–1758," *Agricultural History* 31 (July 1957):21; Extract of an Antigua letter, Mar. 2, 1757, CO 338/47, Ff43; Tullideph to Sydserfe, Nov. 8, 1755, Tullideph Letter Book, MS; *Pennsylvania Gazette,* Oct. 3, 1751.

42. For RAC papers the most useful are PRO, T70/2, 3, 7, 8; see also Antigua Shipping Returns, CO 157/1. Official correspondence is scattered through CO 152, but the detailed slave trade returns in CO, 152/15, 16, 18, 19 are informative. Additional sources are provided in notes following.

43. Separate Traders to BT, Dec. 31, 1708 (enclosing report), CO 388/11, I77, 79; Mins. of Council in Assembly, Aug. 1, 1716, CO 9/3.

44. Mins. of Council in Assembly, Nov. 26, 1729, CO 9/6; Codrington to Bethell, Apr. 1, 1720, fol. 46, Codrington Papers, D1610/C3; also undated letters, fols. 10, 44. Writing to his Barbados attorneys in 1718, Codrington instructed that "as soon as my guinny Sloop arrives with you to put ye Cargo of 500 £ on board her as I have allready mentioned & to send her for Antigua directly to take in rum provided she has not yt her rum on board but if she has to order her directly for ye gold coast of Guinny & to return back to Barbados to you but if you cannot purchase ye Cargoe for ye Sloop yn write to my attorneys at Antigua to let ym know yt they must not send her up but tell ym its my orders yt they send her to new found land for her loading of fish & some oyle & to Consign her to ye master." Codrington also had a "ship" making trips to the coast. "You are on ye arriveall of my ship Pearl," he told the attorneys in Barbados, "to Pick 10 of ye Choicest of ye whole Cargoe for my Planta in Barbados of Negrs & place ym on my Planta. Then you are to pick out 20 of ye next choicest of ye whole Cargoe of Slaves 10 men & 10 women for my Planta in Antigua to be sent to Antigua in my said ship when she goes to receive her Cargoe there to my attorneys for my Planta. of Rooms." Codrington's instructions, Oct. 30, 1718, fols. 40–41 D1610/C2; Hart to BT, July 12, 1724, CO 152/14, R101; Hamilton to BT, July 20, 1719, CO 152/12, P207; CSP, 1734–35, 41, no. 457, p. 360. The direct trade from the islands to the coast had started years before, for in 1708 Gov. Parke reported to the Board of Trade that there had been "since my time but three Sloops & one Brigantine fitted from my Govermt for that trade, two by the Comp. Agent & two by private traders two of whch arrived safe the Other two 'tis feared are lost." Parke to BT, Aug. 23, 1708, CO 152/7, L95. By 1715 the company itself was doing business with plantation vessels arriving on the coast. To its chief merchants on the coast came the following instructions: "We direct You to be buying up, for our Accot. all the Negroes You Can at reasonable rates, and dispose of them for the most You Can get to any Ships Coming on the Coast in Exchange for their Vendible goods, Which you must also Vest in Negroes to be Disposed again in like manner untill You have our further Orders, preferring always Brittish Vessells from the English Settlements in the West Indies. You may likewise to encourage them to Deal with You. Lett them have Such Corn Mallagetta, or Other Necessaries as they Shall want paying a reasonable price for ye Same." Extract of letter from the RAC, Feb. 28, 1715, CO 388/18, O116.

45. CSP, 1685–88, no. 1,773, p. 553. "The Island of Statia neare St. Christophers," Clement Tudway wrote the RAC, "[is a place] from whence Interlopers with Dutch commissions doe supply these Islands with Negroes." Tudway to RAC, Jan. 7, 1687, PRO, T70/12, f78.

46. Holt to BT, received Dec. 15, 1709, CO 388/12, K66. Helden wrote that "within this four Years last past" he had observed that "the Dutch have imported to the Island of Eustatia Several Thousand of Negroes from the Coast of Africa, & there sell them to the English and French that come down in Sloops for that purpose, by which means they are not only supply'd without Vending any of our Commodities and carry our ready Money from the Island, but also Stock of great Quantities of Sugar, which is prejudicial to His Majesties Customs and carryed to a foreign Markett." Helden "Seized Several of these Negroes, after they have been landed in St. Christophers and brought them to Tryall as Dutch Merchandize illegally Imported, but the Judge of the Admiralty have always acquitted them." Helden to RAC, Sept. 19, 1719, CO 388/21, Q19. See also Hamilton to BT, Sept. 10, 1718, CO 152/12, P140; Hamilton to BT, Dec. 19, 1718, CO 152/12, P166; Hart to BT, July 12, 1724, CO 152/14, R101; Hart to BT, Feb. 15, 1727, CO 152/15, R188. Goods were also smuggled in from Curaçao, another Dutch island depot far to the south, off the Venezuelan coast. Memorials from Holt to BT, received Dec. 15, 1709, CO 388/12, K66, K67. For a discussion of illegal trade to the British islands during the first half of the eighteenth century, see Pitman, *British West Indies,* pp. 74–75, 271–333.

47. Ibid., pp. 271–96.

48. Sheridan, "Letters from a Sugar Plantation," pp. 3–23.

49. Ibid., Tullideph to Thomas, Aug. 20, 1748, Apr. 3, 1749, p. 18, June 19, 1749, p. 19, Dec. 3, 1752, p. 23. Although planters may have thought it easier to purchase rather than breed slaves, they could not exercise that option because of the general irregular arrival of slave cargoes. A planter in Antigua told John Newton that "it was cheaper to work slaves to the utmost, and by 'little relaxation, hard fare, and hard usage, to wear them out before they became useless, and unable to do service; and then to buy new ones, to fill up their places' "; but this would have been dependent upon reliable slave supplies. Leeward planters may have used their slaves more judiciously than Newton's report would have us believe. John Newton, *The Journal of a Slave Trader, 1750–1754,* ed. Bernard Martin and Mark Spurrell (London: Epworth Press, 1962), p. 112, as quoted in Sheridan, "Africa and the Caribbean, pp. 26–27.

50. Tullideph to Russell, Mar. 16, 1759, Tullideph Letter Book; Oliver to Swete, July 24, 1745, Swete Papers, 388M/E11, Devon Record Office, Exeter, England; Report on Betty's Hope Plantation, undated, Codrington Papers, D1610/C5; Mackinen to Redwood, Oct. 18, 1753, *Commerce of Rhode Island,* 1:505.

51. Edwin F. Gay, "Letters from a Sugar Plantation in Nevis, 1723–1732," *Journal of Economic and Business History* 1 (Nov. 1928):164, Stalker to Stapleton, June 5, 1730; General Report.

52. Tullideph to Leonard, Dec. 11, 1755 and Apr. 7, 1756, Tullideph to Russell, Feb. 22, 1760, Tullideph Letter Book, MS.

53. Codrington to Redhead, Nov. 5, 1751, Codrington Papers, D1610/C6. On the recruitment of Africans, Edward Long, historian and resident of Jamaica, wrote in the third quarter of the eighteenth century: "The introduction of too many recruits at once has sometimes proved fatal to them. It is very evident, that a small number can be much easier and better provided for, lodged, fed, and taken care of, than a multitude. The planter therefore, who buys only eight or ten at a time,

will in the end derive more advantage for them, than the planter who buys 30; for, by the greater leisure and attention in his power to bestow upon them, he will greatly lessen the ordinary chances against their life, and the sooner prepare them for an effectual course of labor. The comparison, indeed, founded upon fact and observation, is, at the end of three years, the former may possibly have lost one-fifth, but the other will most probably have lost one-half, of their respective numbers." Edward Long, *History of Jamaica*, 3 vols. (London, 1774), 2:435, quoted in Ulrich B. Phillips, "A Jamaica Slave Plantation," *CQ* 1 (Apr.-June 1949):5-6.

54. For a good example of combination of such strategies see J. H. Bennett, Jr., "The Problem of Slave Labor Supply" (Barbados); Bennett, *Bondsmen and Bishops*, pp. 44-74.

55. Daniel C. Littlefield, *Rice and Slaves: Ethnicity and the Slave Trade in Colonial South Carolina* (Baton Rouge: Louisiana State University Press, 1981); W. Robert Higgins, "The Geographical Origins of Negro Slaves in Colonial South Carolina," *South Atlantic Quarterly* 70 (Winter 1977):34-47; Darold D. Wax, "Preferences for Slaves in Colonial America," *JNH* 58 (Oct. 1973):371-401; Edwards, *West Indies*, 2:265-83; A.J.R. Russell-Wood, *fidalgos and Philanthropists: The Santa Casa da Misericordia of Bahia, 1550-1755* (Berkeley: University of California Press, 1968), p. 68; Curtin, *Atlantic Slave Trade*, pp. 155-62, 181-83, 189-90, 208-9 and passim; Long, *History of Jamaica*, 2:352-53, 403-4, 445; Roger Bastide, *African Civilisations in the New World* (New York: Harper & Row, 1971), p. 106; Mackinen to Redwood, Oct. 18, 1753, *Commerce of Rhode Island*, 1:505; Patterson, *Sociology of Slavery*, p. 119; Ivor Wilks, "The Mossi and Akan States 1500-1800," in *History of West Africa*, 2 vols., ed. J.F.A. Ajayi and Michael Crowder (New York: Columbia University Press, 1972-74), 1:344-86; A. B. Ellis, *A History of the Gold Coast of West Africa* (New York: Negro Universities Press, 1969), pp. 94-95.

56. Edwards, *West Indies*, 2:74.

57. Rev. William Smith, *A Natural History of Nevis, And the Rest of the English Leeward Charibee Islands in America* (Cambridge, 1745), letter 9, p. 225; Patterson, *Sociology of Slavery*, p. 276. For Coromantee involvement in Caribbean slave resistance see also Patterson, "Slavery and Slave Revolts: A Socio-Historical Analysis of the first Maroon War, 1655-1740," *SES* 19 (Sept. 1970):289-325; Monica Schuler, "Ethnic Slave Rebellions in the Caribbean and the Guianas," *JSocH* 3 (1970):374-85; Schuler, "Akan Slave Rebellions in the British Caribbean," *Savacou* 1 (June 1970):8-29; Schuler, "Slave Resistance in the Caribbean," manuscript, University of the West Indies, 1966; Long, *History of Jamaica*, 2:446-75.

58. Curtin, *Atlantic Slave Trade*, pp. 154, 187, 245; Ellis, *History of the Gold Coast*, p. 95.

59. Absentee Abraham Redwood's representatives wrote in 1755 that "In December we bought from Blizard and Bannister Twenty three Gold Coast slaves Eighteen men at Thirty five pounds Sterling and five women at Thirty four pounds Sterling, amounting to Eight hundred pounds Sterling; they prove well hitherto, and will always answer better than any Slaves from Africa except Papaws, and those are seldom brought hither." Mackinen and Blizard to Redwood, Feb. 20, 1755, Donnan, *Documents*, vol. 2; no. 240, pp. 510-11; Edwards, *West Indies*, 2:72.

60. Curtin, *Atlantic Slave Trade*, pp. 154-55, (table 43); Patterson, *Sociology of*

Slavery, p. 123; Edwards, *West Indies,* 2:73; Smith, *Natural History of Nevis,* letter 9, p. 225; Littlefield, *Rice and Slaves,* p. 16.

61. Donnan, *Documents,* vol. 2, no. 16, p. 15.

62. Ira Berlin, "The Slave Trade and the Development of Afro-American Society in English Mainland North America, 1619-1775," *SS* 20 (Summer 1981):122-36; Philip D. Curtin, "The African Diaspora," in *Roots and Branches: Current Directions in Slave Studies,* ed. Michael Craton, special issue of *Historical Reflections/ Réflexions Historiques* 6 (Summer 1979):9-11; Faust, "Culture, Conflict, and Community."

Chapter 5: From the Negroes' Labor

1. Frederick Cooper, "The Problem of Slavery in African Studies," *JAH* 20, 1, (1979):111; E. P. Thompson, *The Making of the English Working Class* (New York: Vintage, 1966), pp. 711-12; George Rudé, *Ideology and Popular Protest* (New York: Pantheon, 1980), pp. 7-11; Eugene D. Genovese, "The Treatment of Slaves in Different Countries: Problems in the Applications of the Comparative Method," in *Slavery in the New World: A Reader in Comparative History,* ed. Laura Foner and Eugene D. Genovese, (Englewood Cliffs, N.J.: Prentice-Hall, 1969), pp. 202-10.

2. Wood, *Black Majority;* Cooper, "Problem of Slavery," p. 111; CSP, 1669-74, no. 680, p. 291.

3. John MacPherson, *Caribbean Lands,* 4th ed. (London: Longman, 1980), pp. 112-17; Harris, *Plants, Animals, and Man,* pp. 7-18, 85-99; 98-107; letter 11, May 31, 1786, John Luffman, *A Brief Account of the Island of Antigua, together with the customs and manners of its inhabitants, as well white as black: as also an accurate statement of the food, cloathing, labor, and punishment, of slaves. In Letters to a Friend. Written in the Years 1786, 1787, 1788* (London, 1789), reprinted in Oliver, *History of Antigua,* 1:128-38; Ward Barrett, "Caribbean Sugar Production Standards in the Seventeenth and Eighteenth Centuries," in *Merchants and Scholars: Essays in the History of Exploration and Trade,* ed. John Parker, (Minneapolis, Minn.: Lund Press, 1965), pp. 147-70; S. Ivan Smith, "Functional Ecology of Sugarcane in the American Tropics," *CS* 15, 3 (Oct. 1975):58-60; CSP, 1734-35, 41, no. 314 ii, p. 207; Deerr, *History of Sugar,* 1:195.

4. The lists are reprinted in Oliver, *History of Antigua,* 3:394-97; Dunn, *Sugar and Slaves,* pp. 141-43.

5. Barrett, "Caribbean Sugar Production," p. 165; Sheridan, *Development of the Plantations,* p. 46; Dunn, *Sugar and Slaves,* p. 189.

6. Stuart B. Schwartz, "Patterns of Slaveholding in the Americas: New Evidence from Brazil," *AHR,* 87, 1 (Feb. 1982). Using new evidence from Bahia, Brazil, Schwartz argues for careful analysis of patterns of slaveholding in order to better understand plantation systems in the Americas and variations among them.

7. Sheridan, *Development of the Plantations,* p. 17; John Yeamans to BT, May 27, 1734, CO 152/V29; Council Mins., Jan. 31, 1737, Vallentine Morris report, Jan. 24, 1737; CO 9/10; CSP, 1734-35, no. 314 ii, p. 207; anon., *Some Observations; Which May Contribute to Afford A Just Idea of the Nature, Importance, and Settlement of*

Our New West-India Colonies (London, 1764), cited in R. B. Sheridan, "Samuel Martin, Innovating Sugar Planter of Antigua 1750–1776," *Agricultural History* 24 (July 1960):132; "A fair Estimate of Samuel Martins Plantation in New Division in Antigua, according to the general rule of Appraisement," June 24, 1768, Martin Papers, Add. MSS 41,353, fol. 84; Richard Pares, *Yankees and Creoles: The Trade between North America and the West Indies before the American Revolution* (1956; reprint, New York: Archon, 1968), p. 111.

8. Hamilton to BT, Sept. 13, 1720, CO 152/13, Q62. I have used the list as reprinted in Oliver, *History of Antigua*, 1:92–93. Table 5.1 is also slightly different in presentation from that given by Frank W. Pitman, "The Settlement and Financing of British West India Plantations in the Eighteenth Century," *Essays in Colonial History by Students of Charles McLead Andrews* (Freeport, N.Y., 1966), p. 258.

9. Antigua, map no. 2, "The Island of Antigua by Herman Moll, Geographer," (1 inch to 1⅓ miles), CO 700/2. Tooley gives the first edition date as 1729; there were other editions in 1732 and 1739. R. V. Tooley, *The Printed Maps of Antigua 1689–1899*, Map Collectors' Series, 6, no. 55 (London: Map Collectors' Circle, 1969), p. 5. See also P. A. Penfold, ed., *Maps and Plans in the Public Record Office*, 2 vols. (London, 1974), vol. 2. Petitions of inability to pay taxes on property periodically came from the "Ten Acre Men" of Falmouth Division in the Parish of St. Paul. See below, chap. 4, n. 35. Predominance of windmills in Moll's map should be expected. During the early years of sugar cultivation, cattle mills were widely used, but when the plantations expanded and an increasing proportion of their total acreage was put under sugar cane, less land was left to pasture cattle for cattle mills or even for consumption. Moreover, these mills had a very limited crushing capacity and, especially during harvest, took a heavy toll of livestock. Before long planters switched to the more economical windmill, which could use the trade winds sweeping steadily across the island. Water mills were not used because of the absence of rivers. In 1705 there were 34 windmills, 136 cattle mills, and 4,139 black cattle, which increased to 5,000 the following year. This early, relatively widespread use of cattle mills contrasts strikingly with Moll's new estimates of 1729. By 1748 such mills were still outnumbered by windmills, there being approximately 64 of them to about 175 windmills. R. B. Sheridan, "Samuel Martin," p. 131, n. 39; Sheridan, *Development of the Plantations*, pp. 16–17; Sheridan, *Sugar and Slavery*, p. 192; Oliver, *History of Antigua*, 1:75.

10. See Tooley, *Printed Maps of Antigua*, pp. 5–7. Antigua, map no. 3, "A New and Exact Map of the Island of Antigua in America, According to an Actual and Accurate Survey Made in the Years 1746, 1747, and 1748," by Robert Baker, Surveyor General of Lands (2 inches to 1 mile), (London, 1748–49), CO 700/3; Antigua, map no. 4, "A New and Accurate Map of the Island of Antigua or Antegua taken from Surveys and Adjusted by Astronomical Observations," by Emanuel Bowen (1 inch to 2 miles), (London, 1752), CO 700/4.

11. Michael Craton, *Sinews of Empire: A Short History of British Slavery* (London: Temple Smith, 1974), pp. 121, 122.

12. Ibid., pp. 122–26.

13. Ibid., p. 127; Goveia, *Slave Society*, p. 119; Samuel Martin, "An Essay upon Plantership," *Annals of Agriculture and Other Useful Arts* 18 (1792):266–72; Goveia, *Slave Society*, p. 119; Ulrich B. Phillips, "An Antigua Plantation, 1769–1818," *North*

Carolina Historical Review, 3 (1926):440. See, for example, Farley to Tudway, July 23, 1758, Tudway Papers, DD/TD, box 15; Samuel Martin, "Essay upon Plantership," pp. 263–66; Sheridan, "Africa and the Caribbean," p. 22; Goveia, *Slave Society,* pp. 119–20; Michael Craton, *Searching for the Invisible Man: Slaves and Plantation Life in Jamaica* (Cambridge, Mass.: Harvard University Press, 1978), pp. 203–4.

14. Sheridan, "Samuel Martin," p. 134; Accounts, Sept. 10, 1738–Aug. 13, 1739, Swete Papers, 388M/E4; Tullideph to Thomas, Aug. 1, 1742, Sheridan, "Letters from a Sugar Plantation," p. 7; Tullideph to Thomas, Nov. 16, 1745, ibid., p. 13. Undermanned plantations were more heavily dependent on hired hands than others better supplied with labor. "I think your estate would make near [as] much sugar as Mr. Langford's," William Mackinen wrote Abraham Redwood in 1753, "if it was equally slaved, where [as] now, it does not make about half so much, and your expence [for] task work last year was within a trifle of five hundred [po]unds." Mackinen to Redwood, Oct. 8, 1753, *Commerce of Rhode Island,* 1:505. For a most enlightening discussion of the dynamics and implications of slave hiring in a particular slave society, see Sarah S. Hughes, "Slaves for Hire: The Allocation of Black Labor in Elizabeth City County, Virginia, 1782–1810," *WMQ,* 3d ser. 35 (Apr. 1978):260–86.

15. Sheridan, "Samuel Martin," p. 134.

16. Ibid.; Barrett, "Caribbean Sugar Production," pp. 152–54. To lighten the laborious work of holing and planting, slaves improvised work songs. "The Negroes when at work, in howing Canes or digging round Holes to plant them in, (perhaps forty Persons in a row)," wrote Rev. William Smith of Nevis, "sing very merrily, i.e. two or three Men with large Voices, and a sort of Base Tone, sing three or four short lines, and then all the rest join at once, in a sort of Chorus, which I have often heard and seemed to be, La, Alla, La, La, well enough, and indeed harmoniously turned, especially when I was at a little distance from them. They sing too at Burials," he added. William Smith, *Natural History of Nevis,* pp. 230–31.

17. Sheridan, "Samuel Martin," pp. 128–39; Sheridan, "The West Indian Antecedents of Josiah Martin, Last Royal Governor of North Carolina," *North Carolina Historical Review* 54 (July 1977):259; Samuel Martin, "Essay upon Plantership," pp. 273, 276–78; Barrett, "Caribbean Sugar Production," p. 154; S. Ivan Smith, "Functional Ecology of Sugarcane," p. 58.

18. Samuel Martin, "Essay upon Plantership," pp. 278 (for his most interesting discussion of the proper care of "negroes, cattle, mules, and horses [which] are the nerves of a sugar-plantation," see pp. 236–52), 243; "Orders & directions for Mr. John Griffith Manidger of Bettys Hope Plantation," June 27, 1715, Codrington Papers, D1610/C2. On the evolution of the slaves' use of Sunday, which they came to regard as a right, see the illuminating discussion in Robertson, *Letter,* pp. 44–46.

19. Long to Redwood, Mar. 14, 1733, *Commerce of Rhode Island,* 1:35. "The occasion of your Sloop being detain'd here so long," wrote John Tomlinson, Jr. one week later, "has been intirely owing, to the great Rains we had after Xmas, which continued untill the middle of Feb: so that no mills were at work, till about that time; However as the Rains were general over all the Islands; I hope your Effects will come-to so good a Market as to make amends, for the long time she has been out." Tomlinson to Redwood, Mar. 21, 1733, *Commerce of Rhode Island,* 1:36. An observation about the variable length of crop season indicated that

Antigua "Crops are sometimes Earlier in one Year than another According to the Different Seasons, And consequently our Trading Ships sooner loaded & ready for Sailing to Great Brittain one Year than Another, And we Apprehend that almost every Year our Fleets will be loaded & ready for Sailing before the 24th of June which is the Day Stated for the first Convoy; we likewise apprehend our Crops are generally at an End the latter End of July And Consequently the Trade ready for the 2d Convoy Sooner than the 29th of September." Council Mins., Aug. 22, 1747, CO 9/18. Writing to a Jamaica planter in 1755, Walter Tullideph noted that the crop was in general a good one; "our's begins in January & finish abot the beginning of July, when we expect rains, but I hear your rains are expected in May & therefore Imagine you may begin to grind in November or Decr, some Estates here are still grinding, but to great disadvantage as we have had a good deal of rain these two months past." Tullideph to Clark, "Hannover" Parish, Jamaica, Aug. 20, 1755, Tullideph Letter Book, MS. See also Pares, *West-India Fortune*, pp. 114–15.

20. Dunbar to Tullideph, July 18, 1757, Tullideph Letter Book, MS; Sydeserfe to Tullideph, Mar. 4, 1757, ibid.; "Observations on the Inventory sent Sr. William Codrington Augst. 12, 1751," information related to Betty's Hope Plantation, Codrington Papers, D1610/E5; Tullideph to Leonard at Tortola, Dec. 11, 1755, Tullideph Letter Book, MS; Bennett, *Bondsmen and Bishops*, pp. 20, 44.

21. John W. Blassingame, "Status and Social Structure in the Slave Community: Evidence From New Sources," in *Perspectives and Irony in American Slavery*, ed. Harry P. Owens, (Jackson: University Press of Mississippi, 1976), pp. 137–51; James M. Clifton, "The Rice Driver: His Role in Slave Management," *SCHM* 82 (Oct. 1981):331–53. For perceptive discussion of the role of slave drivers in the United States, see William L. Van Deburg, *The Slave Drivers: Black Agricultural Labor Supervisors in the Antebellum South* (Westport, Conn.: Greenwood Press, 1979); Leslie Howard Owens, *This Species of Property: Slave Life and Culture in the Old South* (New York: Oxford University Press, 1977), pp. 121–35 and passim; Eugene D. Genovese, *Roll, Jordon, Roll: The World the Slaves Made* (New York: Vintage, 1976), pp. 365–88 and passim. Parham Plantation Inventory, Feb. 1737, Tudway Papers, DD/TD, box 16; Parham Plantation (Old Work) Inventory, 1750, ibid., box 14.

22. Pitman, "Slavery on the British West India Plantations," p. 598.

23. Inventory of Bridge Plantation, 1708, Tyrell Papers, D/DKe, T33, Essex Record Office, Chelmsford, England. This plantation seems to have been a small one or heavily undermanned, to judge from the small number (25) of slaves listed.

24. Pitman, "Slavery on the British West India Plantations," p. 598; Tullideph to Jordan, Oct. 25, 1753, Tullideph Letter Book, MS.

25. Pares, *West-India Fortune*, pp. 116–19; Samuel Martin, "Essay upon Plantership," pp. 285–308; Barrett, "Caribbean Sugar Production," pp. 159–63.

26. Report on Betty's Hope Plantation, undated, Codrington Papers, D1610/C5; Craton, *Searching for the Invisible Man*, pp. 206–7; Bennett, "Problem of Slave Labor Supply," pp. 433–34; Martin Papers, Add. MSS 41,353, fol. 84.

27. Patterson, *Sociology of Slavery*, pp. 57–58; Blassingame, "Status and Social Structure," pp. 139–40; Darlene C. Hine, "Female Slave Resistance: The Economics of Sex," *Western Journal of Black Studies* 3 (Summer 1979):123–27; Goveia, *Slave Society*, p. 231.

28. For inventories of small, undermanned plantations without real slave specialists, see inventories of Bridge Plantation for 1706-7, 1716, 1723, 1734, 1753, 1754, 1792, Tyrell Papers, D/DKe, T33. Over this period the plantation was leased out to several people. It contained up to 250 acres and was leased with less than 30 slaves on it. On two separate plantations of 337 and 90 acres, planter Main Swete, deceased, had 88 slaves. In an inventory of 1737 only Jackey the driver and Old Nanny "ye Doctress" were identified by occupation. Swete Papers, 388M/E3.

29. Inventory, 1737, box 16, Inventory, 1772, box 14, Tudway Papers, DD/TD. Inventory of Betty's Hope Plantation, July 26, 1751, Codrington Papers, D1610/E5; "Observations on the Inventory sent Sr. William Codrington Augst. 12, 1751," ibid.; J.R.V. Johnston, "The Stapleton Sugar Plantations in the Leeward Islands," *Bulletin of the John Rylands Library* (Manchester) 48 (Autumn 1965):199.

30. Richard C. Wade, *Slavery in the Cities: The South 1820-1860* (New York: Oxford University Press, 1964); Frederick P. Bowser, *The African Slave in Colonial Peru 1524-1650* (Stanford, Calif.: Stanford University Press, 1974), pp. 100-104; Frederick Cooper, *Plantation Slavery on the East Coast of Africa* (New Haven, Conn.: Yale University Press, 1977), pp. 184-89.

31. Parke to BT, Aug. 4, 1707, CO 152/7, C27. Commenting on the general cost of living in Antigua in 1729, Gov. Londonderry observed to Bishop Edmund Gibson that very few Antigua proprietors kept white servants "but only Negro's to wait on them (and who do it mightly well) which cost so little in maintaining them, that they dont stand in twenty shillings sterling an year each, so that in generall, I look on liveing to be much cheaper than in England." Londonderry to Gibson, June 8, 1729, Fulham Papers, 19, fol. 189, Lambeth Palace Library.

32. "An Act for the further promoting the Number of the Inhabitants of this Island, and more particularly encouraging the King's Soldiers, now to be disbanded, to continue therein, by enabling them to become Settlers amongst us," act no. 118, Dec. 24, 1700, clause 9, *Laws of Antigua*. The act banned employment of blacks in taverns, eating houses, and punch houses and also restricted the number who could be employed on vessels.

33. Mins. of Council in Assembly, Apr. 17, 1725, CO 155/6.

34. "I have hired a Negro man-servant," John Luffman wrote on May 31, 1786, "for whose services I am to pay his owner half a Joannes (eighteen shilling sterling) per month; and also a Mulatto woman cook and washer, for whom I am to pay three dollars per month." Luffman, *Antigua*, letter 2.

35. Bowser, *African Slave in Colonial Peru*, p. 103.

36. How urban slavery undermined control of slaves in that environment is one of Wade's central themes in *Slavery in the Cities*. See especially pp. 80-110. See also Cooper, *Plantation Slavery*, pp. 188-89; Hughes, "Slaves for Hire," pp. 283-84; Gerald W. Mullin, *Flight and Rebellion: Slave Resistance in Eighteenth-Century Virginia* (New York: Oxford University Press, 1972), pp. 162-63.

37. For these tax acts see CO 8/11, 12, 13.

38. "An Act raising a Tax for paying Public Debts and Charges & particularly Applying the said Tax," June 14, 1755, CO 8/11. See also tax resolutions of the assembly in committee, Assembly Mins., Apr. 29, 1755, CO 9/22.

39. Tullideph to Sydserfe, Dec. 28, 1755, Tullideph Letter Book, MS. On June 9, 1755 Tullideph wrote absentee Sydserfe that "We are raising a high tax

this year; those who make no Sugar are to pay 13/6 on their negroes, besides 2/6d Cash tax for the barracks, those who make Sugar, pay 10d pr 100 wt & one penny I hear on Rum; it is not sent up yet to the Upper house; it is thought the most reasonable taxation, your's will run high this year." Ibid.

40. "An Act against Jews ingrossing Commodities imported in the Leeward Islands and trading with the Slaves belonging to the Inhabitants of the Same." Aug. 31, 1694, CO 8/1. As the title of the act suggests, the Jews were also accused of "buying up, & engrossing all Manner of Goods brought thither to be sold." The act was passed to terminate this practice, but more importantly to plug the loophole that did not allow slave evidence against whites, evidence that might have been extremely damaging to the Jews and their trade with slaves.

41. "An Act to repeale a certain Act against the Jewes," Dec. 10, 1701, CO 8/1.

42. Council Mins., July 30, 1742, CO 9/14; Assembly Mins., July 2, 1734, CO 9/7; Council Mins., July 2, 1734, CO 9/8.

43. General Report.

44. "Petition of James Howison, John Waton and Thomas Newey of the said Island Barbers and Peruke Makers praying that a Law might be passed to prevent Slaves from carrying on the said Trades, Read and Order'd to lie on the Table." Assembly Mins., Oct. 4, 1764, CO 9/28. In Nevis in 1682 "The coopers' petition [was] granted, on condition that no more negroes or slaves be taught the trade." CSP, 1681–85, no. 557, p. 248.

45. Act no. 118, Dec. 24, 1700, Laws of Antigua. In 1794 and again in 1800 acts were passed to deal with the problem of runaways obtaining work on vessels. Goveia, Slave Society, p. 160.

46. Hamilton to BT, Aug. 22, 1720, encl. 62, CO 152/13, Q51. The generally larger types of craft — ships, brigantines, snows, and sloops — can be distinguished according to type of rig. In the eighteenth century a "ship" was normally three-masted and square rigged; brigantines and snows were almost identical as two-masted, square-rigged craft except that snows had "a try-sail mast clost abaft the mainmast." Webster's New International Dictionary, 3d ed. unabr. (Springfield, Mass.: G. & C. Merriam, 1960). Sloops were one-masted. See Davis, Rise of the English Shipping Industry, pp. 73–80; Roger Anstey, The Atlantic Slave Trade and British Abolition 1760–1810 (Atlantic Highlands, N.J.: Humanities Press, 1975), p. 9; Jay Coughtry, The Notorious Triangle: Rhode Island and the African Slave Trade 1700–1807 (Philadelphia: Temple University Press, 1981), pp. 70–76.

47. Antigua was deforested quite rapidly during the race to acquire cultivable land in the first decades of the sugar revolution. Harris, Plants, Animals, and Man, pp. 86–87.

48. Inventory, 1772, Tudway Papers, DD/TD, box 14; Pares, West-India Fortune, p. 36; Olaudah Equiano, The Life of Olaudah Equiano or Gustavus Vassa: The African (1837; reprint, New York: Negro Universities Press, 1969), pp. 108–14.

49. Ibid., p. 114.

50. Coughtry, Notorious Triangle, p. 74. Reporting on shipping of the Leeward Islands in 1724, Gov. Hart observed that "There are great Numbers of Sloops belonging to these Islands which are Sailed by the Inhabitants." Hart to BT, July 12, 1724, CO 152/14.

51. When such patterns of communication are better understood it will become

possible to establish more direct links between similar events, such as slave unrest in the 1730s and 1790s, occurring in the various territories of the circum-Caribbean and even perhaps extending to include North America. It would be enlightening to discover whether patterns of interterritorial slave communication followed established trade networks. During the black revolution in St. Domingue, Jamaican authorities, fearing its spread to their island, placed limitations on activities of foreign slaves in port. That act also implied the use of Jamaican slaves, some originally from other colonies, on vessels. "An Act to prevent any intercouse and communication between the slaves of this island, and foreign slaves of a certain description, and for other purposes," 39 Geo., 3 c, 29, 1799, in John Lunan, *An Abstract of the Laws of Jamaica Relating to Slaves* (Jamaica, 1819). For the Leeward Islands there are valuable scattered references to slave sailors. Joe worked on Codrington's sloop. Cotton Plantation Inventory, June 3, 1715, Codrington Papers, D1610/C2; "To Sir William Codrington's Planta. for hire of 5 Negro Sailors from 1st. Jan.: last to this day [Dec. 31. 1758] at 45/- per month each." Plantation Accounts, 1758, ibid., D1610/A4; "I send you two Negroes," wrote Walter Nugent to Abraham Redwood in Rhode Island, "if you like them keep them and give my Account credit for what you think they are worth; the Negroe man is a Peice of Saylor and a fine Papa Slave — cost thirty pounds Sterling out of the Ship." Nugent to Redwood, Apr. 11, 1731, *Commerce of Rhode Island*, 1:15. Gov. Hart reported Spanish capture of several vessels off St. Croix aboard which were black sailors. Hart to BT, Mar. 5, 1727, CO 152/15, R193, Apr. 10, 1727, CO 152/15, R199; for a similar case of seizure of a vessel with a black sailor see Mins. of Council in Assembly, Oct. 20, 1710, CO 9/2; Walter Tullideph to David Tullideph, Nov. 3, 1738, Tullideph Letter Book, MS. Tullideph reported a most interesting case in 1754: "I understand from Mr. Blount that your old man Cuffee who lived a long time with him had left him, and that about a month agone he had a letter from him in the downs, telling him he had hired himself on board of Capt. Johnston for Jamaica at 25/ pr. month as a Cook. I presently acquainted Mr. Thomas & Cousin Sydserfe of it, & I fancy they spoke to Mr. Gray about it and Suppose they have wrote you what can be done it it; I fancy he might be easily secured there, if any body was there that knew him to be your Slave, provided you think it worth your while. I think he deserves at least to be plagued by you." Tullideph to Sydserfe, Apr. 5, 1754, Tullideph Letter Book, MS. For service of blacks, slave and free, on Rhode Island vessels going as far away as Africa, see Coughtry, *Notorious Triangle*, pp. 60–61, 154; *Commerce of Rhode Island*, 1:47. In South Carolina in the years before 1740 the talents of slaves used to water or the sea were of great value. Wood, *Black Majority*, pp. 122–24, 200–205, 230–31.

52. Equiano, *Life*, pp. 122, 131–37, 143–50.

53. Assembly Mins., Jan. 19, 1722, CO 9/5.

54. Mathew to BT, Apr. 15, 1746, CO 152/25, Y154. As late as 1814 an Antigua act declared that "by far the greater Part of the Flats or Boats, now plying in the said Harbour [of Saint John's], are owned wholly by Slaves, without any Responsibility, in consequence of Notes given to them by Free Persons, and addressed to the Harbour-Master, requiring him to license Boats in the Name of the Persons writing these notes, although such Persons have not any Interest whatever in such Boats." "An Act to alter and amend a certain Clause of an Act, intituled, An Act

for the better Regulation of Porters, Jobbers, and Watermen, and all such Persons as shall ply as Porters, Jobbers, or Watermen in any of the Towns or Harbours of this Island, and for the Regulation of small Boats, and Craft of every Description, which ply for Hire in the said Harbours," act no. 644, Mar. 7, 1814, *Laws of Antigua.*

55. Talbot to Dalzell, Mar. 27, 1749, CO 7/1.

56. Richard Pares, *War and Trade in the West Indies, 1739-1763* (1936; reprint, London: Frank Cass, 1963), p. 227. This work is still the best on eighteenth-century warfare in the Caribbean.

57. For general information on English and French island practice, see ibid., pp. 240-42.

58. Mathew to BT, Apr. 15, 1746, CO 152/25, Y154. Fortifications included Monk's Hill, Great George Fort, Rat Island Barracks, Fort Byam, Fort William, Fort Issac, Road Fort, Gulph Point, Dickinson's Bay Platform, Drop Point, Fort Christian, Johnston's Point Fort, James Fort, Corinson Point, Cochran's Island, Indian Creek Battery, Black's Point Battery, Fort Charles, and Fullerton's Point.

59. William Laws, *Distinction, Death & Disgrace* (Kingston: Jamaica Historical Society, 1976), pp. 27-28; CSP, 1734-35, 41, no. 314ii, pp. 214-15.

60. "An Act For ye Further carrying on the Fortifications on Monks Hill," Apr. 25, 1702, CO 8/3. For a seventeenth-century requisition of slave labor for the fortifications, see "An Act for the erecting a Fort on the uttermost Point on the North Side of the Harbour of Saint Johns," Mar. 25, 1683, CO 8/1; "An Act for ye Further carrying on the Fortifications on Monk's Hill," Jan. 30, 1704, CO 8/3.

61. Parke to BT, Mar. 29, 1707, CO 152/7, L8. Four months earlier the assembly informed the lieutenant governor and council that "Wee are of Opinion there is no great Necessity for the going on with Monks hill at present, And as most persons are fitting up their Works in order to begin their Crops, behove the Masons & other Workmen cannot well be spared." Council Mins., Dec. 4, 1706, CO 9/1.

62. Oliver to Swete, July 24, 1745, Swete Papers, 388M/E11; letter dated Oct. 10, 1742, ibid., 388M/E8; Tullideph to Thomas, May 15, 1745, Sheridan, "Letters from a Sugar Plantation," p. 11.

63. There was a case in 1707 when the assembly agreed not to include a clause for paying slave laborers in the act under preparation for continuing work on Monk's Hill. Mins. of Council in Assembly, Feb. 5, 1707, CO 9/1.

64. Council Mins., July 28, 1731, CO 9/7, Aug. 21, 1707, CO 9/1.

65. Society of the Friends of English Harbour, *English Harbour: A Guide* (Barbados: Advocate Co., 1951); "Copy of Comrs. Trades Report to a Committee of Councill," Oct. 2, 1729, Legal Records, Masters Exhibits, C108/415; Hart to BT, May 20, 1726, CO 152/15, R166; papers in CO 152/17; Friends of English Harbour, *The Romance of English Harbour,* 5th ed. (Antigua, 1972); Luffman, *Antigua,* letter 7, Oct. 7, 1786.

66. Tullideph to Thomas, May 15, 1745, Tullideph Letter Book; CSP, 1734-35, 41, no. 314 ii, p. 210; "An Act for Granting the Work of a Number of Slaves to promote the Carrying on the Buildings and Enlarging the Wharff at English Harbour," Jan. 23, 1744, CO 8/9; Mins. of Council in Assembly, May 24, 1707, CO 9/1.

67. Plantation Accounts, 1756, Codrington Papers, D1610/A4.

68. Pares, *War and Trade,* p. 274. In 1749 Commodore Francis Holbourne wrote to the Sec. of the Admiralty from aboard the *Tavistock* about refitting work at English Harbour with references to slave labor: "The Hill Mr. Osborne began to level is not finished, and dare say it will be two Months before it is, 120 Negroes from the Island are now at work on it, and we only at the Expense of victualling them at two thirds Allowance from the Hulk; when that is finished am in hopes 20 or 30 of these Negroes will do all the Jobs we shall want here except their Lordships shall direct Stone Platforms to be layed at the Batteries which I shall give no Directions about till I have their Lordships Orders. I find by General Mathew they cheerfully lend us any Negroes we want for the Support of this Harbour." Holbourne to Sec. of the Admiralty, Apr. 21, 1749, Adm. 1/306, PRO. Three months later Holbourne reported that "the Work we were on there with the Country Negroes is finished and they all Discharged, so that we are now only at a small Expence." Holbourne to Sec. of the Admiralty, July 18, 1749, Adm. 1/306, PRO. Slaves were employed sometimes in careening ships: "I have been obliged to hire Negroes to heave down the Roebuck & Bonetta, the former I with great difficulty got to Sea on the 4th Inst. to join the Cambridge." Commodore John Moore to Sec. of the Admiralty, Nov. 13, 1758, Adm. 1/307.

69. On Antiguan residents' reliance on stored water, see Luffman, *Antigua,* letter 15, May 12, 1787; Janet Schaw, *Journal of a Lady of Quality; Being the Narrative of a Journey from Scotland to the West Indies, North Carolina, and Portugal, in the Years 1774 to 1776,* ed. Evangeline and Charles McLean Andrews (New Haven, Conn.: Yale University Press, 1921), pp. 84–85. *Slebech Papers,* 9402, National Library of Wales, "A Journey through the Caribbean in 1775," Clare Taylor ed. (1974), p. 11; "An Act for makeing, cleaning, and repairing common Ponds, and making and mending Bridges on the High Roads of this Island," June 28, 1702, CO 8/3.

70. Assembly Mins., Aug. 22, 1715, CO 9/4. This aspect of the cost of labor on ponds was never fully explained, but it might be suggested that prohibitive costs could sometimes have inhered from the grudging way in which slaves worked, so that jobs on which they were employed took longer to complete. There are other possibilities. During the period Jan. 1, 1726–Jan. 1, 1727 the government spent £1,623 16s. 9d. on ponds. Treasury Accounts, CO 152/18, T79.

71. See for example, "An Act for cleaning and amending the Highways in this Island, and to repeal an Act for cleaning and enlarging Common Paths and Highways within this Island," act no. 180, Aug. 11, 1724, *Laws of Antigua.*

72. Benjamin Quarles, "The Colonial Militia and Negro Manpower," *Mississippi Valley Historical Revue* 45, (March 1959):643–52; Cooper, *Plantation Slavery,* pp. 190–95; Wood, *Black Majority,* pp. 124–30; Jerome S. Handler, "Slaves, White Migration, and the Colonial Militia of Barbados," manuscript. On the role of the colonial militia see, for example, Brian Holden Reid, "A Survey of Militia in 18th Century America," *Army Quarterly and Defence Journal* 110 (Jan. 1980):48–55; John W. Shy, "A New Look at Colonial Militia," *WMQ,* 3d series 20 (Apr. 1963):175–85. Within Islam slaves were systematically obtained, trained, and used as professional soldiers. Daniel Pipes, *Slave Soldiers and Islam: The Genesis of a Military System* (New Haven, Conn.: Yale University Press, 1981).

73. Wood, *Black Majority,* pp. 124–25; Williams, *Capitalism and Slavery* (London: André Deutsch, 1964), p. 40. Mins. of Council in Assembly, July 31, 1731, CO 9/7.

74. CSP, 1734–35, 41, no. 314ii, pp. 216–18.

75. Ibid., p. 217; Pares, *War and Trade,* p. 255.

76. "An Act for regulating the Militia of this Island," act no. 131, June 28, 1702, clause 1, *Laws of Antigua.* In 1731, the Antigua council ordered 22 physicians who had not done militia duty for many years to begin to do so. These men included Drs. Crump, Williams, Cressy, Lavington, Tullideph, Husband, Young, Buckshorne, Sydserfe, Boyle, Carron, Michaelson, Mignan, Sheffield, Webb, Scott, Dunbar, Archbould, Boylstone, Chardovoine, Pringle, and Turnbull. Council Mins., Dec. 2, 1731, CO 9/7.

77. Council Mins., Aug. 10, 1704, CO 9/1.

78. Assembly Mins., July 31, 1739, CO 9/12. In the early 1740s the legislature made absentee sugar planters contribute toward the island's defense by increasing their taxes.

79. Ibid. He proposed to raise the fund from a tax of a shilling a head on all slaves except those of the poor for the first year, "and Six pence per head on them for a Second and Third Year, if the Warr last so long." Also, a fund was to be established for rewarding slaves doing meritorious service and for compensating owners whose slaves were lost or maimed.

80. Parke to Sec. of State, Sept. 9, 1710, CO 7/1; Plantation Accounts, June 13, 1739, Swete Papers, 388M/E4.

81. Act no. 78, Feb. 13, 1689, clause 3, *Laws of Antigua.* Codrington the younger may have been tempted to arm slaves in the Leewards in 1701, realizing that the French at Guadeloupe had "arms for three companys of lusty negroes, which they have listed and are disciplining." CSP, 1701, no. 401, p. 208.

82. Act. no. 131, June, 1702, clause 17, *Laws of Antigua.* "Jos. Jorye," agent for Nevis in 1701, reported that slaves so heavily outnumbered the small white population there that "in war time, for want of white men, the Government are inforced to make choice of companies of the best blacks to be in posture of defence, lined between two companies of white one black company, which they would never do, had they sufficient of white men for the defence of H. M. Island and their own security." CSP, 1701, no. 941, p. 574.

83. Act no. 131, June 28, 1702, clause 2, *Laws of Antigua.*

84. "An Act for the better Security of this Island in case the Same Should be attacked by the Enemy," Jan. 5, 1705, clause 2, CO 8/3. The act was to be in force for twelve months.

85. Ibid., clauses 3, 8, 5, 7, 9, respectively.

86. Assembly Mins., June 14, 1711, CO 9/2; Dunn, *Sugar and Slaves,* p. 144.

87. Assembly Mins., Oct. 15, 1740, CO 9/12; "A State of the Leeward Islands for their Defence," Oct. 16, 1742, enclosed in Mathew to BT, Oct. 17, 1742, CO 152/24, Y54; "An Act for the better Securing and Defending this Island in time of War and for Encouraging People of Low Fortunes and Indentured Servants to behave gallantly in the Defence of this Island and for Rewarding Slaves Signalizing themselves against the Enemy," June 6, 1743, CO 8/9; "An Act to Render the Rounds Necessary to be Observed during the Christmas Holydays & for the Night time during the present Warr with France more Numerous & to make the duty fall in an Equal manner upon all Persons," June 1, 1744, CO 8/9; Assembly Mins., Apr. 1, 6, 1745, CO 9/16.

291   Notes to Pages 122–23

88. A Supplementary Act to an Act entitled An Act for Regulating the Militia of this Island, and for altering and amending the same," Apr. 7, 1745, CO 8/9. The act was to be in force for only six months. In 1746, a similar act was passed to last two years "Or during the present War with France and Spain, if the same (or either of them) should Continue so long and not otherwise." See "A Supplementary Act to an Act for the Regulating the Militia of this Island and for altering and amending the Same," Mar. 27, 1746, CO 8/9.

89. "An Act Supplementary to an Act inituled, An Act for regulating the Militia of this Island and for altering and amending the same; and for making a proper provision for the said Militia in Time of War," act no. 208, July 5, 1756, clause 47, *Laws of Antigua*; Council Mins., Aug. 11, 1756, CO 9/21.

90. Assembly Mins., July 14, 1757, CO 9/22.

91. Appointed in Oct. 1758, Hopson commanded the land forces of the British expedition to the West Indies, while Moore, senior officer on the Leeward Islands station, was put in command of naval forces. See Marshall Smelser, *The Campaign for the Sugar Islands, 1759: A Study of Amphibious Warfare* (Chapel Hill: University of North Carolina Press, 1955), p. 19. This volume is a detailed study of the campaign against Guadeloupe and Martinique. See also Richard Pares, *War and Trade*, pp. 177–95, 252–57; Thomas Southey, *Chronological History of the West Indies*, 3 vols. (London: Frank Cass, 1968), 2:324–66; Alan Burns, *History of the British West Indies* (London: Allen & Unwin, 1954), pp. 480–500; Rupert Furneaux, *The Seven Years War* (London: Hart-Davis, MacGibbon, 1973), pp. 105–10.

92. Council Mins., Feb. 26, 1759, CO 9/23; Thomas to Pitt, Feb. 28, 1759, CO 152/46; Council Mins., Mar. 2, 5, 1759, CO 9/23; Barrington to Pitt, Mar. 2, 1759, Gertrude Selwyn Kimball, ed., *Correspondence of William Pitt*, 2 vols. (New York: Macmillan, 1906), 1:50.

93. Thomas to Pitt, Mar. 19, 1759, CO 152/46. Barrington had succeeded Hopson, who died of fever on Feb. 27, 1759, as commander. Marshall Smelser, *Campaign for the Sugar Islands*, p. 102.

94. Thomas to Pitt, Apr. 21, 1759, CO 152/46; Council Mins., Mar. 21, 1759, CO 9/23. In regard to the assembly's earlier proposal to send a reinforcement of whites to Guadeloupe, the council replied that it would be "inconsistent with our present or future safety to lessen or divide our small force especially as so many of our White Men are already engaged on board our Privateers." Council Mins., Mar. 1, 1759, CO 9/24. Under the circumstances the council preferred to send black recruits, "Though we are not without apprehensions, that the report which prevails here, of the desertion of some of the Barbadoes Negroes to the enemy, for want of a due allowance of provisions may be a great discouragement to the owners of Negroes unless an especial compulsive law be immediately past, to ascertain the number in an equitable proportion." Assembly Mins., Mar. 1, 1759, CO 9/24. By Apr. 27, Thomas had raised eight companies of white and black volunteers from Antigua, St. Christopher, Nevis, and Montserrat, amounting to 800 men. Thomas to Pitt, Apr. 27, 1759, CO 152/46. One Antiguan, Col. Crump, performed outstandingly in Guadeloupe and was left in command in June after Barrington left for England. Southey, *Chronological History*, 2:327–37; Oliver, *History of Antigua*, 1:118.

95. To many who must have had no property worth protecting on shore,

privateering proved attractive because privateers kept any plunder taken from the enemy. Against Guadeloupe they apparently did signal service, Gov. Thomas noting that they "brought much greater Terror & Distress upon the Enemy by Landing upon the Sea Coast, and by plundering, & laying waste their plantations than if they had acted altogether on shore." Thomas to Pitt, Feb. 28, 1759, CO 152/46.

96. Thomas to Pitt, Apr. 21, 1759, CO 152/46; Thomas to BT, July 13, 1759, CO 152/29, Cc 43; Council Mins., Feb. 26, 1759, CO 9/23.

97. Assembly Mins., Oct. 29, 1761, CO 9/25; "An Act for raising a Number of able Bodied Slaves to serve as Pioneers against the Island of Martinico or such other Islands in these Seas as shall be attacked by His Majesty's Forces," Nov. 24, 1761, CO 8/13; "An Act for raising a Number of able Bodied Slaves to serve as Labourers and Pioneers upon an intended Expedition under the Command of the Right Honourable The Earl of Albermarle," May 14, 1762, CO 8/3. For preparations in 1761 see Assembly Mins., Oct. 29, 1761, CO 9/25.

98. For preparations in 1762 see Assembly Mins., Jan. 14, May 3, 1762, CO 9/25. A few of the Codrington slaves did service in 1762. "I advised you in mine of January 5th," Samuel Redhead wrote home, "that Negroes were to be raised in the Islands for the expedition under my Lord Albermarle and that your proportion would be seven, which I have sent, and as we had it in our option either to be paid for them or receive hire, almost every one had agreed to the former, I have therefore received General Monckton's bill for the payment of yours— amounting to 440£ Sterling the sum they were appraised at. I chose to sell them as I think they could not be worth so much on your Estates, tho' they are very proper people for the service they are gone on." Redhead to Codrington, June 1, 1762, Codrington Correspondence on microfilm, MF 375, Codrington Papers.

99. Council Mins., Apr. 15, 1762; see Assembly Mins., Jan. 14, May 3, 1762, CO 9/25.

100. Instructions, June 27, 1715, Codrington Papers, D1610/C2. On chegoes see Dr. Collins, *Practical Rules for the Management and Medical Treatment of Negro Slaves, in the Sugar Colonies,* (1811; reprint, New York: Books for Libraries Press, 1971), pp. 345-48.

101. Instructions, June 17, 1715, Codrington Papers, D1610/C2; Tullideph to Thomas, Apr. 3, 1749, Tullideph Letter Book, MS; Tullideph to Russell, Nov. 1758, ibid.

102. Farley to Tudway, July 23, 1758, Tudway Papers, DD/TD, box k5.

103. Instructions, Dec. 21, 1716, ibid., box 16.

104. Pares, *Merchants and Planters,* p. 43; Johnston, "The Stapleton Sugar Plantations," pp. 191-92; Schwartz, "Patterns of Slaveholding," pp. 84-86.

105. Sidney W. Mintz and Richard Price, eds., *An Anthropological Approach to the Afro-American Past: A Caribbean Perspective* (Philadelphia: Institute for the Study of Human Issues, 1976), pp. 14, 20.

106. Ibid. This study by Mintz and Price is an important starting point for rethinking the processes behind the development of society in relation to slavery in the Americas. The idea of "moral economy" as used by scholars owes much to E. P. Thompson's work. See, for example, his *Making of the English Working Class* and "The Moral Economy of the English Crowd in the Eighteenth Century," *Past*

and Present, no. 50 (Feb. 1971):76-136. See also James C. Scott, *The Moral Economy of the Peasant: Rebellion and Subsistence in South East Asia* (New Haven, Conn.: Yale University Press, 1976).

Chapter 6: For the Better Government of Slaves

1. G. Duncan Mitchell, ed., *A Dictionary of Sociology* (London: Routledge & Kegan Paul, 1968), pp. 167-68; George A. Theodorson and Achilles G. Theodorson, *A Modern Dictionary of Sociology* (New York: Barnes & Noble Books, 1969), pp. 386-87; Neil J. Smelser, *Theory of Collective Behaviour* (London: Routledge & Kegan Paul, 1962), pp. 157-68, 261-69, 306-10, 364-79; Joseph H. Fichter, *Sociology,* 2d ed. (Chicago: University of Chicago Press, 1971), pp. 404-28; T. B. Bottomore, *Sociology: A Guide to Problems and Literature,* rev. ed. (London: George Allen & Unwin, 1972), pp. 217-72; Gwendolyn Midlo Hall, *Social Control in Slave Plantation Societies: A Comparison of St. Domingue and Cuba* (Baltimore: Johns Hopkins Press, 1971); Edward Brathwaite, "Controlling the Slaves in Jamaica," paper presented at the Conference of Caribbean Historians, University of Guyana, Georgetown, Apr. 1971; Goveia, *Slave Society;* F.M.L. Thompson, "Social Control in Victorian Britain," *EHR,* 2d ser. 34 (May 1981):189-208.

2. Elsa V. Goveia, "The West Indian Slave Laws of the Eighteenth Century," *Revista De Ciencias Sociales* 4 (Mar. 1960):75-105; Mintz and Price, *Afro-American Past,* pp. 12-21; Orlando Patterson, "Toward a Future That Has No Past — Reflections on the Fate of Blacks in the Americas," *Public Interest,* Spring 1972, pp. 42-44; Faust, "Culture, Conflict, and Community."

3. Genovese, *Roll, Jordan, Roll,* pp. 3-7, 89-93; E. P. Thompson, "Patrician Society, Plebeian Culture," *JSocH* 7 (Summer 1974):382-405; Samuel Martin, "Essay upon Plantership," p. 242; Drew Gilpin Faust, *James Henry Hammond and the Old South: A Design for Mastery* (Baton Rouge: Louisiana State University Press, 1982), pp. 69-104.

4. Genovese, *Roll, Jordan, Roll,* pp. 3-7, 89-93; E. P. Thompson, "Moral Economy of the English Crowd," pp. 94-96. "Paternalism in any historical setting defines relations of superordination and subordination," argues Genovese. "Its strength as a prevailing ethos increases as the members of the community accept — or feel compelled to accept — these relations as legitimate. Brutality lies inherent in this acceptance of patronage and dependence, no matter how organic the paternalistic order." Genovese's sensitive applications of "paternalism" to unravel the complex nature of slavery and master-slave relations seems more rewarding than C.L.R. James's reliance on masters' use of naked terror in the French colony of St. Domingue. "To cow them into the necessary docility and acceptance necessitated a regime of calculated brutality and terrorism," writes James, "and it is this that explains the unusual spectacle of property — owners apparently careless to preserving their property: they had first to ensure their own safety." James, *The Black Jacobins: Toussaint L'Ouverture and the San Domingo Revolution* (New York: Vintage, 1963), p. 12. The origins, meaning, and role of violence against slaves are more central to James's interpretation of slave resistance and social control than to Genovese's.

5. Equiano, *Life,* pp. 53-57. For useful discussions of slave naming, see Genovese, *Roll, Jordan, Roll,* pp. 443-50; Henning Cohen, "Slave Names in Colonial South Carolina," *American Speech* 28 (May 1952):102-7; Newbell Niles Puckett, "Names of American Negro Slaves," in *Studies in the Science of Society Presented to Albert Galloway Keller,* ed. George Peter Murdock (New Haven, Conn.: Yale University Press, 1937), pp. 471-94; John C. Inscoe, "Carolina Slave Names: An Index to Acculturation," *JSH* 49 (Nov. 1983):527-54.

6. Robertson, *Letter,* p. 94; General Report; Council Mins., June 1, 1738, CO 9/13; Ligon, *History of Barbados,* p. 46. See above, chap. 2.

7. Dunn, *Sugar and Slaves,* pp. 237-38; Correspondence with the bishop of London, from Rev. Simon Smith, undated, fol. 119; from Rev. Henry Pope, May 25, 1724, fol. 118; from Rev. James Knox, Apr. 18, 1732, fol. 213; Fulham Papers, 19. For a guide to the Fulham Papers, see William Wilson Manross, *The Fulham Papers in the Lambeth Palace Library* (Oxford: Clarendon Press, 1965).

8. CSP, 1699, no. 458-458 ii, pp. 252-53, no. 766, pp. 422-24.

9. Francis Le Jau, "Some Matters Relating to the Condition of the Clergy Employ'd in the Leeward Islands," Papers of the Society for the Propagation of the Gospel, 17, West Indian section, fols. 291-92, Lambeth Palace Library; Byam to Bishop of London, June 16, 1744, Fulham Papers, 19, no. 275. In the history of the colonies Le Jau is chiefly noted for his work in, and writing about South Carolina. See, for example, Frank J. Klingberg, ed., *The Carolina Chronicle of Dr. Francis Le Jau 1706-1717,* University of California Publications in History, vol. 53 (Berkeley: University of California Press, 1956).

10. Genovese, *Roll, Jordan, Roll,* pp. 25-49; Goveia, "West Indian Slave Laws," pp. 75-105; Howard A. Fergus, "The Early Laws of Montserrat (1668-1680): The Legal Schema of a Slave Society," *CQ* 24 (March-June 1978):34-43; Goveia, "West Indian Slave Laws," pp. 75, 86. On the problem of the property-person contradiction in the law of slave societies in the Americas, see especially David Brion Davis, *The Problem of Slavery in Western Culture* (New York: Cornell University Press, 1966), pp. 244-61; Mintz and Price, *Afro-American Past,* pp. 12-19; M. I. Finely, *Ancient Slavery and Modern Ideology* (New York: Penguin, 1983), pp. 73-75, 96-99. Kenneth M. Stampp, *The Peculiar Institution: Slavery in the Ante-Bellum South* (New York: Vintage, 1956), pp. 141-91; Collins, *Practical Rules,* pp. 169-70; Edwards, *West Indies,* 1:13.

11. Jordan, *White Over Black,* pp. 587-88; William Wiecek, "The Statutory Law of Slavery and Race in the Thirteen Mainland Colonies of British America," *WMQ,* 3d ser. 24 (Apr. 1977):280; Goveia, "West Indian Slave Laws," pp. 81-87; Wiecek, "Statutory Law of Slavery and Race," pp. 269-74.

12. Philip J. Schwartz, "The Adaptation of Afro-American Slaves to the Anglo-American Judiciary," pp. 19-20, paper presented at the 41st conference of the Institute of Early American History and Culture at Millersville State College, Millersville, Penn., Apr. 30, 1981. Slave responses to slavery and punishment would obviously be affected in some degree by their sense of justice, African-derived or colonial. "In Africa," argues R.A.J. Van Lier, "slavery was an established institution, so that the slave accepted his state of submission to the white master in accordance with African convention." R.A.J. Van Lier, *Frontier Society: A Social Analysis of the History of Surinam* (The Hague: Martinus Nijhoff, 1971), pp. 142-43.

13. "An Act for the better Government of Slaves," Dec. 16, 1697, CO 8/3; "An Act for the Governing of Negroes," Act no. 329, Aug. 8, 1688, *Acts of Assembly Passed in the Island of Barbadoes, From 1648, to 1718* (London, 1721), pp. 137–44. The South Carolina slave code of 1696 copied almost verbatim the preamble of the Barbados code justifying the need for special laws. The act stated that slaves being "of barbarous, wild, savage natures, and such as renders them wholly unqualified to be governed by the laws, customs, and practices of this Province," it was necessary "to restrain the disorders, rapines, and inhumanity to which they are naturally prone and inclined." Quoted in Wiecek, "Statutory Law of Slavery and Race," p. 270. Samuel Baldwin, writing to the Board of Trade in 1680, noted that he had examined Barbados laws for 1660–72 and found them "good, though not always consonant with the laws of England, as, for instance that negro slaves are to be tried for capital offences not by a jury but summarily before two justices of peace, and that negroes are punishable more severely than others for like offences. Yet I consider the laws concerning negroes to be reasonable, for by reason of their numbers they become dangerous, being a brutish sort of people and reckoned as goods and chattels in the Island." CSP, 1677–80, no. 1,391, p. 551. The Barbados slave code of 1688, however, still adhering to the principle that slaves "being brutish . . . deserve not, for the Baseness of their Condition, to be tried by the legal Tryal of Twelve Men of their Peers or Neighbourhood" as subjects of the crown, ruled that trial should be by two justices and three jurors or "able, good, and legal Free-holders of the Place nearest where the said Crimes were committed." "An Act for Governing of Negroes," Act no. 329 of 1688, *Acts Passed in Barbadoes*.

14. While the Barbados legislature seemed aware of the relationship between slave rebelliousness and standards of maintenance, the Antigua legislature, if also aware, did not enact legislation or show concern, as had the Nevis legislature. The Nevis assembly observed in 1688 "that the Occasion of many persons going off the island is the great Thefts and Insolencies of Negroes and do Desier that a very Seveire Act may bee made against it and that it may have Respect to the Act for Planting Provisions in all Plantations the want of which is the fundamental Cause." Council Mins., July 7, 1688, CO 155/1. The legislature finally passed an "Act for Planting Provision According to the Proportion of Negroes," Sept. 1, 1688. Council Mins., Aug. 22, Sept. 1, 1688, CO 155/1. An earlier act "for planting Provisions in all Plantations" had been passed in 1682. See "Act for Planting Provision Proportionable to Negroes," Apr. 8, 1682, CO 154/2. Montserrat followed Nevis with an act in 1693 to curb slave theft, one clause of which provided "that one acre of provisions should be cultivated for every eight slaves belonging to a plantation." Goveia, "West Indian Slave Laws," p. 87, citing "An Act to restrain the Insolence of Slaves, and for preventing them from committing any Outrages, as also the better ordering such Slaves, & c.," Act no. 36 of 1693, *Montserrat Code of Laws*.

15. "An Act for reinforcing Severall Acts vizt. An Act for the Better Government of Slaves and An Act for regulating the townes and harbours and Settling of Marketts in this Island, the first Dated the Sixteenth Day of December 1697, And the other Dated the Twenty Second Day of Aprill in the said Yeare abovementioned," Mar. 22, 1700, CO 8/3. For later codes see "An Act for the better Government of Slaves, and Free Negroes," Act no. 130 (hereafter Act no. 130 of 1702), June 28, 1702; "An Act for attainting several slaves now run away from their

Master's Service, and for the better Government of Slaves," Act no. 176 (hereafter Act no. 176 of 1723), Dec. 9, 1723, *Laws of Antigua.*

16. Act no. 130 of 1702, clause 6; Act no. 176 of 1723, clause 18; Neville Hall, "Slave Laws of the Danish Virgin Islands in the Later Eighteenth Century," in Rubin and Tuden, *Comparative Perspectives on Slavery,* p. 174.

17. Act no. 130 of 1702, clauses 1, 20; Assembly Mins., Aug. 9, 1715, CO 9/4; Act no. 144, Sept. 2, 1714, *Laws of Antigua.*

18. "An Act to repeal a certain Act of this Island concerning Negroes," Act no. 174, Feb. 1, 1722, *Laws of Antigua;* Act no. 176 of 1723, clauses 30, 29.

19. Assembly Mins., June 25, 1740, CO 9/12; Act no. 176 of 1723, clause 31. Attempts to enforce these provisions had clearly broken down by 1788, when Luffman observed that "The principal dancing time is on Sunday afternoons when the great market is over. . . in fact Sunday is their day of trade, their day of relaxation, their day of pleasure, and may, in the strictest sense of the words, be called the negroes holiday." Luffman, *Antigua,* letter 30, Mar. 14, 1788.

20. Act no. 130 of 1702, clause 6; Hall, "Slave Laws of the Danish Virgin Islands," p. 179; Act. no. 176 of 1723, clauses 35–36.

21. Council Mins., Feb. 14, 1687, CO 155/1; Act no. 176 of 1723, clause 15; Molefi Kete Asante and Michael Appiah, "The Rhetoric of the Akan Drum," *Western Journal of Black Studies* 3 (Spring 1979):8–13; J. F. Nketia, *Drumming in Akan Communities of Ghana* (London: Thomas Nelson, 1963).

22. Act no. 176 of 1723, clauses 32–33; Schaw, *Journal,* p. 108.

23. Robert Dirks, "Slaves' Holiday," *Natural History,* 84 (Dec. 1975):82; Dirks, "Resource Fluctuations and Competitive Transformations in West Indian Slave Societies," pp. 160–66. In the sugar islands at Christmastime, writes Dirks, "Slaves feasted one another and numerous ritual performances were held, including various ancestral rites and the John Canoe dance." This dance was particularly prominent in Jamaica. For a discussion that portrays it as "playful ritual" and "ritualized aggression," see Dirks, "The Evolution of a Playful Ritual: The Garifuna's John Canoe in Comparative Perspective" in *Forms of Play of Native North Americans,* ed. E. Norbeck and C. R. Farrer (St. Paul, Minn.: West Publishing Co., 1979), pp. 89–109. See also Richardson Wright, *Revels in Jamaica 1682–1838* (New York: Dodd, Mead, 1939), pp. 238–47.

24. Plantation Accounts, Sept. 10, 1738–Aug. 13, 1739, Aug. 10, 1741–Aug. 10, 1742, Swete Papers, 388M/E4, 269 M/F10; Phillips, "An Antigua Plantation," p. 445; Stalker to Stapleton, May 15, 1732, Gay, "Letters from a Sugar Plantation in Nevis," p. 172.

25. Luffman, *Antigua,* letter 26, Jan. 1, 1788; Dirks, "Slaves' Holiday"; Dirks, "Resource Fluctuations," pp. 160–66.

26. Ibid., pp. 137–53, 163–64; "Slaves' Holiday," pp. 86–87.

27. Tullideph to Thomas, Apr. 10, 1742; letter of May 30, 1752, Sheridan, "Letters from a Sugar Plantation," pp. 7, 22; Oliver to Hester Swete, Antigua, Oct. 10, 1742, Swete Papers, 388M/E8; Herbert to Stapleton, Oct. 18, 1725, Gay, "Letters from a Sugar Plantation in Nevis," p. 155; see also letters on pp. 155–58; Hart to BT, May 20, 1726, CO 152/15, R166, Aug. 1726, CO 152/15, R174, Feb. 15, 1727, CO 152/15, R188. Rev. William Smith visited Antigua from Nevis in 1720 or 1721 during what he described as "a time of great drowth," when "the whole

face of the Country looked dismally enough. All their Ponds were then quite dry, and their Cisterns almost empty; so that they were obliged to fetch their fresh Water from Guardeloupe, a French Island, and Montserrat, an English one, which was afterwards sold for Eighteen Pence a Pail-full." Smith, *Natural History of Nevis,* letter 11, p. 305. Drought contributed to great distress and heavy mortality among slaves in the Leeward Islands during the American Revolutionary period, when food supplies from the mainland, on which the islands depended, were cut off. R. B. Sheridan, "The Crisis of Slave Subsistence in the British West Indies during and after the American Revolution," *WMQ,* 3d ser. 33 (Oct. 1976):622–25.

28. Dirks, "Resource Fluctuations," pp. 137–53; Gerald T. Keusch, "Malnutrition and Infection: Deadly Allies," *Natural History* 84 (Nov. 1975):27–34; Herbert to Stapleton, Dec. 20, 1728; Stalker to Stapleton, May 15, 1732, Gay, "Letters from a Sugar Plantation," pp. 160, 172; Johnston, "The Stapleton Sugar Plantations," p. 199.

29. Dirks, "Resource Fluctuations," pp. 141–43, 163–64; Dirks, "Slaves' Holiday," pp. 86–87; Dirks, "Relief Induced Agonism," *Disasters* 3 (1979):195–98; Dirks "Social Responses during Severe Food Shortages and Famine," *Current Anthropology* 21 (Feb. 1980):21–32.

30. Robertson, *A Detection,* p. 49; Harris, *Plants, Animals, and Man,* p. 9.

31. John Singleton, *A General Description of the West-Indian Islands, as far as relates to the British, Dutch, and Danish Governments From Barbados to Saint Croix. Attempted in Blank Verse* (Barbados, 1767), p. 52. During the long drought of the 1720s, the Antigua legislature passed an order "That Fryday next the first of October [1725] be observed as a Solemn day of Fast and Humiliation to avert Gods Judgement now impending from the present Drought and to implore his mercy. And that the Secretary give notice thereof to the Severall Ministers of this Island and recommend to them to prepare Sermons Suitable to the Occasion." Mins. of Council in Assembly, Sept. 25, 1725, CO 9/5. Similar orders were issued in Mar. 1726, and, when some rain fell, a day of thanksgiving was appointed in May. Mins. of Council in Assembly, Mar. 11, May 23, 1726, CO 9/6. The islanders were no doubt familiar with fast sermons common in other colonies and the mother country, where "great occasions had always called them forth. There had been a general fast on the approach of the Armada in 1588, a weekly fast in 1603 until the plague was over, and another general fast for the great plague of 1625." H. R. Trevor-Roper, "The Fast Sermons of the Long Parliament," in *Essays in British History Presented to Sir Keith Feiling,* ed. H. R. Trevor-Roper (London: Macmillan, 1964), p. 86. While homeland tradition influenced island practice, Antigua's susceptibility to disasters, man-made and natural, was early recognized in the establishment in 1678 of June 10 to be "annually kept as a fast and day of humiliation that it may please God to avert" disasters. CSP, 1677–80, no. 823, p. 303. "But after all," wrote Rev. William Smith in 1745 about the Leeward Islands, "let me tell you, we must not look for Paradise, either in the East or West Indies (as I said before), on account of Earthquakes, excessive Heat, Muskitoes, Hurricanes, & c. We have annually three publick Fasts, viz in the first Weeks of July, August, and September; to implore God's mercy in averting his Judgement of a Hurricane from us; and if He is so gracious as to Hearken to our Petitions, we have in October a publick Feast or Thanksgiving for it." Smith, *Natural History of Nevis,* letter 9, pp. 243–44.

32. Schaw, *Journal,* p. 109.

33. "An Act for regulating the Militia of this Island," Act no. 131, June 28, 1702, clause 14, *Laws of Antigua*; Act no. 176 of 1723, clause 33; "An Act declaring the Severall Articles Martiall Law shall Consist off," June 28, 1702, CO 8/3. Militia regulations were updated by "An Act to alter and amend the thirty second and thirty third Clauses of an Act of this Island, intituled, An Act for attainting Several Slaves now run away from their Masters' Service, and for the better Government of Slaves; and for regulating the Duty of the Militia during the Christmas Holidays," Act no. 390, Nov. 30, 1778, clauses 2–4, *Laws of Antigua.* For the 1712 Christmas order see Mins. of Council in Assembly, Dec. 18, 1712, CO 9/2. Law enforcement at Christmas was not always tight all around. In 1756 the assembly told the governor and council concernedly that "The Irregularity of the Patroles in their Rounds at Christmas is so contrary to all the Rules of Good Discipline, that We cannot forbear Representing it to your Board and desiring your Concurrence in Application to the General, that he will order the Colonels of each Corps to issue particular Orders to the Commanding Officer of each Division to see the several Patroles within his Command well armed and kept under the strictest Regularity and good Discipline and to be punctual in making Returns to the Colonel of each Corps of all Delinquents, that they may be fined or punished otherwise by Courts Martial according to Law." For this part, the governor expressed concern "that he should be put under a necessity of giving Orders to the Colonels of the several Militia Regiments to do, what they must know to be their Duty, without any Special Order from him." Council Mins., Dec. 8, 1756, CO 9/21.

34. Assembly Mins., Dec. 9, 1740, CO 9/12; "An Act to Render the Rounds Necessary to be Observed during the Christmas Holydays & for the Night time during the present Warr with France more numerous & to make the duty fall in an Equal manner upon all Persons," June 1, 1744, CO 8/9.

35. Act no. 176 of 1723, clause 32. This law, like so many others, was evidently not strictly enforced, and had to be reinforced in 1778, when granting slave holidays was described as "absolutely necessary and proper." The holidays were now to extend from sunset on Christmas Eve to sunrise on Dec. 28, "Provided always, that the Slaves employed by their owners, Renters, or Possessors, about their Houses or Persons, shall not be allowed the Holidays. . .without the Consent and Permission of their said Owners, Renters, or Possessors, nor shall such Slaves be deemed, or taken to be within the Meaning of Intention of this Act." See "An Act to alter and amend the thirty-second and thirty-third Clauses of an Act of this Island, intituled, An Act for attainting several Slaves now run-away from their Master's Service, and for the better Government of Slaves; and for regulating the Duty of the Militia during the Christmas Holidays," Act no. 390, Nov. 30, 1778, clause 1, *Laws of Antigua.*

36. Goveia, *Slave Society,* pp. 173–74; Schaw, *Journal,* pp. 108–9.

37. Luffman, *Antigua,* letter 25, Dec. 8, 1787.

38. Vestry Mins., St. John's Parish, Jan. 29, 1757, in Oliver, *History of Antigua,* 3:358; Assembly Mins., Jan. 27, 1747, CO 9/17. Maj. George Lucas described the "Negro" burial ground as a "Morass or Swamp and in Rainy Weather Scarce passable, filled with the Graves of Dead Negroes and others." "The Memorial of

Majr. George Lucas Commanding Officer of the Hon'ble Lieut. Genl. Dalziels Regiment of Foot now Quartered in the Leeward Islands," Assembly Mins., June 17, 1740, CO 9/12.

39. Smith, *Natural History of Nevis,* letter 9, p. 231; "An Act for the further Prevention of Damages to the Harbours, and Abuses in carrying on the Inland Trade of this Island; regulating the Hire and Manumission of slaves; and for advertizing Run-aways committed to Gaol," Act no. 212, Nov. 25, 1757, clause 12, *Laws of Antigua;* Goveia, *Slave Society,* p. 167.

40. "An Act for the better Government of Slaves," clause 4, Dec. 16, 1697, CO 8/3; Act no. 130 of 1702, clause 4.

41. Luffman, *Antigua,* letter 31, Mar. 28, 1788; Assembly Mins., June 25, 1740, CO 9/12.

42. In this way, slaves played a key role in the internal economy and marketing system of the island. Schaw, *Journal,* p. 88; Sidney W. Mintz, "Caribbean Marketplaces and Caribbean History," *Nova Americana* 1 (1979):333–34. For the implications of similar developments in Jamaica, see Sidney W. Mintz and Douglas Hall, *The Origins of the Jamaican Internal Marketing System,* Yale University Publications in Anthropology, 57 (New Haven, Conn.: Yale University, Department of Anthropology, 1960), pp. 3–26; Mintz, "The Jamaican Internal Marketing Pattern: Some Notes and Hypotheses," *SES* 4 (Mar. 1955):95–103.

43. Luffman, *Antigua,* letter 16, June 1, 1787.

44. Sidney W. Mintz, *Caribbean Transformations* (Chicago: Aldine Publishing Co., 1974), p. 76; Mintz, "Caribbean Marketplaces"; Hall, *Social Control,* pp. 66–68; Dale Wayne Tomich, "Prelude to Emancipation: Sugar and Slavery in Martinique, 1830-1848," Ph.D. thesis, University of Wisconsin, Madison, 1976, pp. 201–27.

45. Vere Langford Oliver, ed., *Caribbeana: Being Miscellaneous Papers Relating to the History, Geneology, Topography and Antiquities of the British West Indies,* 6 vols. (London: Mitchell Hughes & Clarke, 1910-21), vol. 1, print facing p. 313 (see frontispiece).

46. Luffman, *Antigua,* letter 31, Mar. 28, 1788. In addition to staging open-air dances, Luffman noted, the slaves also played "at dice (as they call it) with small shells," after the market, "and frequently lose, not only every dog that they have been working for through the day, but so great is their love of play, that the very trifling clothes from their backs is a forfeit to their mischance. It is not uncommon for them, when intoxicated, to turn out to fight in Otto's pasture (adjoining the market; they are not confined to rules, like the gentleman brutes with you," said Luffman describing slave fights, "but give their blows — how, and where they can, generally open handed, and it is all fair to pull others wool [hair?], kneel upon, beat when down, or indeed whatever they have power to do, to the hurt of their adversary." Ibid. On the Sunday market in Nevis, Rev. William Smith recorded, "At Charles Town, our Metropolis, we hold a Market every Sunday Morning which begins a Sun-rising, and ends about nine o'clock, whither the Negroes bring Fowls, Indian Corn, Yams, Garden-stuff of all sorts, & c." Smith, *Natural History of Nevis,* letter 9, pp. 231–32. When authorities abolished the Sunday market in 1831, slave disturbances erupted in Antigua. For the official papers on these see CO 7/31.

47. Act no. 130 of 1702, clause 5; Assembly Mins., Sept. 17, 1712, CO 9/2.

48. Act no. 176 of 1723, clauses 34, 19–23.

49. Council Mins., Nov. 29, 1733, CO 9/7.

50. Goveia, *Slave Society*, p. 161; Act no. 212, Nov. 25, 1757, clauses 6–8, *Laws of Antigua.*

51. Thompson, "Patrician Society, Plebian Culture," pp. 387–90; William M. Wiecek, "The Statutory Law of Slavery and Race," p. 276.

52. Act no. 130 of 1702, clause 12; Act no. 176 of 1723, clause 11. Slaves were later (1784) allowed trial by two justices and a jury of six reputable whites. According to Goveia, this new procedure, while arguably humanitarian in certain respects, was far more significant for adding solemnity to slave trials "through the association of a larger number of persons in the judicial process." The 1784 act was later replaced by another of same title of 1798. See "An Act for Settling and Regulating the Trial of Criminal Slaves by Jury," Act. no. 424 of 1784, Act no. 527 of 1798, *Laws of Antigua*; Goveia, *Slave Society,* pp. 168–69.

Chapter 7: Regulating Runaways and Freedmen

1. Act no. 130 of 1702, clauses 10, 2.

2. Act no. 176 of 1723, clauses 24–27; Act no. 130 of 1702, clauses 3, 11.

3. Act no. 130 of 1702, clause 19; Marvin L. Michael Kay and Lorin Lee Cary, " 'The Planters Suffer Little Or Nothing:' North Carolina Compensations For Executed Slaves, 1748-1772," *Science and Society* 40 (Fall 1976):288–306; Ulrich B. Phillips, "Slave Crime in Virginia," *AHR* 20 (Jan. 1915):336–40; Wood, *Black Majority,* pp. 279–81; Robert William Fogel and Stanley L. Engerman, *Time on the Cross: The Economics of American Negro Slavery* (Boston: Little, Brown, 1974), p. 147; "An Act concerning the Payment, out of the Publick Treasury, for Slaves executed and to be executed in this Island for Treasons, Murders, or other felonies," Act no. 186, Aug. 31, 1730, preamble, *Laws of Antigua;* see also Act no. 176 of 1723, clauses 13–14.

4. Act no. 130 of 1702, clause 17; Act no. 176 of 1723, clause 9. In 1722 some members had raised the point in the legislature about "reducing our Debts" with particular reference to fugitive compensation, without apparently much effect. See, for example, Assembly Mins., Jan. 29, 1722, CO 9/5.

5. These petitions can be found in the minutes of the legislature, CO 9/5, CO 155/6. Compensation ordered paid in 1723 was £36 15s. at least, where executed slaves were specifically stated to have run away. Compensation for seven other slaves who were executed for crimes unspecified amounted to £400. Among these could have been some runaways. For 1724, compensation for fugitives was at least £140; in this case too there could have been fugitives among four other slaves executed for unspecified crimes. For 1725, before the new compensation act came into effect Aug. 9, at least £920 was ordered paid out for executed fugitives; five slaves valued together at £260 were also executed for unstated crimes. See also "An Act for explaining a certain Act of this Island, past the ninth Day of December, one thousand seven hundred twenty and three, intituled, An Act for attainting several Slaves now runaway from their Master's Service, and for the better Government of Slaves," Act no. 183, Aug. 9, 1725, *Laws of Antigua.* In a letter to the Board of Trade, Gov. Hart explained that "The intention of this Act is only to ascertain the price of Slaves that shall be Condemned, which is a certain'd at

Thirty-five Pounds for a Man, and Thirty Pounds for a Woman Slave, There having been a very ill use made of the liberty given to the Appraisers in the former Act." Hart to BT, May 20, 1726, CO 152/15, R166.

6. Act no. 182, Aug. 9, 1725, clause 3, *Laws of Antigua.* The law appears to have been interpreted as inapplicable to fugitives hunted down and killed. See the case in 1736 when William Denbow claimed £70 for his slave, French Will, killed in the hills. The council was willing to pay only £35, but the assembly argued that Denbow was entitled to full compensation "for that he Doth not come within the Limittation mentioned in the Act . . . the slave never having been tryed and Condemned and So his Death not by Choice of the Master." Council Mins., July 5, 1736, CO 9/9; Assembly Mins., July 5, July 29, Aug. 3, 1736, CO 9/12.

7. Act no. 176 of 1723, clause 6: "And whereas Negroes sometimes upon slight or no Occasions run away and absent themselves in Gangs from the Service of their Masters, Mistresses, or Renters, to the ruining and impoverishing of them, and to the Terror and Danger of His Majesty's good Subjects, Inhabitants of this Island; be it therefore enacted, and it is hereby enacted by the Authority aforesaid, That if any Negroes, being of the Age of sixteen Years, and upwards, shall hereafter absent or run away in any Number or Gang, amounting to ten in Number, or upwards, from any one Plantation to which such Slaves shall belong, and shall continue runaway or absent from their Service, as aforesaid, for ten Days or more, then one of the said Negroes, such as the [Justices] shall think the greatest Offender, shall suffer Death as a Felon."

8. Act no. 130 of 1702, clauses 7, 9; Act no. 212, Nov. 25, 1757, clause 11, *Laws of Antigua.*

9. Act no. 130 of 1702, clause 8; Jordan, *White Over Black,* pp. 108-9; Van Lier, *Frontier Society,* p. 23.

10. "And whereas the said Clause in the said Act by Experience is sometimes found too severe, by reason of new ignorant Slaves; be it therefore enacted by the Authority aforesaid, That the said Clause is replaced, made null, and void." Act no. 130 of 1702, clause 15, The former act was passed in Antigua in 1680 and confirmed by the crown in 1681. See below, chap. 8, n. 13.

11. CSP, 1685-88, no. 1630, p. 496; Act no. 130 of 1702, clause 16.

12. Act no. 176 of 1723, clause 1. Meaning the "Negro Act" to produce good results, the assembly later expressed concern that it had not been "read in several Churches." The assembly therefore asked the governor, "that Copys may be given to each Minister of a Parish, and that his Excellency will order it to be read-in their Churches, And that one Acting JP in each Division may be furnished with a Copy and the Publick pay for the Copys." Mins. of Council in Assembly, Jan. 23, 1724, CO 9/5. For some deliberations concerning the act see Assembly Mins., Oct. 18, 1723, CO 9/5; Mins. of Council in Assembly, Nov. 15, Dec. 2, 1723, CO 9/5.

13. Mins. of Council in Assembly, Nov. 15, 1723, Assembly Mins., Oct. 18, 1723, CO 9/5; CO 9/5; Act no. 176 of 1723, clause 1.

14. Act no. 176 of 1723, clauses 2-6. Touching on the neglect of commissions of the peace in an address to the legislature in January 1724, the governor observed that, while there were many justices, he found "few Magistrates who Act as such, by which means the penal Laws are neglected. This Evil calls for remedy," added

the governor, seeking the legislature's advice. The assembly remarked on the correctness of the governor's observations and concluded that perhaps the trouble lay with the appointment of such a large number of justices. As a remedy the house recommended "a Law Imposing a Penalty upon such, who refuse acting after being sworn & thatt those who refuse to accept the Commission be immediately struck outt." The governor agreed. Mins. of Council in Assembly, Jan. 23, 1724; Assembly Mins., Feb. 1724, CO 9/5.

15. Act no. 176 of 1723, clauses 8, 17. These are my interpretations of the clauses.

16. Ibid., clauses 10, 12, 16, 28.

17. Mins. of Council in Assembly, Nov. 27, 1724, CO 9/5.

18. Mins. of Council in Assembly, Mar. 17, Dec. 11, 13, 1727, Mar. 15, 1728, CO 9/6.

19. Mins. of Council in Assembly, Mar. 17, 1727, CO 9/6; Council Mins., Dec. 17, 1731, CO 9/7.

20. "An Act for publique recompense to the Masters of Slaves putt to death by Law," Oct. 28, 1669, CO 154/2; "An Act for repealing an Act, intituled, An Act for Publick Recompence to Masters of Slaves put to death by Law," May 24, 1682, CO 154/3; Act no. 186, Aug. 31, 1730, Laws of Antigua. For island expenditures on compensation for slaves, see treasurer's accounts for 1727, 1728, 1729, enclosed in Mathew to BT, Dec. 1, 1727, CO 152/16, S63; enclosed in Mathew to BT, July 10, 1730, CO 152/18, T79. Compensation payments for 1727 were only about one-fifth of overall expenditure for runaways, as there were other charges to be met by government such as those for detention, execution, and receipt of fugitives from captors. For compensation see legislature minutes in CO 9/6.

21. Assembly Mins., Aug. 7, 1739, CO 9/12.

22. CSP, 1699, no. 766, p. 424, no. 458, p. 252. In 1705 Gov. Daniel Parke was instructed upon assignment to the Leeward Islands to get a law passed "(if not already done), for the restraining of any Inhumane Severity, by which ill Masters or Overseers may be used toward their Christian Servants and their Slaves, and that provision be made therein, That the willfull Killing of Indians and Negroes may be punished with Death, and that a fit penalty be imposed for maiming them." There was also a section on promoting Christianization of blacks. Parke's instructions, June 8, 1705, CO 152/39. In their addresses to the legislature of Antigua upon taking up office, most governors referred to these items within their instructions without, it seems, concrete results, especially in regard to the death penalty for murder of a slave, until Gov. Hart made some progress in the 1720s.

23. "An Act for the better Government of Slaves, Dec. 16, 1697, CO 8/3; see also Nevis act, "Act against Killing Negroes," May 26, 1675, CO 154/2; Act no. 130 of 1702, clause 14.

24. Hart to BT, Mar. 11, 1724, CO 152/14, R182. The minutes of the Barbados council show that in 1693 Alice Mills was to be paid ten guineas "for castrating forty two Negroes according to sentence of the Commissioners for trial of rebellious Negroes." CSP, Jan. 1693–May 14, 1696, no. 31, p. 5.

25. Act no. 176 of 1723, clauses 40–41. These two clauses were repealed in 1797 when it became law that

every White or other Free Person, who shall be charged with the Murder, or with the maiming or wounding a Slave,—whether belonging to himself, or to herself, or to any other Person or Persons whatsoever, and whether the same be by excessive Punishment or otherwise; every such Person, so charged, shall be proceeded against in the same manner as he or she would have been proceeded against, or tried, for the Murder of, or for the maiming or wounding a Free Person; and, upon being convicted thereof, shall suffer Death, or such other Punishment as by the Laws of England such Persons would be sentenced to suffer for the Murder of, or for the maiming or wounding a Free Person: Provided always, that such Conviction shall not extend to the Corrupting the Blood, or the Forfeiture of Lands or Tenements, Goods or Chattels; and Law, Custom, or Usage to the contrary thereof notwithstanding.

"An Act to repeal the fortieth and forty-first Clauses of an Act of this Island, intituled, An Act for attaining several Slaves now run-away from their Masters' Services: and for the better Government of Slaves, (dated the ninth day of Dec. 1723); and to make Persons charged with and found guilty of the Murder of Slaves, liable and subject to the same Pains and Penalties, as are inflicted for the Murder of Free Persons," Act no. 522, Nov. 28, 1797, clause 2, *Laws of Antigua.* See also Goveia, *Slave Society,* p. 191.

26. Ibid., p. 173.

27. Ash to Tudway, July 18, 1759, Tudway Papers, DD/TD, box 15; Act no. 212, Nov. 25, 1757, clause 10.

28. Act no. 212, Nov. 25, 1757, clause 9, *Laws of Antigua.*

29. Ira Berlin, *Slaves without Masters: The Negro in the Antebellum South* (New York: Oxford University Press, 1974).

30. Extracts of Antigua wills can be found in Oliver, *History of Antigua,* vol. 3. References to particular acts of manumission also appear in the pedigree descriptions of leading island families in Oliver's volumes. For population data see "Account of no. of White Inhabitants, free Negroes & Slaves in Leeward Islands 1672–1774," CO 318/2; Robert Montgomery Martin, *Statistics of the Colonies of the British Empire* (London, 1839), p. 80; *Parliamentary Papers* 18 (1826–27):4.

31. See, for example, Goveia, *Slave Society,* pp. 218, 221–22. Equiano, *Life,* pp. 139–40.

32. Mins. of Council in Assembly, May 24, Mar. 24, 1707, Mar. 13, 1708, CO 9/1.

33. Berlin, *Slaves without Masters,* p. 318.

34. Act no. 130 of 1702, clauses 22–26; "An Act for the better Government of Slaves," Dec. 16, 1697, CO 8/3; Act no. 130 of 1702, clause 22.

35. Ibid. On patron-client relations see Julian A. Pitt-Rivers, *The People of the Sierra* (New York: Criterion Books, 1954); Eric Wolf, "Kinship, Friendship, and Patron-Client Relations in Complex Societies," in *The Social Anthropology of Complex Societies,* ed. Michael Banton (New York: Frederick A. Praeger, 1966) pp. 1–22; Alex Weingrod, "Patrons, Patronage, and Political Parties," *CSSH* 10 (July 1968):377–400; Anthony Hall, "Patron-Client Relations," *Journal of Peasant Studies*

1 (July 1974):506-9; John Duncan Powell, "Peasant Society and Clientist Politics," *American Political Science Review* 64 (June 1970):411-25. In a recent book two historians have used the concept to probe relations between freedmen and whites in seventeenth-century Virginia. See T. H. Breen and Stephen Innes, *"Myne Owne Ground:" Race & Freedom on Virginia's Eastern Shore, 1640-1676* (New York: Oxford University Press, 1980). See also Berlin, *Slaves without Masters*, pp. 338-40.

36. Act no. 130 of 1702, clause 22; "An Act for the better Government of Slaves," Dec. 16, 1697, CO 8/3; Act no. 130 of 1702, clause 26.

37. Ibid., clause 23.

38. Assembly Mins., Dec. 11, 13, 1727; Jan. 4, 1728, CO 9/6; Goveia, *Slave Society*, pp. 96-7, 218. By the 1820s, when the amelioration of slavery in the West Indies was being tried out, freedmen in Antigua and other islands petitioned their legislatures and the home government to remove their disabilities. For Antigua see, for example, "The Humble Petition of the Free Coloured Inhabitants of Antigua to the Speaker and Assembly," Sept. 4, 1823, CO 318/76; also "Address of the Free Coloured Inhabitants of Antigua to H.M. Commission of Inquiry into the Administration of Justice in the Windward and Leeward Islands," Oct. 8, 1823, CO 318/76. For a discussion of their struggle for citizenship and legal equality at the end of the eighteenth century, see Goveia, *Slave Society*, pp. 96-101, 166, 258-59, 333-35. Several petitions from freedmen to the legislature seeking grants of land during the first half of the eighteenth century are scattered through the legislature minutes.

39. Council Mins., April 19, 1754, CO 9/19.

40. Mintz, "Caribbean Marketplaces," p. 334; Dunn, *Sugar and Slaves*, p. 228; Act no. 130 of 1702, clauses 24-25.

41. Singleton, *General Description*, pp. 151-52; see also Sidney W. Mintz, "Groups, Group Boundaries and the Perception of Race," *CSSH* 13 (1971):437-50; Fernando Henriques, *Children of Conflict: A Study of Interracial Sex and Marriage* (New York: E. P. Dutton, 1975), pp. 93-115.

Chapter 8: "To Make Themselves Masters of the Contry"

1. Cooper, "Problem of Slavery," pp. 116-21; Cooper, *Plantation Slavery*, pp. 153-56; Faust, "Culture, Conflict, and Community"; Faust, *James Henry Hammond*, pp. 69-104; Barrington Moore, Jr., *Injustice: The Social Bases of Obedience and Revolt* (New York: M. E. Sharpe, 1978), pp. 3-116; Mintz and Price, *Afro-American Past*, pp. 12-21.

2. Genovese, *Roll, Jordan, Roll*, 597-98; Wood, *Black Majority*, pp. 285-87; Mintz, *Caribbean Transformations*, pp. 75-81; Mintz, "Review Article: Slavery and the Slaves," *CS* 8 (Jan. 1969):65-70; George M. Frederickson and Christopher Lasch, "Resistance to Slavery," in *American Slavery: The Question of Resistance*, ed. John H. Bracey, August Meier, and Eliott Rudwick (California: Wadsworth Publishing Co., 1971), pp. 179-92; Roy Simon Bryce-Laporte, "Slaves as Inmates, Slaves as Men: A Sociological Discussion of Elkins' Thesis," in *The Debate Over Slavery: Stanley*

Elkins and his Critics, ed. Ann J. Lane (Urbana: University of Illinois Press, 1971), pp. 269-92; Jordan, *White Over Black,* pp. 113-15.

3. Pares, *West-India Fortune,* p. 25. Williamson, *The Caribbee Islands,* p. 149. At that time the English occupied the middle area of St. Christopher, while the French held the two extremes. Britain gained control of the whole island in 1713 by the Treaty of Utrecht.

4. CSP, 1661-68, no. 1,270, p. 409, no. 1,274, p. 411; CSP, 1669-74, no. 680, p. 291; Higham, *Development of the Leeward Islands,* p. 176. In regard to threats from Carib Indians, governor Sir William Stapleton reported in 1676 that their "treacherous and barbarous murders, rapes, and enormities discourage the planters in the Leeward Isles more than anything else." CSP, 1675-76, no. 1,152, p. 502. Stapleton observed that in the islands of St. Vincent, Dominica and St. Lucia to the south there were about "1,500 Indians. . . . six hundred of these bowmen are negroes, some run away from Barbadoes and elsewhere." Ibid., p. 499. Michael Adas, "From Avoidance to Confrontation: Peasant Protest in Precolonial and Colonial Southeast Asia," *CSSH* 23 (Apr. 1981):217-47; David Barry Gaspar, "Runaways in Seventeenth-Century Antigua, West Indies," *BELC* (June 1979): 3-13.

5. "An Act for publique recompense to the Masters of Slaves putt to death by Law," Oct. 28, 1669, CO 154/2. Nevis passed a similar act entitled "An Act for preventing ye barbarism of negroes" (Jan. 14, 1677), but the compensation clause was later repealed. "An Act for repealing one clause of the Act intituled An Act for Preventing ye Barbarism of Negroes," Mar. 26, 1681, CO 154/2. For Antigua see also "An Act declaring the dutys of all Masters of Shipps or Small Vessels Tradeing To this Island & for the Carefull Lookeing after Theire Vessells Whilst they Stay & for the preventions of fugitive and transportation without Tickett," Oct. 28, 1669, CO 154/2; "An Act against Run-away Servants," July 5, 1677, CO 154/3. For similar acts in the other Leewards against slave and servant flight by sea, see: (Montserrat) "An Act for Restraineing the Liberty of Negroes and to prevent the running away of Xtain Servants," Oct. 8, 1670, CO 154/1; "An Act against Small Boats, Barqueloggs and Canoes," Mar. 19, 1672, CO 154/2. (Nevis) "Order making it Felony for any persons to runaway with Boats & c," n.d., · CO 154/1. For another act concerning "Running away with Boats," passed May 26, 1675, see CO 154/2; CSP, 1675-76, no. 570, p. 237 and also "An Act against running away with Boats and Canoes," 1699, confirmed Oct. 22, 1700, in *Acts Passed in Nevis.* (St. Christopher) "An Act touching the Carrying off this Island any Slave or Slaves by Stealth or any white person or persons, servant or servants to bee felony," Oct. 1, 1672, CO 154/2. For the slave act against Antigua runaways, see "An Act for bringing in Runaway Negroes and Incouragement of such who shall bring them in," July 9, 1680, CO 154/2.

6. Leslie F. Manigat, "The Relationship Between Marronage and Slave Revolts and Revolution in St. Domingue-Haiti," in Rubin and Tuden, *Comparative Perspectives on Slavery,* pp. 420-38. There is a sizable body of literature on maroons in the Americas. Among modern works I have found most useful in relation to the process and immediate consequences of slave flight are Richard Price, ed., *Maroon Societies: Rebel Slave Communities in the Americas,* 2d ed. (Baltimore: Johns Hopkins

University Press, 1979), which contains twenty-one important selections, as well as a most helpful introduction, afterword, and bibliography; Price, *The Guiana Maroons: A Historical and Bibliographical Introduction* (Baltimore: Johns Hopkins University Press, 1976); Orlando Patterson, "Slavery and Slave Revolts;" Yvan Debbasch, "Le Marronage: Essai sur la désertion de l'esclave antillais," *L'Annee Sociologique*, 3e série (1961):1–112, (1962):117–95; Gabriel Debien, "Le Marronage aux Antilles Françaises au XVIIIe siècle," *CS* 6 (Oct. 1966):3–44; Debien, "Les Eslaves marrons à Saint Domingue en 1764," *JHR* 6 (1966):9–20; Debien, *Les Esclaves aux Antilles Françaises, (XVIIe-XVIIIe siècles)*, (Basse-Terre/Fort-de-France: Société d'Histoire de la Guadeloupe/Société d'Histoire de la Martinque, 1974); Jean Fouchard, *The Haitian Maroons: Liberty or Death* (New York: Edward W. Blyden Press, 1981); David Buisseret and S.A.G. Taylor, "Juan De Bolas and his Pelinco," *CQ* 24 (March–June 1978):1–7; Mavis Campbell, "The Maroons of Jamaica: Imperium in Imperio?" *Pan African Journal* 6 (Spring 1973):45–55; Campbell, "Marronage in Jamaica: Its Origins in the Seventeenth Century," in Rubin and Tuden, *Comparative Perspectives on Slavery*, pp. 389–419; Silvia W. deGroot, "Maroons of Surinam: Dependence or Independence," ibid., pp. 455–63; deGroot, "The Boni Maroon War 1765–1793, Suriname and French Guiana," *BELC* 18 (June 1975):30–48; Elain White, "The Maroon Warriors of Jamaica and their Successful Resistance to Enslavement," *Pan-African Journal* 6 (Autumn 1973):297–312; Polly Pope, "A Maroon Settlement on St. Croix," *Negro History Bulletin* 35 (Nov. 1972): 153–54; R. K. Kent, "Palmares: An African State in Brazil," *JAH* 6 (1965):161–75; Bernard A. Marshall, "Maronage in Slave Plantation Societies: A Case Study of Dominica, 1785–1815," *CQ* 22 (June–Sept. 1976):26–32; John D. Milligan, "Slave Rebelliousness and the Florida Maroon," *Prologue* 6 (1974):5–18; Gilbert C. Din, "Cimarrones and the San Malo Band in Spanish Louisiana," *Louisiana History* 21 (Summer 1980):237–62; Scott V. Parris, "Alliance and Competition: Four Case Studies of Maroon-European Relations," *NWIG* 55 (1981):174–224; Thomas Flory, "Fugitive Slaves and Free Society: The Case of Brazil," *JNH* 64 (Spring 1979): 116–30; Patrick J. Carroll, "Mandinga: The Evolution of a Mexican Runaway Slave Community, 1735–1827," *CSSH* 19 (Oct. 1977):488–505; Michel-Rolph Trouillot, *Ti Dife Boule sou Istoua Ayiti* (Brooklyn, N.Y.: Koleksoin Lakansiel, 1977); Barbara Klamon Kopytoff, "Jamaica Maroon Political Organization: The Effects of the Treaties," *SES* 25 (June 1976):87–105; Kopytoff, "The Development of Jamaican Maroon Ethnicity," *CQ* 22 (1976):33–50; Kopytoff, "The Early Political Development of Jamaican Maroon Societies," *WMQ*, 3d ser. 35 (Apr. 1978):287–307; Kopytoff, "Colonial Treaty as Sacred Charter of the Jamaican Maroons," *Ethnohistory* 26 (Winter 1979):45–64. Joseph J. Williams, *The Maroons of Jamaica*, Anthropological Series of the Boston College Graduate School, 3 (Boston, Mass.: Boston College Press, Dec. 1938). For older treatment of the Jamaica maroons see Robert C. Dallas, *The History of the Maroons from their Origin to the Establishment of their Chief Tribe at Sierra Leone*, 2 vols. (London: printed by A. Strahan for T. Longman and O. Rees, 1803); Long, *History of Jamaica*, 2:338–50.

7. Mins. of Council in Assembly, July 14, 1684, CO 1/50.

8. Dunn, *Sugar and Slaves*, p. 259; Council Mins., Feb. 14, 1687, CO 155/1.

9. Harris, *Plants, Animals, and Man*, p. 86. The Antigua census is printed in

Oliver, *History of Antigua,* 1:58-61. By 1693 Rowland Williams, a member of the Antigua council, was listed as owning 203 slaves. Mins. of Council in Assembly, Jan. 19, 1693, CO 155/2.

10. Council Mins., Feb. 14, 1687, CO 155/1.

11. Council Mins., Mar. 9, 1687, CO 155/1.

12. Council Mins., Mar. 17, 24, 1687, CO 155/1.

13. Ibid.

14. Council Mins., Mar. 24, 1687, CO 155/1.

15. Price, *Maroon Societies,* pp. 18-19.

16. Curtin, *Atlantic Slave Trade,* p. 125; Donnan, *Documents,* 1:93-95, 274; William Bosman, *A New and Accurate Description of the Coast of Guinea* (London: Frank Cass, 1968), p. 326-29; Donnan, *Documents,* 1:260, n. 3, 398; Price, *Maroon Societies,* pp. 23-24.

17. Council Mins., Mar. 31, Apr. 7, 17, 1687, CO 155/1.

18. Patterson, "Slavery and Slave Revolts."

19. Council Mins., Nov. 24, 1692, Feb. 22, 1694, CO 155/2.

20. Council Mins., Feb. 19, 1695, Mar. 10, 1696, Dec. 28, 1697, Mar. 30, 1694, June 13, 1694, Jan. 25, 1695, Mar. 10, May 21, June 7, 17, 1696, Dec. 28, 1697, Dec. 15, 1699, CO 155/2.

21. Dunn, *Sugar and Slaves,* pp. 238-46; Eugene Sirmans, "The Legal Status of the Slave in South Carolina, 1670-1740," *JSH* 28 (1962):462-73; "An Act for the better Government of Slaves," Dec. 16, 1697, CO 8/3.

Chapter 9: "However They May Disguise It, They Hate Their Masters"

1. Patterson, "Slavery and Slave Revolts"; David Barry Gaspar, "A Dangerous Spirit of Liberty: Slave Rebellion in the West Indies during the 1730s," *Cimarrons* 1 (1981):79-91.

2. Gamble to Codrington, Dec. 29, 1701; Codrington to BT, Dec. 30, 1701, CO 152/4, F35. Maj. Martin was the father of Col. Samuel Martin, Antigua planter and author of "An Essay on Plantership." Oliver, *History of Antigua,* 2:240. John Yeamans was lieutenant governor of Antigua 1698-1711. Ibid., 3:320.

3. [Flannigan], *Antigua and the Antiguans,* 2:79; Luffman, *Antigua,* letter 26, Jan. 1, 1788; Martin Letter Book, 29, fol. 79, Martin Papers, Add. MSS 41, 474; Act no. 176 of 1723, clause 32. Codrington to BT, Dec. 30, 1701, CO 152/4, F35; BT to Codrington, Mar. 24, 1702, CO 153/7; Higham, "The Negro Policy of Christopher Codrington," pp. 151-52.

4. Gamble to Codrington, Dec. 29, 1701, CO 152/4, F35.

5. Codrington to BT, Dec. 30, 1701, Gamble to Codrington, Dec. 29, 1701, CO 152/4, F35. The plot referred to was the alleged Barbados slave plot first brought to the attention of that island's authorities by the wife of a white fisherman on Dec. 16, 1701. Jerome S. Handler, "Slave Revolts and Conspiracies in Seventeenth-Century Barbados," *New West Indian Guide* 56 (1982):29-30; CSP, Jan.-Dec. 1, 1702, no. 8, p. 7, no. 28, p. 21, no. 335, p. 219.

6. Codrington to BT, Dec. 30, 1701, CO 152/4, F35.

7. Ibid.; Le Jau, "Some Matters Relating to the Condition of the Clergy Employ'd in the Leeward Islands."

8. Stampp, *Peculiar Institution*, p. 185.

9. For a useful general consideration of the causes of slave revolt in Jamaica that might be applied to other slave societies, see Patterson, *Sociology of Slavery*, pp. 273–83; see also his "Slavery and Slave Revolts," especially, pp. 318–25.

10. Kilson, "Towards Freedom," pp. 176–77.

11. Robertson, *Letter*, p. 12–13; Tullideph to Sanders in Nevis, Nov. 7, 1748, Tullideph Letter Book MS.

12. Patterson, "Toward a Future That Has No Past," pp. 42–44; Raymond A. Bauer and Alice H. Bauer, "Day to Day Resistance to Slavery," *JNH* 27 (Oct. 1942):388–419; Patterson, *Sociology of Slavery*, pp. 260–65; Bryce-Laporte, "Slaves as Inmates, Slaves as Men," pp. 269–72; Melville J. Herskovits, *The Myth of the Negro Past* (Boston: Beacon Press, 1958), pp. 99–105; Faust, "Culture, Conflict, and Community"; James West Davidson and Mark Hamilton Lytle, *After the Fact: The Art of Historical Detection* (New York: Alfred A. Knopf, 1982), pp. 169–204.

13. Dunn, *Sugar and Slaves*, pp. 238–46; Jordan, *Black Over White*, pp. 103–10, 588.

14. The claim procedure involved a petition that went first to the council, then, if approved, was sent on to the assembly. If the assembly approved, the petition was referred back to the council, and the treasurer was then authorized to make payment. Claims utilized in this study (1722–63) can be found in minutes of the legislature, CO 9/5–26. Petitions for 1751 and 1752 are missing, and sources before 1722 are erratic. For use made of newspaper advertisement, see Mullin, *Flight and Rebellion*, especially pp. 39–47; Wood, *Black Majority*, pp. 239–68; Darold D. Wax, "The Image of the Negro in the *Maryland Gazette*, 1745–75," *Journalism Quarterly* 46 (Spring 1969):73–86; Lorenzo J. Greene, "The New England Negro as Seen in Advertisements for Runaway Slaves," *JNH* 19 (Apr. 1944):25–146; Daniel E. Meaders, "South Carolina Fugitives as Viewed Through Local Colonial Newspapers with Emphasis on Runaway Notices 1732–1801," *JNH* 60 (Apr. 1975):288–317; "Eighteenth Century Slaves as Advertised by Their Masters," *JNH* 1 (Apr. 1916):163–216; Robert C. Twombly, "Black Resistance to Slavery in Massachusetts," in *Insights and Parallels: Problems and Issues of American Social History*, ed. William L. O'Neill (Minneapolis, Minn.: Burgess Publishing Co., 1973), pp. 11–33; Jordan, *White Over Black*, pp. 392–93.

15. Jordan, *White Over Black*, p. 114.

16. Adas, "From Avoidance to Confrontation," pp. 236–37; Eric Hobsbawm, *Bandits* (New York: Pantheon Books, 1981); Hobsbawm, *Primitive Rebels: Studies in Archaic Forms of Social Movement in the 19th and 20th Centuries* (New York: Norton, 1965), pp. 13–29; Assembly Mins., Jan. 8, 1713, CO 9/2.

17. Council Mins., July 18, 1737, CO 9/11.

18. They were Robert Smith, Thomas Harwood, and Dr. John Dunbar. Smith and Harwood said they were present when a sober Woodyatt reported to Morris. Dunbar himself said that on the night of the incident, Woodyatt had ridden up

to his house on Blubber Valley Plantation, told him about it, and "Desired this Examinant to lend him a Servant to go with him to Coll. Morris's House, for that he was Afraid to go alone." He too said Woodyatt was sober, so there seemed no reason to believe the servant had exaggerated or invented the whole affair. Council Mins., July 18, 1737, CO 9/11.

19. Assembly Mins., Jan. 25, 1722, CO 9/5; Mins. of Council in Assembly, July 29, 23, 1774, CO 9/3; Council Mins., July 20, 1730, CO 152/43; Assembly Mins., July 5, 1735, CO 9/9; Assembly Mins., June 22, 1750, CO 9/20; Council Mins., Aug. 6, 1755, Apr. 8, 1756, CO 9/21; Assembly Mins., Nov. 18, 1762, Oct. 7, 1760, CO 9/25, June 28, 1764, CO 9/27; Council Mins., Apr. 4, 1753, CO 9/17; Assembly Mins., Jan. 2, 1761, CO 9/25.

20. Owens, *This Species of Property,* pp. 93–96; Peter Kolchin, "Reevaluating the the Antebellum Slave Community: A Comparative Perspective," *Journal of American History* 70 (Dec. 1983):581–82; Lawrence T. McDonnell, "Slave Against Slave: Dynamics of Violence Within the American Slave Community," paper presented at meeting of the American Historical Association, San Francisco, Dec. 28, 1983; Gerhart Saenger, *The Psychology of Prejudice: Achieving Intercultural Understanding and Cooperation in a Democracy* (New York: Harper & Brothers Publishers, 1953), p. 29.

21. See Table 9.1. Act no. 176 of 1723, clause 28, outlined the mode of compensation to owners of the murdered slave and the executed murderer: "where one Slave murders another, the Price paid by the Publick on executing the Murderer, shall be equally divided between the Owner of the Offender, and the Owner of the Slave Slain." Clauses 13–14 of the act covered cases where slaveowners did not prosecute within three months slaves belonging to them guilty of murder or any felony except running away. Where slaves assaulted others and caused grievous bodily harm, it was possible, by clause 12 of Act no. 130 of 1702, for the owner of the victim to claim damages. The Antigua authorities in 1767 ordered absentee Charles Tudway to pay "for certain damages & losses" £22 12s. to John Braham, whose slave Eve had received a severe beating at the hands of Tudway's slave Sussex, suffering a broken arm. And until such compensation was paid, Sussex was assigned to Braham. Tudway Papers, DD/TD, box 14.

22. Wood, *Black Majority,* pp. 289–92; "An Additional and Explanatory Act to an Act of the General Assembly of this Province, entitled 'An Act for the Better Ordering and Governing Negroes and other Slaves in this Province;' and for Continuing Such Part of the Said Act as is not Altered or Amended by this Present Act, for the Term Therein Mentioned," Act no. 790, May 17, 1751, clauses 7–12, in David J. McCord, *The Statutes at Large of South Carolina,* (Columbia, S.C., 1840), pp. 422–23.

23. Gabriel Debien, *Plantations et Esclaves à Saint-Domingue: Sucrerie Cottineau,* Notes d'Histoire Coloniale no. 66 (Dakar 1962), pp. 61–68; Yvan Debbasch, "Le Crime d'empoisonnement aux îles pendant la période esclavagiste," *Revue Française d'Histoire d'Outre-Mer* 50 (1963):137–88; Hall, *Social Control,* pp. 40–41, 68–74, and passim; Margaret Deanne Rouse-Jones, "St. Kitts, 1713–1763: A Study of the Development of a Plantation Colony," Ph.D. thesis, Johns Hopkins University, 1978, p. 115; Schuler, *Slave Resistance,* pp. 24–33, James, *Black Jacobins,* pp. 20–22.

24. Act no. 176 of 1723, clause 5; Council Mins., Mar. 6, 1746, CO 9/17; Assembly Mins., May 4, 1749, CO 9/20; *Pennsylvania Gazette,* Jan. 3, 1749; Assembly Mins., Aug. 4, 1763, CO 9/25, Nov. 17, 1748, CO 9/20.

25. "Tryal of Quawcoo an Old Cormantee Negroe of Mr. John Pare 9th December [1736]," TR, Council Mins., Jan. 12, 1737, CO 9/10.

26. Council Mins., Sept. 13, Dec. 4, 1706, CO 9/1, June 1, 1738, CO 9/13; Assembly Mins., May 31, 1739, CO 9/12, Sept. 11, 1745, CO 9/16, Apr. 1, 1747, CO 9/17, Dec. 10, 1754, CO 9/22, July 15, 1736, CO 9/12.

27. Esteban Montejo, *The Autobiography of a Runaway Slave,* ed. Miguel Barnet (New York: Vintage Books, 1973); Hart to BT, Dec. 24, 1724, CO 152/15, R121.

28. Council Mins., Dec. 4, 1706; Mins. of Council in Assembly, Dec. 15, 1707, CO 9/1.

29. Assembly Mins., Sept. 17, Oct. 4, Nov. 6, 1712, CO 9/2.

30. Mins. of Council in Assembly, July 27, 1713, Assembly Mins., Jan. 8, 1713, CO 9/2. About this time the legislature had a supplementary act for control of blacks under consideration: "The additional Act for the Better Government of Slaves and free Negroes lyes now before us but we have thought upon Some Amendments which will take up more time than we have to Spare this Evening." Gov. & council to assembly, ibid.

31. Mins. of Council in Assembly, July 16, 1744, CO 9/3; "An Act for the better regulating Negroes, and the suppressing their Conspiracies and Profanation of the Lord's Day," Act no. 144, Sept. 2, 1714, *Laws of Antigua* (cited only, without text).

32. Mins. of Council in Assembly, May 7, 1715, June 12, 1716, Sept. 11, 1717, CO 9/3. In regard to the fugitive Quamino's killing of Archibald Cochran's slaves, the governor and council recommended that Cochran be compensated because his slave was lost "in endeavouring to take the other." The assembly, however, could not agree "believing It may occasion many Inconveniences there being no Instances of that kind." Seven years later, however, the act of 1723 granted compensation in precisely such cases. Mins. of Council in Assembly, June 12, 1716, CO 9/3; Act no. 176 of 1723, clause 28.

33. Mins. of Council in Assembly, Aug. 9, 1725, CO 155/6; Council Mins., Sept. 27, 1726, CO 9/6; Assembly Mins., Jan. 5, 1728, CO 9/6.

34. "An Act for the better Government of Negroes, and other Slaves," Act no. 2 of 1711; "An Act for attainting several Negroes therein mentioned; and for the more effectual preventing Negroes from running away from their Masters Service; and for explaining and rendering more effectual an Act, intituled, An Act for the better Government of Negroes, and other Slaves," Act no. 52 of 1722, *Acts of Assembly Passed in the Island of St. Christopher, From 1711, to 1735, inclusive* (London: printed by John Baskett, 1739), pp. 9–13, 69–74. CSP 1722–23, no. 190, pp. 92–93; Rouse-Jones, "St. Kitts, 1713–1763," pp. 111–18; John Oldmixon, *The British Empire in America,* 2 vols. (London, 1741), 2:262; (St. Christopher) Council Mins., July 28, Aug. 20, 1722, CO 155/6.

35. "An Act for the preventing keeping Canoes, unless sufficient Security be given; and to prevent Members of the Council and Assembly signing any Adjustments out of their respective Houses," Act no. 82, 1722, *Montserrat Code of Laws,*

pp. 40-42; "An Act for the good Government of Negroes, and other Slaves in this Island," Act no. 81, 1717, *Acts Passed in Nevis,* pp. 75-78; Herbert to Stapleton, June 24, 1726, Gay, "Letters from a Sugar Plantation," p. 157.

36. Council Mins., Oct. 12, Nov. 18, 1730, Jan. 15, 1731, CO 152/43, Oct. 18, 1732, CO 9/7; Assembly Mins., Apr. 12, 1731, CO 9/7; Council Mins., Sept. 26, 1732, Apr. 6, 1733, CO 9/7, Nov. 17, 1756, CO 9/21.

37. Price, *Maroon Societies,* pp. 5-16; Fouchard, *The Haitian Maroons,* passim; Stuart B. Schwartz, "The Mocambo: Slave Resistance in Colonial Bahia," *JSocH* 3 (Summer 1970):321-22; Flory, "Fugitive Slaves and Free Society"; Parris, "Alliance and Competition."

38. Phillips, "An Antigua Plantation," p. 444; Plantation Accounts, Sept. 10, 1738-Aug. 13, 1739, Swete Papers, 388/E4; Aug. 10, 1741-Aug. 10, 1742, ibid., 269M/F10; Tudway Papers, DD/TD, box 8, 1750.

39. Martin to Anderson, Oct. 25, 1731, Martin Letter Book, pt. 1, fol. 47, Martin Papers, Add. MSS 41,352; Tullideph to Lowes, Sept. 25, 1756, Tullideph Letter Book, MS; Inventory of Bridge Plantation, Antigua, 1754, Tyrell Papers, D/DKe, T33; Tullideph to Dunbar, Dec. 5, 1747, Tullideph Letter Book, MS; Betty's Hope Inventory, July 26, 1751, Inventory of Cotton Plantation, July 31, 1751, Codrington Papers, D1610/E5. For expenditure on runaways see the plantation accounts.

40. Allan Kulikoff, "The Beginnings of the Afro-American Family in Maryland," in *Law, Society, and Politics in Early Maryland,* ed. Aubrey C. Land, Lois Green Carr, and Edward C. Panenfuse (Baltimore: Johns Hopkins University Press, 1977), pp. 189-90; A.J.R. Russell-Wood, "The Black Family in the Americas," *Societas* 8 (Winter 1978):28-33. "Evidence against Bartons Joe [Jan. 20, 1737]," TR, Council Mins., Feb. 24, 1737, CO 9/11.

41. Debbasch, "Le Marronage," pp. 41-83; Fouchard, *The Haitian Maroons,* pp. 271-78; Rouse-Jones, "St. Kitts, 1713-1763," pp. 118-19; H. H. Breen, *St. Lucia: Historical, Statistical, and Descriptive* (1844; reprint, London: Frank Cass, 1970) pp. 169-81; Chris Searle, "Message to Grenada: An Interview with Edward Brathwaite," *Race & Class* 22 (Spring 1981):392-94; Schuler, *Slave Resistance,* pp. 52-61; CSP, 1661-68, no. 1,717, p. 544; CSP, 1699, no. 74, pp. 39-45, no. 628, pp. 337-38; CSP, Aug. 1717-Dec. 1718, no. 753, p. 394, no. 763, p. 396, no. 767, p. 397; Goveia, *Slave Society,* pp. 255-58; Neville Hall, "Slavery in Three West Indian Towns: Christiansted, Fredericksted and Charlotte Amalie in the late Eighteenth and Early Nineteenth Century," manuscript, 1981, pp. 2-23; Arturo Morales-Carrion, *Puerto Rico* (Rio Piedras, P.R.: University of Puerto Rico Press, 1952), pp. 62-63, 66-68.

42. Mins. of Council in Assembly, Apr. 21, 29, 1708, CO 9/1; Council Mins., Oct. 17, 1759, CO 9/24; CSP, July 1711-June 1712, no. 194, p. 169.

43. Issac Dookhan, "Viegques or Crab Island: Source of Anglo-Spanish Colonial Conflict," *JCH* 7 (Nov. 1973):1-22; CSP, Jan. 1716-17, no. 118, p. 56; Hart to BT, July 12, 1724, "Queries," CO 152/4.

44. Morales-Carrion, *Puerto Rico,* pp. 63, 67, n. 31. Reporting on Crab Island in 1724, Gov. Hart observed that "it would be Impracticable [for the British] to Settle

the same because the Negroes wou'd Continually fly to the Spaniards for Refuge, who give them their Liberty in One Year after they are Baptis'd." Hart to BT, July 12, 1724, "Queries," CO 152/4.

45. J. Hartog, *History of St. Eustatius* (Central U.S.A., Bicentennial Committee of the Netherlands Antilles, 1976), pp. 51–52; Altagracia Ortiz, *Eighteenth-Century Reforms in the Caribbean* (Rutherford, N.J.: Fairleigh Dickinson University Press, 1983), p. 196; Waldemar Westergaard, *The Danish West Indies Under Company Rule (1671–1754)* (New York: Macmillan, 1917), pp. 186, 191, 228; Schuler, *Slave Resistance*, pp. 55–56, John P. Knox, *A Historical Account of St. Thomas, W.I.* (1852; reprint, New York: Negro Universities Press, 1970), p. 65; Elise Pinckney, ed., *The Letterbook of Eliza Lucas Pinckney 1739–1762,* (Chapel Hill: University of North Carolina Press, 1972), pp. 57–58, nn. 72–73; John J. TePaske, "The Fugitive Slave: Intercolonial Rivalry and Spanish Slave Policy, 1687–1764," in *Eighteenth-Century Florida and Its Borderlands,* ed. S. Proctor (Gainesville: University of Florida Press, 1975), pp. 1–12; Alvin O. Thompson, *Some Problems of Slave Desertion in Guyana, c. 1750–1814* (Cave Hill, Barbados: Institute of Social and Economic Research, 1976), pp. 5–15; Ronie C. Tyler, "Fugitive Slaves in Mexico," *JNH* 57 (Jan. 1972): 1–12; Wood, *Black Majority*, p. 260. In 1786 the Jamaica agent in London, Stephen Fuller, reported that in March 1767 he had addressed a communication to the secretary of state about fugitives from Jamaica to Cuba, supplying "a list of 95 Negroes, with the names of the Proprietors. Fifty one of these Negroes deserted in the short space of about 7 Months before." Fuller to Lord Sydney, June 5, 1786, Stephen Fuller Papers (1786–96), Manuscripts Department, William R. Perkins Library, Duke University.

46. Fleming to BT, Jan. 25, 1751, CO 152/41; Fleming to Sec. of State, Dec. 14, 1751 enclosing letter to Pareja, Dec. 14, 1751, CO 152/45.

47. Thomas to BT, Feb. 6, 1754, CO 152/28, B67 enclosing translation of a letter from the governor of Puerto Rico to Mr. Purcell, lieutenant governor of the Virgin Islands, Oct. 1, 1753; Goveia, *Slave Society,* p. 255; Morales-Carrion, *Puerto Rico,* pp. 100–132; Adalberto Lopez, "The Evolution of a Colony: Puerto Rico in the 16th, 17th, and 18th Centuries," in *The Puerto Ricans: Their History, Culture, and Society,* ed. Adalberto Lopez (Cambridge, Mass.: Schenkman Publishing Co., 1980), pp. 39–46; Robert Mann to governor of Puerto Rico, May 2, 1770, CO 152/50. Mann was "Commander in Chief of His Majesty's Ships & Vessels employed & to be employed at Barbados," involved in seeking the return of some fugitives who had fled to Puerto Rico from St. Christopher in 1769. The case can be followed in CO 152/50, fols. 41–58, 61–64.

48. Wood, *Black Majority,* pp. 241–68; Mullin, *Flight and Rebellion,* pp. 34–123.

49. Act no. 176 of 1723, clause 6; Robertson, *Letter,* pp. 12–13; Council Mins., July 31, 1783, CO 9/28, quoted in Goveia, *Slave Society,* p. 257. For discussion of motivation behind slave flight see, for example, Fouchard, *The Haitian Maroons,* pp. 15–110, and passim; Debien, "Le Marronage aux Antilles Françaises au XVIIIᵉ siècle"; Debien, *Une Plantation de Saint-Domingue: La Sucrerie Galbaud du Fort (1690–1802),* Notes d'Histoire Coloniale no. 1 (Cairo: Les Presses de l'Institut Français d'Archéologie Orientale du Caire, 1941), pp. 97–101; Debien, *Plantations et esclaves,* pp. 69–76; Debbasch, "Le Marronage," pp. 3–39; Russell-Wood, "The Black Family in the Americas," pp. 28–33.

50. Council Mins., Dec. 17, 1731, CO 9/7.

51. See letters in Gay, "Letters from a Sugar Plantation in Nevis," pp. 154–57. For example, Herbert to Stapleton, June 12, 1726: "Many negroes and stock lost for want of provisions and water. I have not had the greatest share he says in these misfortunes haveing only lost some old negroes" (p. 156); Herbert to Stapleton, Aug. 25, 1727: "Most of the Negroes that dyed kill'd themselves by running away in the hard times" (pp. 157–58); (Nevis) Assembly Mins., Sept. 27, Oct. 12, 1725, CO 186/1; Hart to BT, Jan. 6, 1726, CO 152/15, R158.

52. Mins. of Council in Assembly, Jan. 24, 28, Feb. 28, 1729, CO 9/6; Gov. Londonderry to BT, Apr. 5, 1729, CO 152/17, T25; "An Act for the Banishment of Several Negroe Slaves Concern'd in the late Conspiracy," Mar. 8, 1729, CO 8/6. In compensation for his four executed slaves Col. Crump received £80 for Hercules, and £50 each for Boquin Prurry, and Hanniball. Thomas Kerby, an assemblyman, petitioned for £50 each for Ando and Teasy, who were banished. For others banished, Crump got £50 for Cuffy and £45 for Glasgo; Edward Byam, the lieutenant governor, £50 for Quashy; Archibald Cochran, a councillor absent in England, £32 for Natty; Nathaniel Gilbert £45 for Joe; George Nichols £60 for Stepney; and Sir William Codrington, also on the council, £50 for Tackey, the valuation of his other slave Cracow not being specified. Council Mins., Mar. 8, 25, 31, Apr. 29, Nov. 12, 1729, CO 9/6. See also provost marshall's accounts, Jan.–Apr. 1729, Council Mins., July 20, 1730, CO 152/43.

53. Council Mins., Mar. 31, Apr. 11, 1737, CO 9/11; "An Act for the Banishment of Several Negro Slaves Concern'd in the late Conspiracy"; Londonderry to BT, Apr. 5, 1729, CO 152/17, T25.

54. David Barry Gaspar, "A Dangerous Spirit of Liberty," pp. 79–91; Oruno D. Lara, "Le Procès de résistance," ibid., pp. 13–15, 21–78; Patterson, "Slavery and Slave Revolts," pp. 289–325; Wood, Black Majority, pp. 219–326; Westergaard, Danish West Indies, pp. 165–68; Herbert Aptheker, American Negro Slave Revolts (New York: International Publishers, 1974), pp. 3–5; 179–95; Jordan, White Over Black, pp. 116–22; Peter Wood has noted that while much work has been completed on slave resistance in separate slave societies, "there have been no successful longitudinal studies, analyzing periods of intensified slave resistance throughout the Atlantic community, such as the late 1730s or the early 1790s." Wood, " 'I Did the Best I Could for My Day:' The Study of Early Black History during the Second Reconstruction, 1960 to 1976," WMQ, 3d ser. 35 (Apr. 1978):216.

55. CSP, 1737, 43, no. 379, pp. 191–92; Fleming to Duke of Bedford, Aug. 13, 1750, CO 152/45; J. Hartog, Curaçao: From Colonial Dependence to Autonomy (Aruba, Netherlands Antilles: De Wit 1968), pp. 119–21; James, Black Jacobins; David Patrick Geggus, Slavery, War, and Revolution: The British Occupation of Saint Domingue 1793–1798 (Oxford: Clarendon Press, 1982), pp. 33–45, 79–99, 290–331, and passim; Geggus, "Jamaica and the Saint Domingue Slave Revolt, 1791–1793," The Americas 38 (Oct. 1981):219–33; T. Ott, The Haitian Revolution (Knoxville: University of Tennessee Press, 1973); Michael Craton, Testing the Chains: Resistance to Slavery in the British West Indies (Ithaca, N.Y.: Cornell University Press, 1982), pp. 180–210.

56. (Montserrat) Council Mins., Mar. 18, 30, 1768, CO 177/11; Woodley to sec. of state, Apr. 22, June 18, 1768, CO 152/48; Woodley to BT, June 21, 1768, CO 152/30, Dd84; "Extract of a Letter from Vice Admiral Pye, Commdr. in Chief

of His Majts Ships at the Leeward Islands, to Mr. Stephens dated the 16th May 1768," enclosed in Admiralty Office to Hillsborough (sec. of state), Oct. 6, 1768, CO 152/48; sec. of state to Woodley, July 14, 1768, CO 152/48.

57. Woodley to sec. of state, Apr. 20, 1770, CO 152/50.

58. Berlin, "The Slave Trade and the Development of Afro-American Society," pp. 126-28; Joseph P. Reidy, " 'Negro Election Day' and Black Community Life in New England, 1750-1860," *Marxist Perspectives* 1 (1978):102-17; Twombly, "Black Resistance to Slavery," p. 29.

59. Darlene C. Hine, "Female Slave Resistance: The Economics of Sex," *Western Journal of Black Studies* 3 (Summer 1979):123-27; Steven E. Brown, "Sexuality and the Slave Community," *Phylon* 42 (Spring 1981):1-10; Angela Davis, "Reflections on the Black Woman's Role in the Community of Slaves," *Black Scholar* 3 (Dec. 1971):3-15; Lucille Mathurin, *The Rebel Woman in the British West Indies during Slavery* (Kingston, Jamaica: Institute of Jamaica, 1975); Mathurin, "Reluctant Matriarchs," *Savacou* 13 (1977):1-6; Barbara Bush, "Defiance or Submission? The Role of the Slave Woman in Slave Resistance in the British Caribbean," *Immigrants & Minorities* 1 (Mar. 1982):16-38; Mintz and Price, *Afro-American Past,* pp. 20-21, and passim; Foner, "Black Conspiracies," p. 40.

Chapter 10: "A Conspiracy Deeply Laid & Extended Wide"

1. The Antigua slave plot made news on the mainland, where several newspapers reported on it in the form of letters from the stricken island, information conveyed by people arriving from there, and publication of parts or the full official report prepared by the first court that tried the rebels. It is interesting that the plot received relatively scant coverage in South Carolina and Virginia, where slavery was a deeply entrenched institution, while in colonies to the north — Pennsylvania, New York, and Massachusetts — coverage was by contrast more substantial. Mainland slaveowners took a very keen interest in developments in the sugar islands, especially slave unrest, seeking in that insular mirror reflections of difficulties they wished to avoid, or control if at all possible. Wood, *Black Majority,* pp. 221-24. For mainland newspaper coverage of the Antigua plot see *Virginia Gazette,* (William Parks), Apr. 8, May 20, 27, 1737; *South Carolina Gazette,* Dec. 4, 1736, Feb. 5, Apr. 23, 1737; *American Weekly Mercury* (Philadelphia), Dec. 2, 1736, Feb. 22, Mar. 17, 1737; *Pennsylvania Gazette,* Nov. 25, Dec. 9, 1736, Feb. 23, Mar. 17, 24, 1737; *New York Gazette,* Dec. 6, 1736, Mar. 1, 28, 1737; *New York Weekly Journal,* Nov. 29, Dec. 6, 1736, Mar. 28, Apr. 4, 11, 18, 25, 1737; *Boston Weekly Newsletter,* Dec. 2, 1736, Mar. 3, Apr. 8, 1737; *Boston Evening Post,* Nov. 29, 1736; *Boston Gazette,* Nov. 29, 1736. General Report.

2. Mintz, "Review Article," p. 70.

3. General Report.

4. This question about perceptions of freedom or other dimensions of slave societal organization requires that students of New World slave society probe deeply into African societies from which slaves came. Recent work on indigenous African slavery has begun to show just how important the African perspective is

to a fuller understanding of New World developments. See Suzanne Miers and Igor Kopytoff, eds., *Slavery in Africa: Historical and Anthropological Perspectives,* (Madison: University of Wisconsin Press, 1977); Paul E. Lovejoy, ed., *The Ideology of Slavery in Africa,* (Beverly Hills, Calif.: Sage Publications, 1981); Lovejoy, "Indigenous African Slavery" in *Roots and Branches: Current Directions in Slave Studies,* ed. Michael Craton, *Historical Reflections/Réflexions Historiques,* 6 (Summer 1979):19–38; Cooper, *Plantation Slavery,* pp. 1–20; Cooper, "The Problem of Slavery." For an interesting discussion of the possible range of meaning of freedom to African slaves, see Thomas L. Weber, *Deep Like the Rivers: Education in the Slave Quarter Community 1831–1865* (New York: W. W. Norton, 1978), pp. 139–53.

5. General Report.

6. Ibid. This section of the official report the judges prefaced with a statement showing they were aware Antiguan slaveowners would be criticized by antislavery Englishmen on account of the plot, but they pleaded that such condemnation was undeserved: "As this horrid Conspiracy cannot but be heard of, wherever People hold Correspondence with Antigua; It will no doubt be variously animadverted upon; and as Slavery is the very Odium of Englishmen, Some of our Countreymen may do it to our disadvantage; Yet let these men cooly consider, and they will think our Circumstances deserve a kinder Treatment, Slavery being among us, not of Choice, but of necessity." This, and the rest of the quotation in chapter 10 of this study, was all the judges apparently thought necessary to include in a brief paragraph, perhaps not wishing to belabor the point that, in regard to the plot, slaveowners should not be blamed too heavily.

It should be pointed out, however, that in the printed copy of the report, which appeared in Dublin, Ireland, in 1737, this section was edited. It thus took precisely the course the judges avoided. The printed version deserves quoting in full.

As this execrable Consispacy must reach the Knowledge of distant Countries, and probably be animadverted upon with Severity, especially in those happy Kingdoms, where Slavery is look'd upon with just Indignation: We think it our Duty to advertise our fellow Subjects of Great Britain, to consider that Slavery is not our Choice, but Necessity; it being impossible to carry on our Sugar Manufacture by white Labourers, since in our present Circumstances, our Estates will scare yield a Subsistence to the Proprietors: But indeed the Slavery of our Negroes is merely nominal, since they are governed by our own Laws, and not by the arbitrary Will of their Masters; and tried in all criminal Cases by lawful and impartial magistrates; since their little Properties are preserved inviolate, and their Corrections much less severe, than of Criminals in free Kingdoms; their Labours more moderate, and their manner of living more comfortable than the poor Inhabitants of the freest Countries: For besides the tender Sensations of Humanity common to us with other Men, it is the Interest of every Master to take all possible Care of his Slaves (or rather Servants) both in Sickness and in Health; since his whole Profit and Subsistence depends absolutely on their Strength and Vigour.

These Considerations we hope will convince our fellow Subjects, that our Calamities deserve their Commiseration; and especially when they are assured, that this wicked Conspiracy took its Rise from too much Lenity and Indulgence of Masters to their Slaves, not one of whom so much as pretended Hardship or Oppression in Excuse of their Crimes; but on the contrary it appeared to us, that mere Lust of Power, and unbounded Ambition were the only Incentives to their unnatural Rebellion, even tho' their Condition in our Colonies, is a State of perfect Freedom, compared to the native Slavery of their own Country. (*A Genuine Narrative*, pp. 17–18)

The above proslavery rationalizations are interesting for the image they portray of rebellious slaves.

7. General Report.

8. CSP, 43, 1737, no. 99, p. 50; Mathew to BT, May 31, 1736, CO 152/22, W47; Bennet H. Wall, "An Epitaph for Slavery," *Louisiana History* 16 (Summer 1975): 237–38. In 1711 there were nearly 5 (4.147) blacks (total pop. 11,838) for every white person (total pop. 2,854: women, children, men fit to bear arms) in the whole island. In St. John's town the number of blacks (834) and whites (760) was close; in outlying St. John's division, however, there were nearly 13 (12.93) blacks (total pop. 1,875) for every white (total pop. 145). Population data for 1711 in Sir John St. Leger to BT, Aug. 23, 1712, CO 152/10, O15. A report on the condition of Main Swete's Body Plantation of about 337 acres around the mid-eighteenth century stated that "the land is not any ways hedg'd or fenced in, it not being cutomary in these parts of the world." Undated inventory of the Body and "Falmouth land," Swete Papers, 388M/E12.

9. For a discussion of these and related issues, see Eugene D. Genovese, *From Rebellion to Revolution: Afro-American Slave Revolts in the Making of the Modern World* (Baton Rouge: Louisiana State University Press, 1979); Genovese, *Roll, Jordan, Roll*; Wood, *Black Majority*; Mullin, *Flight and Rebellion*; Degler; *Neither Black Nor White*, pp. 47–61.

10. Sheridan, "The Rise of a Colonial Gentry: A Case Study of Antigua, 1730–1775," *EHR*, 2d ser., 13 (1961):346. Legislation increasing taxation of absentees was passed in 1706, 1707, 1711, 1714, 1740, 1741, 1742, and 1744. These acts, with the exception of that of 1706, were all tax acts passed in view of a situation of war. Mathew to BT, Apr. 15, 1743, CO 152/24, Y61. Many slaves on the absentee Tudways' Parham Plantation may have been involved in the plot, to judge from slave evidence in the trial record, but it is not possible to discern what conditions were like there. The Tudways lost by execution Watty the mason and Cuffee, also a mason; Cuffee the driver was banished. Among other slaves of the plantation taken up were Attaw, the driver, and George, who were probably released. Parham Inventory, Feb. 1, 1737, Tudway Papers, DD/TD, box 16; lists of slaves executed and banished in Mathew to BT, May 26, 1737, CO 152/23, X7; compensation claims in Assembly Mins., July 24, 1738, CO 9/12.

11. Aptheker, *Slave Revolts*, p. 114; Jordan, *White Over Black*, pp. 102–3; Patterson, "Slavery and Slave Revolts," pp. 318–19, 324–25; Patterson, *Sociology of Slavery*,

pp. 273-75; Twombly, "Black Resistance to Slavery," p. 31; Wood, *Black Majority,* pp. 165-66, 218-29.

12. General Report; CSP, 1737, 43, no. 99, p. 50; Morris to Gov. and Council, Jan. 24, 1737, Council Mins., Jan. 31, 1737, CO 9/10.

13. In 1730 the legislature was made aware of "an immediate Necessity to repair the Gates [at Monk's Hill]." Council Mins., Nov. 30, Dec. 18, 1730, CO 152/43. By 1736 new gates were needed, there being none. Mins. of Council in Assembly, Oct. 15, 1736, CO 9/9; Council Mins., Nov. 15, 1736, CO 9/10. To "remedy this Dangerous State" of Monk's Hill the assembly also agreed to assign a number of "montrosses" who should "reside constantly there for the safety of the Arsenal & Magazine," to "Allow Each of them Twenty Pounds a Year in Cash and a Barrel of Beef," and "that Ten Acres of Land be rented for them adjacent to that Fortification at the Publick Expence." These men would be at "liberty to keep their While Familys with them But no Slaves Either by Night or Day."

14. Mathew to BT, Jan. 17, 1737, CO 152/22, W88.

15. [Flannigan,] *Antigua and the Antiguans,* 1:91; Westergaard, *Danish West Indies,* pp. 166-76.

16. Harry Eckstein, "On the Etiology of Internal Wars," *History and Theory* 4 (1965):140-43; James C. Davis, "Toward a Theory of Revolution," *American Sociological Review* 27 (1962):5-8; Lawrence Stone, "Theories of Revolution," *World Politics* 18 (Jan. 1966); Neil J. Smelser, *Theory of Collective Behaviour,* pp. 1-22, and passim.

17. Sheridan, *Sugar and Slavery,* pp. 426-33; Sheridan, "The Molasses Act and the Market Strategy of the British Sugar Planters," *JEH* 17 (Mar. 1957):62-83. James A. Henretta, *The Evolution of American Society, 1700-1815* (Lexington, Mass.: D. C. Heath, 1973), pp. 51-53; Assembly Mins., July 12, 1734, CO 9/7; CSP, 1735-36, 42, no. 11, p. 5; CSP, 1734-35, 41, no. 314ii, pp. 207-8, no. 138, p. 117; Petition from legislature to the king, Assembly Mins., Oct. 3, 1738, CO 9/12.

18. CSP, 1734-35, 41, no. 314 ii, p. 207; Council Mins., Apr. 12, May 7, July 31, 1731, CO 152/43; Mathew to BT, May 26, 1737, CO 152/23, X6; Deerr, *History of Sugar,* 1:195; Langford to Redwood, Mar. 1731, Byam to Redwood, May 22, 1731, John Tomlinson Jr. to Redwood, Apr. 1732, Gunthorp to Redwood, Apr. 23, 1732, Long to Redwood, Mar. 14, 1733, Pope to Redwood, Mar. 19, Dec. 8, 1733, Tomlinson to Redwood, Mar. 21, 1733, *Commerce of Rhode Island,* 1:12-41; *Gentleman's Magazine,* May 1731, p. 218, June 1731, p. 265; "An Account of the Produce of Parham Plantation Sugar and how Disposed of, for the Year 1737. The Crop begun the 21st. Februa^y 1736/7 and Ended the 23^d June 1737," Tudway Papers, DD/TD, box 16; Martin to Bayard, Dec. 16, 1736, Josiah Martin Letter Book, pt. 1, fol. 113, Martin Papers, Add. MSS 41,352; *Pennsylvania Gazette,* Dec. 2-9, 1736; *New York Weekly Journal,* June 13, 1737; *South Carolina Gazette,* Oct. 23-30, 1736; *Virginia Gazette,* Sept. 17-24, 1736; Council Mins., Jan. 17, 31, 1737, CO 9/10; Sheridan, *Sugar and Slavery,* pp. 428-29; Tullideph to Dunbar, July 23, 1735, Walter Tullideph to David Tullideph, Sept. 1736, Tullideph Letter Book. In 1738 the St. Christopher council complained in London through their agent that "the Inhabitants in the Calamitous Circumstances they are Reduced to by Dry Weather and a Blast or Insect that of late years has Destroyed their Product and still infests them are unable to put the Island in a Tenable Condition or to Erect the Public Buildings so

necessary for the Honor of Your Majesty's Government and safety of the Titles
on which your Subjects Property Depends, or even in Due time or at all without
distress to Discharge the Debts Contracted for the Public Service." (St. Christopher)
Council Mins., July 5, 1738, CO 241/4. On the "blast" Bryan Edwards wrote at
the end of the century: "The sugarcane is subject to a disease which no foresight
can obviate, and for which human wisdom has hitherto, I fear, attempted in vain
to find a remedy. This calamity is called the blast; it is the aphis of Linnaeus, and
is distinguished into two kinds, the black and the yellow; of which the latter is the
most [sic] destructive. It consists of myriads of little insects, invisible to the naked
eye, whose proper food is the juice of the cane; in search of which they wound
the tender blades, and consequently destroy the vessels. Hence the circulation being
impeded, the growth of the plant is checked, until it withers or dies in proportion
to the degree of the ravage." Edwards, West Indies, 2:252-53. Col. Samuel Martin
believed that burning trash upon cane lands was one way of fighting the blast.
"Essay upon Plantership," pp. 259-60, 282-83. Among attorney Walter Tullideph's
worries in 1740 was the blast on one of George Thomas's plantations. "Dr. Sydserfe's
Canes next to you were so much blasted," he wrote, "that I cutt them down both
for his own sake as well as your's. You have both had a large share of it in your
present young Canes but we have had such seasonable weather that I hope with
Care to get the better of it." Tullideph to Thomas, Apr. 22, 1740, Sheridan, "Letters
from a Sugar Plantation," pp. 4-5.

19. Tullideph to Dunbar, July 23, 1735, Walter Tullideph to David Tullideph,
Sept. 1736, Tullideph Letter Book, MS; "Extract of Letters from Two Gentlemen
in Antigua: One dated Aug. 4 [1736]," Virginia Gazette, Sept. 17-24, 1736; "Ordered
that the Deputy Secretary make out a Proclamation for a General Fast to be held
in this Island on the 21st. Day of this Instant to deprecate God's Anger from whence
this Island has been Afflicted with the blast and Dry weather and Issue Letters
to the respective Clergy men of this Island to adapt their Prayer and Sermon
suitable to the Occasion, and that all People white and black abstain from Labour
and that Masters keep their Negroes within their own Plantation," Mins. of Council
in Assembly, July 5, 1736, CO 9/9; Martin to Bayard in New York, Dec. 16, 1736,
Josiah Martin Letter Book, pt. 1, fol. 113, Martin Papers, Add. MSS 41,352.

20. Council Mins., Oct. 18, 1732, CO 9/7; Mins. of Council in Assembly,
July 5, Aug. 23, 1735, CO 9/9; Walter Tullideph to David Tullideph, Oct. 21, 1734,
Tullideph Letter Book, MS; Parham Plantation Inventory, Feb. 1, 1737, Tudway
Papers, DD/TD, box 16.

21. Tullideph to Dunbar, July 23, 1735, Tullideph Letter Book, MS; Martin to
Freeman, Dec. 10, 1736, Josiah Martin Letter Book, pt. 1, fol. 112; Martin Papers,
Add. MSS 41,352; Petition from legislature to the king, Assembly Mins., Oct. 3,
1738, CO 9/12. According to one newspaper report, "Some of the principal
Gentlemen there with their Families are making Provision to leave the Island,
believing the Negroes will accomplish their Designs sooner or later." New England
Weekly Journal, Apr. 12, 1737. See also New York Weekly Journal, June 6, Aug. 8, 1737;
Tullideph to Oliver, Jan. 7, 1757, Tullideph Letter Book, MS.

22. Pitman, British West Indies, p. 115; "Address of president, council and
assembly of Jamaica to the King, offering the distressed and unhappy condition

to which this colony is at present reduced," CSP, 1737, 43, no. 156 ii, p. 79; CSP, 1731, 38, no. 494, pp. 348–50; Council Mins., July 31, 1731, CO 9/7; Tullideph to Johnston, June 27, 1737, Walter Tullideph to David Tullideph, Jan. 15 and May 25, 1737, Tullideph Letter Book, MS; Council Mins., Dec. 17, 1731, CO 9/7; Arbuthnot Report.

23. Aptheker, *Slave Revolts*, p. 117. See also Genovese, *From Rebellion to Revolution*, p. 13.

Chapter 11: "Daring Spirits to Lead Them On"

1. Mathew to BT, May 26, 1737, CO 152/23, X7; TR, Council Mins., Jan. 12, 1737, CO 9/10, Feb. 24, 1737, CO 9/11.

2. General Report.

3. Arbuthnot Report; Genovese, *Roll, Jordan, Roll*, pp. 388–98, 592–93; Genovese, *From Rebellion to Revolution*, pp. 27–28; Hormansden, *New York Conspiracy*, pp. xix–xx; Killens, *Trial Record*, pp. x–xvi; Starobin, *Denmark Vesey*, p. 3; Richard B. Sheridan, "The Jamaican Slave Insurrection Scare of 1776 and the American Revolution," *JNH* 61 (July 1976):290–308; Craton, *Testing the Chains*, pp. 172–94.

4. Robertson, *Letter*, p. 94; Ligon, *History of Barbados*, p. 14; CSP, 1661–68, no. 1,788, p. 586; Carl N. Degler, *Neither Black Nor White: Slavery and Race Relations in Brazil and the United States* (New York: Macmillan, 1971), pp. 54–55.

5. General Report.

6. Mullin, *Flight and Rebellion*, pp. 37–38, 161–62.

7. "Tryal of Ned Chester a Mulatto Carpenter belonging to Caesar Rodney 26th Nov. [1736]," TR, Council Mins., Jan. 12, 1737, CO 9/10.

8. Coromantees' use of Akan day-names as they appear in the lists may be used as only a rough guide to Coromantee participation. For the day-name classification and its Caribbean version, see Schuler, "Akan Slave Rebellions," pp. 28–29, n. 11.

9. General Report; "Tryal of Tilgarth Penezar Commonly Called Targut, a Creole Christian Slave belonging to the Widow Roach, a Carpenter & Caulker and a very Stout, Resolute, Sensible fellow that has been to the Northward & Can read & Write, say Prayers & ca., 26th Novem. [1736]," TR, Council Mins., Jan. 12, 1737, CO 9/10; "Evidence against Vernons Cudjoe [Jan. 26, 1737]," TR, Council Mins., Feb. 14, 1737, CO 9/11. In relation to the baptized Creole slave Ned belonging to Col. Jacob Morgan, Jemmy told the judges "how Morgan's Ned one Day in Goal preached to his Fellow Prisoners & Endeavour'd to Influence them by Fasting, Reading, Preaching, praying, giving the Sacrament & Absolution to them, not to Disclose the Plot." "Tryal of Budinots Dick a Negro Carpenter 19th Novem. [1736]," Council Mins., Jan. 12, 1737, CO 9/10.

10. Stanley M. Elkins, *Slavery: A Problem in American Institutional and Intellectual Life* (Chicago: University of Chicago Press, 1959), pp. 137–38; Kilson, "Towards Freedom," pp. 174–75; Eugene D. Genovese, "On Stanley Elkins's Slavery: A Problem in American and Institutional and Intellectual Life," in *American Negro Slavery: A Modern Reader*, ed. Allen Weinstein and Frank Otto Gatell (New York: Oxford University Press, 1968), p. 339; Genovese, *In Red and Black: Marxian*

Explorations in Southern and Afro-American History (New York: Vintage, 1971), pp. 137–38; Genovese, *Roll, Jordan, Roll,* pp. 365–88. George F. Tyson, Jr., ed., *Toussaint L'Ouverture* (Englewood Cliffs, N.J.: Prentice-Hall, 1973), p. 13.

11. "It would appear reasonable," writes Patterson, "and the available comparative literature lends support to the hypothesis that the higher the proportion of slaves recruited from outside the system, the greater was the probability of rebellions taking place. Clearly, people socialized within the slave system would have been more adapted to such a system, more aware of the risks involved in revolting and less inclined to bring down the known wrath of the ruling caste upon themselves than would slaves recruited as adults to the system." Patterson, "Slavery and Slave Revolts," p. 319.

12. Genovese, "On Elkins's Slavery," p. 339; General Report; "Extract of a Letter from Antigua," Nov. 10, 1736, CO 152/23, X32.

13. By the end of the eighteenth century and during the early nineteenth century, the memory of Africa as a catalyst for revolt was to some extent replaced, especially in relation to Creoles, by the powerful example of the Haitian Revolution, which culminated with the establishment of a black republic.

14. General Report. I have used the estimate of Court's age as it appeared in this report in Council Mins., Jan. 24, 1737, CO 9/10, because it corresponds with Thomas Kerby's claim that Court was an "Elderly Distemper'd Fellow." Arbuthnot Report. In the copy of the judges' report in Mathew to BT, Jan. 17, 1737, CO 152/22, W94, as also in *Genuine Narrative,* Court's age is given as thirty-five. In the Gold Coast in 1701 an Asante army won a major victory over that of Denkyira and established Asante supremacy. If my guess that Court was enslaved in that year is correct, it would seem possible, even probable, that it was as a result of the Asante-Denkyira war. Court may thus have come from Denkyira. See J. K. Flynn, *Asante and Its Neighbours 1700–1807* (London: Longman, 1971), pp. 37–40.

15. Madeline Manoukian, *Akan and Ga-Adangme Peoples of the Gold Coast* (London: Oxford University Press, 1950), pp. 36–37; K. A. Busia, *The Position of the Chief in the Modern Political System of Ashanti* (London: Oxford University Press, 1951); Busia, "The Ashanti," in *Perspectives on the African Past,* ed. Martin A. Klein and G. Wesley Johnson (Boston: Little, Brown, 1972), pp. 220–25; R. S. Rattray, *Ashanti Law and Constitution* (Oxford: Clarendon Press, 1929), pp. 99–107.

16. General Report.

17. Ibid.; Arbuthnot Report. Sam Sharpe led a slave rebellion in the island of Jamaica in 1831/32. On this revolt see, for example, M. Reckord, "The Jamaican Slave Rebellion of 1831," *Past & Present,* July 1968, pp. 108–25; E. Brathwaite, "Caliban, Ariel and Unprospero in the Conflict of Creolization: A Study of the Slave Revolt in Jamaica 1831–32," in Rubin and Tuden, *Comparative Perspectives on Slavery,* pp. 41–62. See also Eckstein, "On the Etiology of Internal Wars," pp. 133–63. This is a useful source for sorting out problems connected with explaining internal war or "any resort to violence within a political order to change its constitution, rulers, or policies." (p. 133).

18. Fynn, *Asante and Its Neighbours.*

19. Manoukian, *Akan and Ga-Adangme Peoples,* p. 37; Busia, "The Ashanti," p. 222–23; Busia, *Position of the Chief,* pp. 26–27.

20. Manoukian, *Akan and Ga-Adangme Peoples,* p. 37; Busia, *Position of the Chief,* pp. 13–14; Phillip Longworth, "Peasant Leadership and the Pugachev Revolt," *Journal of Peasant Studies* 2 (Jan. 1975):186; General Report.

21. I am indebted to Prof. Tim Garrard for bringing this interpretation of the plot to my attention. Private correspondence, Sept. 13, Oct. 1, 1984.

22. The reference to a "long coldness" between Court and Tomboy is certainly intriguing. If the young men could pose a political threat to Akan rulers, one wonders whether Tomboy had earlier challenged or appeared to challenge Court's leadership role among the slaves. And, were the judges in fact not far from the truth when they claimed that the Creoles planned to subjugate all others who would not follow their lead after the revolt had succeeded? General Report.

23. For recruitment tactics in Prosser's revolt see Mullin, *Flight and Rebellion,* pp. 142–51; "Tryal of Tom Hansons Quashee, his Mother a Cormantee 24th November [1736]," "Tryal of Ned Chester 26th Nov. [1736]," TR, Council Mins., Jan. 12, 1737, CO 9/10.

24. Ibid.; "Tryal of Budinots Dick 19th Novem. [1736]," TR, Council Mins., Jan. 12, 1737, CO 9/10.

25. "Evidence against Pares Cudjoe a Boyler," TR, Council Mins., Feb. 24, 1737, CO 9/11.

26. The judges' translation of the Akan vernacular is correct. Private correspondence with Prof. Ivor Wilks, Northwestern University, Evanston, Ill., Sept. 5, 1983. Prof. Tim Garrard, Sept. 13, Oct. 1, 1984; Sam Dakwa, ghanaian student, University of California, Los Angeles, Nov. 26, 1984.

27. "Tryal of Quawcoo an Old Cormantee Negroe of Mr. John Pare [Dec. 9, 1736]," "Tryal of Troilus 10th Dec. [1736]," Quawcoo also complained of the overseer's ill "usage breaking and Starving them." He had planned to poison the overseer. TR, Council Mins., Jan. 12, 1737, CO 9/10. "Tryal of Col. Lucas driver Caesar [Jan. 20, 1737]," TR, Council Mins., Feb. 14, 1737, CO 9/11.

28. "Evidence against Bartons Joe [Jan. 20, 1737]," TR, Council Mins., Feb. 24, 1737, CO 9/11.

29. See, for example, "Tryal of Budinots Dick 19th Novem. [1736]," "Tryal of Tom a field Negro of Edward Otto's the 24th Novem. [1737]," "Tryal of Skerrets Billy apprentice to Rodney's John, 19th Nov. [1736]," "Tryal of Cubbinah a Negro Creole Driver belonging to the Estate of Henry Osborne 8th December [1736]," TR, Council Mins., Jan. 12, 1737, CO 9/10.

30. "Tryal of Tom a field Negro of Edward Otto's the 24th Novem. [1736]," TR, Council Mins., Jan. 12, 1737, CO 9/10.

31. See TR in Council Mins., Jan. 12, 1737, CO 9/10; Council Mins., Feb. 14, Feb. 24, 1737, CO 9/11.

32. "Tryal of Tilgarth Penezar 26th Novem. [1736]," TR, Council Mins., Jan. 12, 1737, CO 9/10.

33. General Report; "Tryal of London a Creole slave belonging to the Estate of John Goble Dece'd. [Nov. 1736]," TR, Council Mins., Jan. 12, 1737, CO 9/10; "Tryal of Parham Watty [Jan. 14, 1737]," TR, Council Mins., Feb. 14, 1737, CO 9/11.

34. "Evidence-against Vernons Cudjoe [Jan. 26, 1737]," Evidence against

Warner's Johnno a Cooper belonging to the Folly Plantation [Jan. 21, 1737]," TR, Council Mins., Feb. 14, 1737, CO 9/11; Schuler, "Akan Slave Rebellions," pp. 15–17, 23.

35. E. J. Hobsbawn, *Primitive Rebels*, pp. 150–74; Benjamin C. Ray, *African Religions: Symbol, Ritual, and Community* (Englewood Cliffs, N.J.: Prentice-Hall, 1976), pp. 165–71; E. P. Modum, "Gods as Guests: Music and Festivals in African Traditional Societies," *Présence Africaine* 2nd Qtly. (1979); Monica Schuler, *"Alas, Alas, Kongo": A Social History of Indentured African Immigration into Jamaica, 1841–1865* (Baltimore: Johns Hopkins University Press, 1980), p. 33; Eric O. Ayisi, *An Introduction to the Study of African Culture* (London: Heinemann, 1979), pp. 89–93; Johns S. Mbiti, *African Religions & Philosophy* (London: Heinemann, 1969), pp. 58–71, 166–87; Manoukian, *Akan and Ga-Adangme Peoples*, pp. 55–59; Busia, "The Ashanti," pp. 221–22; Busia, *Position of the Chief*, p. 24–27. Oath swearing played an important part in Akan culture, and in some cases it has specialized meaning. On oaths see especially R. S. Rattray, *Religion & Art in Ashanti* (Oxford: Clarendon Press, 1927), pp. 205–15. The oath the Antigua slaves employed would seem to be the Akan/Asante *nsedie* which meant that they called upon "some supernatural power to witness what has been said and to impose a supernatural sanction should the statement be false." Rattray, *Religion & Art*, p. 215.

36. "As most of these were the favorite Negroes, brought up in the Families, which laid this Scheme, so they could carry it on with greater secrecy, many of the Heads being capable of Writing and Reading, and has been taught the Christian Religion, comformable to the frequent Admonition of our worthy Diocesan the Bishop of London and therefore in Swearing the Multitude into their Scheme, they swore them and administered the Sacrament to all such as professed themselves Christians according to the Rites of the Bishops' Church, the others they swore according to their several Country Forms; which gives us a Specimen of what may be expected from Converting Negroes." *New York Gazette*, Mar. 28, 1737 (account said to be based on a letter from Antigua, Jan. 15, 1737). Another account stated that "ye usual" form of swearing "for ye Coromantees was by a mixture of Grave dirt in rum or beer, which they drank, holding their hand over a white dunghill cock; to the Creoles was added alsoe kissing ye new testament." Tullideph Letter Book, Jan. 15, 1737. See also General Report.

37. "Tryal of Quawcoo an old Oby Man & Physition & Cormantee belonging to Mr. Wm. Hunt 11th December [1736]," TR, Council Mins., Jan. 12, 1737, CO 9/10; Schuler, "Akan Slave Rebellions," pp. 9, 16–17; Schuler, "Ethnic Slave Rebellions," pp. 382–83; Schuler, *"Alas, Alas, Kongo,"* pp. 40–42; Patterson, *Sociology of Slavery*, p. 192; C.L.R. James, *The Black Jacobins*, p. 86; William C. Suttles, Jr., "African Religious Survivals as Factors in American Slave Revolts," *JHN* 56 (Apr. 1971):97–104.

38. General Report; "Tryal of Vernons Cudjoe [Jan. 26, 1737]," TR, Council Mins., Feb. 14, 1737, CO 9/11; Execution List, enclosed in Mathew to BT, May 26, 1737, CO 152/23, X7.

39. "Tryal of Quawcoo an old Oby Man [Dec. 11, 1736], TR, Council Mins., Jan. 12, 1737, CO 9/10. A chequeen was a local coin. Craton, *Testing the Chains*, p. 359, n. 21.

40. Ibid.

41. "Tryal of Tilgarth Penezar 26 Novem. [1736]," "Tryal of Sydserfs Robin als: Boggo a Creole Carpenter 15th November: 1736," "Tryal of Monk's Mingo [Nov. 1736]," "Tryal of Budinots Dick 19th Novem. [1736]," "Tryal of Ned Chester 26th Nov. [1736]," TR, Council Mins., Jan. 12, 1737, CO 9/10; "Tryal of Vernons Cudjoe Jan. 26, 1737," TR, Council Mins., Feb. 14, 1737, CO 9/11. Councillor Vallentine Morris believed that "the Negro Women by their Insolent behavior and Expressions had the utter Extirpation of the white as much as heart, as the Men, and would undoubtedly have Done as much Mischief by Butchering all the Women and Children." Council Mins., Jan. 31, 1737, CO 9/10.

42. "Tryal of Quawcoo an Old Cormantee Negroe of Mr. John Pare [Dec. 9, 1736]," TR, Council Mins., Jan. 12, 1737, CO 9/10; "Tryal of Parham Watty [Jan. 14, 1737]," TR, Council Mins., Feb. 14, 1737, CO 9/11.

43. Schuler, "Akan Slave Rebellions," p. 15; Long, *History of Jamaica*, 2:455–56.

44. Manoukian, *Akan and Ga-Adangme Peoples*, p. 39; R. S. Rattray, *Ashanti* (Oxford: Clarendon Press, 1923), pp. 77–85 and passim; Busia, *Position of the Chief*, pp. 19–21.

45. Though we cannot be certain, it is more than likely that Queen was a Coromantee if she filled the role of queen-mother.

46. "Tryal of Monk's Mingo [Nov. 1736]," "Tryal of Tom Hansons Quashee 24th November [1736]," "Tryal of Ned Chester 26th Nov. 1736]," "Tryal of Morgans Newport 9th of November 1736," "Tryal of Lavington's Sampson 17th November [1736]," TR, Council Mins., Jan. 12, 1737, CO 9/10.

47. See, for example, "Tryal of Col. Tomlinsons Barryman," "Tryal of Tom a field Negro of Edward Otto's the 24th Novem. [1736]," "Tryal of Tilgarth Penezar 26 Novem. [1736]," "Tryal of Quawcoo an Old Cormantee Negroe of Mr. John Pare [Dec. 9, 1736]," TR, Council Mins., Jan. 12, 1737, CO 9/10. "Tryal of Olivers Quaw," TR, Council Mins., Feb. 14, 1737, CO 9/11.

48. "Tryal of Budinots Dick 19th Novem. [1736]," TR, Council Mins., Jan. 12, 1737, CO 9/10; Arbuthnot Report; "Tryal of Monk's Mingo [Nov. 1936]," TR, Council Mins., Jan. 12, 1737, CO 9/10; General Report. It is interesting that Court's and Tomboy's festivities were held in October and that they were one week apart. This suggests that the festivities may have been related to the great annual Akan celebrations known as Odwira, held immediately after the harvest (September-October), which many Europeans called the "Yam festivals." Generally nearby towns would try to avoid holding their Odwira festivals on the same day. During the festival, the chief, holding a sword, may dance publicly before his people. Fetish priests and executioners may also dance, jump around, and go through various celebratory exercises. The *akyem* or shield dance, similar to the one that Court staged, may also be performed at the Odwira for entertainment. Private correspondence with Prof. Tim Garrard, Oct. 1, 1984. For a famous description of the Asante Odwira festival, see T. E. Bowdich, *Mission from Cape Coast Castle to Ashantee* (London: Griffith & Farran, 1873), pp. 226–29.

49. Ibid.

50. Large umbrellas were part of Akan ceremonial regalia. "An umbrella was obviously used to keep the chief physically cool, but it was also intended to promote a condition of spiritual peace and coolness (*dwo*) and to create around him a particular symbolic space." The umbrella "serves to isolate the King from above

in the way that his sandals prevent his ever coming into direct contact with the earth beneath." M. D. McLeod, *The Asante* (London: British Museum Publications, 1981), p. 109.

51. The headgear of an Akan chief even today often consists of a velvet cap adorned with gold ornaments. Private communication with Prof. Tim Garrard, Oct. 1, 1984. See also McLeod, *The Asante*, chaps. 5–6.

52. Ibid. Court, who had left the Gold Coast as a child, was apparently instructed in the details of the *ikem* dance. The slave Billy testified that he saw the Coromantee *obeah* man Quawcoo "Once at Kerby's Warfe with Court a Month before Courts Dance Shewing Court how they played with the Ikim in his Country and he had a Wooden Cutlace to Shew how they fought there and had a Sheep Skin on his Thigh and blowed with an Oben i.e. an Elephants Tooth." "Tryal of Quawcoo an old Oby Man [Dec. 11, 1736]," TR, Council Mins., Jan. 12, 1737, CO 9/10. Billy also reported that the *ikems* or shields were made at Court's house and that Court showed Troilus "the Ikem and one of the Wooden Cutlasses and Troilus Flourished the Cutlace & Ikem and Blew the Horn." "Tryal of Troilus [Dec. 10, 1736]," TR, Council Mins., Jan. 12, 1737, CO 9/10. For an interesting discussion of the *ikem* dance in relation to Akan regalia see Marion Johnson, "Ekyem, the State Shield," British Museum Occasional Paper no. 3 (1979), pp. 6–12. I am indebted to Stanley E. Engerman for bringing this source to my attention. On the shield, see also McLeod, *The Asante*, pp. 103–4.

53. On enstoolment in Asante, see Busia, *Position of the Chief*, pp. 12–13. The stool was the symbol of the authority of prominent figures in Akan government. In Asante the most important stool was the Golden Stool, first introduced during the reign of Osei Tutu by the priest Okomfo Anokye, who made it the repository of the spirit of the Asante nation. On the Golden Stool see Rattray, *Ashanti Law*, pp. 270–84; Rattray, *Ashanti*, pp. 287–93.

54. Private correspondence from Prof. Ivor Wilks, Sept. 5, 1983, and Prof. Ray Kea, June 8, 1973. Rattray, *Ashanti*, p. 263.

55. Robert S. Smith, *Warfare and Diplomacy in Pre-Colonial West Africa* (London: Methuen, 1976), pp. 18, 53; Rattray, *Ashanti Law*, pp. 120–26; General Report. The word *Conguo* may stand for the Akan for "stool," or "throne," as it were. Private correspondence with Prof. Ivor Wilks, Sept. 5, 1983, and Prof. Tim Garrard, Oct. 1, 1984.

Conclusion

1. Genovese, *From Rebellion to Revolution*, p. 3; Craton, *Testing the Chains*, chaps. 13–22.

2. On slave resistance in Barbados see Dunn, *Sugar and Slaves*, pp. 256–58; Craton, *Testing the Chains*, pp. 105–14, 254–66; Handler, "Slave Revolts and Conspiracies," pp. 5–42; Handler, "The Barbados Slave Conspiracies of 1675 and 1692," *Journal of the Barbados Museum and Historical Society* 36 (1982):312–33; Jill Sheppard, "The Slave Conspiracy That Never Was," *Journal of the Barbados Museum and Historical Society* 34 (Mar. 1974):190–97.

3. I am preparing a book on the emergence of Afro-Caribbean (Creole) revolt

that will explore the historical context in which three such events occurred: in Barbados in 1692, Antigua in 1736, and Jamaica in 1776. These episodes of collective slave resistance were the first of their kind in the respective territories. On the impact of creolization on slave society, see, for example, Edward Brathwaite, *Development of Creole Society in Jamaica 1770–1820* (Oxford: Clarendon Press, 1971); Craton, *Testing the Chains,* pp. 241–53; Mintz and Price, *Afro-American Past.*

4. Eric R. Wolf, *Peasant Wars of the Twentieth Century* (New York: Harper & Row, 1973), p. 290.

5. James, *Black Jacobins,* p. 85.

6. For comparative treatment of styles of slave resistance in the Americas, see, for example, Genovese, *From Rebellion to Revolution*; Genovese, *Roll, Jordan, Roll,* pp. 287–98; Degler, *Neither Black nor White,* pp. 47–61.

7. Dunn, *Sugar and Slaves,* pp. 258–59; Patterson, *Sociology of Slavery,* p. 273; D. W. Thoms, "Slavery in the Leeward Islands in the Mid Eighteenth Century: a Reappraisal," *Bulletin of the Institute of Historical Research* 42 (May 1969):84.

Index

Books in the Series